Exposing the Reich

How Hitler Captivated and Corrupted the German People

David Harper

ROWMAN & LITTLEFIELD
Lanham • Boulder • New York • London

Published by Rowman & Littlefield
An imprint of The Rowman & Littlefield Publishing Group, Inc.
4501 Forbes Boulevard, Suite 200, Lanham, Maryland 20706
www.rowman.com

86-90 Paul Street, London EC2A 4NE

British Library Cataloguing in Publication Information Available

Library of Congress Cataloging-in-Publication Data

Names: Harper, David Ray, 1953- author.
  Title: Exposing the Reich : how Hitler captivated and corrupted the German
    people / David Harper.
  Other titles: How Hitler captivated and corrupted the German people
  Description: Lanham : Rowman & Littlefield, [2023] | Includes
    bibliographical references and index.
  Identifiers: LCCN 2023027320 (print) | LCCN 2023027321 (ebook) | ISBN
    9781538180891 (cloth) | ISBN 9781538180907 (ebook)
  Subjects: LCSH: Hitler, Adolf, 1889-1945. | Nazis. | National socialism. |
    Germany—Politics and government—1933-1945 |
    Germany—History—1933-1945.
  Classification: LCC DD253 .H283 2023 (print) | LCC DD253 (ebook) | DDC
    943.086—dc23/eng/20230721
  LC record available at https://lccn.loc.gov/2023027320
  LC ebook record available at https://lccn.loc.gov/2023027321

Contents

Acknowledgments

Special thanks to the following people whose assistance and support is most appreciated: Dr. Mathias Irlinger and Karin Wabro of the Leibnitz Institute for Contemporary History; Arthur Magida, for his valuable help in writing the book proposal and searching for publishers; Ronnie Landau, for opening the door to publication; and Pawel Sawicki of the Auschwitz Memorial Press Office.

I wish to thank the following centers for the complimentary use of their photographs: Auschwitz Concentration Camp Memorial Site and Dokumentation Obersalzberg (Leibnitz Institute for Contemporary History).

Above all, my gratitude goes to my wife, Christine Dundas-Harper, for her indispensable proofreading, corrections, and suggestions, as well as for her patience in putting up with a recluse for a year.

This work is dedicated to my aunt Noor Inayat-Khan, code name Madeleine.

Introduction

As I ponder the motivation behind writing *Exposing the Reich*, my mind wanders back to a sunny day in the summer of 1995. I can still see my uncle, with his shock of white hair wildly flying about, ardently waving a wispy baton in the direction of an improvised choir and piecemeal orchestra. The music performed was a conventional enough piece—Johann Sebastian Bach's Mass in B Minor—yet the setting was anything but ordinary: the infamous Dachau concentration camp. Surrounded by guard towers, barbed-wire fencing, and the very crematorium where his sister had met her tragic end in 1944, my uncle, a teacher of meditation and Indian Sufi mysticism, had gathered this musical group and a small but attentive audience to pay homage to his beloved sister, Noor Inayat-Khan, half a century after her untimely passing.

Noor, who had volunteered to assist in the war effort and trained as a secret agent, was sent into German-occupied France in 1943 as a radio operator for the Special Operations Executive (SOE), an organization created to sabotage German occupation in Europe and help the Resistance in German-controlled countries. At great risk and despite many near captures, Noor operated in Paris clandestinely for months, carrying out crucial work in preparation for the Allied landings, pinpointing drop zones for parachutes to deliver weapons and money, and liaising the French resistance organizations with London's supportive military command. She facilitated the escape of thirty Allied airmen shot down over French soil and organized false papers for fellow agents. For some time, Noor acted as the sole communications link between resistance agents in the Paris region and London intelligence and military headquarters until she could be replaced.

Ultimately, arrangements were made to repatriate Noor to the safety of England, an offer she had repeatedly refused until she felt she had fulfilled her duty. However, tragically, just days before her return to London, Noor was betrayed to the Gestapo, as there was a bounty on her head. She was then incarcerated in the German Security Headquarters in Paris, where she attempted to escape twice but failed. Later, Noor was transferred to a German prison where she was subjected to the horrors of solitary confinement and kept in chains for close to a year.

In September 1944 orders came from Hitler via Ernst Kaltenbrunn that all Allied agents who were currently held in German captivity should be made to disappear in a *"Nacht und Nebel"* (night and fog) operation. Noor, along with three fellow women agents serving in Churchill's SOE, were taken to Dachau, where they were executed.

Though, by a twist of fate, I had been living only a couple of hours' drive from Dachau for nearly ten years, it was not until my uncle invited me to the musical commemoration for Noor that I finally visited the camp to pay tribute to my aunt's acts of bravery and call of duty to the free world. As the product of a mixed-race heritage—born in Russia to an Indian father and an American mother—Noor had spent much of her life in England and France. Yet her allegiance lay not with any one country or nationality but with the cause of justice and righteousness. The young woman who aspired to devote her life to music, writing children's stories, and working in child psychology, was tortured and murdered at the age of thirty while fearlessly battling against Hitler and his regime of terror.

My initial reluctance and procrastination in visiting the Dachau Memorial Site likely stemmed from a fear of facing the quandary about how the German people could be responsible for the unimaginable horrors of the concentration camps. I had been living in Bavaria all these years and perceived the German people as being no different from those I had lived among before, namely, British, American, and French.

A decade after my first visit to Dachau, I received an invitation to return while participating in a BBC documentary about my aunt, Noor Inayat Khan. It was during this visit that the center's curator divulged shocking details about Noor's death. He presented me with a photo of SS *Obersturmbannführer* Wilhelm Ruppert, the man in charge of executions at Dachau, and revealed that he was the one who had personally beaten my aunt before fatally shooting her.

Standing in solemn silence at the "execution wall," where Noor and countless others had met their tragic end, we also paid our respects at the nearby "ash pit," where their remains had been unceremoniously disposed of. This experience left me with a multitude of unanswered questions, including the necessity of Noor's sacrifice and the culpability of the German people for the atrocities of World War II and genocide. With these questions weighing heavy on my mind, I hope that through *Exposing the Reich* readers can gain a deeper understanding of this dark chapter of history and comprehend how ordinary citizens could turn into killers.

Upon my arrival in Germany during the 1980s, I quickly learned that it was best not to bring up the topics of Hitler, World War II, or the Holocaust.

The older generation would dismissively categorize that period as "difficult times" and preferred not to discuss it further. The younger Germans at the time had limited knowledge of those dark days and would often deflect any national culpability by pointing out the transgressions of other nations, such as British colonization or American oppression of Native Americans and African slaves. However, nearly four decades later, the situation has significantly improved.

Like most western children born in the 1950s, I was exposed to the Hollywood-stereotyped movies portraying us as "the good guys" versus the "bad" Germans, the "Nazis." At the French elementary school I attended in the 1950s, children parroted their parents' nickname for the Germans, referring to them as *"les sales Boches,"* a contemptuous term the Allies used for Germans during both world wars and derived from the French slang *tête de caboche*, meaning "cabbage head." Yet now I lived and interacted with Germans, people like you and me, gifted with the same qualities and faults as the rest of humanity. Where were these monsters? Were they my friends' and neighbors' parents or grandparents? Could they have been so different from the other inhabitants of Europe or of North America?

Stephen E. Ambrose recounts a timeless anecdote in his best-selling World War II history book *Band of Brothers*. It involves American soldiers describing, often in a derogatory manner, the people they met as they advanced from England to France, Belgium, and ultimately Germany. However, the story takes an unexpected turn when the average G.I. discovers that the Europeans they liked the most, related to the most, and even enjoyed being around were the Germans. Many American soldiers found the Germans to be similar to themselves: clean, hardworking, disciplined, educated, and with middle-class tastes and lifestyles.

Working as a tour guide for over three decades on "Hitler's Mountain" in Berchtesgaden, I have become accustomed to inquiries surrounding Hitler and his Nazi Party. Visitors are often eager to venture beyond the mere facts and figures concerning Hitler's mountaintop Eagle's Nest retreat, asking thought-provoking questions such as these: What motivated the Germans to vote for Hitler? Why did Hitler harbor such hatred toward the Jewish people? Did all Germans support the Nazi Party? How could the German people be aware of the concentration camps yet do nothing to prevent them? Providing satisfactory responses to such complex and multilayered questions can be challenging, as it requires contextual knowledge to comprehend the intricate historical events that led ordinary individuals to actively participate in heinous acts against their fellow human beings.

What educational material could I recommend to my tour participants to better understand the quandary of the Third Reich? What book or books could answer their questions easily, could fill in the blanks? An exhaustive list of

Hitler biographies, Hitler personality analyses, World War II histories, and voluminous academic studies on specific aspects of his regime spun around in my head. Yet I could not point a finger at a single work that would, in simple language and condensed into a reasonably short read, offer an understanding of one of the greatest calamities that mankind has ever experienced.

For this reason, I felt compelled to gather material that would help us understand what transpired in Germany during the first half of the twentieth century. I was determined to do this without either placing a burden of guilt on the German people or attempting to plead their innocence. I deemed it important to follow the time line of Hitler's rise and reign and, in easy-to-read terminology, to guide a reader step-by-step to gain insight to the how and why of the Third Reich tragedy. Chapter by chapter, *Exposing the Reich* aims to list the most important facts and events that allowed a frail and skinny young man who, at the age of twenty-four, was found unfit to fulfill Austrian military service to become, arguably, history's most ruthless dictator and warmonger.

Part 1 of the book offers readers a chronological journey through Adolf Hitler's life, starting from his youthful ambitions of becoming a "great artist" and his life-shaping experiences in Vienna. The section also covers Hitler's time serving in the First World War and his return to Munich as a decorated veteran. Additionally, readers will learn about Hitler's training in the army's political propaganda, his entry into the world of politics, and the challenges faced by the Weimar Republic, the German postwar government. We also follow the events that shaped Hitler's worldview and led to his rise to power. The last chapter in this section questions the commonly held belief that Hitler restored Germany's floundering economy. Surprising as it may sound, the much-touted drop in unemployment and the concurrent resumption of industry did not produce a solid economy, the desired self-sufficiency, or long-term wealth for Germany.

Part 2 delves into the Third Reich's use of multiple forms of propaganda, ranging from education and art to media and entertainment, as well as the *Führer* myth. Through subtle and theatrical means, National Socialism aimed to appeal to the senses and emotions of the public. Readers will become familiar with Hitler's skills as an orator, his use of dramatic staged events, and the public's constant forced exposure to manipulated worldviews. Above all, the Reich's well-oiled propaganda machine aimed to instill in Germans a fear and hatred of so-called international Jewry and Judeo-Bolshevism.

Part 3 reveals the mechanisms by which Germany's population was monitored, in particular by the police force and the terror apparatus such as the Gestapo and the SS. It describes the targeting of actual or perceived enemies of the Reich, such as Jews, dissidents, political opponents, and those who, for social or religious reasons, did not conform to the new norm. The development of the German concentration camp system is also elucidated, from its first official establishment near Dachau to its repurposing as extermination facilities in Eastern Europe. In this section we also learn about those who did not embrace Hitler's ways and who, at the risk of their lives, to a lesser or greater extent did what they could to counter, resist, or topple the regime and its dictatorship.

Part 4 delves into additional themes related to the Third Reich, providing answers to common questions and topics of interest. Among these are whether Hitler and his top officials studied occult or esoteric themes, the truth about Eva Braun's role as Hitler's mistress, the significance of the swastika as the National Socialist symbol, and the similarities between Hitler's and Mussolini's regimes. The often overlooked role and status of women during the Third Reich is also explored, and finally, the section reviews Hitler's unpublished "Secret Book" or "Second Book," written in 1928, which sheds light on the foreign policy plans that Hitler would later implement during his twelve-year reign of terror.

Part 5 delves into the level of involvement of the average German in National Socialist beliefs during Hitler's regime. It investigates the extent to which Germans, from soldiers to housewives, teenagers to civil servants, supported the regime's ideology and persecution from 1933 to 1945. This section further explores the Germans' retrospective assessment of the Third Reich, World War II, and the Holocaust, both in East and West Germany, in the decades following the war. The final part of this section provides insight into how the German state and its people perceive and remember their past today, particularly the Germany of their parents and grandparents, and how they are dealing with the recent surge in xenophobia in the country.

Through the systematic presentation and development of various themes, this book aims to provide a comprehensive understanding of Germany and the Germans during the period of the National Socialist German Workers Party's rise to power and eventual downfall at the end of World War II. In keeping with my effort to explore and understand the Third Reich in an objective manner, I have purposely avoided the employment of the non-German derogatory designation of the party as "Nazi" or its adherents as "Nazis" but have chosen to use the official terms "National Socialist" or "NS" Party.

By following developments along the time line during which they unfolded, it is my intention to present this complex era of history in a clear and easily comprehensible manner, accessible to a diverse readership, including students, scholars, World War II history enthusiasts, visitors to Germany, and anyone with an interest in history. I hope that this book will provide insightful and thought-provoking information to all who engage with its pages.

David Harper

P.S. If you find this work interesting and illuminating, please look out for my next book. Wishing to share my knowledge of the numerous historically significant sights—many of which have remained obscure and that are often overlooked by even the most educated travelers to Europe—I have put together a "guide book" to identify and visit both perpetrator sites and victim sites. Few have explored, for instance, the remnants of Third Reich Germany's monumental underground fortifications, such as the *Ostwall* or the *Westwall*, once stretching hundreds of miles along the country's eastern and western borders.

The book also describes how to visit over forty historic sites in Europe, nearly half of which have remained unknown, such as the fortress-like training center for the Reich's future political leaders, Himmler's mysterious Wewelsburg Castle, and the two salt mines in which Hitler stockpiled the world's largest art collections. Other sites of great historic interest include vast hidden bunkers in Poland, German V-weapon factories in France, and Hitler's once-secret HQ in Belgium.

Better known travel destinations such as the Normandy Landing beaches, the Nuremberg Trials' courtroom, and the infamous concentration camps of Dachau and Auschwitz are also described among the book's listing of numerous historic and educational sites dotted across ten countries.

PART I

From Artist to Dictator

"If you would judge, understand."

—Marcus Annaeus Seneca (writer, ancient Rome)

Chapter 1

Adolf Hitler's Humble Beginnings

MYSTERY AND SCANDAL

Adolfus Hitler's family history has been the object of disproportionate research and speculation. "People must not know who I am," Hitler reportedly ranted when he learned of one of the early investigations into his family history. "They must not know where I am from."[1] Motives for these inquiries into the future dictator's background range from discreditation of the supposedly pure Aryan Austrian ("but didn't he have a Jewish grandfather?") to tabloid-style sensationalizing of his father's somewhat scandalous relationships and marriages.

A SEMINAL SECRET

The great mystery of Hitler's ancestry remains unsolved: Maria Schicklgruber took this "seminal" secret to her grave in 1847, over forty years prior to her grandson Adolf's birth. The church registry of Döllersheim in Austria's Waldviertel, some seventy miles northwest of Vienna and not far from the Czechoslovakian border, recorded the birth of her illegitimate son, Alois Schicklgruber, on June 7, 1837. Maria, an unmarried housemaid of forty-two, refused to disclose the identity of the boy's enigmatic progenitor.

Rumors have abounded to the effect that Adolf Hitler's grandfather could have been a wealthy Jew named Frankenberger or even a Baron Rothschild from Vienna, also a Jew. However, a more likely candidate for Alois's fatherhood is Johann Georg Hiedler, an itinerant mill worker from the nearby town of Spital who finally married Maria Schicklgruber when Alois was five years old. Despite this turn of events, it's noteworthy that Johann Georg Hiedler never claimed paternity of the illegitimate boy. Alois was only ten when his mother died, forcing him to live on the farm of his father's brother, Johann Nepomuk, who some researchers also believe to be a candidate for the mysterious fatherhood.

At the age of forty, Alois Schicklgruber returned to the church in Döllersheim where his illegitimate birth, as well as his mother's subsequent marriage, had been registered many years before. Most likely against his better judgment, the parish priest allowed himself to be coerced into retroactively modifying Alois's last name from Schicklgruber to Hitler. Surely the registry clerk must have known that it was illegal to alter Alois's surname based solely on assurances that his deceased father had allegedly wished to adopt the boy. Without this historically significant change, Alois's future baby boy would have been christened Adolf Schicklgruber.[2]

The various forms of the name Hiedler or Hitler can be traced back to Czech names such as Hidlar or Hidlarček. Variants include Hydler, Hytler, and Hidler. Coincidentally, a seventeenth-century direct ancestor of Hitler's mother was Georg Hiedler, some of whose descendants spelled their name "Hüttler" as well as "Hitler." It may have been a well-hidden embarrassment to Adolf Hitler to know that his last name's origins were Slavic, as he would later classify the Slavic people as subhuman and unworthy of populating Eastern European lands.[3]

THE PLAYBOY

Alois left home at the age of thirteen and went to Vienna, where he started working as an apprentice cobbler. However, he soon felt a desire for more and enlisted in the border guards to improve himself. Extremely motivated to succeed in his new role, Alois spent much of his time studying and preparing for exams. His efforts were rewarded as he advanced through the ranks and eventually attained the position of full inspector of customs at Braunau on the River Inn, which served as the border between Austria and Germany.

When on leave from his duties, Alois would return to his hometown of Spital. The sight of the dashing young man in uniform drew the attention of many, including the beautiful Klara Pölzl, a sixteen-year-old girl with luxuriant dark brown hair and striking features. True to his reputation as a womanizer, Alois determined to seduce Klara, but two obstacles stood in his way. Firstly, he was already married, and secondly, Klara was his first cousin once removed. Undeterred, Alois saw an opportunity to be close to Klara when his wife became sickly. He convinced Klara's parents to allow her to accompany him back to Braunau to assist with his wife's care. And thus, Alois and Klara's journey together began, a journey that would change the course of history forever.

When Klara arrived at the inn where Alois Hitler resided with his wife, Anna, she was immediately caught in a web of deceit and infidelity. Though she may have felt drawn to Alois, her feelings quickly changed upon discovering his relationship with the kitchen maid, Fanni. The arrival of Klara proved to be the final straw for Alois's wife, who soon left him and filed for separation. Fanni, however, saw an opportunity to further entrench herself in Alois's life and promptly moved in, acting more as a wife than a mistress. Acutely aware of Alois's weakness for women, she hastily sent Klara back to her hometown. Eventually, Alois's first wife, Anna, passed away, clearing the way for him to legitimize his relationship with Fanni and their two children.

Soon it was Fanni's health that began to deteriorate, and she was moved to a country village for treatment, leaving Alois alone to care for their two children at the Pommer Inn in Braunau. As can be expected, Alois seized the opportunity to call for Klara to return from Spital, and she soon assumed the roles of housemaid, nursemaid, and mistress. Conveniently for Alois, though, Fanni passed away soon after, leaving the path clear for his third marriage: this time to his cousin Klara. Despite their incestuous relationship, Alois managed to obtain a special marriage dispensation from Rome, likely due to the fact that Klara was already pregnant.

The couple wed on January 7, 1885, in Braunau am Inn, and Klara continued to address her husband as "Uncle," as he was twenty-three years her elder. Two years later, Klara gave birth to a baby boy named Adolfus Hitler. At the age of three, Alois was promoted and the family moved to the larger town of Passau, further down the Inn River. There, young Adolf spent the next two and a half years playing with German children, a period which, he later claimed, shaped the distinctive lower Bavarian dialect that would remain his "mother tongue." At the age of six, the family moved back to Austria and settled in Hafeld, some thirty miles southwest of Linz, where Alois had been reassigned.

"A SCRUBBY LITTLE ROGUE"

As Adolf and his half sister Angela walked along the dusty road to the local school, they both felt the weight of the lackluster learning environment that lay ahead of them. Adolf would later describe the school as "shabby and primitive," but despite its shortcomings, he quickly emerged as a standout student, remembered by his teacher as "mentally very alert, obedient but lively." Throughout his school years, Adolf excelled in subjects such as history and language but struggled with mathematics. However, his talent for drawing was consistently praised. Additionally, he was known to possess a pleasant singing voice and would often participate in choir classes at the local monastery. Upon entering the establishment, Adolf was immediately struck by the stone archway featuring the monastery's coat of arms, prominently displaying an ancient symbol: the swastika. The abbey made a profound impact on the young boy, who was said to be "intoxicated by the solemn splendor" of the magnificent church festivals and held the abbot in high regard, even aspiring to become a priest himself.

Father Alois was prone to violence and, despite other siblings and half siblings being present in the home, Adolf usually bore the brunt of the customs officer's harsh discipline. According to his younger sister Paula, "He was a scrubby little rogue, and all attempts of Father to thrash him for his rudeness and to cause him to love the profession of an official of the state were in vain. How often on the other hand did my mother caress him and try to obtain with her kindness, where Father could not succeed with harshness!"

As a child, Adolf possessed natural leadership skills and would lead his schoolmates in playful battles between cowboys and Indians. When the Boer War broke out, he became deeply passionate about German patriotism and incorporated the conflict into his games. Adolf would cast himself as the leader of the Boers, and his classmates were forced to play the role of the British in numerous battles. Throughout his childhood, Adolf displayed a strong interest in all things German, openly sharing his Pan-German views and even drawing portraits of Otto von Bismarck, the statesman who had unified Germany in 1870. These actions were considered bold and dangerous in the conservative Austrian society in which he grew up.

Adolf's educational journey took him to the Realschule in Linz at the age of eleven. There, he was mesmerized by the legendary figures of German mythology and was introduced to the world of Wagnerian opera. His first year in Linz was filled with challenges as he struggled to adjust to his new environment and was labeled a "country bumpkin" by his classmates. The class photo no longer showed a cocky Adolf but rather a lost and dejected youth. In his second year, however, he regained his confidence and leadership skills and steadily improved his drawing abilities.

A year following his father's death from a pleural hemorrhage, Adolf began failing in French. Although he managed to pass the makeup exam in the autumn, he was only allowed to proceed to the next grade if he attended a different school. He resided with a local family in Steyer, but his academic performance remained average, with the exception of history, geography, and drawing. Despite passing his summer exams, Adolf did not wish to take the Matura, the Austrian exam for college education. He relied on a recent lung condition as an excuse and persuaded his mother to allow him to take a break from his studies.

With no father to keep him in check, a teenage Adolf who loathed authority began to immerse himself in literature, filled sketchbooks with drawings, visited museums, and attended the opera. His father had left the family with a comfortable sum of money, meaning he had no need to worry about seeking employment. Not being a sociable person, Adolf finally found someone he could "tolerate," a local boy named August Kubizek. The son of an upholsterer and known as "Gustl" to Adolf, he dreamed of becoming a world-famous musician. Gustl already played several instruments and was studying music theory in Linz. The two young men began attending almost every opera performance and enjoyed strolling along the picturesque boulevards of the city. They spent hours and days in each other's company, with Adolf sketching or painting watercolors, while sharing his hopes and plans and revealing his wild dreams and imaginings. Kubizek recalled those days: "He always knew what I needed and what I wanted. Sometimes I had a feeling that he was living my life as well as his own."[4]

A MAMA'S BOY

In the spring of 1906, a dream came true for Adolf when his mother allowed him to visit Vienna, the capital of art, music, and architecture. For a month, he roamed the streets, immersing himself in the city's culture and keeping Gustl updated on his visits to the opera, theater, and museums. However, shortly after his return from this unforgettable trip, his mother fell ill and was treated by Dr. Edward Bloch, a Jewish physician known in the area as "the poor people's doctor." The doctor summoned Adolf and his sister Paula, explaining to them that Klara had breast cancer and that surgery was the only hope of saving her. Bloch was moved by Adolf's reaction, recalling that "his long, sallow face was contorted. Tears flowed from his eyes. Did his mother, he asked, have no chance? Only then did I recognize the magnitude of the attachment that existed between mother and son."

Klara underwent the operation and several weeks later was allowed to return home. Although Adolf was relieved, he soon became restless and felt that Linz no longer had anything to offer him. Vienna's artistic pull proved too strong, and with his mother's permission, he withdrew his inheritance, a sum that would sustain him for a year in the capital. He was thrilled at the prospect of fulfilling his dream. The only thing that marred his mood was the fact that his mother's health was gradually deteriorating. The admission exam to Adolf's dream school, Vienna's Academy of Fine Arts, took place only in October, so he left despite his concern for his mother's health.

Some weeks later, it became clear that Klara Hitler was dying, and Adolf rushed back home. Dr. Bloch recommended a drastic treatment involving large and painful doses of iodoform to be applied to Klara's open wound. Adolf gladly paid for the costly medication in advance and promised to

Figure 1.1.   Adolf Hitler as a child

pay for the treatment later. Klara was soon installed in the only room in the house that was heated all day, the kitchen. Adolf slept on a couch and tended to his mother with devotion. According to Gustl, during those bleak days Adolf "lived only for his mother." Dr. Bloch recalled that "she bore her burden well, unflinchingly and uncomplaining. But it seemed to torture her son. An anguished grimace would come over him when he saw pain contract her face."

On December 20, as the Christmas tree was illuminated, Klara whispered to Gustl as he was leaving, "Go on being a good friend to my son when I'm no longer here. He has no one else." Later that night, Klara passed away quietly. When Dr. Bloch came the next morning to sign the death certificate, he noticed that Adolf's sketchbook featured a last drawing of his mother. Dr. Bloch attempted to ease Adolf's grief by saying that in this case "death had been a savior." The teenager, however, could not be comforted. Dr. Bloch, who had experienced many deathbed scenes in his career, stated, "I never saw anyone so prostrate with grief as Adolf Hitler."

Many historians and researchers have pointed to Dr Bloch's inability to cure Hitler's mother as a source of his hatred of Jews. This supposition is highly unlikely when we consider the fact that after his mother's death Hitler wrote Bloch grateful missives thanking him for his devoted care and, later, even singled him out as worthy of praise and special protection.[5] In addition, in exchange for Bloch to turn over the records of his treatment of Klara Hitler, he was given a prized exit visa to emigrate to the United States in 1938—a privilege denied to nearly every other doomed Jew in Austria.[6] With his mother buried, nothing stood in the way of Adolf's grand future in Vienna.

NOTES

1. Ron Rosenbaum, *Explaining Hitler: The Search for the Origins of His Evil*, updated ed. (Boston: Da Capo, 2014), 4.

2. John Toland, *Adolf Hitler: The Definitive Biography* (New York: Ancho, 1992), 6.

3. Ibid.

4. Ibid.

5. Rosenbaum, *Explaining Hitler*, 147.

6. Ibid., 243.

Chapter 2

Vienna and the Roots of Hitler's Antisemitism

At the age of eighteen, Adolf Hitler moved to Vienna, where he intended to become a "great artist." Sharing an apartment with his best friend, Gustl Kubizek, the young man who had shown promising creative talent in his school days was eager to conquer the art world.

ARTISTIC PURSUITS

To Hitler it was essential that he attend the capital's Academy of Fine Arts, but despite having taken art lessons in Vienna to better prepare for the entrance examination, Hitler was rejected. Outraged and feeling dejected, Hitler found consolation in the form of music. He and Kubizek shared a love of music, and the two attended as many concerts and operas as possible. Hitler's passion for Wagner's operas intensified in these early days; their enchantment was so strong to him that he attended *Lohengrin* ten times.[1]

Sensing, perhaps, that the art world may not be his future, Hitler tried his hand at other artistic pursuits. One day Kubizek found Hitler working on a play. Hitler was extremely excited about the theme, describing it as a conflict between the pagan natives of the Bavarian mountains and the early Christian missionaries who were trying to convert them. His theme and setting were entirely Wagnerian and may also have been inspired by a book Hitler was reading during his time in Vienna, *Legends of the Gods and Heroes: The Treasures of Germanic Mythology.*[2]

Nothing came of the play project because Hitler switched to writing an opera about *Wieland der Schmied* (Wayland the Smith), an ancient heroic tale filled with rape and murder. Hitler had taken piano lessons in Linz, but as he had no formal musical training beyond that, he suggested that he could compose the music for the opera and Kubizek could write it down.[3] But despite his plans, Hitler's operatic attempts hit a dead end.

Hitler also revealed a keen interest in architecture and became captivated by the ostentatious buildings along Vienna's Ringstrasse—a potpourri of styles, predominantly dating from the mid-nineteenth century. He would drag an unwilling Kubizek on tours of the Ringstrasse, explaining in detail the various facets and histories of the buildings they were passing. These buildings became Hitler's impromptu training ground, and the Ringstrasse became an "object against which he could measure his architectural knowledge and demonstrate his opinions."[4]

During Hitler's stay in Vienna, the city emerged as a leading center for new artistic, architectural, musical, and literary movements. However, Hitler remained oblivious to these exciting developments and instead preferred to immerse himself in the classicism and historicism of the nineteenth century. He would later envision the grandiose and ostentatious buildings of his "thousand-year Reich" as modeled on his Ringstrasse ideal. Although Hitler would dabble in the arts for the next few years, his enduring passion was for architecture. Even during his final days in the Berlin bunker, Hitler occupied himself with studying and revising the architectural details of his plans for cultural buildings in Linz.[5]

THE CRUMBLING HABSBURG EMPIRE

In the early twentieth century, the Vienna that Hitler encountered was a decaying city, clinging to its former grandeur. Emperor Franz Joseph, who took control at the age of eighteen during the turbulent period of the 1848 revolutions, presided over an empire of fifty-two million subjects spanning Central and Eastern Europe, comprising twelve ethnic groups from the Adriatic Sea to the Carpathians and the Alps. By the turn of the century, Franz Joseph's outdated methods of governance were faltering, and the modern era of nationalism and democracy loomed on the horizon. While many people recognized the inevitable collapse of the Habsburgs' six-century-long rule, the Austrians themselves remained oblivious to the impending collapse.

At some point during his time in Vienna, Hitler became interested in Austrian politics and even attended parliament sessions as a visitor. Following one such gathering, Hitler and Kubizek stumbled upon a demonstration where protesters carried a large banner with the word "HUNGER" blazoned in red letters. According to Kubizek, this experience ignited in Hitler a passion for the cause of the "poor betrayed masses" and for the "storm of revolution," and imbued him with a renewed sense of purpose as a struggling artist.[6]

Hitler came to the realization that Emperor Franz Joseph was "a king in the age of democracy; an imperialist in the era of nationalism," an anachronism in the twentieth century.[7] Vienna, six centuries earlier, had been the capital of the small principality belonging to the Habsburg family and had grown over time to become an empire of more than fifty million souls. The Habsburg monarchs had attempted to rule and unify twelve different nationalities: Germans, Hungarians, Italians, Slovaks, Romanians, Czechs, Poles, Slovenes, Croats, Serbs, Transylvanian Saxons, and Ruthenes. However, Emperor Franz Joseph was unwilling to forfeit the absolute power of the Habsburg dynasty's sovereignty even as his grip on the empire progressively weakened. In the year after Hitler left Austria, Emperor Franz Joseph's severe response to the assassination of his nephew and heir in Sarajevo led to the outbreak of World War I. This would prove to be a catastrophic turning point in history.

Hitler's perception of the Habsburgs' Austria was that of the degradation of the Germanic element within the empire. Hitler recalled his observation of the artifice and inadequacy of the Habsburgs' rule in *Mein Kampf*: "What repelled me was the way the press curried favor with the court. There was scarcely any event at the Hofburg which was not imparted to the readers either with raptures of enthusiasm or plaintive emotion, and all this to-do, particularly when it dealt with the 'wisest monarch of all time,' almost reminded me of the mating cry of the mountain cock."[8] In the same tirade, the xenophobic Hitler talks about this "impossible state which condemned ten million Germans to death. The more the linguistic Babel corroded and disorganized Parliament, the closer drew the inevitable hour of the disintegration of the Babylonian [i.e., Habsburg] Empire."[9]

The early twentieth-century Vienna that Hitler was discovering had not only become a melting pot of multiple ethnic groups but was also a major European capital where many Jewish citizens had attained prominent positions in various areas of society and in many professions. The Jewish population in Vienna had grown rapidly, increasing from just 2 percent of the city's population in 1857 to 8.6 percent by 1910. However, not all of Vienna's Jews fit the stereotype of the successful entrepreneur, a cliché that was prevalent in antisemitic beliefs. Living in the lower-income districts of Vienna, a significant portion of the Jewish population was less fortunate, ranging from 17 percent in the poor neighborhood of Brigittenau to 33 percent in Leopoldstadt.[10]

The Austrians' perception of a Jewish "threat" was based not so much on the percentile of Jews in the empire but, rather, on their sphere of influence in Vienna. In 1909, for instance, over a quarter of university enrollment in the capital was Jewish.[11] Jewish student presence was the greatest in the faculties of law and medicine, and Jews were, generally speaking, successful in big business and the stock exchange. In 1820 the Jewish Rothschild family established the first bank in Vienna and, throughout Austria's early industrialization, financed sizable development projects. The Rothschilds were also generous lenders to Austrian Chancellor Prince Klemens von Metternich and granted substantial credits to the empire's aristocracy. In 1855 the Austrian Rothschilds founded the Credit-Anstalt, which soon became the Austrian Empire's largest bank.

THE TOLERANT MONARCH

When, still in his teenage years, Franz Joseph acceded to the imperial throne of Austria, he intervened on behalf of the Jewish population, stating that "the civil rights and the country's policy are not contingent upon the people's religion." The next year, in 1849, he did away with the prohibition against Jewish organizations within the community, and by 1867 Jews were formally granted full equal rights.

In 1869, Emperor Franz Joseph was warmly welcomed by Jews on a visit to Jerusalem. He later established a fund with the aim of financing the development of Jewish institutions and also founded the Talmudic School for Rabbis in Budapest. In the 1890s, several Jews were even elected to the Austrian parliament. During Franz Joseph's sixty-eight-year reign, despite the Jewish population being small (about 4.5 percent at the turn of the century), Jews made significant contributions to Austrian culture as a whole, and Vienna became a center of Jewish culture. Many notable Jewish minds and talents, such as composers Mahler and Schoenberg; authors Kafka, Hofmannsthal, Schnitzler, Zweig, Kraus, Canetti, Roth, and Baum; as well as doctors like Sigmund Freud, Viktor Frankl, and Alfred Adler and philosophers Martin Buber and Karl Popper, among others, influenced and enriched Austria's artistic and intellectual society.

AUSTRIAN ANTISEMITISM

As the twentieth century began, the Habsburg Empire was home to over two million citizens who practiced the Hebrew faith. Thanks to Franz Joseph's policies of liberalism and legal equality, Austrian Jews, whether they were longtime citizens or new immigrants, were able to realize their aspirations for social integration. However, during this time, rising antisemitism threatened the Jewish population.

In the 1895 elections for Vienna's municipal council, the Christian Socialists won two-thirds of the seats and elected Karl Lueger as mayor. According to imperial law, the emperor was obliged to confirm the mayor's appointment. Franz Joseph, however, refused to comply because he considered Lueger a dangerous revolutionary and disapproved of his outspoken antisemitism. Despite the emperor's objections, the Christian Socialists maintained their overwhelming majority and repeatedly reelected Lueger. It was only after the mayor's fourth election and a personal appeal by Pope Leo XIII that Karl Lueger's appointment was finally sanctioned in late 1897.

Though Austrians also remember Karl Lueger for having transformed Vienna into a modern city with a supply of clean tap water, electricity, and gas, his legacy is tainted with vile antisemitic rhetoric. For all his talk and slander, however, Lueger's active persecution of the country's Jewish citizens did not match the level of his verbal attacks. He did manage, nevertheless, to forbid Jews from working in Vienna's factories or to be employed in the city's services, and he limited their numbers in high schools and universities. In an 1890 speech at the Reichsrat (Imperial Assembly), he declared that the Jews should all be put on a large ship, sent to sea, and the ship sunk with no survivors.[12]

Lueger succeeded in creating a party that channeled social discontent and that depicted capitalism and Marxism alike as products of the Jewish mind, combining these new themes with the centuries-old hatred of the Jews stemming from church doctrine. In the words of the historian Léon Poliakov, "it soon became apparent that, especially in Vienna, any political group that wanted to appeal to the artisans had no chance of success without an antisemitic platform. Though in 1887, Lueger raised the banner of antisemitism, the enthusiastic tribute that Hitler paid him in *Mein Kampf* does not seem justified, for the Jews did not suffer under his administration."[13] In retrospect, the mayor's antisemitism was opportunistic rather than racist, but it is evident that Lueger's leadership during Adolf Hitler's early years in Vienna had a significant impact on the young man's political development.

The *Deutsches Volksblatt, Alldeutsches Tagblatt,* and Catholic *Das Vaterland* were three Austrian newspapers that fostered antisemitic views. Hitler was undoubtedly aware of these widely circulated newspapers, but he reportedly became captivated by a monthly magazine called *Ostara*, which was named after an ancient Germanic goddess and promoted unabashedly antisemitic ideas. The brainchild of a defrocked monk named Adolf Lanz, who gave himself the aristocratic title of *von* to mask his humble origins, *Ostara* was a strange concoction that combined a weak understanding of anthropology, an interest in the occult, and a dash of eroticism. Lanz von Liebenfels, as he later called himself, created a "magical" philosophy that pitted the blond, blue-eyed *"Heldlinge"* (little heroes) against dwarfish and apelike creatures he dubbed *"Äfflinge"* (little apes). It was not difficult to see the parallels between his ideas and the notion of the Aryan race versus the Jews.

The magazine was a calculated blend that played on the anxieties of the lower middle class. Lanz's "ape-men" not only competed with poor citizens for jobs but also destroyed the German race through interbreeding. The magazine included explicit illustrations that depicted blond women being abducted by dark, hairy men. Lanz's portrayal of the overpotent ape-man luring Aryan women to him in order to violate them was intentionally disturbing.[14]

Lanz von Liebenfels believed that man had degenerated from the heroic being he had once been—created in God's image—and that this original demigod condition could be recaptured by a strict regime of pure breeding of Nordic-looking Aryans among themselves. He advocated "the extirpation of the animal-man and the propagation of the higher man" and promised to implement a breeding program "to the hilt of the castration knife." Genetic selection, sterilization, deportation to the "ape jungle," and liquidations by forced labor all featured among the Ariosophist's recommendations for the creation of a master race.

According to some accounts, Hitler was so fond of *Ostara* that he gathered every issue he could obtain and treasured them like a child cherishing a comic book collection. It's been said that he carried these magazines with him as he moved from one address to another. Hitler was even rumored to have visited Lanz von Liebenfels at his office to acquire some back issues of *Ostara* that he was unable to purchase. As the story goes, Liebenfels gave the "pale, serious, and impoverished" young man the missing copies for free, along with some money for his trip home.[15]

Curiously, Hitler did not acknowledge any debt to Lanz von Liebenfels or his magazine, which reportedly boasted a circulation of up to one hundred thousand copies. In fact, when Austria was annexed by the Third Reich in 1938, Lanz hoped for Hitler's support, but the formerly Austrian leader banned him from publishing and had copies of *Ostara* removed from the shelves. After World War II, Lanz accused Hitler of not only stealing his ideas but also corrupting them.

Despite this, it is evident that Hitler's views on Jews can be traced back to his days in Vienna. More than a decade later, Hitler wrote in *Mein Kampf* that the Jews he encountered in Vienna "were no lovers of water, and, to your distress, you often knew it with your eyes closed." He claimed to have discovered that these people had despicable professions, ranging from pimps to white slavers. Hitler came to believe that the Jews were responsible for destroying culture, claiming that "all the filth written in his Vienna days was perpetrated by the Jews." Invoking an aura of religious justification in his tirade, Hitler summed it up when he stated, "By defending myself against the Jew, I am fighting for the work of the Lord."[16] Rehashing the images and messages of the *Ostara* booklets of his Vienna days, Hitler later wrote of the "nightmare vision of the seduction of hundreds of thousands of girls by repulsive, crooked-leg, Jew bastards."[17]

Another probable influence on Hitler while he lived in Vienna was the writing of Guido von List, who developed his own brand of mysticism. He promulgated Aryan supremacy and a reverence for the "Old Ones"—allegedly the progenitors of the Aryo-Germanic people. List called this ancient race the "*Armanen,*" with whom he claimed to have a psychic connection. Guido von List was forced to flee Vienna due to rumors of rituals that involved sexual perversion and the practice of black magic. Regardless of the truth of List's alleged "blood lodge," Lanz von Liebenfels became a member of the List Society, and whether Hitler ever met Guido von List or not, he possessed at least one of his books in his personal library.

In turn, Guido von List was a reader of Lanz's *Ostara* and an active member of Lanz's personal Order of the Templars. List, Liebenfels, and Hitler alike were fascinated by archaic symbols. Liebenfels used the ancient swastika as a logo, as did other secret societies and occult orders at the time. List was also captivated by the jagged runic letters *SS* shaped like lightning bolts, which Hitler later chose for his private army.[18] Before he died in 1919, Guido von List prophesied that a racially pure Reich would be established in Germany in 1932—Hitler seized power in January 1933.[19]

Figure 2.1. Vienna Opera House (watercolor by Adolf Hitler)

THE STRUGGLING ARTIST

After failing the entrance exam for Vienna's Academy of Fine Arts, Hitler was determined to make a second attempt the following year. Confident in his artistic abilities, he brought a selection of his artwork but was rejected once again. The nineteen-year-old was so devastated by the rejection that he secretly moved out of the apartment he had shared with his schoolmate Kubizek. Soon, Hitler's small inheritance from his parents began to run out. He moved to simpler and cheaper accommodations several times and briefly worked for a construction company, but he quit when he was required to join a labor union, claiming he didn't want to be coerced into anything.

Hitler, who was unemployed and had no source of income, eventually resorted to seeking aid from charitable institutions, where he would wait in line for a bowl of soup or spend the night at a homeless shelter. Amusingly, one of these institutions, the Asylum for the Shelterless in Meidling, was mainly sponsored by the wealthy Jewish Epstein family.[20]

In February 1910, Hitler moved into a residence for destitute men, where he stayed for the next three years. He collaborated with his friend Reinhold Hanisch, who was in a similar situation, to sell Hitler's drawings and paintings. Hanisch found a market for handmade postcards that featured famous Vienna landmarks and simple images that were useful for frame manufacturers. It was easier to sell a frame if it had a picture in it. Ironically, much of Hitler's meager income came from Jews in the art industry, the very people he had started to despise.[21]

At the Männerheim, Hitler spent his days painting by the window, reading newspapers, and pontificating his views on politics, society, and the arts to anyone who would listen. Other residents of the home usually made a point of disagreeing with him, which Hitler couldn't tolerate.[22] Whenever he became impassioned while arguing or expounding his views, he would jump to his feet, seemingly unable to express himself with fervor unless he was standing.

HITLER'S GRANITE FOUNDATION

While Hitler lived in Vienna, a new form of entertainment made its debut in society: the cinema. Cheaper than a ticket for the opera—which Hitler was no longer able to afford—this new medium fascinated Hitler for the rest of his life (later, he regularly watched movies at his home at Obersalzberg). During the showing of a film called *The Tunnel*, Hitler became mesmerized by a scene in which the orator makes a speech in a tunnel, turning it into "a great popular tribune." Upon his return to the men's home, Hitler sought out his friend Hanisch, who recalled that Hitler was "aflame" with his new idea and, excitedly grabbing Hanisch by the arm, recounted his film experience and concluded that "this was the way to found a new party." Hanisch laughed at his overzealous friend and retired to bed.[23] In those days, Hitler had grown used to people not taking him seriously, even belittling his often inflammatory views. Someday he would prove them wrong to have ridiculed his opinions and visions.

Thanks to his partnership with Hanisch, Hitler's sketches and watercolors of Viennese scenes and landscapes provided him with a sporadic income. His first splurge was to purchase two mottoes that he framed and hung in his room. The one translated as "Without Jews, without Rome, we will build Germany's Cathedral. Heil!" and the other: "We gaze freely and openly, we gaze unflinchingly / We gaze happily over there into the German fatherland. Heil!"[24] These two adages, which became engraved in Hitler's ideological agenda, were in fact the touchstones of the Austrian political extremist Georg von Schönerer and his Pan-German Party, founded in 1885. In *Mein Kampf*, Hitler wrote, "When I was in Vienna, my sympathies were fully and wholly on the side of the Pan-German movement."[25]

Schönerer was a strong antisemite and pro-Prussian advocate whose antidemocratic and left-wing liberal ideas during the final years of the Habsburg Empire attracted support from the Viennese lower middle class and fraternities. One of his program points stated that "To carry out the reforms aspired to, the removal of Jewish influence from all spheres of public life is essential."[26] Despite becoming a national political figure in Austria, Schönerer's violent temperament eventually discredited his Pan-German Party. However, his lasting ideological influence on other extremists such as Lueger, Guido von List, and his admirer Adolf Hitler was not weakened.

In *Mein Kampf*, Hitler provides a detailed account of the political lessons he learned during his time in Vienna. His six years in the Austrian capital coincided with a period when the political climate reflected the shortcomings of liberalism. The 1873 stock market crash and the grim working-class suburbs stood in stark contrast to the empire's superficial and glossy high society, which was characterized by unbridled capitalism. These opposing realities were the everyday experience of the average Viennese resident as well as the wider population of Austria. Dissatisfied with the empty promises of the liberal parties, various groups began advocating for reform. The Pan-Germans, the Christian Socialists, and the Social Democrats all promised to restructure the electoral process, improve working conditions, and address the social injustices of "unproductive capitalism."[27]

Hitler observed the progress of each of these parties, noting their agendas and their rhetoric. He noticed how Lueger and his party understood "the value of large-scale propaganda . . . in influencing the psychological instincts of the broad masses of its adherents."[28] He also remarked on the weaknesses of the main parties and intimated that it fell upon him, the humble postcard painter living in the poorhouse, to devise the perfect plan for the liberation of the hard, honest worker from capitalist oppression.

Hitler's description omitted the early iteration of what he later presented to the German public. In fact, as early as 1903, a proponent of Schönerer's Pan-German ideology established the German Workers Party in the Bohemian and Moravian regions of the Habsburg Empire.

The German Workers Party aimed to safeguard German interests in the Czech lands and was intensely anti-Slavic, anti-Catholic, anti-Marxist, and anticapitalist. During the Imperial Council's 1911 election, which coincided with Hitler's growing interest in the empire's politics, the party won three seats. This precursor to the German Workers' Party that Hitler would later join and take over, it represented an early fusion of nationalism and socialism. It even included the term *Volksgemeinschaft* (people's community) in its ideological framework—the quasi-mystical and reassuring ideal that Hitler would later propagate.[29]

Though a failure at marketing his own artwork, Hitler valued the talent of his friend Hanisch and other agents in the art of salesmanship. One morning, while leafing through the papers, he came upon an ad that particularly pleased him. It was a sketch of a woman with floor-length hair, recommending an extraordinary hair pomade that was guaranteed to make hair grow "even on a billiard ball." Hitler laughed when he read this and exclaimed, "Now that's called advertising. Propaganda, propaganda, until the people believe this trash will help them."[30] Some days later, when arguing with Hanisch about sales tactics, he claimed that oratory and propaganda were the essential ingredients needed to sell anything.[31] "Propaganda," Hitler continued, "is the essence of every religion, whether it be for heaven or hair pomade."[32]

Shortly after his twenty-fourth birthday and after nearly six years in Austria's capital, Hitler took leave of Vienna. A "longing arose stronger and stronger in me," he recounted of his decision later, "to go at last wither since childhood secret desires and secret love had drawn me."[33] His sudden move to Munich, where he planned to enroll at the Art Academy and, moreover, to learn architecture, was also prompted by the fact that he was allegedly trying to dodge the Austrian military draft.

Upon arriving in Vienna, Hitler had expected that his artistic accomplishments would elevate him and distance him from his humble origins. While in Vienna, he was able to indulge in his passion for opera, theater, and the fine arts, although he had managed to ignore the art nouveau revolution that was taking place in this pioneering art capital.

Vienna also exerted a strong influence on young Hitler's antisemitic views. He soon began blaming Jews for everything wrong in history and society.

In the Habsburg Empire, Hitler shaped his political views and learned how demonstrations, cinema, and various forms of propaganda could be used to change a nation's political agenda. The very nation that Hitler had referred to as moribund was the school in which he learned how to charm, hypnotize, and ultimately conquer the German people.

Out of the potpourri of Vienna's opposing beliefs and movements—even despite his lack of personal political involvement at the time—Hitler brewed a cynical view of the world around him.[34] Hitler famously stated, "At that time [1907–1913], I formed a view of life which became the granite foundation of my actions."[35] Vienna's "granite foundation" was to become not only the cornerstone but the entire premise of Hitler's Third Reich.

As Hitler left Vienna for Germany, he carried with him not just the contents of his worn-out suitcase but also a plethora of experience and beliefs that he would exploit in the years to come. During his time in the Austrian capital, Hitler endured profound disappointment from his failure to be accepted at the Art Academy and the ensuing years of financial hardship. These trying moments allowed him to connect with his family's farming background and the working-class origins he shared with them. The *Weltanschauung* that Hitler gained in Vienna ultimately led to the horrific and ignominious calamities that the *Führer*'s twelve years of terror left in their wake.

NOTES

1. J. Sydney Jones, *Hitler in Vienna 1907–1913: Clues to the Future* (New York: Stein and Day, 1983), 36.

2. August Kubizek, *The Young Hitler I Knew* (Boston: Houghton Mifflin, 1955), 154.

3. Ibid., 195.

4. Ibid., 164.

5. Jones, *Hitler in Vienna*, 53.

6. Kubizek, *Young Hitler I Knew*, 246.

7. Jones, *Hitler in Vienna*, 84.

8. Adolf Hitler, *Mein Kampf* (Boston: Houghton Mifflin, 1942), 39.

9. Ibid., 38.

10. Leo Goldhammer, *Die Juden Wiens* (Leipzig: R. Löwit Verlag, 1927), 9.

11. Ibid., 39–40.

12. William A. Jenks, *Vienna and the Young Hitler* (New York: Octagon Books, 1976), 50.

13. Léon Poliakov, *The History of Anti-Semitism* (Philadelphia: University of Pennsylvania Press, 2003), 4:25.

14. Jones, *Hitler in Vienna*, 117.

15. Ibid.

16. Hitler, *Mein Kampf*, 57–65.

17. Alan Bullock, *Hitler: A Study in Tyranny* (New York: Harper & Brothers, 1953), 16.

18. Jones, *Hitler in Vienna*, 123–25.

19. Robert G. L. Waite, *The Psychopathic God: Adolf Hitler* (New York: Basic Books, 1977), 97.

20. Jones, *Hitler in Vienna*, 133.

21. Ibid., 144–48.

22. Ibid., 151.

23. Reinhold Hanisch, "I Was Hitler's Buddy," *New Republic*, April 5, 1939, 242.

24. Josef Greiner, *Das Ende des Hitler-Mythos* (Zürich: Amalthea-Verlag, 1947), 81.

25. Hitler, *Mein Kampf*, 124.

26. Jenks, *Vienna and the Young Hitler*, 84.

27. Jones, *Hitler in Vienna*, 170.

28. Hitler, *Mein Kampf*, 119.

29. Jones, *Hitler in Vienna*, 172.

30. Greiner, *Das Ende des Hitler-Mythos*, 40–41.

31. Hanisch, "I Was Hitler's Buddy," 241.

32. Greiner, *Das Ende des Hitler-Mythos*, 42.

33. Hitler, *Mein Kampf*, 124.

34. Jones, *Hitler in Vienna*, 174.

35. Hitler, *Mein Kampf*, 30.

Chapter 3

The Great War

FROM HOPE TO DEFEAT

It was May 1913 when the dilettante Austrian artist first showed up in Munich. Leaving Vienna behind, as well as the embarrassment of his repeated failure to enter its Academy of Fine Arts, Hitler hoped to attend Munich's art academy for a period of three years.[1] Upon registering with the police in Munich, he listed his profession as Kunstmaler (painter).

THE DABBLING ARTIST

During his time in the Austrian capital, Hitler relied mainly on watercolors, as they were less expensive than oil paints, to create intricate depictions of renowned landmarks. In Munich, some of Hitler's preferred subjects were the famed beer hall, the Hofbräuhaus, and the Opera House. He would spend days working on his paintings before visiting art dealerships and popular bars to showcase his art. Hitler expressed his affection for Munich and felt right at home in the Bavarian capital, which had around six hundred thousand inhabitants at the time.

A firsthand account of Hitler in those early years is given by one of his first customers, Dr. Hans Schirmer. Sitting in the Hofbräuhaus Biergarten, he noted:

> Around eight o'clock I noticed a very unassuming, quite shabby-looking young man, whom I took for an impoverished student, pass by my table offering to sell a small oil painting. Around ten o'clock I observed that he had still not managed to sell his painting. . . . At length I met his price. It was a mood piece, called Evening. As soon as the painter left me I noticed that he went to the buffet and

bought a piece of bread and two Viennese sausages. He ate this alone, without any beer.[2]

Ineptitude at depicting the human form (the unschooled artist's attempts at drawing people resembled stick figures) limited Hitler's subjects to land-scapes and buildings. Even with the help of his Munich roommate, who had accompanied him from Vienna, Hitler had very little success selling his work.

UNFIT TO SERVE?

To make matters worse, in January 1914 Hitler received devastating news from Austria: the officials had tracked him down for having allegedly failed to report for military service in his homeland. Rejecting conscription in a peacetime army, he pleaded with the Austrian authorities, depicting himself as a down-and-out artist struggling to make a living in a city where "three thousand artists" were trying to get by. Hitler was, however, obliged to report to the authorities in Salzburg, where, after he failed his physical, the Austrian officials took pity on him and deemed him unfit to serve.[3] Soon after, Hitler's luck improved as he found more buyers for his inexpensive, run-of-the-mill artwork. He obviously abandoned his ambition of enrollment at Munich's art academy and recalled in *Mein Kampf* that, at that time, "he was painting to live rather than living to paint."[4]

OR FIT TO FIGHT?

Adolf Hitler was thrilled when, a few months later, World War I broke out. He recalled the opportunity it presented to him: "Even today, I am not ashamed to say that, overcome with rapturous enthusiasm, I fell to my knees and thanked heaven from an overflowing heart for granting me the good fortune of being allowed to live at this time." In his mind, the war at hand represented the realization of the Greater Germany he had dreamed of since youth.

As the country mobilized for war, excitement swept through Germany, with many embracing the idea of going to battle. The belief that war would bring national unity and the opportunity for the German Empire to assert its power in Europe played a key role in this enthusiasm. A sense of national pride, coupled with the desire to defend Germany's perceived place in the international order, fueled the eagerness of many Germans to go to war. The idea that a conflict with France and Russia could lead to the reclaiming of lost territory and the expansion of the German Empire also contributed to the fer-vor. This was not a result of individual reasoning but rather a mass outpouring of emotions, as large gatherings saw people close to hysteria and willing to make sacrifices for the "cause." The idea of a pan-Germanic nation, with a master race directing the progress of mankind, was also a popular sentiment. Although such statements may have been echoed by an older Adolf Hitler, at that time he was merely eager to join the Bavarian armed forces.

On the fateful day of August 3, 1914, Germany declared war against France, and Hitler was filled with excitement and eagerness to play his part in the conflict. Just half a year after the Austrian army had deemed Hitler "unfit to serve," he now submitted a personal petition to King Ludwig III of Bavaria, asking to join the army as a volunteer. To Hitler's delight, his request was granted, and he was accepted into the 2nd Bavarian Infantry Regiment. This was a significant moment for Hitler, as he was now free to fight under the German flag instead of the Austrian, which he had grown to dislike. Joining the army also meant he no longer had to worry about paying for his basic needs such as food, clothing, and shelter. Hitler had finally found a purpose in life and was determined to play his part in the grand scheme of things.

After several months of basic military training at the Munich barracks, Hitler, now wearing a uniform and armed with a rifle, took an oath of loyalty to King Ludwig III in person, as well as to Emperor Wilhelm in absentia. He then joined his regiment and embarked on a journey that began with a seventy-mile march through the rain to Lerchfeld Camp for further, more intense training. Eventually, Hitler and his comrades were shipped off to the front lines, where they soon found themselves thrown into the hellhole of battle near Ypres in Belgium.

OF MUD AND MEDALS

"Private" Hitler was now faced with the well-known horrors of World War I warfare: vast expanses of mud-filled craters, barbed-wire defenses, concealed landmines, rat-infested water-filled trenches, and persistent deadly assaults. In his first battle, Hitler served as a regimental dispatch carrier and, under heavy enemy fire, assisted in retrieving a wounded lieutenant colonel with the help of a medic.

In November 1914, Hitler's regiment underwent significant reductions in personnel. While serving with the new commander, Lieutenant Colonel Engelhardt, Hitler and another enlisted soldier embarked on a perilous mission near the front lines to observe the enemy's position. Their presence was detected, and they were met with an unexpected burst of machine-gun fire. Hitler and his comrade acted quickly, shielding the commander and pushing him into a ditch. The lieutenant colonel silently shook their hands in gratitude. Later, Hitler was awarded the Iron Cross Second Class, a medal

Figure 3.1. Hitler (r) and his dog during World War I

typically reserved for soldiers who demonstrate exceptional bravery in combat. He was also promoted to corporal for his willingness to aid injured soldiers and undertake dangerous missions, establishing himself as a dependable and trustworthy soldier.

During the trench warfare in Ypres, Hitler had the opportunity to indulge in his artistic pursuits. He had brought some art supplies with him and, when the opportunity arose, created drawings and watercolors. This hobby made him popular among his fellow soldiers, who enjoyed seeing their experiences and memories captured in his sketches and cartoons. When more serious topics arose in their conversations, Hitler would passionately share his opinions on topics such as art, architecture, and politics, impressing his comrades with his fluency and knowledge. Despite being more reserved when the topic turned to food or women, Hitler was admired for his ability to engage in thoughtful discussions.

By the end of summer 1915, Hitler had established himself as a valuable asset to his regiment's officers. As communication lines were constantly incurring damage from enemy artillery, trustworthy human messengers became crucial to military operations. Hitler demonstrated his daring and stealth by quietly crawling to the front lines, much like he used to do in his childhood Indian games. In September, when the British made a night advance that threatened Hitler's entire regiment and disrupted the phone lines, he ventured out with another soldier to gather information on the enemy. Despite the dangerous mission, they were able to make it back "by the skin of their teeth."[5]

Throughout the years on the front, time and time again, as if by miracle, Hitler managed to narrowly escape death. He once recounted to an English correspondent,

> I was eating my dinner in a trench with several comrades. Suddenly a voice seemed to be saying to me, "Get up and go over there." The command was so clear and insistent that I obeyed mechanically, as if it had been a military order. I rose to my feet at once and walked twenty meters along the trench, carrying my dinner in its tin-can with me. Then I sat down to go on eating, my mind being once more at rest. Hardly had I done so, than a flash and deafening report came from the part of the trench I had just left. A stray shell had burst over the group in which I had just been sitting, and every member of it was killed.

During the course of World War I, Hitler was fortunate in many ways, but he also suffered two injuries: one from an exploding shell and another from a gas attack that temporarily caused him blindness. Hitler also received a second award, the Iron Cross First Class in 1918, for his bravery in an open warfare attack, where messengers played a crucial role.

World War I brought immense hardship not just to soldiers but also to the German civilian population. With food shortages, many people were reduced to eating dogs and cats, and bread made from sawdust and potato peels was common. Strikes erupted, fueled not only by hunger but also by Germany's inability to reach a peace agreement with Russia's newly established Bolshevik government. In January 1918, the situation reached a breaking point as workers across Germany went on strike, calling for workers' representation in negotiations with the Allies, increased food rations, the removal of martial law, and a nationwide democratic government. Upon hearing of these events, Hitler blamed the lack of action on "lazy workers" and the Communists. This is "the biggest piece of chicanery in the whole war," he grumbled. "What was the army fighting for if the homeland itself no longer desired victory? For whom the immense sacrifices and privations? The soldier is expected to fight for victory and the homeland goes on strike against it!"[6]

It was during Hitler's hospital stay to recover from the effects of mustard gas that the announcement of President Wilson's ultimatum was broadcast, requiring Kaiser Wilhelm's resignation before an armistice would be accepted. The ultimatum led to the breakdown of Germany's military and a mutiny among the sailors, snowballing into revolution. This marked a pivotal moment in Germany's involvement in World War I, culminating in the signing of the Armistice and, later, the infamous Versailles Treaty. As Hitler sat in his barracks in Munich, he pondered his uncertain future. After four years of serving Germany, what lay ahead for him in civilian life? Would Adolf Hitler resume his failed art career, or would destiny proffer an unexpected path?

NOTES

1. Frederic Spotts, *Hitler and the Power of Aesthetics* (London: Hutchinson, 2002), 129.

2. Hans Schirmer, Niederschrift im Hauptarchiv der NSDAP, reel 2, file 30.

3. Spotts, Hitler and the Power of Aesthetics, 131.

4. Adolf Hitler, *Mein Kampf*, trans. Ralph Manheim (Boston: Houghton Mifflin, 1971), 126.

5. Toland, *Adolf Hitler*, 63.

6. Ibid., 69.

Chapter 4

The Failure of Democracy

The conclusion of World War I did not bring significant relief to the German population. Hunger, human loss, and a sense of despair were experienced throughout the Reich. During the negotiations leading up to the Armistice, U.S. President Woodrow Wilson advocated for the abdication of Emperor Wilhelm II and the eradication of military autocracy in Germany. As a result of these efforts, not only did the Hohenzollern Kaiser abdicate and flee to Holland but all German monarchies and dynasties were dissolved.

THE WEIMAR REPUBLIC

The period was marked by fear and hatred, which manifested in the form of violence, including gun battles, assassinations, riots, massacres, and general civil unrest. Though an interim democratic government had been put in place in an effort to avoid the total breakdown of services and order, the existing environment was not conducive to the establishment and growth of the fragile German democracy. However, when faced with the imminent threat of the Communist-led Spartacist group proclaiming a soviet republic in Berlin, Philipp Scheidemann of the Majority Social Democratic Party ran to the window of the Reichstag building and to the masses assembled below proclaimed the forthcoming establishment of a republican government. This impromptu declaration led to the formation of a committee of prominent figures from the labor movement who convened in Weimar, a historical town closely associated with celebrated German writers Johann Wolfgang Goethe and Friedrich Schiller. Far from the uprisings and crises plaguing the capital, this small town is where the founding group discussed and drafted Germany's future constitution.

The elections held in January 1919 resulted in the formation of a Constituent Assembly that was controlled by a coalition comprising the Social Democrats, the left-liberal Democrats, and the Center Party. The resulting

German constitution for the new state, later known as the Weimar Republic among the National Socialists, was regarded as one of the most progressive and democratic documents of its era. It included provisions that were seen as effective safeguards for the establishment and operation of an almost perfect democracy. The constitution was inspired by the constitutions of other countries, incorporating ideas such as the cabinet government from Britain and France, the concept of a powerful president elected by popular vote from the United States, and the notion of a referendum from Switzerland. Additionally, a sophisticated and comprehensive system of proportional representation and list voting was implemented, with the intention of avoiding wasted votes and providing representation for minority parties in parliament.[1]

The original German National Constitutional Assembly, as it was known, briefly united the two wings of the Social Democratic movement: the Majority faction, which had supported the war, and the Independents, who had opposed it. The council was led by Friedrich Ebert, a long-serving official of the Social Democratic Party. Ebert, the son of a master tailor, learned the saddler's trade and traveled throughout Germany as a journeyman saddler. He subsequently became a Social Democrat and trade unionist, promoting revisionist and liberal trade-union socialism. However, he did not display a deep interest in the ideological disputes of Marxism, instead focusing on practical improvements in the living conditions as well as the social and moral betterment of the German working class. Ebert was not renowned for his oratory skills or charismatic leadership, but he demonstrated himself to be a calm and patient negotiator, able to bring opposing factions to a mutual agreement.[2]

It must be acknowledged that Ebert, as first president of the Weimar Republic, may have exercised his power excessively during the early years of the republic. The Reich president was granted the power to rule by decree, a clause intended for use only in the event of a national emergency. However, Ebert employed this special power on 136 separate occasions.[3] It goes without saying that the task of leading Germany following its defeat in World War I and the acceptance of the harsh terms of the Treaty of Versailles would have been a formidable challenge for any government, and particularly difficult for a democratically focused government that was inexperienced in navigating such complex issues. The task of addressing the significant problems presented by the treaty and complying with its demands was a legacy that the idealistic yet inexperienced postwar government was forced to face.

Though Ebert throughout his six years as Reich president entertained a close rapport with the "old order" military leaders, this did nothing to immunize him from ongoing attacks from the far-right press. His opponents unsparingly depicted him as a squat and pudgy figurehead instead of a dignified and idealized leader, all the while attempting to dig up dirt by associating him with financial scandals. The unending onslaught of disapproval directed at Ebert not only contributed to undermining his political standing but wore him down both mentally and physically.[4] A ruptured appendix for which he neglected to seek treatment led to his early death on February 28, 1925, at the age of fifty-four.

The elections for a new president revealed more than ever the government's severe political fragmentation. As no single party gained sufficient support to legitimize a candidate, it was the right-wing groups that shone the spotlight on Field Marshall Paul von Hindenburg. A perfect example of the archaic military and imperial *Weltanschauung*, Hindenburg cut a bulky, stoic, and larger-than-life figure. Awarded numerous medals and honors—many underserved—he came across as an aging military man of some experience and integrity now holding the nation's future in his hands. To many, this *Ersatz-Kaiser*'s succession to power was a decisive step away from democracy and toward the reestablishment of the old monarchical order.

Nevertheless, to the surprise of many, the elderly military man stuck to the letter of the constitution, though once in his eighties he began to show his support for monarchical sovereign power. Like Ebert before him, Hindenburg began to make use of the constitution's presidential emergency powers to exercise a conservative dictatorship and thereby demonstrated that he had no faith in democratic institutions and no intention of defending them from their enemies.[5]

GERMANY'S PUNISHMENT AND THE TREATY OF VERSAILLES

In order to better grasp what Germany's World War I children and youth—as well as the rest of the population—experienced following the war, we should briefly review the main international punitive measures imposed on the nation.

Germany was dependent on imports of food and raw materials, most of which had to be shipped across the Atlantic Ocean. The Blockade of Germany (1914–1919) was a naval operation implemented by the Allied Powers to prevent the supply of raw materials and foodstuffs from reaching the Central Powers. This blockade was not lifted until eight months after Germany ceased fighting. In December 1918, the German Board of Public Health stated that 763,000 German civilians had died during the Allied blockade, although an academic study in the same year put the death toll at 424,000 people.[6] The terms of the November 11, 1918, Armistice allowed Allied troops—later, predominantly French—to occupy Germany's Rhineland region and forced Germany to demilitarize the said zone.

During the first half of 1919, some seventy delegates from twenty-seven nations met in Paris to discuss the punitive measures that should be taken against Germany. Among them were the "Big Four": French Prime Minister Georges Clemenceau, Italian Prime Minister Vittorio Emanuele Orlando, British Prime Minister David Lloyd George, and U.S. President Woodrow Wilson met in no less than 145 closed sessions to reach the most important decisions.[7] Under threat of Allied invasion, Germany was forced to sign the so-called Versailles Treaty on June 28, 1919, at Versailles. Already viewed by economists at the time as excessively harsh and bordering on unrealistic, the treaty has sometimes been cited as one of the causes of World War II. Although the Versailles Treaty's actual impact was not as severe as feared, its terms led to great resentment in Germany, which many historians believe powered the rise of Hitler and National Socialism.

The Versailles Treaty stripped Germany of twenty-five thousand square miles (65,000 km²) of territory and seven million inhabitants. Among these regions or protectorates were Alsace-Lorraine, German-speaking Moresnet and Eupen-Malmedy, the Saarland (for fifteen years), Czechoslovakia (actually controlled by Austria), parts of Upper Silesia, the province of Poznan, Eastern Pomerania, Danzig and parts of East Prussia, as well as the Memel. Germany's prized colonies and possessions in Africa and Asia were likewise redistributed to members of the Allied nations.

At the end of World War I, Germany's army still comprised six million men. The Versailles Treaty's provisions allowed Germany an army of no more than one hundred thousand soldiers in a maximum of seven infantry and three cavalry divisions.[8] Germany was prohibited from trading arms, limits were imposed on the type and quantity of weapons permitted, and the nation was barred from manufacturing or stockpiling chemical weapons, armored cars, tanks, and military aircraft.[9] For defense purposes, the German navy was allowed six battleships, six light cruisers, twelve destroyers, and twelve torpedo boats but was forbidden the possession of submarines.[10] The navy's manpower was not to exceed fifteen thousand men, and Germany was not allowed to own an air force. Compared to the European pre–World War I efforts to balance the great powers' respective armed forces, Germany's postwar "puppet army" would be visibly insufficient to counter a potential enemy invasion and was, above all, an embarrassment to Germany's strong military tradition.

The treaty obliged Germany to compensate the Allied Powers and also created an Allied Reparation Commission to establish the exact sum that Germany should pay in reparations and war damages and the form that such payment would take. The commission was required to "give to the German Government a just opportunity to be heard" and to submit its conclusions by May 1, 1921. In the interim, the treaty required Germany to pay the equivalent of twenty billion gold marks ($5 billion) in gold, commodities, ships, securities, or other forms.[11] In hindsight, many experts agree that the astronomical sums that Germany was expected to hand over in the wake of an economically draining war were utterly exaggerated and that the "debt" could not be honored.

Rather than be forced to sign the Versailles Treaty, Germany's first democratically elected head of state, Philipp Scheidemann, resigned. In an impassioned speech delivered to the National Assembly on May 12, 1919, he termed the treaty a "murderous plan" and exclaimed, "Which hand, trying to put us in chains like these, would not wither? The treaty is unacceptable."[12]

HUNGER AND HATRED

A major turning point in World War I was the sailors' rebellion of October 1918 and the ensuing revolution that gradually swept through Germany. As most of Germany's old elite refused to concede that the German army had been defeated—which was facilitated by the lack of a decisive battle in the autumn of 1918—the "stabbed in the back" legend found widespread acceptance.[13] This myth held that the German army did not lose World War I on the battlefield but, instead, was betrayed by the civilians on the home front, in particular by Jews and republicans who overthrew the Hohenzollern monarchy in the German Revolution of 1918–1919. Advocates of this opinion denounced the German leaders who signed the Armistice on November 11, 1918, as the "November criminals." Myth or no myth, the Versailles Treaty, and in particular its War Guilt Clause, was viewed with quasi-universal rebuff. The main party, the Social Democrats, only admitted cautiously that the leadership of imperial Germany was to bear responsibility for the war to a limited extent.[14]

The first four years of the Weimar Republic's existence were marked by severe food shortages, and the situation for Germany's civilians remained dire. The economic burden imposed by the treaty, coupled with mass inflation, presented a dark and desperate future to the German population in the postwar years. As an example, in 1919, one loaf of bread cost about one mark, but by 1923 the same loaf cost one hundred billion marks.[15]

By 1923, the Weimar Republic claimed it could no longer afford the reparations payments demanded by the Versailles Treaty, and the government began defaulting on payments. As a result, French and Belgian troops occupied the Ruhr area, Germany's most productive industrial region and, in January 1923, seized control of most mining and manufacturing companies. Strikes were called, and passive resistance was encouraged. The strikes lasted eight months, further damaging both the economy and society. In November

1923, a new currency, the Rentenmark, was introduced at the rate of one trillion (1,000,000,000,000) paper marks for one Rentenmark, a correction known as redenomination. Reparation payments were resumed, and the Ruhr region was returned to Germany.

In 1924, in an effort to help Germany meet reparation obligations, the American Dawes Plan was put into effect. This agreement between U.S. banks and the German government allowed American banks to grant loans to German banks with German assets as collateral.[16] This heralded the beginning of five years of economic stability known as Germany's Golden Twenties. During this time, various international agreements were signed, and Germany joined the League of Nations.

When the New York Stock Exchange crashed in October 1929, U.S. loans dried up, and the severe decline of the German economy brought the Golden Twenties to an abrupt close. The Great Depression hit Germany just as hard as it did America. Unemployment in Germany soared, and the last years of the Weimar Republic were marred by even more systemic political instability than in the previous years, while political violence increased.

A BURDENSOME LEGACY

In retrospect, it is apparent that the Weimar Republic faced numerous challenges that contributed to general mistrust and skepticism toward its legitimacy. One such challenge was the instability of its leadership and representation. The republic experienced a high turnover of government officials, with a total of twenty different cabinets and thirteen chancellors appointed during its fourteen-year existence. This frequent change in structure further weakened the government and added to its instability.

Another major problem was the infighting and lack of cooperation among multiple political parties. Many of the prominent parties that had existed during the imperial and monarchical regime carried on into the Weimar Republic, but instead of merging with similarly minded parties, they tended to splinter and function independently. These parties were deeply entrenched in their own distinct milieux, which were both rigid and homogenous. They had their own newspapers, clubs, and social events, and even everyday social life became politicized. This mind-set of political activists, who were more interested in promoting their own ideology than in seeking compromise and cooperation with rival parties and officials, made it difficult to form larger and more operational political parties, further hindering the stability and effectiveness of the Weimar Republic.

The Weimar Republic also faced difficulties in its constitutional structure, which was inherited from the federal structure established by Bismarck during the formation of the Second Reich in 1871. Despite the removal of princes and kings during the 1918 revolution, their states were still intact and retained significant autonomy in key areas of domestic policy. These were now endowed with democratic and parliamentary governing bodies but managed to preserve significant autonomy in fundamental areas of domestic policy. Certain states, such as Bavaria, which held strong traditional identities, were often inclined to resist and obstruct the national government's directives and policies. This presented another significant challenge to the successful functioning of the republic.

The Weimar government also struggled to gain the support of the army and the civil service, as both institutions found it difficult to adjust to the transition from an authoritarian regime under Kaiser Wilhelm to a democratic structure. Without the support of the army, it was unlikely that the government would also receive support from civil servants. The civil service, which maintained a significant presence in many areas of society, including the central administration, federal states, state enterprises such as the police, railway and postal service, and educational institutions, also provided little support to the Weimar government.

REASONS FOR FAILURE

To sum it up, there are multiple causes for the malfunction of the Weimar Republic. To begin with, the state struggled with economic instability, including the economic crisis caused by the First World War and the hyperinflation of the early 1920s, which made it problematic for the government to pay for public services and led to widespread poverty. The Great Depression in 1929 led to a severe economic downturn and mass unemployment, famine, and general upheaval: by 1932, 10 percent of Germans were unemployed.

Another issue was the political instability as a result of frequent crises, as a number of succeeding governments and coalitions formed and fell apart. This made it most difficult for the government to pass any necessary reforms or implement effective policies. The Weimar Republic faced significant opposition from both the far right and the far left, with the rise of extremist groups such as the National Socialists and the Communist Party. These groups were able to exploit the state's economic and political instability to gain support and destabilize the government.

The heavy reparations imposed on Germany, as well as the loss of territory and restrictions on the nation's sovereignty and defense, led to resentment toward the Weimar Republic and the belief that the government had betrayed the German people. The republic also struggled to establish itself as a legitimate government, in part because it was seen as having been imposed by the victorious Allied Powers, and also because it was unable to provide effective governance. Furthermore, lack of support from the military, police, and employees of the civil service made it hard for the government to maintain order and control over the country.

By this time, the stage was set for a "savior" to enter the scene. The events that followed successively would bring an unprecedented turnaround to Germany's political leadership, and Adolf Hitler would steer the nation first toward tangible hope, then to total disaster.

NOTES

1. William Shirer, *The Rise and Fall of the Third Reich* (New York: Simon & Schuster, 1990), 89.

2. Richard Evans, *The Coming of the Third Reich* (New York: Penguin, 2005), 78.

3. Ibid., 80.

4. Ibid., 81.

5. Andreas Dorpalen, *Hindenburg and the Weimar Republic* (Princeton, NJ: Princeton University Press, 1964), cited in Evans, *Coming of the Third Reich*, 83.

6. Leo Grebler (1940): The Cost of the World War to Germany and Austria-Hungary p. 78

7. Antony Lentin, "Germany: A New Carthage?," *History Today*, January 2012, 20–27.

8. Versailles Treaty, articles 159–63.

9. Ibid., articles 165, 179, 171, 172, and 198.

10. Ibid., articles 181 and 190.

11. Ibid., articles 232–35.

12. Wolfgang Lautemann, ed., *Geschichte in Quellen*, vol. 6 (Munich: Bayrischer Schulbuch-Verlag 1975), 129.

13. Boris Barth, *Dolchstosslegenden und politische Desintegration: Das Trauma der deutschen Niederlage im Ersten Weltkrieg, 1914–1933* (Dusseldorf: Droste Verlag, 2003).

14. Ulrich Heinemann, *Die verdrängte Niederlage: Politische Öffentlichkeit und Kriegsschuldfrage in der Weimarer Republik* (Göttingen: Vandenhoeck & Ruprecht, 1983).

15. Alan Farmer, *Democracy and Nazism: Germany, 1918–1945* (London: Hodder Education, 2016), 27.

16. Martin Kitchen, *The Cambridge Illustrated History of Germany* (Cambridge: Cambridge University Press, 1996), 241.

Chapter 5

From Soldier to *Führer*

In order to better grasp how Hitler shaped his National Socialist views, it is important to take into account the dramatic events that took place in Munich in 1918 and 1919. Considering Bavaria's moderate and conservative political tradition, it probably came as a shock to most Germans to learn of Kurt Eisner's coup d'état and its ensuing left-wing revolution.

THE PEOPLES' REPUBLIC OF BAVARIA

Eisner, a Jewish politician, journalist, and leader of the centrist USPD (Independent Social Democratic Party), became the first republican head of government in Bavaria. Though the November revolution of 1918 first emerged in Munich, it spread through Germany like wildfire and resulted in toppling monarchic leadership and even the emperor himself. In hindsight, the revolution of 1918 was not a move toward social or political reform as much as it was a direct rebellion against the war. During the weeks leading up to the Bavarian uprising, a deep longing for peace at any price could clearly be discerned.

Regardless of justifications for the revolution, many were those in Bavaria who fiercely denounced the new government as being run by Jews: even worse—by non-Bavarian Jews (Eisner hailed from Berlin). Over the next few months, it became apparent that the feeling of discontent in Bavaria was not a result of the new leader's goals but, rather, that the revolution had put an end to Bavaria's institutions and political traditions.[1]

Eisner's ascent to power coincided with the November 11 Armistice, a cease-fire that led most Germans to believe erroneously that they had won the Great War. The truce, however, did not lift the ongoing international blockade aimed at punishing the German people. Though the war had come to an end, the borders remained closed and hunger persisted. Worse than the Allied blockade was that Kurt Eisner, for all that he aspired to represent, possessed no governing skills and hadn't the faintest clue as to the workings of high politics or how to inspire and lead the Bavarian people.

THE BAVARIAN SOVIET REPUBLIC

Following the Armistice, Hitler decided to remain in the army, conceivably for financial reasons, as well as possibly due to the fact that he had neither family nor friends to whom he might return.[2] Ironically, the defense of Eisner's new regime against antisemitic attacks fells to the 2nd Infantry Regiment to which Hitler belonged at war's end. This responsibility was obviously not implemented effectively enough to protect Eisner from armed attack. Only two days after a failed coup led by a sailor, Eisner was assassinated on February 21, 1919. Earlier that year, his party had gleaned a pitiful 2.5 percent of the votes in the state election.

The assassination of Eisner paved the way for the radical left's fast-growing movement to undermine parliamentary democracy and seize control. In just a few days, a fresh surge of revolutionary zeal swept through the Bavarian capital. Red flags were flown, martial law was enforced, and a new administration was established. This new government was headed by Ernst Niekisch, a left-wing social democrat who espoused National Bolshevism, advocating for Germany's future to be tied with the East, specifically, through collaboration with Russia.

Hitler's superiors recognized his remarkable oratory skills and appointed him to act as an intermediary between his regiment's propaganda department and the revolutionary regime. Officially designated as a *Vertrauensmann* (man of confidence) of his company, Hitler underwent a transformation from an obedient soldier, a solitary figure, and a wanderer to a respected leader of others by April 1919.[3] Despite the proclamation of a "Soviet Republic" in Bavaria, Hitler chose to remain stationed at his army headquarters, presumably hoping to weather the storm. If he had deserted the army and rejected the Communist revolutionary regime, he may have had to give up the relative comfort and stability of his new position. Notwithstanding the widespread opposition to the Bavarian Communist Soviet Republic, Hitler continued to interact with the Communist regime and was elected deputy battalion councilor for his unit.

In theory, Munich's military units, including Hitler's, were part of the Communist regime's "Red Army." For the greater part, though, the military did not support the Soviet government and attempted to remain neutral at all costs: Hitler was among those who did not join active units of the Red Army. By the end of April 1919, the thirty to forty thousand troops of the government in exile (which had meanwhile retreated to Bamberg) stormed Munich.

Though mass desertion took place among members of the Red Army, Hitler, who chose not to defect, was taken prisoner and detained for a short time by the "white" troops.

THE RISE OF ANTISEMITISM AND ANTI-BOLSHEVISM

The brief existence of Munich's Soviet Republic resulted in a dramatic surge in antisemitism. This form of xenophobia did not target all Jews equally, in the manner that National Socialist antisemitism would later develop. Instead, it was primarily directed at Jewish revolutionaries and was expressed through anti-Bolshevik antisemitism, particularly aimed at political activists such as Eisner. In addition, Munich's antisemitism assumed a religious character, with the Catholic Church openly denouncing all non-Catholic religious customs.[4] Hitler's experiences with revolution and the Soviet Republic in Munich are thought to have exacerbated his already active hatred for anything foreign, international, Bolshevik, and Jewish, which may have originated during his time in Vienna.

Following the reinstatement of democracy in Munich, the armed forces turned their attention to removing rebels and revolutionaries in order to prevent the resurgence of left-wing extremism. They singled out for retribution any military personnel who had fervently backed the Soviet Republic in Bavaria. Hitler saw this as a significant chance to offer his services as an informant. From May 1919, he served on a three-member board and carried out operations to identify soldiers who had served in the Red Army before being discharged.

The military leadership conducted propaganda classes in southern Bavaria to propagate counter-revolutionary notions, and Adolf Hitler and other officers attended them. The classes featured knowledgeable speakers on subjects such as history, economics, and politics, emphasizing the notion that ideas, not material conditions, shape the world. The course curriculum dealt with themes such as resource management for survival and the devastation caused to society by international capitalism and finance, seen as the fundamental causes of inequality and suffering. This final message, coupled with the classes' anti-Bolshevik agenda, would have a profound and long-lasting impact on Hitler.

HITLER'S MENTOR KARL MAYR

It fell to the propaganda department's head, Captain Karl Mayr, to set up courses that would not only help Hitler shape his political views but led him to realize that he possessed oratory skills and could capture the listener's attention. Karl Mayr was a General Staff officer and Adolf Hitler's immediate superior in the Army Intelligence Division in the Reichswehr, to which Hitler now belonged. Mayr would later be known as the person who introduced Hitler to politics, as well as becoming his first mentor. In 1919, Mayr directed Hitler to write the so-called Gemlich letter, in which he first expressed his antisemitic views in writing.

kKarl Mayr produced pamphlets that were distributed to troops throughout Bavaria, covering a wide range in their political orientation. One of the pamphlets, titled "What You Should Know about Bolshevism," was aimed at proving that "leaders of Bolshevism are chiefly Jews who ply their dirty trade." Others showed up a dark side of communism or were written with the aim of appealing to Catholics or to members of the Socialist Democratic Party.[5]

It was at precisely this time, in early July 1919, that Germany was forced to ratify the Treaty of Versailles, a history-making event that would give Hitler an incentive to become active in the country's politics. The Armistice of November 11, 1918, had brought an end to the fighting of World War I, but it was not until June 1919 that the Allies declared that war would resume if the German government did not sign the treaty they had agreed to among themselves. One of the most significant and contentious provisions of the treaty was the so-called War Guilt Clause, which stated that Germany and its allies accepted responsibility for causing all the losses and damages suffered by the Allied countries and their citizens as a result of the war. The treaty also required Germany to disarm, cede territory, and pay reparations to the Allied Powers. Some Allied leaders viewed these sanctions as excessive and counterproductive, while others, including French Marshal Ferdinand Foch, believed that, on the contrary, the treaty was too lenient on Germany.

In Munich, the peace terms were perceived as excessively harsh, and the Allied Powers' decision to exclude the Provisional National Assembly of German Austria from the peace negotiations and deny Austria the right to self-determination was also controversial. It is very likely that Hitler, among others, anticipated that the international humiliation of Germany and the crushing of national pride would fuel a desire for revenge among the German people. Hitler would always view the events of November 1918 as the root of all Germany's problems. He spent the rest of his life revisiting Germany's defeat and trying to prevent a similar disgrace from occurring again. At this time, Hitler selected the parts of the course that resonated with him and simply discarded the rest. As a result, the societal and political ideas that began to form in his mind included the celebration of work, how to ensure a steady food supply for the population, the rejection of Bolshevism, and the elimination of the influence of international finance and capitalism.[6]

The propaganda courses completed, Hitler began working for Captain Mayr, who was only six years his senior. Born in Bavarian Swabia and the son of a judge, Mayr was raised in a Catholic middle-class family, had seen considerable action in the war, and had suffered a bad injury. Following his service on the western front, on the alpine front, in the Balkans, as well as in the Ottoman Empire, he was perceived by his commanders as a "highly talented, versatile officer of extraordinary intellectual vitality."[7]

Back in Munich after the war, Mayr served first in the Ministry of War and ended, finally, as a company commander of the 1st Infantry Regiment, at the heart of which he actively fought, from within, against the short-lived Communist regime. Mayr's goal was to shape the small group of army veterans who worked for him into representatives and propagators of his political vision. He considered himself a teacher and mentor to these men, despite plenty of opposition and disapproval on behalf of Munich's civilian and military authorities. Though for a few short years Karl Mayr served as Hitler's first mentor, he would gradually turn against Hitler's policies and the future National Socialist Party. As a result, he was eventually interned in the Sachsenhausen concentration camp and, later, in the Buchenwald camp. A British bomb killed him while he was working at a nearby munitions factory in Weimar, just three months before the end of World War II.

HITLER JOINS THE GERMAN WORKERS' PARTY

Following his activities as a speaker for the army's propaganda department in Munich's postrevolutionary period, Hitler was given the task of discretely attending meetings of various groups, especially those of a political nature. As a trusted political agent of the army, he was now to spy on and provide a report on one of Munich's budding political parties, the Deutsche Arbeiterpartei (DAP) or German Workers' Party. After listening to a talk by Baumann, the chairman of the *Bürgerverein* who advocated for Bavarian separatism, Hitler felt compelled to stand up and deliver an impassioned speech in which he argued that all ethnic Germans should be united under one national roof. Later that evening, the tiny party's cofounder and chairman, Anton Drexler, handed Hitler a pamphlet and asked him if he'd return in a week's time. When Hitler read Drexler's manifesto, he felt a strong connection to the ideas it expressed and claimed that he and Drexler had, over the years, experienced a similar political transformation.

Through his propaganda classes, Hitler had been exposed to the idea that Jews were seen by many as having contributed to Germany's recent defeat. At this time, Hitler's hatred of Jews was primarily directed at their role in capitalism, rather than at their involvement with Bolshevism. Drexler, who shared Hitler's views, believed that Jewish finance capitalism was driving capitalist internationalism and that international socialism was being used by Jewish bankers to destroy and take over nations.

In a letter penned that year, Hitler exposed in no uncertain terms what he felt about Jews. He spoke about the "pernicious effect that Jews as a whole, consciously or unconsciously, have on our nation." He added that Jews acted like "leeches" and that "Jewry is absolutely a race and not a religious community." Furthermore, he believed that Jewish materialism caused the "racial tuberculosis of the nations" because Jews corrupted the character of their hosts. Hitler's solution was, rather than carry out pogroms against Jews, that governments should limit the rights of the Jews and ultimately remove Jews altogether from their host nations.[8]

In the course of Hitler's propaganda-fueled discourses to the soldiers, his oratory skills had been perceived as "spirited lectures . . . that included examples taken from life," and he was acclaimed as "a natural speaker for the people, whose fanaticism and popular demeanor force his listeners in a rally to pay attention to him and to follow his thoughts."[9] Now, as he began to address groups of civilians, Hitler's newfound radical antisemitism and racism did not, however, form the core of his political message but merely aspects of his *Weltanschauung*. Foremost on Hitler's political agenda was to build a state that could avoid any future German defeat.

After accepting Drexler's invitation to attend German Workers' Party (DAP) meetings, Hitler became a member of the executive committee, serving specifically as a propagandist.[10] The DAP, led by Drexler, aimed to convert the working class from Marxism and recruit members to support the Pan-German movement. As a publicist and spokesperson for the party, Hitler was motivated to leave the army and dedicate himself to political agitation. His oratory skills were largely attributed to his ability to connect with his audience's desires and sentiments, employing simple and direct language, emotive slogans, and powerful rhetoric. Many noted that he spoke from the heart and shared his personal hopes and fears with those in attendance.

ECKART, THE ANTISEMITIC AUTHOR

Johann Dietrich Eckart, born in 1868 in Bavaria, was overly enthused to meet Adolf Hitler at a German Workers' Party speech that the future *Führer* delivered in 1919. The year before, in December 1918,[11] Eckart founded, published, and edited the antisemitic weekly *Auf gut Deutsch* (In Plain German). This was made possible with financial assistance from the Thule Society,[12] as well as with the input of Alfred Rosenberg, whom Eckart called his "co-warrior against Jerusalem,"[13] an antisemitist who eventually became the "ideologist" of the National Socialist Party.

Though his membership in the organization has long been the subject of experts' debate, Eckart was known, at the very least, to have had occasional involvement in the Thule Society, a Munich occult study group promoting a political agenda. This Pan-German, *völkisch*, and antisemitic sect with roots in the prewar Germanic Order, named itself after *Thule* (Iceland), supposedly the symbol of Aryan purity. The members' objective was to research the origins of German antiquity and the roots of the German race. The order's logo was a stylized form of the swastika, an ancient symbol that was in use in numerous cultures for over five thousand years before Adolf Hitler adopted it as the centerpiece of the National Socialist flag. Signifying good fortune in Sanskrit, the swastika had already been adopted by several European organizations even prior to World War I. Among the Thule Society's members were some who would later become active in high positions in the National Socialist Party: Rudolf Hess (secretary and successor to the *Führer*), Alfred Rosenberg (party ideology chief), and Hans Frank (head of the General Government in National Socialist–occupied Poland during World War II).

The antisemitic members of the Thule Society studied the occult and believed in the coming of a "German Messiah" who would redeem the nation after its defeat in World War I.[14] Eckart expressed his anticipation in a poem he wrote months before he first met Hitler, in which he refers to the "Great One," the "Nameless One," or "Whom all can sense but no one saw." When Eckart met Hitler, he was convinced that he had encountered the prophesied redeemer.[15]

Serving as a blueprint for Hitler's later political doctrine, Eckart's *Weltanschauung* heftily criticized the German Revolution and the Weimar Republic, deplored the Treaty of Versailles—which the author equated to treason—and believed in the widely propagated "stabbed in the back" legend that blamed the Jews and the Social Democrats for Germany's defeat in World War I. Eckart also became the first publisher of the party's newspaper, the *Völkischer Beobachter*, a paper that the NSDAP later purchased from the Thule Society.

In early 1923, as a result of Eckart's publication of a libelous poem deriding Germany's president, Friedrich Ebert, he escaped arrest by hiding out, under the name of Dr. Hoffman, in the Bavarian Alps near Berchtesgaden, close to the German-Austrian border. It was there that Hitler paid him a visit in the spring, a sojourn that served to introduce the future *Führer* to the area where he would later build his home and Alpine headquarters, the Berghof at Obersalzberg.

Twenty-one years Hitler's senior, Eckart would greatly contribute to the creation of the future dictator's public persona[16] as well as the Hitler Myth.[17]

Beyond their common political opinions, a deep emotional and intellectual bond developed between the two men,[18] and in private Hitler later acknowledged Eckart as having been his teacher and mentor[19] and the spiritual cofounder of National Socialism.[20] As Hitler's early guide, Eckart exchanged ideas with him and helped to establish the theories and beliefs of the party.[21] He lent Hitler books to read, gave him a trench coat to wear, and made corrections to Hitler's style of speaking and writing[22] and taught him proper manners.[23]

The two men found many interests in common, in particular in the fields of art and politics, and Eckart introduced Hitler to the painter Max Zaeper and his salon of like-minded antisemitic artists, as well as to the photographer Heinrich Hoffmann, who became instrumental in marketing the Hitler Myth.[24] Using his connections within the *völkisch* movements,[25] Dietrich Eckart facilitated meetings between Adolf Hitler and affluent potential donors. Collaboratively, the duo endeavored to gather funds for the German Workers' Party in Munich.[26] However, their efforts proved futile in the beginning. On the other hand, Eckart was better connected with the rich and powerful in Berlin, where the two party campaigners managed to collect substantial funds. On one such visit to the capital, Eckart introduced Hitler to his future etiquette tutor, socialite Helene Bechstein, thanks to whom Hitler began to mingle among the upper circles of Berlin's high society.[27] Eckart also made recommendations to Hitler as to who should assist him within the party, bringing the likes of Julius Streicher on board, the publisher of the virulently antisemitic *Der Stürmer*.

Later, Hitler would dedicate part two of his book *Mein Kampf* to his former friend and mentor, and named a hospital, a stadium, and a school after him. Hitler told one of his secretaries that his friendship with Eckart was "one of the best things he experienced in the 1920s" and that he never again had a friend with whom he felt such "a harmony of thinking and feeling."[28]

THE APPEAL OF THE PARTY

One of the key factors that contributed to the success and growth of the German Workers' Party, later renamed the National Socialist German Workers' Party (NSDAP), was its perception of itself as a movement rather than a political party. The idea of a party connoted loyalty to parliamentary democracy, whereas Hitler promoted the National Socialist "movement," a term that evoked a sense of energy and progression toward a shared objective. On February 24, 1920, Hitler and Drexler drew up an official twenty-five-point program for the fledgling movement that called for the revocation of the Versailles Treaty, the "union of all Germans in a Greater

Germany," and the denial of civil rights for Jews, among other items. By July of the next year, Hitler had insisted on becoming the NSDAP's chairman "with dictatorial powers." Having gained complete control over the National Socialist Party, Hitler could now implement his propaganda campaign.

Over the next couple of years, Hitler's movement drew a lot of attention, not only through its leader's regular inflammatory speeches but because of repeated violent outbreaks between the NSDAP's ruffians and members of competing groups and parties on the streets of Munich. This function of protecting Hitler and other National Socialist leaders or being aggressive toward the opposition fell into the hands of Ernst Röhm, a Free Corps veteran with a penchant for ruthless violence, in the form of the *Sturmabteilung* (Storm Division), better known as the SA.

THE MUNICH PUTSCH

Mussolini's "March on Rome" in late October 1922 inspired Hitler's so-called Beer Hall Putsch, also known as the Munich Putsch. On November 8, 1923, with a crowd of over two thousand supporters, Hitler endeavored to overthrow the government. The plan was first to seize the Bavarian government before marching on Berlin to overthrow the Weimar Republic. The key figures in the uprising were Adolf Hitler, World War I veteran Hermann Göring, Ludwig Siebert (the leader of another right-wing group), and Ernst Röhm, with close to two thousand members of his SA fighters.

The uprising was quashed by the police and army. Subsequently, Hitler was arrested and tried for high treason in a Munich court starting from February 26, 1924, with the trial lasting for twenty-four days. During the proceedings, Hitler exploited the opportunity to propagate his nationalist and antisemitic views and gain public attention. He acted as his own defense counsel and delivered speeches blaming the government and Jews for Germany's defeat in World War I and for its economic woes. Hitler also contended that the putsch was not a criminal offense but a move to protect Germany from the Communists and Jews.

Hitler's speeches at the trial were reported in the newspapers, catapulting him to widespread public attention. Nevertheless, he was found guilty of high treason and handed a five-year prison sentence. However, he served a mere nine months of his term in Landsberg Prison, where he dictated the first volume of his book *Mein Kampf* (My Struggle) to his deputy Rudolf Hess. Ultimately, the trial and Hitler's defense speeches played a crucial role in his eventual rise to power, as it helped him to gain considerable public notice and promote his ideas.

Figure 5.1. Hitler behind bars at Landsberg Prison in 1924. *AKG Images*

THE WRITTEN WORD

As Hitler was forbidden to speak in public for four years, he devoted this time to resurrect the National Socialist Party by writing articles for the party's press. He also set in motion the party's propaganda directorate, with Gregor Strasser as its head, assisted by Heinrich Himmler.[29] Julius Streicher, the Nuremberg Party Leader, and Party Leader Joseph Goebbels in Berlin were each responsible for inflammatory newspapers that greatly contributed to the dissemination of propaganda material.

The NS Propaganda Directorate launched a nationwide campaign of recruitment through carefully designed leaflets, pamphlets, and posters. The propagandists established precise guidelines regarding the organizing of meetings as well as the design, color, and wording of visual advertising. They focused on simple messages such as "Work and Bread," and unlike their political adversaries, they promoted the persona of the party leader, Adolf Hitler. The Propaganda Directorate "carefully crafted images of the *Führer* that emphasized his charisma, his roots among the common people, his heroism as a soldier in World War I, his quasi-messianic nature as a savior, and his respectability."[30]

TARGETING THE MASSES

Though in the campaigning years Hitler and his followers generally banged away at Liberals, Communists, Social Democrats, and Jews, Hitler's anti-semitic jibes were toned down after 1928 as his party began to see a strong increase in general support and because he realized that he needed to gain respectability as a future national leader.[31]

In the party's fourteen-year-long electoral campaign, violence walked hand in hand with propaganda. Recurrent bloody outbreaks took place between the NSDAP's ruffians and members of competing groups and parties on the streets of Munich and elsewhere in Germany. The function of protecting Hitler and other National Socialist leaders or aggressing the opposition fell upon Ernst Röhm and the SA.

The SA storm troopers were repeatedly responsible for bloody—even fatal—clashes with the paramilitary organizations of the Social Democrats and the Communists. National Socialist media often presented this violence as self-defense or as heroic battles against the "Marxists" who otherwise would lead to a "Bolshevist" Germany.

In 1930, Hitler named Goebbels director of the party's national propaganda apparatus. Known for his fiery oratory and loyalty to the *Führer*, Goebbels organized the election campaigns of 1930 and 1932, including the slogan "Hitler over Germany." This novel marketing sensation consisted of chartering a plane to fly Hitler all over the country. His propagandists arranged for Hitler to speak at some twenty rallies, "electrifying" nearly one million Germans. Goebbels pioneered the use of radio and, as an inveterate film buff, ordered the production of motion pictures of rallies, speeches, and other events to show at meetings with the aim of further inspiring and mobilizing core supporters.[32]

Voters had varying reasons to cast 33.7 percent of votes for Hitler and his party in the November 6, 1932, elections, a couple of months before he seized power. For the most part, support for Hitler was not due to antisemitic reasons but, rather, in hopes of ending the ongoing economic crisis and the political division and disorder that Germans experienced under the Weimar Republic. In 1929, the U.S. stock market crash had triggered a wave of financial panic and a global economic downturn that initiated the Great Depression in Germany, a catastrophic turn of events that greatly exacerbated the nation's already untenable financial devastation.

A large proportion of young people were drawn to the party because it came across as dynamic, heroic, and youthful, as opposed to the tired, old established parties. The National Socialists groomed their image as standing above class and confessional differences and as representing blue-collar and white-collar workers, peasants, soldiers, women, students, the middle class, Protestants, and Catholics.[33]

Thanks to propaganda, the National Socialists appeared as the only viable political alternative and the only way to save Germany. The party's underlying antisemitism did not stop those millions of Germans from voting for the National Socialists.[34] In general, most voters overlooked Hitler's antisemitism, thinking that, given time, it would disappear or they disregarded it, as it did not "affect them."

Hitler's promise to restore the economy—as well as Germany's national pride—along with numerous other alluring assurances touted by his political agenda did not fall on deaf ears. Years of National Socialist propaganda, coupled with Hitler's often mesmerizing rhetoric, allowed the Third Reich to commandeer power in 1933. Few people foresaw then that this was not the dawning of a glorious "thousand-year Reich," but the beginning of a twelve-year reign of terror.

NOTES

1. Thomas Weber, *Becoming Hitler: The Making of a Nazi* (New York: Basic Books, 2017), 13.

2. Ibid., 10.

3. Ibid., 40.

4. Ibid., 58.

5. Ibid., 92.

6. Ibid., 82–86.

7. Ibid., 102.

8. Ibid., 119.

9. Sönke Neitzel and Harald Welzer, *Soldaten: On Fighting, Killing, and Dying*, trans. Jefferson S. Chase (New York: Alfred A. Knopf, 2012), 122.

10. Ernst Dauerlein, *Der Aufstieg der NSDAP in Augenzeugenberichten* (Dusseldorf: Rauch, 1968), 98.

11. Ian Kershaw, *Hitler: A Biography* (New York: W. W. Norton, 2008), 154.

12. Volker Ullrich, *Hitler: Ascent, 1889–1939*, trans. Jefferson Chase (New York: Vintage, 2017), 105–7.

13. Toland, *Adolf Hitler*, 78.

14. John Michael Greer, *The New Encyclopedia of the Occult* (St. Paul, MN: Llewellyn, 2003), 322.

15. Claus Hant, *Young Hitler* (London: Quartet Books, 2010).

16. Ullrich, *Hitler: Ascent*, 105–107.

17. Joachim C. Fest, *Hitler*, trans. Richard Winston and Clara Winston (Harmondsworth, UK: Penguin, 1975), 136.

18. Weber, *Becoming Hitler*, 288.

19. Ibid., 143.

20. Karl Dietrich Bracher, *The German Dictatorship: The Origins, Structure, and Effects of National Socialism*, trans. Jean Steinberg (New York: Praeger, 1970), 119.

21. Kershaw, *Hitler*, 94–100.

22. Toland, *Adolf Hitler*, 99.

23. Fest, *Hitler*, 132–33.

24. Weber, *Becoming Hitler*, 142–43.

25. Ian Kershaw, *Hitler: Profiles in Power* (London: Routledge, 1991), 41.

26. Kershaw, *Hitler*, 155.

27. Weber, *Becoming Hitler*, 212–13.

28. Ullrich, *Hitler: Ascent*, 105–107.

29. Steven Luckert and Susan Bachrach, *State of Deception: The Power of Nazi Propaganda* (Washington, DC: United States Holocaust Memorial Museum, 2009), 36–38.

30. Ibid., 39.

31. Sarah Gordon, *Hitler, Germans, and the "Jewish Question"* (Princeton, NJ: Princeton University Press, 1984), 69.

32. Luckert and Bachrach, *State of Deception*, 56–57.

33. Ibid., 48.

34. Christopher Browning, *The Origins of the Final Solution* (London: Arrow, 2004), 8.

Chapter 6

Hitler's Swift Rise to Power

We struggle to grasp how a people who gave the world Luther, Bach, Mozart, Goethe, Brahms, Haydn, and Schubert could commit the acts of sadistic brutality that were carried out during Hitler's abuse of power.

Our first clue to the circumstances and processes that made this possible should be searched for in the First World War and its ruinous consequences. It is easy to identify the stigma imprinted on the German people in the wake of the savagery of trench warfare on the western front and the resentment and void created by Germany's ensuing defeat and the subsequent punishment, loss, and shame of the postwar years. The war and its aftermath as experienced by the children and youth of that time clearly shaped the nature and success of National Socialism. The young adults who became politically operative after 1929 and who filled the ranks of the SA, SS, and other paramilitary organizations such as the Hitler Youth or the League of German Girls were the children and teenagers socialized during or in the shadow of the First World War.[1]

NATIONAL SOCIALISM: A YOUNG PEOPLE'S MOVEMENT

The Great War was a particularly traumatic experience for younger Germans and synonymous with prolonged hunger, false or misleading war propaganda, the absence of fathers—sometimes even of both parents, as some 1.2 million German women were employed in factories or in the war industry—as well as the bankruptcy of all political values and norms.[2] Among the consequences of these years of deprivation and hardships, these youths later often reacted to internal personal stress with externalized violence, and they projected all antinational and antisocial characteristics onto foreign and ethnic individuals and groups.[3] This cohort also yearned for an idealized, though distant, father figure who is all-knowing and all-powerful, who expounds the merits of military valor, and who encourages his sons and daughters to honor him by proudly donning a uniform and joining the fight for the national cause.[4]

It has been said that the children of World War I were a fatherless generation. Over two million German soldiers never made it home, while millions more returned to their families mutilated and mentally or emotionally traumatized. The National Socialist movement's principal adherents, and later, perpetrators, were the younger generation. The demographer and sociologist Norman Ryder states, "The Great War weakened a whole cohort in Europe to the extent that normal succession of personnel in roles, including positions of power, was disturbed. Sometimes the old remained in power too long; sometimes the young seized power too soon."[5]

In the early years, the National Socialists successfully targeted German youth. An official slogan of the party stated that "National Socialism is the organized will of youth,"[6] and the Party's propagandist Gregor Strasser shouted "Step down, you old ones!" National Socialism was, in essence, a youth movement,[7] and its ideology and organization matched those of the elitist principles of the German youth movement, the *Wandervogel*. This extremely popular group prized the virtues of a rustic life on the moors and heaths and in the forests, where the bonds of group life and group activities could develop.

The National Socialist principle of "blood and soil," as well as the ideal and preservation of the German *Volk*, nation, language, and culture, appealed to the romantic notions of the postwar German youth associations. The National Socialists' use of pageantry, flags, songs, war games, uniforms, and the "*Führer* Principle" struck a chord in the hearts of these lonely youths, who found purpose in comradery, group discipline, allegiance, sacrifice, and dedication to nation and leader.

Germany's youth contributed greatly to the rapid surge in votes that the National Socialist Party gleaned from the late 1920s into the early 1930s. According to the Reich's 1933 census, those aged eighteen to thirty represented nearly one-third of the German population. Among these, the newly enfranchised, having reached voting eligibility, actively participated in politics: in 1930 alone, there were 5.7 million new voters.[8] In the elections of March 5, 1933, there were 2.5 million new voters over the previous year, and voting participation rose to 88 percent of the electorate as opposed to 75 percent in 1928.[9] Another aspect of young people's voting influence is that three million (mostly older) voters died in the period from 1928 to 1933, whereas the number of first-time voters in the same period was 6.5 million.[10] It is no wonder that the National Socialist campaign specialists explicitly targeted Germany's students.

PROMISES, PROMISES

During the politically turbulent years of the republic, plagued by major economic problems and the perceived injustices of World War I and the Versailles Treaty, Hitler and the National Socialists formulated clear and promising goals. Hitler's charismatic speeches, the relentless propaganda articles printed in the party's paper the *Völkischer Beobachter*, and the prospect of strong leadership greatly boosted the National Socialists' popularity, especially after the onset of Germany's economic depression.

Hitler gained the support of many of the tycoons in business and industry who controlled political funds and were anxious to use them to promote a strong right-wing, antisocialist government. The financial backing Hitler received from the industrialists positioned his party on a secure financial footing and allowed him to make effective his emotional appeal to the lower middle class and the unemployed, based on the proclamation of his faith that Germany would emerge from its sufferings to resume its natural greatness.

Hitler promised a new German order to replace what he viewed as an incompetent and inefficient democratic regime. In reality, his new order was distinguished by a despotic political system based on a leadership structure in which authority flowed downward from a supreme national leader.[11]

Many contemporaries claimed that, during his speeches, Hitler appeared to be addressing them directly and personally. In truth, Hitler artfully responded to the wishes and goals of a wide spectrum of Germans. To the socialists, he promised that farmers would be given their land, pensions would increase, and public industries such as electricity and water would be state owned. To the nationalists, he promised that the German-speaking *Volk* would be united in one country, that the Versailles Treaty would be discarded, and that special restrictions would apply to foreigners. To the racially biased, he promised that Jews would be deprived of German citizenship and that immigration would be halted. To the fascists, he promised a strong central government and control of the press. To industrialists, business owners, landowners, the wealthy, and the army, he promised the remilitarization of Germany and that contracts would be awarded to Germans ("Only through the rebuilding of the military can peace be ensured," he stated). To the workers, he promised an end to unemployment, an increase in wages, and protection from the Communist-Bolshevist threat.[12]

Hitler used such meetings to tell many Germans what they wanted to hear—that there was a political party that would solve all their problems. He used simplistic language and short phrases to convey his message and came across as energetic and passionate—as someone who cared about the plight of the German people. The National Socialists' propagandists employed modern campaigning methods that included radio, mass rallies, newspapers, posters, and the novel idea of Hitler flying from city to city to deliver his allegedly mesmerizing speeches in person.

Figure 6.1.   Propaganda poster: "Our last hope: Hitler." *Courtesy of USHMM*

SEIZING CONTROL

Totaling four hundred thousand in 1932[13]—four times the number of army soldiers permitted in Germany—the paramilitary SA stormtroopers came across as a strong organization that could protect Germany from its enemies, both within the nation and abroad.[14] By the end of 1932, the SS counted fifty-two thousand members[15] at a time when political parties depended on paramilitary formations to protect their leaders and activists at events during election campaigns.

National Socialist strategy encouraged the use of violence to intimidate or sidetrack political rivals, while allowing Hitler plausible claim that he sought election through legal means and blaming the violence on his opponents or on crisis disorders brought about by the weakness and corruption of the Weimar democracy. Although the National Socialist paramilitary and terror apparatus often provoked violence, their opposition, the Communist, Social Democratic, and German Nationalist paramilitaries, countered in kind.[16]

The elections of July 31, 1932, were an extraordinary triumph for Hitler. The NSDAP captured 37.3 percent of the vote, becoming the largest party in the Reichstag, though later that year, the November 6 elections proved to be a setback for the party when the vote dipped to 33.7 percent.[17]

Though Hitler's popularity had slightly dropped, the National Socialists were still the largest political party. Aware of the fact that he held a strong position by virtue of his unprecedented mass following, Hitler entered into a series of intrigues with conservatives such as Franz von Papen, Otto Meissner, and President Hindenburg's son Oskar. The threat of Communism and the rejection of the Social Democrats bound them together, and Hitler insisted that the chancellorship was the only office he would accept. Under pressure and with no other leader able to gain sufficient support to govern, President Paul von Hindenburg appointed Adolf Hitler chancellor of Germany on January 30, 1933.[18]

FROM DEMOCRACY TO DICTATORSHIP

A few short weeks later, a fire broke out in the Reichstag (Parliament) building in Berlin, and authorities arrested a young Dutch Communist who confessed to starting it. Hitler used this episode to convince President Hindenburg to declare an emergency decree suspending many civil liberties throughout Germany, including freedom of the press, freedom of expression, and the right to hold public assemblies. The police were authorized to detain citizens without cause, and the authority usually exercised by regional governments

Figure 6.2.   Chancellor Hitler bowing to President Hindenburg, March 1933. *Courtesy of USHMM (#78587)*

Figure 6.3.   The Reichstag fire. *Alamy 2FN48YN*

became subject to control by Hitler's national regime. Almost immediately, Hitler began dismantling Germany's democratic institutions and imprisoning or murdering his chief opponents, the Communists in particular.

The final step toward Hitler's totalitarian goal was the eradication of parliamentary democracy and the rule of law. Although the National Socialists possessed a stable working majority in the Reichstag, they sought to gain complete de facto political power by means of an amendment to the Weimar Constitution. This could be achieved through the "Act for the Removal of the Distress of the People and the Reich," more commonly known as the *Ermächtigungsgesetz* or Enabling Act, by which the government of the Reich would be conferred near unlimited powers to enact laws, even in cases where legislation encroached on core bylaws of the constitution. As the Enabling Act required an amendment to the Weimar Constitution, its adoption neces-sitated both a two-thirds majority in parliament and the presence in the Reichstag of at least two-thirds of all its members.[19]

The prospects of achieving the requisite number of votes were good since the mandates of the eighty-one deputies from the Communist Party of Germany had been rescinded under the Reichstag Fire Decree. Moreover, many members of the Reichstag had already fled or been imprisoned or mur-dered. Hitler and his National Socialists entered into a series of negotiations with, and promises to, the remaining parties and to the representatives of the church. Only the deputies of the Social Democratic Party voted en masse against the bill, in spite of the considerable intimidation implemented by SA and SS men who surrounded the Kroll Opera House, where the parliament members were assembled.[20]

A mere ninety-four deputies voted against the bill while 444 voted in favor. The adoption of the Enabling Act on March 23, 1933, authorized Adolf Hitler's government to enact laws without the consent of the Reichstag (which continued to exist), without the countersignature of the president of the Reich, and without the endorsement of the Reichsrat (Reich Council, which consisted of members appointed by the German states and participated in legislation affecting all constitutional changes).

The passing of this act marked the final collapse of the democratic state based on the rule of law and the abolition of parliamentary democracy. All legislation in the National Socialist state was now based on the Enabling Act and served to centralize public administration, the judiciary, the security apparatus, and the armed forces in accordance with the "*Führer* Principle"; to standardize political life in accordance with National Socialist ideology by banning political parties and mass organizations; and to obliterate freedom of the press.[21]

This concentration of power in the hands of the National Socialist govern-ment, and thus in the person of Adolf Hitler, completed the transition to dicta-torship. When Reich President Paul von Hindenburg died the following year, Hitler claimed the titles of *Führer*, chancellor, and commander-in-chief of the German armed forces. The following years would be marked by masterful propaganda, the alleged "restoration of German pride," intimidation through the terror apparatus, persecution or elimination of all opposition and minority groups, and ultimately, war and genocide.

NOTES

1. Peter Loewenberg, "The Psychohistorical Origins of the Nazi Youth Cohort," *American Historical Review* 76, no. 5 (December 1971): 1457–58.

2. Ibid., 1463.

3. Fritz Redl and David Wineman, *The Aggressive Child* (Glencoe, IL: Free Press, 1957), 76–78.

4. Loewenberg, "Psychohistorical Origins," 1458.

5. Norman B. Ryder, "The Cohort as a Concept in the Study of Social Change," *American Sociological Review* 30 (1965): 848.

6. Lebendiges Museum Online, "Alltagsleben," https://www.dhm.de/lemo/kapitel/ns-regime/alltagsleben.html.

7. Walter Z. Laqueur, *Young Germany: A History of the German Youth Movement* (London: Routledge & Kegan Paul, 1962), 191.

8. Loewenberg, "Psychohistorical Origins," 1469.

9. Koppel Pinson, *Modern Germany: Its History and Civilization* (New York: Macmillan, 1954), 603–604.

10. Heinrich Striefler, *Deutsche Wahlen in Bildern und Zahlen: Eine soziografische Studie der Reichstagswahlen der Weimarer Republik* (Dusseldorf: Wende-Verlag W. Hagemann, 1946), 16.

11. National World War II Museum, "How Did Adolf Hitler Happen?," https://www.nationalww2museum.org/war/articles/how-did-adolf-hitler-happen.

12. BBC, "Nazi Rise to Power," https://www.bbc.co.uk/bitesize/guides/zpknb9q/revision/1.

13. United States Holocaust Memorial Museum, "Adolf Hitler: 1930–1933," *Holocaust Encyclopedia*, http://encyclopedia.ushmm.org/content/en/article/adolf-hitler-1930-1933.

14. BBC, "Nazi Rise to Power."

15. "The SS," History.com, https://www.history.com/topics/world-war-ii/ss.

16. United States Holocaust Memorial Museum, "Adolf Hitler."

17. Ibid.

18. "Rise to Power of Adolf Hitler," *Encyclopedia Britannica*, https://www.britannica.com/biography/Adolf-Hitler/Rise-to-power.

19. Historical exhibition presented by the German Bundestag, "The Enabling Act of 23 March 1933," Administration of the German Bundestag, Research Section WD 1, March 2006.

20. Ibid.

21. Ibid.

Chapter 7

Germany's Economic Recovery

MIRACLE OR DECEPTION?

A chief factor in Hitler's popularity and rise to power was his promise to rescue Germany from the financial collapse caused by the Great Depression. Bankruptcies and business failures plagued the economy, and around six million German workers were unemployed when the National Socialists came to power in 1933. By 1936 government propaganda claimed that it had all but eradicated unemployment. How did such a remarkable reversal take place in just a few years, making Hitler's achievements appear, at the time, nothing short of a miracle?

STATE CAPITALISM

A commonly held belief is that, while Hitler was a monstrous individual, he was able to significantly restore Germany's struggling economy. However, it is important to note that a global economic recovery was already underway during this time, albeit in a hesitant manner. The promised stability of the Third Reich's political structure helped to instill greater confidence in businesses, leading to increased investment and growth. However, the National Socialist regime came to power when the economy was already showing signs of improvement, and the government's actions did little more than to restore the pre-Depression status quo.[1]

Hitler and the National Socialist Party held a vehement anticapitalist stance, regarding western capitalism as a corrupt and decadent system. They contended that capitalism caused the working class to be exploited and wealth to be concentrated in the hands of a select few, resulting in social and economic inequality. Additionally, they perceived it as a system that disregarded the importance of community and national unity and promoted individualism and materialism. Hitler further regarded it as a system controlled by Jews and attributed many of Germany's economic difficulties to Jewish influence.

As an alternative, the National Socialist regime implemented a form of capitalism that was heavily influenced by fascist ideology. This system is often referred to as "state capitalism" or "corporatist capitalism." Under state capitalism, the government exercised a significant degree of control over the economy and private businesses. It intervened in the economy through measures such as price controls, regulation of production, and the allocation of resources. The government also established a system of "corporatism," in which different industries were organized into state-controlled cartels and trade associations. These groups were expected to work together to promote the interests of the state and the economy as a whole rather than pursuing their own self-interest.

Figure 7.1.   **Hitler inaugurating a section of Autobahn construction (1933).** *Courtesy of USHMM (Provenance William O. McWorkman)*

Figure 7.2. Propoganda poster: "Hitler is rebuilding—do your part: buy German goods" (ca. 1934). *AKG Images*

MEFO BILLS AND BUILDING ON A DEFICIT

In March 1933, Hitler appointed Hjalmar Schacht president of the Reichsbank and, the following year, minister of economics. Schacht supported public-works programs, most notably the construction of the Autobahn network, one of the programs that Paul von Hindenburg had planned during the Weimar Republic but that the National Socialists appropriated as their own.[2] In September 1934, Schacht introduced the "New Plan," Germany's effort to attain economic self-sufficiency. The nation had accumulated a large foreign currency deficit during the Great Depression, which persisted into the early years of Hitler's regime. Schacht negotiated trade agreements with several countries in South America and southeastern Europe, allowing Germany to import raw materials in exchange for Reichsmarks. This led to the deficit's stabilization while Germany could attempt to close the financial gap that had already developed.

Hjalmar Schacht created a plan for deficit financing, by which capital projects were paid for with the issuance of promissory notes called Mefo bills, which could be traded between companies.[3] These promissory notes were named after the Metallurgische Forschungsgesellschaft (Metallurgical Research Corporation) and served, in reality, to fund the rearmament program. The notes were particularly convenient in enabling the Third Reich to rearm because the Mefo bills were not the official Reichsmark currency and did not appear in the federal budget, thus helping to conceal rearmament.[4]

Hitler proposed the construction of a new road system that aimed to connect key economic regions of Germany and promoted the expansion of motor vehicle production with the goal of providing each German family with a "People's Car" or Volkswagen. However, this so-called motorization of Germany turned out to be a false promise made by the National Socialist regime. Road workers were subjected to poor pay and unfavorable working conditions, and car manufacturing decreased as military production increased. A large-scale advertising campaign encouraged workers to invest a significant portion of their wages in purchasing a car, but in reality, these unsuspecting employees were unknowingly contributing to the country's rearmament. By the end of 1939, through this tactic, approximately 270,000 Germans had loaned 110 million Reichsmarks to the National Socialist government. None of them received a Volkswagen in return as the factory was converted to war production by September 1939.[5]

The primary economic focus of the new government, which differentiated it from earlier German administrations, was the reconstruction of the military. Apart from serving defense needs, a powerful military would enable the nation to reclaim territories taken from Germany and, more importantly, expand their *Lebensraum* (living space) in the east.[6] As per historian Richard Evans, the National Socialists anticipated recovering their prewar debt by looting the riches of conquered countries during and after the war.

Contrary to popular perception, Germany's economy during Hitler's regime was not as strong as it appeared to be. For example, in 1938, taxes paid to the state only covered slightly more than half of the state's spending. One may question how Hitler was able to finance his massive rearmament and job creation programs. The answer lies in the implementation of "creative credit production," a practice that involved deficit financing. Hitler believed that this method was only a short-term measure, as the deficit would be recouped through territorial expansion in the future.[7]

Hitler claimed right from the start that "the future of Germany depends exclusively and solely on the reconstruction of the *Wehrmacht*. All other tasks must cede precedence to the task of rearmament."[8] This policy was immediately put into effect so that military expenditure quickly grew far larger than the civilian work-creation programs, with the share of military spending rising from 1 percent to 10 percent of national income in the first two years of the regime alone[9] and peaking as high as 75 percent by 1944.[10] Germany's massive rearmament goals unashamedly contravened the military limits imposed by the Versailles Treaty, and the unprecedented size of the rearmament program rendered it impossible to totally mask from foreign observers. When an explanation was demanded of Hitler, he justified the action by claiming that Germany was "engaged only in essential maintenance and renewal expenditure."[11]

PRIVATE ENTERPRISE

Starting in June 1933, the so-called Reinhardt Program was put into effect, with the aim of eliminating unemployment. It combined indirect incentives, such as tax reductions, with direct public investment in waterways, railroads, and highways and resulted in a large expansion of the German construction industry. Between 1933 and 1936, employment in the field of construction soared from only 666,000 to over 2,000,000. The automobile and other forms of motorized transport became increasingly attractive to the population, and the German motor industry boomed.[12] Despite propaganda generally depicting German families as well dressed and driving new Volkswagen cars, consumption actually slumped in the prewar economy, with few people being able to afford cars.[13]

As the new chancellor in January 1933, Hitler made a personal appeal to German business leaders to contribute to government funding during the

Figure 7.3. German tank factory. *Bundesarchiv, BILD 146-1985-100-33/Unknown author/CC-By-SA 3.0*

crucial months that were to come. He contended that business owners should support him in establishing a dictatorship because "private enterprise cannot be maintained in the age of democracy" and because democracy would allegedly lead to communism. Within a matter of weeks, the National Socialist Party raked in contributions from seventeen different business groups, the highest sums coming from IG Farben and Deutsche Bank.[14] Many of these businesses continued to support Hitler even during the war and also profited from the persecution of Jews.

In the same move, the National Socialist government launched a large-scale privatization of businesses and industry: several banks, as well as shipyards, railway lines, shipping lines, welfare organizations, and more were privatized.[15] One of the reasons for the regime's privatization policy was to cement the partnership between the government and business interests, as well as increasing the government's control of business.[16]

As the National Socialist regime faced budget shortages due to its military spending, privatization was one of the means by which it raised more funds.[17] Behind these moves one can also discover an ideological motivation: National Socialism held entrepreneurship in high regard, and, according to an economic study, "private property was considered a precondition to developing the creativity of members of the German race in the best interest of the people" and "private property itself provided important incentives to achieve greater cost consciousness, efficiency gains, and technical progress."[18] The "Second Reinhardt Program" provided half a billion Reichsmarks in credit to private businesses, mainly in construction, to spur new projects and job creation. With other similar programs, the government likely invested over five billion Reichsmarks in job creation in 1933.[19]

FREE LABOR AND CONTROLLED LABOR

Another factor that aided the economy was the adoption of the RAD (Reich Labor Service) by which young men between eighteen and twenty-five years of age were obliged to perform a minimum of six months of "voluntary and charitable" work, mainly for military and, to a lesser extent, civic and agricultural construction projects. Many continued to serve for the maximum period, which was two years, often working up to seventy-six hours a week. The sexist National Socialist policy was to discourage women from working a job and to stay at home in order to produce and raise children for the Reich, a practice that freed up a large number of jobs for unemployed men. However, from 1939 on, young women were also obliged to join the Reich Labor Service.

National Socialists condemned the welfare system of the Weimar Republic, as well as private charities, and accused them of supporting people they viewed as "racially inferior" and weak, who should have been weeded out in the process of natural selection. However, in the face of mass unemployment and poverty, the leadership decided to set up charitable institutions to help "racially pure" Germans in an effort to increase popular support, while emphasizing that this assistance was to be considered a means of "self-help" and not to be considered indiscriminate charity or universal social welfare. Programs such as the Winter Relief of the German People (WHW) and the broader National Socialist People's Welfare (NSV) were created as quasi-private institutions, relying on private donations—though "donating" was often compulsory.[20]

In order to avoid the problem of workers' strikes as experienced at the end of World War I, the National Socialists banned and dissolved all trade unions that had existed prior to their rise to power, to replace them with the DAF (German Labor Front). Controlled by the party, the German Labor Front did not intend to protect workers but to increase output and to control wages.[21]

Figure 7.4. Propaganda poster: "Yes! Führer, we follow you!" (1934). *Courtesy of USHMM (#2004.286.2)*

JOBS FOR THE PEOPLE?

To promote the perceived success of the National Socialist regime in elimi-nating unemployment, various methods were implemented. In addition to the automobile industry and highway construction, the government reinforced traditional gender roles by encouraging women to become homemakers through offering a "marriage loan." If the future bride had been employed for a sufficient period, the couple was eligible for an interest-free loan of up to one thousand Reichsmark, provided they did, indeed, get married and that the bride gave up her job immediately after. However, this solution did not lead to the creation of a significant number of jobs for men as women were not typically competing for the same roles, though it did have a positive impact on overall employment statistics.

Another tactic used in manipulating statistics was to categorize occasional workers as permanently employed. Some branches of trade and industry implemented policies that reduced working hours, which created jobs for new workers but resulted in cuts to workers' wages. Young people were heav-ily pressured to enroll in the "Voluntary" Labor Service or be drafted into agricultural work, further reducing official unemployment figures: nearly a half million people were registered in the program by 1935. The final step was the reinstatement of compulsory military service in May 1935, which required men aged eighteen to serve for one year in the German armed forces, extended to two years by August 1936. As the number of enlisted men grew in the following years, there were nearly no able-bodied men officially recorded as unemployed.

A HEALTHY ECONOMY?

From the very beginning, Hitler aimed for Germany to become economically self-sufficient and, in preparation for an inevitable war, to no longer rely on foreign imports. The experience of the First World War's blockade of Germany and its resulting deprivations had led Hitler to prioritize autarky, regardless of the restrictions it imposed on the population. In order to prevent a return of the devastating inflation of the early 1920s, the government imposed a compulsory freeze on prices in October 1936. Starting on New Year's Day the following year, Germans experienced the rationing of butter, margarine, and fat. Though the country had undoubtedly become self-sufficient in certain essential foods such as meat, potatoes, bread, and sugar just prior to the onset of war, imports were still needed for the German people's supply of fat, beans, and eggs. Rationing now included fruit, coffee, and other foodstuffs for the population, while the government, on the other hand, was secretly stockpiling supplies in preparation for war.

In 1936, as evidence of the failure of Schacht's New Plan grew, Hermann Göring introduced the Four-Year Plan to prepare Germany for war, a plan that emphasized the perceived threat from the Soviet Union. "The essence and goal of Bolshevism," Hitler announced in the plan's preamble, "is the elimination of those strata of mankind which have hitherto provided the leadership and their replacement with worldwide Jewry." He added that Germany should take the lead in combatting it as Bolshevism's victory would cause "the annihilation of the German people."

The Four-Year Plan aimed to increase the production of strategic materials such as coal, aluminum, rayon, crude oil, and synthetic fuel. However, despite a significant increase in production, Germany remained dependent on imports throughout World War II. By 1937, shortages of raw materials led to severe consequences for the population. The government implemented measures such as requesting that citizens collect and deliver scrap metal to support the steel and iron industries. By 1938, the run on metal escalated to the removal of metal garden fences and iron railings from family graves, as well as searches by the Hitler Youth for any metallic objects, including old radiators and keys, in homes and attics.

CHALLENGES AND CRIMES OF THE WAR YEARS

The war brought about a British blockade that seriously constrained German access to world markets and to the supply of fuel, sugar, coffee, chocolate, and cotton—all of which became scarce. Coal gasification replaced fuel imports to a limited extent, and Germany was forced to rely on Romanian oil fields. Germany depended on Sweden for the majority of its iron ore production and turned to Spain and Portugal to provide tungsten. Switzerland maintained trade agreements with Germany, and until the declaration of war on the Soviet Union, the Third Reich received large supplies of grain and raw materials from the USSR in exchange for industrial machinery and weapons.[22]

At the onset of war in 1939, Germans were forced to ration, but rather than increasing citizens' taxes to fund the war, as was the policy in Great Britain, the German government instead funded much of its military effort through plunder, especially appropriating the wealth of Jews and political enemies, both domestically and in the conquered territories.[23] As the Reich acquired new regions in the east, these lands were obliged to sell raw materials and agricultural products to Germany at exceptionally low prices. A large quantity of goods flowed into Germany from occupied lands in the west as well: two-thirds of all French trains in 1941, for instance, carried goods to Germany.[24] Fiscal policy also aimed at exploiting conquered nations, from which capital was gathered for German investments and German-run banks that were set up to manage local economies.

From the very beginning of the National Socialist regime, the unpaid labor in the concentration camps boosted the economy. The work was provided at first by political opponents, the wide range of "asocial" Germans, alleged criminals, Jews, Roma, and Sinti, later to be joined by prisoners of war brought into Germany from occupied territories following the German invasion of Poland. With Germany's subjugation of Eastern European territories, hundreds of forced labor camps were established in which millions of victims, both Jewish and non-Jewish, were exploited for the war industry and, often, worked to death. Among the slave laborers from the occupied lands, hundreds of thousands were hired out to leading German corporations, including Thyssen, Krupp, IG Farben, Bosch, Blaupunkt, Daimler-Benz, Demag, Henschel, Junkers, Messerschmitt, Siemens, and Volkswagen, as well as the Dutch corporation Philips.[25] By 1944, slave labor made up one-quarter of Germany's entire workforce, and the majority of German factories kept a contingent of prisoners.[26]

In hindsight, the Third Reich achieved no economic "miracle." Hitler's dictatorial regime aided the economy through its illegal rearmament program, by issuing promissory notes, printing bank notes, providing jobs, privatizing businesses, striving for self-sufficiency, utilizing slave labor, and exploiting the resources of occupied lands. Despite initial alleged economic successes for which the regime actively lauded itself, the National Socialist regime soon led Germany to war, which resulted in years of shortages and suffering for the civilian population and, ultimately, in the country's economic ruin.

NOTES

1. Richard Evans, *The Third Reich in Power* (New York: Penguin, 2005), 338.

2. W. Dick and A. Lichtenberg, "The Myth of Hitler's Role in Building the German Autobahn," *Deutsche Welle*, August 4 2012.

3. R. J. Overy, *The Nazi Economic Recovery, 1932–1938*, 2nd ed. (Cambridge: Cambridge University Press, 1996), 42.

4. William L. Shirer, *The Rise and Fall of the Third Reich: A History of Nazi Germany* (New York: Simon & Schuster, 2011), 260.

5. Evans, *Third Reich in Power*, 342–43.

6. Adam Tooze, *The Wages of Destruction: The Making and the Breaking of the Nazi Economy* (New York: Penguin, 2006), 38.

7. Evans, *Third Reich in Power*, 342.

8. Tooze, *Wages of Destruction*, 38.

9. Ibid., 66.

10. Richard J. Evans, *The Third Reich at War* (New York: Penguin, 2008), 333.

11. Tooze, *Wages of Destruction*, 59.

12. Hans-Joachim Braun, *The German Economy in the Twentieth Century* (London: Routledge, 1990), 83–84.

13. Niall Ferguson, *Civilization: The Six Killer Apps of Western Power* (London: Penguin, 2012), 232.

14. Tooze, *Wages of Destruction*, 99–100.

15. Germà Bel, "Against the Mainstream: Nazi Privatization in 1930s Germany," *Economic History Review* 63, no. 1 (April 2006): 34–55.

16. Ibid., 18.

17. Ibid., 42.

18. Christoph Buchheim and Jonas Scherner, "The Role of Private Property in the Nazi Economy: The Case of Industry," *Journal of Economic History* 66, no. 2 (June 2006): 408.

19. Evans, *Third Reich in Power*, 330.

20. Ibid., 484–87.

21. Shirer, *Rise and Fall of the Third Reich: A History of Nazi Germany*, 263.

22. Tooze, *Wages of Destruction*, 422.

23. Allan Hall, "Confiscated Jewish Wealth 'Helped Fund the German War Effort,'" *Telegraph*, November 9, 2010.

24. Braun, *German Economy in the Twentieth Century*, 121.

25. Marc Buggeln, *Slave Labor in Nazi Concentration Camps* (Oxford: Oxford University Press, 2014), 335.

26. Michael Thad Allen, *The Business of Genocide* (Chapel Hill: University of North Carolina Press, 2002), 1.

PART II

The Overwhelming Power of Propaganda

Chapter 8

Hitler and the Arts

CULTURE AS PROPAGANDA

Goebbels viewed culture as a means of propaganda and considered it to be the very sustenance of the *Volksgemeinschaft*, the people's community. He maintained that "the essence of propaganda must always be simplicity and repetition." The framework of National Socialist propaganda was constructed from a mixture of truth, half-truths, and blatant falsehoods, providing a flexible structure that could be molded and reshaped to accommodate the regime's evolving policies. Despite the arts being portrayed to Germans as instruments of edification and entertainment, the Third Reich's utilization of culture served as a means of disseminating the National Socialist worldview.[1]

THE "GREAT" ARTIST

To speak about Hitler as a warmonger and a monster responsible for brutality and genocide is easily acceptable, as it conforms to the facts that we have learned and that are public knowledge. To describe Hitler as a lover of the arts makes most people uncomfortable and sometimes irate. Any attempt to narrate Hitler's life that in any way humanizes the man or might present him in a remotely positive light is usually squelched or condemned as being "pro-Nazi."

However, this present work strives to remain open-minded in its study of the numerous aspects of the Third Reich. The aim is to help the reader to view a larger picture and to acquire a deeper understanding of all the elements that enabled Hitler to play pied piper to a majority of the German people. Art, architecture, and music were favored topics in Hitler's speeches, and his regime would later confirm to the nation that German culture and the

71

fine arts occupied an elevated position in the Third Reich. Hitler's alleged aim, after his wars and racial genocide had cleansed Europe, was to create a culture-state in which the arts would be the first priority.[2]

According to his sister Paula, as a child Adolf Hitler displayed an "extraordinary interest in architecture, painting and music."[3]

While in Vienna, Hitler produced mainly dreamy watercolor landscapes or renditions of well-known Vienna landmarks such as the Karlskirche. His work, though middle-of-the-road artistically, eventually increased in detail, particularly in its architectural elements. One feature that stood out, however, was a gaping absence of people: Hitler was inept at painting figures. Sometimes completing a picture per day, Hitler estimated, years later, that he had turned out some seven to eight hundred pictures during his stay in Vienna. His artwork was bought by those who could not afford anything better—often tourists wishing to take a souvenir back from Vienna or, occasionally, by frame shops.[4]

Awkward at hawking his own work, apart from the assistance he received from his friend Hanisch, Hitler teamed up with two other men from the hostel, Neumann and Löffner, both Jews, who occasionally made a sale on his behalf. Hitler also personally frequented two art dealers who occasionally purchased his work: Altenberg and Morgenstern. It was especially the latter, a Jew, who was not only the first person to offer a good price for Hitler's pictures but occasionally gave him a commission. Hitler said later of Morgenstern that he had been his "savior."[5] The art dealer kept a card file of his clients' purchases: ironically, most of those buying Hitler's artwork were local Jewish residents.[6]

All the while, Hitler devoured books; his favorite pastime was reading histories of art, culture, and architecture. His secretary Christa Schroeder remembered him saying that in his young days in Vienna he had purportedly consumed the entire five hundred volumes of a city library.[7]

Hitler viewed and described himself as an artist ad nauseam. "If someone else had been found," he later commented, "I would never have gone into politics; I would have become an artist or a philosopher."[8] It is of interest to note that, once he had risen to power, the first building Hitler erected was an extensive art gallery: the Haus der Kunst in Munich. Hitler's grip on the German people was twofold: on the one side, he created a police state that monitored and controlled people's views and freedoms; on the other, he seduced the Germans through symbols, pseudo-religious rites, spectacles, and his personal dramatized showmanship. It has been said that Hitler motivated the German people into active political participation by transforming them from spectators into participants in the National Socialist "theater."

According to the cultural historian Frederic Spotts, "Hitler aimed at creating a German culture state where the arts were supreme and where he could construct his buildings, hold art shows, stage operas, encourage artists and promote the music, painting and sculpture he loved." He also "held a deep and genuine interest in music, painting, sculpture and architecture. He regarded politics, not art, as a means to an end, the end of which was art. Hence the paradox of a man who wanted to be an artist but lacked the talent, who hated politics but was a political genius."[9]

It has been said that all totalitarian leaders deem the control of culture to be as important as the control of the economy. The loud flaunting of cultural ideals creates a sense of national pride and unity, lends the leader an allure of respectability, and helps to veil the ugly acts that a totalitarian government invariably commits. It might appear that Hitler's struggle for power was not for political glory but, rather, a means to achieve his personal cultural gratification.

In a speech delivered in Nuremberg in 1923, Hitler stated, "All great art is national. Great musicians, such as Beethoven, Mozart, Bach, created German music that was deeply rooted in the very core of the German spirit and the German mind. . . . That is equally true of German sculptors, painters, architects."[10] About a year or so later he wrote in *Mein Kampf* that twentieth-century culture had degenerated due to a social decline, not because of military or economic failures. Cubism and Dadaism were, in Hitler's opinion, "art Bolshevism" and could drive people "into the arms of spiritual madness."[11] Foreign art and aesthetics would ultimately threaten the very foundations of Western civilization. In a chapter of *Mein Kampf* titled "Nation and Race," Hitler attempts to prove that the Aryan race is at the root of "all human culture, all art, science and technology."[12]

Hitler saw culture and homeland as living hand in hand and, as the Jews were "a disorganized tribe without a territory," they "lacked the basis on which alone culture can arise."[13] His opinion was that "the Jewish people, despite all apparent intellectual qualities, is without any true culture, and especially without any culture of its own . . . the two queens of all the arts, architecture and music, owe nothing original to the Jews."[14] In conclusion, Hitler ascertained that "the Jew" contaminated art, literature, and the theater, and that through control of the press, Jews promoted international, Modernist, Bolshevist, and cosmopolitan, rather than German, works of art.[15] We can conclude that Hitler's early denigration of the Jewish people aimed at making them appear as a threat to the allegedly unique standards of Aryan culture. In his hateful assertations, Hitler chose to totally ignore the excellence of Jews in the fine arts and performing arts on both national and international levels.

Hitler described modern society as one of cultural decay and believed that a *Kulturkampf* (cultural struggle) had been taking place in Germany since 1871, the beginning of Germany's Second Reich. Political degeneration and cultural decay walked hand in hand, and at the 1935 party rally he exclaimed that the perpetrators of Modernism were "criminals of world culture," "destroyers of our art."[16] He also claimed that "art is the clearest and most immediate reflection of the spiritual life of a people. It exercises the greatest conscious and unconscious influence on the masses of a people. . . . In its thousand-fold manifestations and influences it benefits the nation as a whole."[17]

It remains an enigma how the man who built up an army in which up to seventeen million served also regretted that so much money had to be spent on warfare rather than on art. In the heat of the war, he commented, "It is a pity that I have to wage war on account of that drunk [Churchill] instead of serving the works of peace."[18] And again, in line with the idea that art was his ultimate goal and that war and persecution were a means to an end: "The whole point of power," Hitler said, "was to produce cultural wonders. . . . If I were to assess my work, I would first emphasize that in the face of an uncomprehending world I succeeded in making the racial idea the basis of life, and the second that I made culture the driving force in German greatness."[19]

STATE-CONTROLLED CULTURE

Once a police state was established in Germany, the new leaders carried out a *Säuberung*, a racial and cultural purge, a cleansing "of the collective body of the nation." This included the entire education system, the cinema, literature, press, and radio. A few months after Hitler came to power, the Reichskulturkammer, or RKK (Reich's Culture Chamber), under Josef Goebbels was founded with the aim of overseeing—and controlling—the various professional cultural associations. The RKK was composed of professional chambers for film, radio, music, theater, the fine arts, press, and literature. In early 1935, the RKK implemented racial regulations that forbade Jews as well as Romani and Sinti from becoming members.

As no one was allowed to practice a profession in the arts unless he or she was a member of this association, a massive wave of discrimination and exclusion soon followed the creation of this "cultural" ministry, an institution ensuring that state and culture were inseparably linked. Those targeted also included members embracing an opposing political view, such as Communists, Social Democrats, and Liberals. Needless to say, thousands of professionals thus lost their customary and essential source of income. Countless musical works and books were banned, the entire theatrical repertoire purged, and on May 10, 1933, about twenty thousand books were burned in several German university cities. By 1938, some three thousand Jews had been removed from German artistic life.[20]

Goebbels and the Ministry of Propaganda employed various cultural mediums to establish and reinforce their political agenda and ideology. Film was considered by Goebbels to be a key "leadership tool of the state" due to its ability to create a manipulative narrative. The German theater occupied a secondary position to film but could be transformed to emphasize political objectives, thereby fostering a new "political consciousness at the theater." The visual arts were utilized to depict the beauty and strength of the pure German race, while music had the power to evoke emotions at political mass events. Literature could create archetypes of racially correct behavior and outline the goals of National Socialism, while the press could be tailored to each social class and target group. And, finally, the radio attracted listenership through light entertainment interspersed with a political message.[21]

AWARDS AND REWARDS

Perhaps it was Hitler's "struggling artist" days in Vienna and in Munich that pushed him to lavish money on his favorite artists. "My artists should live like princes and not have to inhabit attic rooms," he stated.[22] He presented them with grants, awards, commissions, titles, tax rebates, studios, and even houses—some of which had been confiscated from Jews.[23] These generous tokens of recognition were also bestowed on conductors, photographers, sculptors, architects, singers, and those in diverse branches of the fine arts

Figure 8.1. Ministry of Public Enlightenment and Propaganda, Berlin (ca. 1938). *AKG Images*

Figure 8.2.   Hitler as "Patron of German art" (1934). *AKG Images*

and performing arts. Goebbels noted, "No royal patron was ever so generous to artists as he."[24] Hitler saw himself as the successor to Bavaria's patron of the arts and fellow Richard Wagner fan King Ludwig II, builder of the world-famous fairy-tale castles.

Hitler's subsidies to the arts surpassed anything seen before in Germany. Money flowed into cultural institutions and into the pockets of individual artists to the extent that Goebbels complained about Hitler's "excess of unrestricted spending."[25] Hitler personally disposed of vast sums gained legally and semi-legally. One source was royalties from the sale of *Mein Kampf*—required reading for Germans or, at least, encouraged ownership of a copy—as well as royalties earned from the sale of postage stamps bearing the *Führer*'s image. The cultural fund also received donations from the film industry and other assorted sources. Hitler used these funds to reward his artists of choice, as well as for his personal art purchases and toward building projects. Funds were also donated by German industrialists and stolen from Jews by the state's sale of their confiscated property.

Though Hitler's cultural chamber mercilessly stripped Jews of their right to work in the art world, he resentfully gave recognition to several Jewish artists such as the composers Gustav Mahler and Max Rheinhardt, the director of the Berlin theater. He promoted the career of one of his favorite opera singers, Margarete Slezak, who was half Jewish, as was one of Hitler's art dealers, Maria Almas Dietrich. He reinstated a Jewish composer, Arthur Piechler, at Augsburg's Conservatory and was amicable toward a number of artists whose spouses were Jewish.[26] These were, of course, just a few exceptions to Hitler's untiring discrimination and oppression of the Jewish community in his Reich.

Another award Hitler granted to artists was that of military exemption. It is estimated that more than twenty thousand discharges were approved, much to the chagrin of Germany's military leaders—especially as the war dragged on and drained the number of able-bodied soldiers by the millions (World War II resulted in an estimated 4.3 million German casualties).

MASSES AND MONUMENTALITY

Hitler's long-term plans for the Greater German Reich encompassed stunning edifices, theaters, opera houses, and museums. He meant to reshape the Reich on a grand scale, as well as on a regional scale with the fine arts and performing arts present in even small towns. Munich was to become the capital of German art, and Hitler's hometown Linz, in Austria, was to be lavished with the world's greatest art gallery. Even in February 1945, when Germany's defeat was imminent and inevitable, as already stated, Hitler focused his wholehearted attention on his cultural plans for Linz. He seemed to find solace in examining and discussing architectural plans even while his Reich was crumbling around him.[27]

As a suborganization of the Deutsche Arbeitsfront (German Labor Front), the *Kraft durch Freude* (Strength through Joy) program, also known as KdF, aimed at making it possible for the German masses to take vacations. It intended to stimulate the enjoyment of life and the joy of working and promote health, physical performance, and community spirit so as to boost the nation's economic productivity. Formerly restricted to the wealthy, leisure activities and the arts now became affordable to the working class. In some cases, art exhibitions and music were even brought directly to the factories. Many viewed the KdF programs, allowing them inexpensive access to the arts and to family vacations, as one of the most positive aspects of the National Socialist regime.[28]

The flipside of KdF is that it strengthened the implementation of the Third Reich's racial discrimination: Jews, "gypsies," and the government's political opponents did not qualify for participation. Though the purposes of *Kraft durch Freude* included breaking down class divisions and stimulating the German economy, the actual goal was part of the party's effort to control all aspects of life in the Third Reich. In 1937 alone, close to ten million Germans took part in KdF programs, many on organized hikes.[29]

Though, with the onset of war, the *Kraft durch Freude* program petered out, Hitler insisted that museums and theaters should remain open in Germany throughout World War II. He told Goebbels that if the cultural activities stopped, the quality of artistic life would be seriously damaged. He wished to boast that the Third Reich remained the world's great cultural state and that culture was the essential element he was fighting for. He also wanted to prove that Germany could wage a full-scale war without the disruption of social life. By so doing, he would convince the German people that victory was just around the corner.

People saw in this Hitler's confidence that Germany would win the fight, and they viewed the cultural opportunities as an escape from the horrors of war. Like never before, masses filled the museums, opera houses, theaters, and cinemas.[30] Only the bombing of such buildings put a damper on Germans' cultural drive. After a final discussion with Hitler about cultural issues, Goebbels noted, "I can easily foresee that once the war is over he [Hitler] will once again devote himself with the most passionate enthusiasm to such matters."[31]

His great admiration of Grecian architecture and that ancient civilization's fondness of sporting competitions led Hitler to emulate the Greek style in both architecture and events. At the BDM (League of German Girls) performances at the Nuremberg party rallies, thousands of girls donned outfits resembling Greek tunics to present gymnastics and dances. Also typically Grecian in essence, the strong naked male figure became a major feature of National Socialism's imagery. The prototype of a tall and muscular Nordic Aryan male, often brandishing a sword, was widely incorporated into sculptural works of the time. The symbology suggests, on the one hand, the power and superiority of the new Germany—proud of its beauty and strength—and, on the other, the German willingness to fight and die for state and *Führer*.[32]

Hitler's appreciation of the arts was, above all, shaped by the nineteenth century, the "golden age" of Germany's intellectual and cultural achievements. Hitler often reaffirmed his admiration for the German accomplishments of that era and lamented how, suddenly, an extensive cultural degeneration had cut off the creative flow. "Up to 1910," Hitler said, "we displayed an extraordinarily high level in our artistic achievement. After that, unfortunately, everything went ever more precipitously downhill."[33]

Hitler found it alarming that art and science were headed in drastically new directions and were earmarked by novel ideas. He was uncomfortable with this trend and wished to end it at any cost, in order to return to the accustomed styles. In his opinion, the Modernist style was corrupting not only the art world but society itself, and he maintained that a Jewish influence was behind it. To him avant-garde painting, the works of Bolshevists, Cubists, and Futurists, were "the products of spiritual degenerates" and "the hallucinations of lunatics or criminals."[34]

THE STATE VERSUS MODERNISM

Following World War I, many German artists were inspired to make a fresh start and embarked on a journey of innovative experimentation with new forms, themes, and techniques in art. The *Novembergruppe*, named after the end of the war in November, was comprised of prominent figures such as Walter Gropius and aimed to bring about a unified approach to art, architecture, craftsmanship, and urban design. The group proclaimed that "the future of art and the gravity of the current moment compels us, the revolutionaries of the spirit (Expressionists, Cubists, Futurists), to unite and work closely together." This artistic resurgence became known as the Bauhaus movement, centered in Weimar, the same town where the new postwar political regime was established. Walter Gropius and other Bauhaus leaders explored new ways of designing and painting and even formed their own jazz band, capitalizing on the growing popularity of the genre in Germany.[35]

In *Mein Kampf*, Hitler criticized "Cubism and Dadaism" as types of "Bolshevist art." He subsequently publicly disavowed any art movement, including Impressionism and Expressionism, that he considered to be a reflection of sickness and degeneracy caused by physical and mental illness and associated with Jews.[36] The National Socialist "revolution" was, above all, supposedly, a "cultural revolution," and once Hitler could exercise total political control of Germany, his cultural jurisdiction followed. The National Socialists discharged hordes of museum directors and curators nationwide, to be replaced by authorities chosen thanks to their political allegiance rather than their artistic competence. These new "experts" now became responsible for separating classic and time-honored art from Cubism, Dadaism, Futurism, and the "Modernist and Cultural Bolshevist monstrosities" of the twentieth-century styles. Germany had, interestingly, reared the highest number of Modernist artists and works (totaling about eighteen thousand). Hitler's attack and ban resulted in countless contemporary German artists losing both income and cultural standing in National Socialist Germany, and many fled the country.

In 1936, the regulation of the press was further tightened by suppressing analytical commentary. During the Weimar Republic, analysis and criticism were established features of the intellectual world. Under the new restrictions, only authorized National Socialist writers were allowed to critique books, films, theater productions, art, and other cultural forms. The role of the critic changed from *Kunstkritiker* (art critic) to *Kunstbetrachter* (art observer), and this effectively limited the critic to offering approval rather than engaging in analytical criticism.[37]

In order to show the German people the type of art that Hitler considered to fall in the category of Modernist horrors and a corruption of the high standards of German culture, in 1937 an exhibition was put together, titled Images of Decadence in Art (not to be confused with the works of the late nineteenth-century Decadent movement). The Degenerate Art Exhibition made its debut in Vienna before traveling to Nuremberg to coincide with the annual party rally and, finally, to the newly opened House of German Art in Munich. Hitler's aversion to modern art can be expressed in his view of it as "thought-provoking, unconventional, uncomfortable, shocking, abstract, pessimistic, distorted, cynical, enigmatic, disorderly, freakish." Hitler simplified his opinions on art when he stated, "*Deutsch sein heißt klar sein*"—to be German means to be clear. Hitler wanted art to provide escape from pain, not confrontation with it. Hitler opined that art and society are moved by similar forces and that art not only reflects but promotes social upheaval.[38] Most of the confiscated "degenerate" artwork was sold overseas, often to enrich Göring or Hitler personally, or traded with Swiss art dealers. Art objects that could not be sold were burned, resulting in an irretrievable loss for the civilized world.[39]

With the banning of "degenerate" or "culturally and socially corruptive" artwork, there proved to be a vacuum in the field of good contemporary art. Hitler realized this when trying to organize an exhibition of German contemporary art at Munich's brand-new art museum in 1937. Of fifteen thousand entries, some nine hundred works were selected for consideration, but Hitler had a fit when he reviewed the works. Goebbels recounted the event as follows: "The sculptures are alright, but some paintings are a downright catastrophe. Pieces were hung that made one positively cringe. . . . The *Führer* was beside himself with rage."[40]

Hitler's anger was likely caused by the realization that his National Socialism had not succeeded in inspiring great works. "These paintings demonstrate," Hitler seethed, "that we in Germany have no artists whose works are worthy of being hung in this splendid building."[41] Hitler stormed off to the Berghof in Berchtesgaden and left his personal photographer, Heinrich

Figure 8.3.   Hitler at the Haus der Kunst, Munich

Hoffmann, to carry out the contemporary art exhibition's selections. Over the next years, other temporary and permanent art shows of a wider period and "acceptable" styles opened throughout Germany, attracting countless visitors.

THE UNSCRUPULOUS COLLECTOR

In June 1939, just months before Hitler set the wheels of World War II in motion, he summoned Dresden's famous Picture Gallery director, Hans Posse, to the sumptuous Berghof, his home at Obersalzberg. He proposed for Posse to take on the task of supplying the artwork for a world-class museum to be established in Hitler's hometown, Linz, in Austria. His choice of Linz was, on the one side, for it to become a superlative city of the arts vying with Florence or Paris. On the other, he didn't want his museum to have to compete side-by-side with the unmatched museums of the Greater Reich, such as those of Berlin, Munich, or Vienna. It would house "only the best of all periods from the prehistoric beginnings of art . . . to the nineteenth century and recent times."[42] The decision to create a museum on German soil as a lasting monument to himself was more than likely inspired by his recent trip to Italy, where in the company of Mussolini he marveled at classic masterpieces in the museums of Florence and Rome.

Figure 8.4.   Hitler with architect Giesler and Martin Bormann discussing the rebuilding of Linz. *Walther Frentz Collection*

In his younger days, Hitler had sketched a detailed design of his ideal museum structure, titled "Sketch of a German Museum for Berlin." Now he possessed the authority and the means to commission the construction of the museum of his dreams—a Hitler Museum—in the city of his youth and to turn it into an enviable treasure chest of world renown. To complement Hitler's already extensive collection of German Romantic paintings, Posse's mission would be to locate and procure the artwork that Hitler would personally select and acquire by "purchase or confiscation." Although Hitler favored German and Austrian paintings from the nineteenth century, Posse's focus included early German, Dutch, French, and Italian paintings.[43]

Hitler set up a small task force of about twenty members, the Linz Special Commission, headed by Martin Bormann and with Hans Lammers, head of the Reich Chancellery, in charge of the financing. For the first four years of its existence, the Linz cultural center project was kept secret from the public. Finally, in April 1943, at a time when the war was wearing down on the nation and Germany's cities were being relentlessly bombed, Hitler allowed the Linz plan to be revealed. In a special edition of Heinrich Hoffmann's art magazine *Kunst dem Volk* (Art for the People), the idea was presented in a carefully worded text—personally examined by the *Führer*—announcing the creation of a great art gallery in Linz as part of the postwar beautification of the Reich. The article boasted how little time it had taken to make the acquisitions for the art gallery, as opposed to other nations that had required centuries to collect their museums' content. Of course, no mention was made of the number of these art treasures having been "acquired" through the confiscation of Jewish or other private property. The article ended with the notion that Hitler had bestowed the German people with a gift it could never forget and that the people would never be able to repay "its debt of gratitude to the *Führer*."[44]

Though a large portion of the works acquired by Posse for Hitler's selection and possible approval was legally purchased, the bulk of it was conveniently confiscated under the designation of *staatsfeindliches Vermögen* (property of enemies of the state). This category applied to the possessions of Jews or citizens considered by the authorities as undesirable, or those who had fled the country. A further means of acquiring artwork was by forced sale through blackmail. The bane of the National Socialists' illegal art collecting raked in roughly 220,000 works of art and began with the annexation of Austria in March 1938. It continued unabashedly in Germany following the shameful *Kristallnacht* in November of the same year.

The next year, when Hitler seized Czechoslovakia, the systematic looting of valuables was not limited to Jewish homes but to all private, public, and religious property as well. Following Poland's invasion, the German rape of art treasures grew even more savage and included several Old Masters such as works of Rembrandt, da Vinci, and Raphael. The ransacking of the Netherlands began in May 1940 with the customary confiscation of Jewish property and the fevered purchasing of valuable artwork.

The German occupation of France in June 1940 secured Hitler some of the world's most valuable art collections, many belonging to Jewish families such as the Rothschilds. Hitler issued a decree declaring that all private artworks and antiquities, including those of the French state, should be "taken into provisional custody . . . [as] guardianship of property to be used as collateral in peace negotiations." Nearly twenty-two thousand items soon filled the Jeu de Paume pavilion in Paris, from which Hermann Göring helped himself to some six hundred pieces.[45] On his mission to acquire outstanding artwork for Hitler's Linz Museum, Hans Posse also traveled to Italy on three occasions, where he purchased some twenty-five items. These acquisitions were certainly not to the liking of the Italians in general, who view their art heritage in a more nationalistic way than even their own social identity.

"BOOKS, BOOKS, AND MORE BOOKS"

Thus commented Hitler's childhood friend Kubizek about Hitler's lifelong passion for reading. By 1941, World War II was well underway, and Hitler could not find sleep unless he spent several hours looking at picture books on art or architecture. Hitler's personal library, distributed between Berlin,

Munich, and Berchtesgaden and allegedly consisting of some twelve thousand books, was discovered at the Altaussee salt mines in Austria. About three thousand were shipped to the United States, but unfortunately, many were "duped out"—discarded or recycled—over the years. Today, some 1,200 are housed in the rare book collection at the Library of Congress in Washington, DC.[46]

In keeping with Hitler's passion for books, he intended to include a library in his plans for Linz. Originally, some 250,000 volumes were to form this collection, but with time and his inherent megalomania, Hitler determined it should become the largest library in the world.[47] The more Hitler collected, the more he wanted, and he soon decided to add two more collections to his Linz museum: one for coins, the other for arms and armor. As the requisitioning of art treasures continued, Hitler's ambitions for Linz grew even greater. In addition to the art museum and library, he eventually made plans for an opera house, a music hall, a theater, and a cinema. Sketching himself the outlines of the types of structures he wanted, Hitler's "European Culture Center," as it was often referred to, was not to stand out as just the largest and best in the German Reich but to dazzle as one of the leading cultural centers of the world.

Hitler's secretary Christa Schroeder stated that "the Linz museum was one of his favorite conversation topics at late afternoon tea."[48] Hitler wished for each display to have plenty of space, as opposed to the cluttered way the artwork in the Louvre was exhibited. He wanted the different schools to be grouped into specific periods, complete with furniture and decoration corresponding to the time.

It is likely that Hitler viewed the collected artwork as symbols of personal power and wealth and took pride in the number and value of the works that he had selected for the "*Führer* Museum" in Linz. Hidden in various castles and monasteries, according to some, the total number of looted or purchased artworks destined for Linz is estimated at around seven thousand. Among the main depositories for that collection were the iconic Neuschwanstein Castle, the Kremsmünster Monastery, and the remote Altaussee Salt Mine in Austria. The latter is where the bulk of the Linz selection was painstakingly stored, deep in the mountain. The exciting story of these art treasures' close escape from destruction at war's end was featured in the *Monuments Men* film, based on the book of the same name.

TREASURES IN SALT MINES

As early as 1939, the Viennese art museum curators visited the old salt mines near Altaussee, in a remote corner of the Austrian Alps, to evaluate them for the possible safe storage of valuable artwork. An interesting factor about these particular mines is that wood used in construction projects appeared freshly cut even decades after having been installed, and pine twigs used in the decorating of the miners' chapel remained fresh smelling after months. Tests led to the conclusion that the mine's unique atmosphere of 75 percent humidity and a constant 8 degrees Celsius (46° Fahrenheit) offered ideal conditions for the long-term preservation of artwork. In 1943 the miners developed proper rooms with upright props to avoid cave-ins, with boarding on floors, walls, and ceilings. To complete this massive undertaking beneath the mountain, the workers used 1,200 square meters (42,000 ft³) of wood and some five kilometers (3.1 mi) of electric cable.

By the end of the year, Hitler suggested transferring the large collection hidden at Kremsmünster Monastery to the Altaussee Salt Mine. By January 1944, the transfer was completed, soon to be followed by further transfers from the Führerbau in Munich, Hitler's artwork from the Berghof, his personal library, and his entire coin, weapon, and armor collections intended for the Linz museum. Due to the mine's inaccessibility in snow, additional transports in the winter of 1944–1945 were carried out by caterpillar trucks originally manufactured for the Russian campaign.

Among the looted masterpieces from Belgium, such as Michelangelo's *Bruges Madonna*, perhaps the most famous piece of the entire hoard was the *Ghent Altarpiece*. This fifteenth-century masterpiece, marking the transition from the art of the Middle Ages to that of the Renaissance, has been stolen seven times, in part or in its entirety, thus making it one of the most coveted pieces in history. In the 1800s the wings of this triptych altar were pawned by the Ghent diocese and, as they were never reclaimed, eventually purchased by the king of Prussia and, finally, exhibited in Berlin's Gemäldegalerie.

During World War I, German forces confiscated the main part of the altarpiece, but the entire work was returned to Belgium soon after, as part of the reparations agreement under the Treaty of Versailles. After Germany's invasion of Belgium in 1940, Belgian authorities shipped the priceless altar to the Vatican for safekeeping, but it did not travel farther than the south of France before Hitler ordered it to be seized and brought to Neuschwanstein Castle in Germany. Along with another Flemish altarpiece, the precious *Last Supper of Leuven*, the *Ghent Altarpiece* now rested deep under the mountain in the relative safety of a secret repository of some seven thousand exhibits: the world's largest museum at the time.[49]

Just weeks before the end of the war in Europe, Adolf Hitler gave instructions that the stockpile of art should be preserved and, in the event of the enemy's approach, the entrance tunnels to the mine destroyed. However, *Gauleiter* Eigruber, the regional governor, refused to accept the *Führer*'s order. In his steadfast National Socialist conviction, he considered it his duty to guard the artwork from the enemy and destroy it rather than allow its possible return into the hands of "world Jewry."

Determined to destroy the world's largest art collection, Eigruber ordered eight aircraft bombs to be placed inside the mines. Their transport cases were marked "careful, marble, do not drop." When the salt mine's director, Pochmüller, found out about the half-ton bombs, he and the miners became determined to prevent the mine's destruction. Their motivation in this endeavor was, on the one hand, to save the inestimably valuable art treasure and, on the other, to preserve their mining jobs.[50]

Employing a ruse, Pochmüller traveled to Linz to speak with *Gauleiter* Eigruber, where he explained to him that the explosive devices would not suffice to destroy the artwork unless the mines' entrance tunnels were capped. The quickest way to block them, he said, was to blast them shut with explosives before detonating the half-ton bombs by cable from a distance. Little did the *Gauleiter* know that Pochmüller never intended on setting off the devastating bombs. On April 22, 1945, renewed instructions arrived from Hitler, again forbidding the artwork's destruction and instructing that the mine's entrances be sealed, if necessary.

Pochmüller interpreted this as permission for him to take the bombs out of the mine. As soon as the miners managed to remove all eight bombs from the mines, they blew up the mine's access tunnels with explosives, thus successfully saving the monumental treasure hoard from imminent destruction.[51] A few days later, on May 8, 1945 (VE Day), Major Ralph Pearson of the U.S. 3rd Army secured the Altaussee site, to be followed on May 20 by a team of the so-called Monuments Men. In the months to follow, the contents were transported by truckload to the "central collecting point" in the former National Socialist Party headquarters in Munich.[52]

In the months and years following World War II, the various nations that had lost art in a legal or illegal manner made an indecorous scramble for not only Hitler's Linz collection but the rest of the art now stockpiled in Germany and Austria. A substantial portion of these works and collectibles had been legally purchased by the German state or by Hitler's "Linz art fund," the small fortune accumulated through industrialists' donations and from postage stamp royalties. Nonetheless, ostensibly due to the fact that much of the artwork had been obtained by looting private, public, and above all Jewish-owned collections, the American army was instructed to return works to the country of origin, to be left in the care of each nation's authorities.[53]

Two additional mines were used as repositories for sizable amounts of art: one in Austria, the other in Germany. Not far from the Altaussee mine in the Salzkammergut region, extensive collections of priceless artwork and objets d'art, principally from Vienna's museums, were stowed nearly three kilometers (almost 2 mi) deep in Bad Ischl's mines.[54] These included works of such artists as van Eyck, Velazquez, Dürer, Munch, and Monet[55] as well as masterpieces by Rembrandt, Raphael, Rubens, and Bruegel.[56] In addition, crates arrived with Egyptian finds and the more than two-thousand-year-old Venus of Willendorf statuette.[57] Though more shipments from Vienna arrived later, Bad Ishl's inventory at the end of February 1945 included 518 crates, 668 paintings, and 171 tapestries.[58]

Toward the end of the war, with increased air raids over Berlin, Merkers's giant potash mines, about 380 kilometers (236 mi) southwest of the capital, were selected as a secret repository for most of Germany's gold reserves, currency totaling a billion Reichsmarks bundled in one thousand bags, a considerable quantity of foreign currency, piles of confiscated valuables, as well as one-fourth of the major holdings of fourteen of the principal Prussian state museums. At war's end, the find was so sensational that it was celebrated by a joint visit to the mine by the three top U.S. armed forces generals: Eisenhower, Patton, and Bradley.[59]

HITLER AND THE WAGNERS

During Adolf Hitler's younger years in Vienna, he made three attempts to meet Alfred Roller, a professor of fine arts and stage designer. Though Hitler was hoping to work for Roller in creating stage sets, each time the insecure artist got cold feet and left just before the meetings took place.

Though the visual aspect of operatic stage sets was of significant importance to Hitler, it was above all Richard Wagner's music that exerted a hypnotic fascination on him. He attended his first opera, Wagner's *Lohengrin*, at the age of twelve and, after that, became obsessed with not only the composer's operas but the man himself. Christa Schroeder said of Hitler, "Wagner's musical language sounded in his ear like a revelation of the divine."[60]

As an obsessed fan, Hitler was intimately familiar with both the stories and the musical content of Wagnerian operas. The American German theater director Carl von Schirach, father of the National Socialists' Reich Youth Leader, Baldur von Schirach, stated, "In all my life I never met a layman who understood so much about music, Wagner's in particular."[61] Despite the poverty of his Vienna days, Hitler managed to attend *Tristan und Isolde* thirty or forty times and, in the course of his life, saw *Die Meistersänger* about a hundred times.[62] Notwithstanding the Reich Youth Leader's adulation, it has often been suggested that Hitler possessed a limited understanding of music; in all likelihood, his admiration for Wagner arose from the composer's combination of traits that Hitler himself sought to embody: a blend of drama and action that reflected his own inclination toward pathos and ideology, a

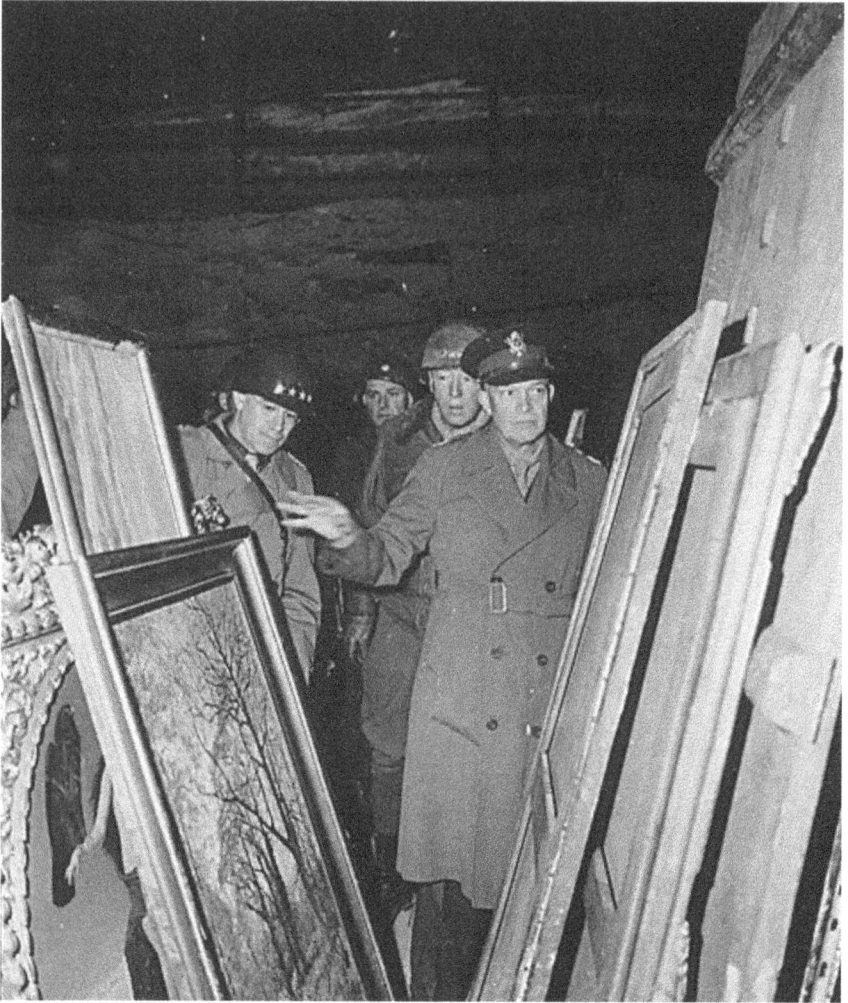

Figure 8.5.   Three U.S. generals visit the art cache at Merkers Mine (April 12, 1945)

platform from which to perform and speak to the masses, and a visually stunning stage created through the use of color and form.[63]

In his youth, Hitler produced stage sketches for Wagner's operas, and from the mid-1930s on, he enjoyed working on Wagnerian productions with Benno von Arent, whom he appointed "Reich stage designer." Hitler personally funded several joint productions with Arent, one of which included a setting reminiscent of the Nuremberg party rallies, complete with a sea of banners and a martial chorus.[64]

In a 1923 speech in Bayreuth, Hitler expressed heroism as the essential attribute of human greatness and stated that this quality was possessed by three men: Luther, Frederick the Great, and Richard Wagner. While in Bayreuth, Hitler was hosted by the influential piano manufacturers Edwin and Helene Bechstein, who also owned a holiday home at Obersalzberg, Berchtesgaden, just a stone's throw from Hitler's future residence and headquarters, the Berghof. On this occasion, he met Winifred Wagner, the composer's English-born daughter-in-law, who would later run the Wagner Festival in Bayreuth from 1930 to 1945.

Winifred's invitation to visit Haus Wahnfried, the villa that Richard Wagner constructed for himself in 1874, thanks to King Ludwig II's generosity, was a moving moment for Hitler, one that he repeatedly reminisced about for years to come. This first visit was the start of a lifelong personal friendship with Winifred and her family. She and her husband, Siegfried, backed numerous National Socialist activities and campaigns. Hitler turned a blind eye to the fact that Siegfried leaned toward homosexuality and had married Winifred to save himself from public scandal. Hitler often stopped by the house—usually after dark and hidden from the prying eyes of Bayreuth's residents—to spend the night. Haus Wahnfried not only became a refuge for him, but Winifred and her four children became like family to Hitler. According to Frederic Spotts, Winifred was the woman Hitler never married, and her children were the offspring he lacked.[65]

Rumors of romance between Hitler and Winifred Wagner—even the possibility of marriage—abounded, but all such allegations were shrugged off. Nonetheless, he doted on Wieland, the eldest of the Wagner children and grandson of Hitler's idol. Hitler gifted him a Mercedes, allowed him to work at the Bayreuth Festival instead of completing the compulsory Reich's Labor Service, and exempted him from military service during the war.

With near religious regularity, Hitler attended the Bayreuth Festival every summer from 1933 to 1940. By this time, Winifred Wagner had become the director of the festival and was expected to become a member of the Reich Theater Chamber—an instrument of "cultural cleansing"—which, despite Goebbels's urging, she was able to refuse thanks to Hitler's intervention on her behalf. Notwithstanding the Cultural Chamber's nationwide purge, Winifred refused to fire anyone for political or racial motives, and she employed Jews in the festival up until their final "emigration."[66]

Though Winifred came under fire from the National Socialist authorities, Hitler's patronage paradoxically resulted in the Bayreuth Festival becoming the only cultural establishment not subjected to the National Socialists' control and censorship.[67] At some point in each festival season, Hitler summoned the entire theater crew for an evening at the Wagners' residence. His social invitation included the team's Jewish members, as well as those who had a Jewish spouse. According to Winifred Wagner, those of Jewish descent accepted Hitler's invitation "with pleasure and out of a sense of curiosity."[68]

The upheaval of war in no way deterred Hitler from implementing "his" Wagner Festival. In his mind, what could be more comforting and rewarding to a wounded or convalescing soldier than to attend an opera of the divine Wagner? Bayreuth was promoted to the mythical status of exerting miraculous and curative powers on those whose psyches had suffered in their heroic duties on the front.

Stukas, a 1941 popular propaganda film of the war years, glorified young Luftwaffe pilots' victories during the Battle of France, and featured the story of a handsome hero who, after France and Poland's defeat, lay comatose in a clinic. It was only after attending a performance of Wagner's *Götterdämmerung* that he regained his lust for dive-bombing and decimating Germany's enemies. From 1940 to 1944, Hitler's "War Festival" in Bayreuth was attended by an impressive 142,000 "guests of the *Führer*," whether these war-weary or fight-happy soldiers chose to or not.[69]

MUSIC FOR THE MASSES

In addition to his adulation of Wagner, Hitler encouraged the public's appreciation of other German and Austrian composers such as Ludwig van Beethoven, Anton Bruckner, and Franz Lehár in particular. By the same token, the Reich Culture Chamber's State Music Institute condemned and purged "modern" artwork and its creators from the new Germany. Mahler, Mendelssohn, Offenbach, and Schoenberg were just a few of the great "Jewish-born" composers whose works were now banned. Debussy drew disfavor simply because he had married a Jew, and among other political dissidents, Alban Berg's music was ousted. So-called *Negermusik*, as well as jazz or swing music, fell into the general "degenerate" category. The same applied to any Jewish bandleaders and composers such as Bennie Goodman, Irving Berlin, and George Gershwin.

The National Socialists' principal attack on Modernist music focused on its alleged "atonality and dissonance," which, for propaganda's sake, were strung together with the terms "social chaos, Bolshevism, Jewish influence and Internationalism." In the same way that Hitler's art appreciation was mired in late nineteenth-century Romanticism, his musical tastes remained trapped in the past. Hitler's aim was to provide music with the same standing that he imagined it had enjoyed in ancient Greece. Art and music's sole purpose was to elevate the finer emotions of the *Volk*, and thus it should not only be readily available but aesthetically accessible to the general public.

This meant that a composer's duty was to create a medium that people from every walk of life could understand and be moved by.

To Hitler, atonality and dissonance in music was a perversion of reality, similar to the work of Cubists and Expressionists. An insult to finer senses, modern music was, to Hitler, elitist. Artists should not compose for a small minority, but rather, as culture was the glue that bound society together, music should hold the same appeal to everyone. As Hitler was of the opinion that music had reached its zenith at the turn of the century and declined ever since, he said, "We need not create any new art; if we cannot achieve anything great, then let us concentrate on what is already there, which is immortal."[70]

The Music Chamber's censorship board oversaw every aspect of musical recording, broadcasting, programming, and publication and was responsible for categorizing works as either acceptable or "degenerate" music. In a 1935 speech, Goebbels stated that "we do not intend to tell a conductor how he should conduct a score. But we do claim the sovereign right to decide *what* is played and *what* conforms to the spirit of *our* time."[71]

As one cannot physically destroy music as one can artwork, the National Socialists' aggressiveness in the music purge of Germany was not quite as assertive and rigorous as with painting or sculpture. In hindsight, Hitler managed to inflict less harm on music than on the other fine arts.[72] Music was undoubtedly Germany's chief cultural legacy, and Hitler used it to drown out the sounds of his underlying dictatorial policies and his totalitarian state. Hitler's untiring control and promotion of the fine arts would create an image of Germany's "New Order" as one of culture rather than political terror. This appearance was intended to fool not only the German people but the rest of the world as well.

With the removal of Modernism and Jews, Hitler believed that he had pruned the German music world in such a way that a new blossoming could now take place. Indeed, an overwhelming number of compositions streamed in, honoring Hitler, the New Order, the party, or the military—overall more quantity than quality. Hitler was disheartened by the scarcity of outstanding new composers and likely realized that he had set his own expectations too high by anticipating a new Wagner to emerge like a phoenix.

In a 1938 speech at the Nuremberg rallies, Hitler defined the music for the German *Volk* as follows:

Music must follow the broad rules of national life and therefore produce not a confusion of sounds that will bewilder a perplexed listener but, instead, move the heart through the beauty of sound. . . . Whether in architecture, or music, or sculpture or painting, one fundamental principle should never be overlooked: every true art must in its expression bear the stamp of beauty. The ideal for all of us lies in the cultivation of what is healthy. Only what is healthy is right and natural, and what is right and natural is therefore beautiful.[73]

With no precise direction as to what might be deemed by the *Führer* to be "healthy and beautiful," musicians were left with no clear guidance. Some reverted back to the accepted classic Romanticism; others experimented with a mixture of genres that they hoped would earn the Third Reich's stamp of approval.

THE THEATER

Hitler deemed himself an authority on numerous topics, especially in cultural affairs. Although the National Socialists aimed to politicize all performing arts, the theater received less attention than the film, music, and art industries. Differing opinions on taste and direction made it challenging to establish clear guidelines for the theater's mission. Goebbels believed that the theater should provide nonsentimental, heroic entertainment that reflected the National Socialists' desired portrayal of life rather than reality. Hitler's dramatic values were relatively straightforward: he reportedly favored *Snow White and the Seven Dwarves*, *Gone with the Wind*, and *King Kong* as his top three movies.[74]

Though the National Socialist dictatorship implemented an anti-Jewish policy, parallel to German non-Jewish actors, Jewish-born theater practitioners in Germany also found creative niches for their artistic flow. Despite the bans and restrictions, a wealth of cultural production persisted, even in places one may think impossible for any kind of creativity. Forms of theater and related musical events endured until 1941 in a cultural organization solely for Jews: the Jewish Kulturbund.[75]

The Kulturbund (Cultural League) of German Jewry, later renamed the Kulturbund for Jews in Germany, was established with the approval of National Socialist officials in Joseph Goebbels's Ministry of Propaganda. Under the directorship of the musicologist Dr. Kurt Singer, a network of cultural leagues across the *Führer*'s Reich provided theaters with musical and theatrical events for Jewish subscribers from October 1933 to September 1941. This permission was restricted to Jews to perform in, attend, and review play productions, operas, cabarets, and orchestral concerts at Kulturbund-sponsored theaters. The dramatic repertoire, however, was limited mainly to works written by non-German Jewish artists, though some pieces succeeded in escaping censorship.[76]

The Reich's Dramaturgical Bureau published a "List of Abusive and Undesirable Literature for the Stage." Some playwrights, such as Franz

Arnold, Bertolt Brecht, Carl Zuckmayer, and Bruno Frank, were relegated to the list right from the start and remained there till the oppressive regime's demise. Sidestepping the laws regarding repertoire selection was not as difficult in the field of comedy. The idea of performing comedy—and a lot of comedy was presented—during a reign of terror may seem out of place. The fact is that of the more than forty-two thousand productions that were staged between 1933 and 1944 during the Third Reich, the majority were comedies.[77]

THE CINEMA

Within two months of Hitler's rise to power, he and Goebbels decided that the motion picture industry was important enough to create a separate department, the Reichsfilmkammer (Reich Film Chamber), within the Ministry of Propaganda. Formally established as early as July 1933, the department comprised ten different branches to deal with every aspect of filmmaking. A "Reich film dramaturg" was appointed for the censorship of film scripts and for the rating of distributed films.[78] By so doing, filmmakers and actors opposed to the ideology of the Third Reich were simply banned. Three years later, the chamber created a special commission for *Weltanschauung*, with the aim of ensuring that films would present ideologically correct views to moviegoers. Similarly to the theater world, by the midthirties, the cinematographic industry was nearly *Judenrein* (cleansed of Jews) in personnel and content.[79]

Throughout the duration of the regime, the Reich Ministry of Culture made significant efforts to boost the film industry. While there is disagreement among researchers regarding the exact number, it is estimated that between 1,150 and 1,350 movies received censorship approval during the Third Reich.[80] These films aimed not only to shape public opinion on various issues but also to distract from the severity of Germany's situation during the war years. It is challenging to differentiate between politically charged films and those created purely for entertainment, but most experts agree that all movies distributed during the Third Reich contained some element of propaganda, to varying degrees. Those most steeped in National Socialist ideology were documentaries and newsreels.

The "dream factory" of the film industry was a powerful tool in the hands of propaganda masters Goebbels and Hitler. The main themes included an idealized portrayal of Hitler Youth, the plight of Germans residing outside the Reich homeland, great leaders of Germany's past, the breeding of animosity against enemy nations, antisemitism, invincibility in the war effort, honoring the dead, and the *Führer* cult. This last theme, which consisted of offering gratitude and paying tribute to Adolf Hitler, is best exemplified by Leni

Riefenstahl's film *Triumph of the Will*, for which she earned medals not only in Germany but in the United States and other countries as well.

ARCHITECT OF THE REICH

Although Hitler was unable to extract new and valuable music from the Jewish and Modernist-free Reich, he sought to enhance the performance and presentation of classical music. To improve musical standards, he carefully selected and supported numerous conductors and provided ample funding for musicians. One of his first acts upon assuming power was to refurbish Nuremberg's opera house. Even during his Vienna years, Hitler had been intrigued by opera house architecture and was familiar with the world's most prominent opera houses. The fact that a room full of illustrated opera house architectural books was found in his Berlin bunker confirms his keen interest in this area. Hitler's aim was to provide everyone, regardless of their financial status, with access to the opera. The "illusion" provided by the opera was what people needed in order to cope with life's struggles. "Opera belongs to the people," he said, "and must therefore be available to the people. Prices should accordingly be kept down. . . . Opera must also be accessible to youth."[81]

To make opera available to all, opera houses were to be refurbished and their number increased. Apart from the opera houses of Vienna and Dresden, which he liked, Hitler planned on replacing the rest with *his* style of opera house. Over the years, he sketched and developed plans for numerous opera houses. The plan for Munich—the world's largest, with seating for four to five thousand spectators—was the only architectural drawing he fully completed and that he wished to use as a model for others. At the time, there were some ninety opera houses in the Reich, but if Hitler had completed his opera house project, this number would have easily doubled. Despite all the planning, only two opera houses were built during his time in power.

Hitler's obsession with opera houses was so great that during World War II, Albert Speer remembered that "the bombing of an opera house pained [Hitler] more than the destruction of whole residential quarters."[82] As a result, when the opera houses in Berlin, Mainz, and Munich were bombed, Hitler ordered their immediate reconstruction.[83] This prioritization of rebuilding a theater over a destroyed residential neighborhood is a clear indication of his fixation on a utopian future rather than empathy for or assistance to the suffering civilian population impacted by his belligerent policies.

A few weeks after Hitler's appointment as chancellor in 1933, a fire conveniently destroyed the Reichstag (Parliament) building. Hitler seized the

opportunity to set its reconstruction in motion, the first of hundreds of buildings that he would plan for the "Thousand-Year Reich." With the unstop-
pable passage of time, a civilization's most visible cultural legacy is that of
its architecture. A culture's physical monuments bear witness to the artistic
achievements of its people as much as its literature, music, or art. Though
mostly in ruins, Athens' Parthenon and Rome's Colosseum are monumental
stone reminders of the greatness and grandeur of civilizations dating back
thousands of years.

Though over the centuries many artists have romanticized ruins in painting
and sculpture, it is one of Hitler's architects, Albert Speer, who is attributed
with the term *Ruinenwert*, literally, "ruin value," in architecture. He reflected
on the depressing sight of rusting iron debris of a building he observed under
reconstruction. He wondered if, by using special materials and by applying
certain principles of statics, one could erect buildings that, centuries later,
might resemble Roman ruins. In Speer's *Inside the Third Reich*, he wrote,

> To illustrate my ideas, I had a romantic drawing prepared. It showed what the
> reviewing stand on the Zeppelin Field would look like after generations of
> neglect, overgrown with ivy, its columns fallen, the walls crumbling here and
> there, but the outline still clearly recognizable. In Hitler's entourage this draw-
> ing was regarded as blasphemous. That I could even conceive of a period of
> decline for the newly founded Reich destined to last a thousand years seemed
> outrageous to many of Hitler's closest followers. But he himself accepted my
> ideas as logical and illuminating. He gave orders that in the future the important
> buildings of his Reich were to be erected in keeping with the principle of this
> "law of ruins."[84]

In addition to shaping new German politics, military goals, and foreign
diplomacy, Hitler assumed the role of the nation's primary architect
for its reconstruction. His motives were undoubtedly a combination of
self-aggrandizement and megalomania, evident in his plans for exaggeratedly
oversized structures like the future German stadium in Nuremberg, which had
a seating capacity of over four hundred thousand. Rather than creating new
ideas for the Reich, Hitler handpicked approximately ten architects, including Albert Speer, to execute his own concepts and plans. He selected the sites
for state buildings, whether for political or entertainment purposes, appointed
individual architects, provided rough outlines, approved final plans, arranged
financing, and supervised the construction work as it progressed.[85]

Architecture's appeal to Hitler undoubtedly began when he was a teenager
roaming the streets of his native Linz, examining its buildings and landmarks. Viewing architecture, as well as music, as the "queens of the arts,"
Hitler wrote in *Mein Kampf*, "I was firmly convinced that I should someday

make a name for myself as an architect."[86] In one of his early speeches at Munich's Hofbrauhaus, he stated that great architecture is the outward sign of inward political greatness. In a subsequent Munich address, he announced that Germans needed to adopt a totally new way of thinking and a wholly new view of the state's cultural role. The new Germany was not going to be known for its department stores and factories but for "documents of art and culture" that would last for centuries. Great structures of the past were not just an inspiration for the ages but had at one time prompted a sense of identity and communal unity.[87]

MEGALOMANIA AND MONUMENTALITY

Hitler viewed the columns of ancient Greece and the arches of the Romans as symbols of enduring empires. This inspiration is evident in the design of Third Reich structures, particularly in Nuremberg's monumental congress hall. The Third Reich's major state buildings were modeled after the austere grandeur of neoclassicism. In a speech at the 1935 party rally, Hitler emphasized that Germany's cultural greatness would be demonstrated through its architectural accomplishments.[88] He also believed that state and party buildings should be more impressive than other structures and rival the great structures of the past to showcase their ideological superiority. Initially, Hitler criticized modern buildings, such as American skyscrapers, but eventually changed his stance and allowed functional and Modernist public buildings like schools, airports, factories, and railway stations.[89]

At the 1937 Nuremberg party rally, Hitler shared quite openly that the buildings of the Third Reich "exist to strengthen our authority."[90] Examples of this so-called intimidation architecture are also easy to distinguish not only in projected plans for the Third Reich monuments but in many of the buildings that subsist today, either in part or in their entirety. This type of architecture utilized natural stone to cover concrete or brick shells, enlarged the structures to make viewers feel small and insignificant, and created the impression of timelessness by emulating the colossal structures of past civilizations, which were meant to endure for a thousand years. All of these elements combined to create, on the one hand, a sense of awe and, on the other, a feeling of admiration.

The Olympics venue for the 1936 games in Berlin, Tempelhof Airport, and the *Luitpoldhain* grounds for massive party rally events in Nuremberg serve as testimonies to the immense size the Reich foresaw for public structures and mass venues. Today, of these former statements of power and colossal architecture, we can still see the unfinished congress hall, the zeppelin field, and the SS training center in Nuremberg, as well as the former Luftwaffe ministry building in Berlin and, in a different style, the so-called Eagle's Nest perched on a mountaintop in the Bavarian Alps, a building that was to convey an impression of loftiness and domination.

"*Wort aus Stein*" (word out of stone) is how Hitler referred to his architectural creations or, simply said, Third Reich ideology manifested in monumental structures.[91] It is well known that Hitler viewed the German people as suffering from an inferiority complex, but by February 1939, in a secret speech delivered to the army troop commanders, he assured them that the Germans were the "strongest people not only in Europe but . . . for all intents and purposes, in the world."[92] Linking this development to his personal rebuilding program for Germany, he declared that it had restored Germans' self-assurance. His plans were to elevate Berlin to the world's greatest city, Munich the world's prime cultural center, Linz the greatest art center, and Hamburg the greatest port. He also stated that the autobahn network had helped restore the self-confidence that the nation deserved and needed.[93]

"*Bauen, bauen!*" (Build, build!)[94] was Goebbels's entry in his diary in September 1937 after the laying of the cornerstone for the oversized German Stadium in Nuremberg, which, incidentally, was never built. Speaking to Speer, Hitler assured him, "We are going to create a huge Reich combining all Germanic people, starting in Norway and going all the way down to Northern Italy. . . . And your Berlin buildings will be the crowning achievement."[95]

In January 1938, Hitler appointed Albert Speer as the general building inspector for the nation's capital and tasked him with overseeing the extensive remodeling of Berlin, to transform it into the greatest city in the world. Hitler described his vision as follows: "As world capital, Berlin will only be comparable with Ancient Egypt, Babylon, and Rome! What is London, what is Paris compared to that!"[96]

Hitler's grandiose plan included slicing through existing neighborhoods to create wide boulevards for military parades, with a triumphal arch towering four hundred feet high at the center and a Great Hall with a dome of 825 feet in diameter, the largest on the planet. The main avenue would lead to the Great Hall, and four other boulevards would lead to airports. Due to the project's enormity, Hitler did not expect it to be completed until 1950.[97] Though the main colossal undertaking was to be carried out after Germany's victory, some of the projects were completed before, such as the establishment of a great east–west city axis, which included widening Charlottenburger Chaussee (today Strasse des 17. Juni) and placing the Berlin victory column in the center, a long distance from the Reichstag building, where it originally stood.

When Norway fell, Hitler confided to Goebbels that he had "great plans" for that country. He would build "a great German city" near Trondheim and, from there, an autobahn would link the far north to the Austrian-Italian border at Klagenfurt: "In no time at all, these countries will be Germanified."[98] Implicit in all these programs, Speer confessed, was Hitler's design for world domination. All the building projects would be finished by 1950, by which time Hitler would have reached his political and military goals. The *Führer*'s final victory would be manifested in stone, and Berlin, now renamed Germania, would be recognized as "capital of the world."[99]

Hitler was so confident of his political future that he developed elaborate plans for state structures even before coming into power. As early as 1932, he created designs for party headquarters and two other sizable buildings in Munich. Once he assumed the position of chancellor, he wasted no time in ordering the renovation of Berlin's old chancellery. Soon after, construction began in Nuremberg for the party rallies, as well as for the refurbishment of the opera house. In Munich, he embarked on the reconstruction of the grand, neoclassical Königsplatz, where his personal offices and the party's headquarters would be located. As if this were not enough, Hitler's projects elsewhere included museums, opera houses, autobahns, bridges, railway development, war monuments, and special schools for party ideology. As "architect-builder," Hitler flourished in his element.[100]

According to Christa Schroeder, Hitler's architectural knowledge and skills were impressive,[101] and Albert Speer said of Hitler regarding planning and sketching, "An architect could not have done better."[102] Though Hitler may have favored simplicity and austerity in his architectural ideal, he endeavored to impress the viewer through overbearing massiveness. Perhaps following the examples set by the pyramids, Persepolis, New York skyscrapers, and Gothic cathedrals, Hitler used intimidation architecture to humble the individual, as well as the world, through gigantism. By so doing, Hitler could aggrandize himself and debase human beings into tiny objects.[103]

NOTES

1. Michael H. Kater, *Culture in Nazi Germany* (New Haven, CT: Yale University Press, 2019), 62.

2. Spotts, *Hitler and the Power of Aesthetics*, 1.

3. "Interview with Hitler's Sister on 5th June 1946," transcript provided by Michael Williams, https://www.oradour.info/appendix/paulahit/paula01.htm.

4. Spotts, *Hitler and the Power of Aesthetics*, 127.

5. Billy F. Price, *Adolf Hitler: The Unknown Artist* (Houston: B. F. Price, 1984), 15.

6. Spotts, *Hitler and the Power of Aesthetics*, 128.

7. Werner Jochmann, ed., *Monologe im Fürerhauptquartier 1941–1944* (Hamburg: Knaus, 1980), 235.

8. Spotts, *Hitler and the Power of Aesthetics*, 8.

9. Ibid., 10.

10. Eberhard Jäckel and Axel Kuhn, *Sämtliche Aufzeichnungen 1905–1924* (Stuttgart: Deutsche Verlags-Anstalt, 1980), 779.

11. Hitler, *Mein Kampf*, 259.

12. Ibid., 290.

13. Ibid., 302.

14. Ibid.

15. Spotts, *Hitler and the Power of Aesthetics*, 19.

16. Adolf Hitler, "Art and Politics," in *Liberty, Art, Nationhood: Three Addresses Delivered at Seventh National Socialist Congress, Nuremberg 1935* (Berlin: M. Müller & Sohn, 1935).

17. Spotts, *Hitler and the Power of Aesthetics*, 27.

18. Henry Picker, *Hitlers Tischgespräche im Führerhauptquartier: Hitler wie er wirklich war* (Stuttgart: Seewald Verlag), 21 March, 1942, p. 128.

19. Adolf Hitler, Monologue im Führerhauptquarier: Die Aufzeichnungen Heinrich Heims, ed. Werner Jochmann (Hamburg: Albrecht Knaus,1980), October 21–22, 1941, pp. 101–102.

20. Boguslaw Drewniak, *Das Theater im NS-Staat* (Dusseldorf: Droste, 1983), 163.

21. Kater, *Culture in Nazi Germany*, 63–65.

22. Arno Breker, *Im Strahlungsfeld der Ereignisse* (Preussisch Oldendorf, Germany: K.W. Schütz, 1972), 100.

23. Spotts, *Hitler and the Power of Aesthetics*, 79.

24. Goebbels's diary, November 19, 1936, quoted in Spotts, *Hitler and the Power of Aesthetics*, 80.

25. Goebbels's diary, February 8, 1939, quoted in ibid., 81.

26. Ibid., 84.

27. Ibid.

28. Volker Dahm et al., eds., *Die Tödliche Utopie: Bilder, Texte, Dokumente, Daten zum Dritten Reich* (Munich: Institut für Zeitgeschichte, 1999), 267.

29. Graham Land, "Tourism and Leisure in Nazi Germany: Strength through Joy Explained," HistoryHit.com, July 23, 2018, https://www.historyhit.com/tourism-and-leisure-in-nazi-germany/.

30. Spotts, *Hitler and the Power of Aesthetics*, 38–39.

31. Goebbels's diary, December 2, 1944, quoted in ibid., 39.

32. Ibid., 111.

33. Henry Picker, ed., *Hitlers Tischgespräche im Führerhauptquartier* (Bonn: Athenäum, 1951), 142.

34. Hitler, *Mein Kampf*, 258, 262.

35. Kater, *Culture in Nazi Germany*, 2.

36. Ibid., 18.

37. Ibid., 23.

38. Spotts, *Hitler and the Power of Aesthetics*, 159–60.

39. Kater, *Culture in Nazi Germany*, 46.

40. Goebbels's diary, June 6, 1937, quoted in Spotts, *Hitler and the Power of Aesthetics*, 171–72.

41. Heinrich Hoffmann, *Hitler, wie ich ihn sah* (Munich: Herbig, 1974), 143.

42. Hans Posse's diary, June 21, 1939, quoted in Spotts, *Hitler and the Power of Aesthetics*, 187.

43. Angelika Enderlein, Monika Flacke, and Hanns Christian Löhr, "Database on the *Sonderauftrag* Linz (Special Commission: Linz): History of the Linz Collection," German Historical Museum.

44. Spotts, *Hitler and the Power of Aesthetics*, 194.

45. Ibid., 197–207.

46. Timothy Ryback, "Hitler's Forgotten Library," *Atlantic*, May 2003.

47. Spotts, *Hitler and the Power of Aesthetics*, 211–12.

48. Christa Schroeder, *He Was My Chief: The Memoirs of Adolf Hitler's Secretary* (London: Frontline Books, 2009), 218.

49. Veronika Hofer and Hannes Androsch, "Introduction," in *Berg der Schätze* (Scharnstein, Austria: Prospera Verlag, 2006), 9.

50. Veronika Hofer and Hannes Androsch, eds., *Berg der Schätze* (Scharnstein, Austria: Prospera Verlag, 2006), 24.

51. Ibid., 25–26.

52. Ibid., 33.

53. Spotts, *Hitler and the Power of Aesthetics*, 220.

54. Katharina Hammer, *Glanz im Dunkel: Die Bergung von Kunstschätzen im Salzkammergut am Ende des 2. Weltkrieg* (Altaussee, Austria: Burgverein Pflindsberg, 1996), 80.

55. Ibid., 95.

56. Ibid., 100.

57. Ibid., 103.

58. Ibid., 106.

59. Greg Bradsher, "Nazi Gold: The Merkers Mine Treasure," *Prologue Magazine* 31, no. 1 (Spring 1999), https://www.archives.gov/publications/prologue/1999/spring/nazi-gold-merkers-mine-treasure.html.

60. Schroeder, *He Was My Chief*, 189–90.

61. Spotts, *Hitler and the Power of Aesthetics*, 235.

62. Joachim Fest, *Hitler: Eine Biographie* (Frankfurt am Main: Propyläen, 1973), 520, 712.

63. Kater, *Culture in Nazi Germany*, 60.

64. Spotts, *Hitler and the Power of Aesthetics*, 239.

65. Ibid., 247–50.

66. Interview in Hans Jürgen Syberberg, dir., *Winifred Wagner und die Geschichte des Hauses Wahnfried* (1975).

67. Spotts, *Hitler and the Power of Aesthetics*, 258.

68. Interview in Syberberg, dir., *Winifred Wagner und die Geschichte des Hauses Wahnfried*.

69. Spotts, *Hitler and the Power of Aesthetics*, 262.

70. Adolf Hitler, speech on January 26, 1928, in Munich, quoted in ibid., 271.

71. Helmut Heiber, *Göbbels-Reden 1932–1945* (Bindlach, Germany: Gondrom Verlag, 1998), 227–28.

72. Spotts, *Hitler and the Power of Aesthetics*, 276.

73. Michael Walter, *Hitler in der Oper: Deutsches Musikleben 1919–1945* (Berlin: Springer, 1995), 155–57.

74. Glen W. Gadberry, *Theatre in the Third Reich, the Prewar Years: Essays on Theatre in Nazi Germany* (Westport, CT: Greenwood, 1995).

75. Music and the Holocaust, https://holocaustmusic.ort.org/.

76. Ibid.

77. William Grange, "Rules, Regulations, and the Reich: Comedy under the Auspices of the Propaganda Ministry," in *Essays on Twentieth Century German Drama and Theatre*, ed. Helmuth Rennert (Frankfurt am Main: Lang, 2004), 196–97.

78. David Weinberg, "Approaches to the Study of Film in the Third Reich: A Critical Appraisal," *Journal of Contemporary History* 19, no. 1 (January 1984): 109.

79. Ibid., 111.

80. Ibid.

81. Klaus Backes, *Hitler und die Bildenden Künste* (Cologne: Dumont, 1988), 181.

82. Albert Speer, *Spandau: The Secret Diaries* (New York: Macmillan, 1976), 104.

83. Spotts, *Hitler and the Power of Aesthetics*, 286.

84. Albert Speer, *Inside the Third Reich* (New York: Macmillan, 1970), 97–98.

85. Spotts, *Hitler and the Power of Aesthetics*, 312.

86. Hitler, *Mein Kampf*, 35.

87. Spotts, *Hitler and the Power of Aesthetics*, 315.

88. Hitler, "Art and Politics."

89. Spotts, *Hitler and the Power of Aesthetics*, 319.

90. Norman Baynes, *The Speeches of Adolf Hitler, April 1922–August 1939* (London: Oxford University Press, 1942), 592.

91. Spotts, *Hitler and the Power of Aesthetics*, 321.

92. Jochen Thies, *Architekt der Weltherrschaft: Die Endziele Hitlers* (Dusseldorf: Droste, 1976), 79–80.

93. Spotts, *Hitler and the Power of Aesthetics*, 321.

94. Goebbels's diary, September 10, 1937, quoted in ibid., 330.

95. Gitta Sereny, *Albert Speer: His Battle with the Truth* (New York: Random House, 1995), 185.

96. Werner Jochman, *Monologe im Führerhauptquartier 1941–1944* (Hamburg: Knaus, 1980), 318.

97. Speer, *Inside the Third Reich*, 117–22.

98. Goebbels's diary, July 9, 1940, quoted in ibid., 331.

99. Speer, *Inside the Third Reich*, 69.

100. Spotts, *Hitler and the Power of Aesthetics*, 331–33.

101. Christa Schroeder, *Er war mein Chef* (Munich: Langen Müller, 1985), 219.

102. Speer, *Inside the Third Reich*, 143.

103. Spotts, *Hitler and the Power of Aesthetics*, 335–36.

Chapter 9

Antisemitic Propaganda

To most of the western world, the knowledge of antisemitic sentiment in Germany during Hitler's Third Reich and the ensuing Holocaust is a familiar historical fact. Yet how did Hitler manage to impress upon the German people that "Jewry" was secretly planning not only to undermine but to exterminate the Germans. According to him, any action taken against Jews in Germany, or elsewhere in the world, was not a wanton act of aggression but, rather, a justifiable act of self-defense.

In this chapter, we will examine the historical background of anti-Jewish sentiment and pogroms both internationally and in Germany. Understanding the past instances of Jewish persecution highlights the reality that the mistreatment, theft, and even murder of Jewish communities long existed prior to the National Socialist regime. We also take a look at the National Socialist regime's deceitful efforts to portray everyday Germans as innocent victims and Jews as cunning and dangerous perpetrators. Additionally, we'll demonstrate that Hitler's form of antisemitism was based on racial animosity rather than the conventional religious intolerance.

ANTISEMITISM IN ANTIQUITY

From the Assyrian Captivity around 740 BCE, the Jewish people's harassment, persecution, relocation, expulsion, and massacre can be documented in Persia, Iraq, Iran, Egypt, Greece, the Roman Empire, the Byzantine Empire, Arabia, North Africa, Yemen, France, Spain, Portugal, Italy, England, the Holy Roman Empire of the German Nation, Belgium, the Netherlands, Switzerland, Hungary, Bohemia, Slovenia, Croatia, Poland, Lithuania, Russia, and Austria.

There is evidence that Semitic peoples were forced to work as slaves in ancient Egypt,[1] and a clear example of anti-Jewish sentiment can be traced back to Alexandria in the third century BCE.[2] The Ancient Greek ruler

Antiochus Epiphanes desecrated the Temple in Jerusalem and banned Jewish religious practices, such as circumcision, Shabbat observance, and the study of Jewish religious books. Relations between the Jews in Judea and the occupying Roman Empire were antagonistic from the very start and resulted in several rebellions. It has been argued that European antisemitism finds its roots in Roman policy.[3] When Christianity became the state religion of Rome in the fourth century, Jews became the object of religious intolerance and political oppression. This hostility was reflected in the edicts both of church councils and state laws. In the early fourth century, under the provisions of the Synod of Elvira, intermarriage between unconverted Jews and Christians was prohibited.

EUROPEAN ANTISEMITISM IN THE MIDDLE AGES

While Venice is renowned for its timeless charm and romantic canals, it also has a dark history for the Jewish community. It was here that the world's first ghetto was established, and the quality of life for Jews in Venice was subject to the whims of those in power.[4] Although Jewish merchants and money-lenders had been working in the city as early as the tenth century, Venetian captains were forbidden from accepting Jews on their ships in 945 and 992, respectively. Due to restrictions on where they could live, Jews established a community on the island of Spinalunga, now known as Giudecca, in 1252.[5]

In 1516, Venice's ruling council, after debating whether Jews should be allowed to remain in Venice, decided to let them stay, but their residence would be restricted to Ghetto Nuova, a small, dirty island: the world's first ghetto. The moniker *ghetto* stems from the Italian *getto*, signifying "casting," or Venetian *geto*, meaning "foundry." In February 2016, Venice marked the five hundredth anniversary of the establishment of the world's first Jewish ghetto with a year-long commemoration including keynote speakers, concerts, exhibitions on Jewish life in Venice, workshops, art installations, conferences, and more.[6] The program was aimed at bringing about world awareness of the historical persecution of the Jewish people and other minorities.

During the Middle Ages, Jewish people in Europe were subject to persecution, including forced conversions, expulsions, and killings. In the twelth century, some Christians believed that Jews possessed magical powers obtained from making deals with the devil, and this belief led to the appearance of *Judensau* (Jewish pig) images in Germany. The Crusades also resulted in the persecution and banishment of Jews from England, Spain, France, and Germany. In 1290, all Jews were banished from England, and in 1396, approximately one hundred thousand Jews were expelled from France.

Similarly, in 1421, thousands of Jews were expelled from Austria. Many of those who were forced to leave their homes sought refuge in Poland.

German imperial authority, which was traditionally responsible for the protection of the Jews, temporarily collapsed during the period of dispute between two contenders to the crown of the Holy Roman Empire, King Adolf of Nassau and Duke Albert of Austria. During that time, in 1287, the unexplained death of a sixteen-year-old boy in the Rhineland was blamed on Jews, and in retaliation, some five hundred Jews were killed, followed by a series of blood libels.

Jews in the Franconian town of Röttingen were accused of having desecrated a consecrated host from the church. The local lord, a brute named Rintfleisch, assembled a mob and burned Röttingen's Jews on April 20, 1298. Rintfleisch claimed to have been given a mandate from heaven to avenge the sacrilege and to decimate the Jews. Contemporary sources contend that the local lord of Röttingen was, in fact, burdened with debts to Jewish lenders. Rintfleisch and his mob traveled from town to town killing all the Jews they came upon, subsequently destroying the Jewish communities in Rothenburg ob der Tauber, Würzburg, Bamberg, Dinkelsbühl, Nördlingen, and Forchheim. Nuremberg's six hundred some Jews[7] took refuge in the castle and were aided by Christian citizens, but Rintfleisch overpowered their defenses and slaughtered the Jews on August 1. The pogroms continued to spread from Franconia to Bavaria and on to Austria, resulting in the annihilation of 146 Jewish communities and the murder of about twenty thousand Jews.[8]

ETHNIC CLEANSING IN THE FOURTEENTH CENTURY

The devastating plague known as the Black Death in Europe lasted from 1348 to 1351 and killed an estimated fifty million people, about 60 percent of Europe's population.[9] In the fourteenth century, people had no medical understanding of this devastating disease and were searching for an explanation. For centuries, Jews had often been targeted as scapegoats for society's ills, and in the face of the growing pandemic, the rumor spread that Jews had caused the disease by deliberately poisoning wells.[10] This conclusion was possibly reached because Jews were less affected than others. The reason for their relative immunity was because Jews chose not to use the cities' common wells[11] or, in some cities, were isolated in ghettos with their own source of water.[12] In addition, a number of Jewish rules promote cleanliness, such as washing hands before eating bread and after using the bathroom, as well as bathing once a week.[13] Despite the lack of any evidence, Jews were often tortured until they "confessed" to having poisoned the wells.[14]

Now that "the culprits" for the Black Death had been found, massacres of Jews began in April 1348 in Toulon, southern France, followed by reprisals in Barcelona, Spain,[15] and in Nuremberg, where 582 Jews were burned alive.[16] The next year, persecution and massacres swept across Europe like wildfire, mainly in Germany, Switzerland, Northern Spain, and Flanders.[17] Some two thousand Jews were burned alive in Strasbourg, even though the plague had not yet reached the city.[18] During this period, over five hundred Jewish communities were destroyed in cities that included Frankfurt am Main, Cologne, and Mainz, where in the latter alone some three thousand Jews were murdered.[19]

By the end of 1349, the Rhineland pogroms subsided, but the bloodbaths of Jews continued near the Hansa townships of the Baltic coast as well as in Eastern Europe. By 1351, about 350 anti-Jewish pogroms had been carried out in these regions and over two hundred Jewish communities wiped out. The widespread persecution of Jews in Northern Europe forced many to migrate to Poland and Lithuania, where their descendants remained for the next six centuries.

During the Black Death period and its Jewish persecutions, Pope Clement VI attempted to protect the Jewish communities by issuing two papal edicts in 1348, stating that those who blamed the plague on the Jews had been "seduced by that liar, the Devil."[20] The pope urged the clergy to protect Jews and even offered them papal protection in the city of Avignon. Clement's efforts, however, were opposed by the newly elected Holy Roman emperor, Charles IV, who decreed that the property of Jews killed in riots was forfeit, a ruling that resulted in local authorities viewing oppressive action against the Jewish communities as a means to financial gain.[21]

The period of the Black Death was not unique in history for the mass killing of Jews: just twenty years later, the Brussels massacre (1370) wiped out the Belgian Jewish community.[22] Following the genocide of the Black Death period, Jews in all German towns continued to live in constant fear of persecution as many civil authorities implemented a plan of expulsion in their efforts to "solve the Jewish question." By the end of the fifteenth century, only three major communities were left in the whole of Germany.[23]

In Europe, throughout the centuries, local rulers, as well as church officials, forbade the practice of numerous professions to Jews, forcing them into marginal roles considered socially inferior, such as tax and rent collecting or moneylending, occupations only tolerated as a "necessary evil." Catholic doctrine maintained that lending money for interest was a sin and hence was a trade forbidden to Christians. Not being subject to this restriction, insofar as loans to non-Jews were concerned, Jews made this business their own, despite possible criticism of usury in the Torah and later sections of the Hebrew Bible. Sadly, this led to many negative stereotypes of Jews as insolent, greedy usurers, and the understandable tensions between creditors (typically Jews) and debtors (typically Christians) added to social, political, religious, and economic strains. Peasants who were forced to pay their taxes to Jewish tax collectors could see them as personally taking their money while remaining unaware of those on whose behalf these Jews worked.

While one generally associates the historic series of Inquisitions with Spain and Portugal, by 1255, with the exception of England and Scandinavia, these often violent inquiries were also actively implemented throughout Central and Western Europe. To start with, the Inquisition targeted only supposed Christian heretics, such as the Albigensians (aka Cathars) and did not affect the Jews. However, doctrinal disputes provided a pretext for persecuting Jews, and in 1242, the Inquisition condemned the Talmud and burned thousands of books. In 1288, the Inquisition's first mass burning of Jews at the stake took place in Troyes, France.[24]

In 1481, the Inquisition arose in Spain and ultimately surpassed the medieval Inquisition, in both scope and intensity. *Conversos* (Secret Jews) and New Christians were targeted because of their close relations to the Jewish community: many of them were Jews in all but name. In hopes of destroying ties between the Jewish community and *Conversos*, the Jews of Spain were expelled in 1492 and fled to Portugal. However, a Spanish-style Inquisition was soon instituted in Portugal, and courts were set up in Lisbon and other cities. It was not until 1808, during the short reign of Joseph Bonaparte, that the Inquisition was finally abolished. An estimated 31,912 "heretics" had burned at the stake, 17,659 were burned in effigy, and 291,450 made reconciliations in the Spanish Inquisition. In Portugal, about forty thousand cases were tried, though "only" 1,800 were burned, the rest making penance.[25]

From the sixteenth to the early twentieth centuries, the maligning of Jews and pogroms against the Jewish citizens of many European countries persisted. In Russia, for instance, a mix of pogroms and repressive legislation resulted in the mass emigration of Jews to Western Europe and the United States. Between 1881 and the outbreak of the First World War, an estimated two and half million Jews left Russia—one of the largest mass migrations in recorded history.

VILIFYING THE JEW IN ART, FOLKLORE, AND THE PRESS

For hundreds of years, anti-Jewish hatred permeated western art, politics, and popular culture. Throughout history, a biased perception of Jews and their culture was manifested in objects—from fine arts and crafts for the elite to everyday toys, knickknacks, and household items. A large number of these objects fostered damaging attitudes toward Jews and created deprecating stereotypes of them. Prejudiced views and discriminatory treatment of Jews have a shameful Europe-wide past and can be documented in countries from England to Italy and from Spain to Russia.

The United States Holocaust Memorial Museum mentions a few of the antisemitic themes used in various parts of Europe over the centuries. One of the recurrent myths was that of the "martyrdom" of Simon of Trent, which supposedly took place in Italy in the fifteenth century. In 1475, a two-year-old Christian boy named Simon was found dead. Shortly before Simon went missing, an itinerant Franciscan preacher had delivered a series of sermons in Trent in which he vilified the local Jewish community. After pinning Simon's murder on the Jews, a myth soon became popular within the Catholic community according to which Jews were blamed for killing Christian children in a religious ritual. Over the centuries, the propagation of such "blood libel" accusations resulted in expulsions, executions, and mob attacks against Jews.

From the Middle Ages to the modern era, the dehumanization of Jews frequently portrayed them as vermin and various other animals—pigs in particular, probably because Judaism considers pigs unclean and forbids the consumption of pork. In the nineteenth century, European artisans commonly adorned everyday items such as ceramics, toys, and even walking sticks with caricatures of Jewish faces. Such walking sticks, of which the handle represented an exaggeratedly long nose, are examples of racial antisemitism becoming accepted as part of everyday life.

After medieval expulsions, Jews were only gradually readmitted to England starting in 1656. In 1753, Jews gained naturalization only to lose it the following year due to fierce public protest. In a move to malign England's Jews, an eighteenth-century illustration in England featured a Jew holding some dentures in hopes of extracting a gold tooth from his patient.

In France, from 1892 to 1924, a rabidly antisemitic and racist illustrated newspaper was published with the slogan "*La France aux Français!*" (France for the French!). The paper was founded by the journalist Edouard Drumont, who claimed in an 1896 book, *La France Juive* (Jewish France), that Jews were responsible for everything that had gone wrong in France and were a threat to all good Frenchmen. In 1889, Drumont founded the Ligue Nationale Antisémitique de France (National French Antisemitic League), and he was elected to the national legislature in 1898.[26]

In Vienna in 1848, an antisemitic and antirevolutionary leaflet read,

There can be no mistaking the partiality of some Jews for a republican government form so as to come into unlimited possession of all civil rights (emancipation) and hence to achieve all the more certainly the most complete domination
over you and even greater control of the state treasury and of the more lucrative

positions. The Jew twists and turns, allows himself to be taunted and trodden on, deceives and pretends to be harmless and even supports a good cause merely to surreptitiously acquire popular favor so as to obtain profit and the customary interest from the victim of his cringing humility and with his innate arrogance to dominate and exert even greater pressure.[27]

EARLY DISCRIMINATION IN THE UNITED STATES

During the late nineteenth century, Jews, along with Italians, Irish, and Eastern and Southern Europeans, encountered discrimination in employment, education, and social advancement in the United States. Organizations like the Immigration Restriction League labeled these new arrivals, along with Asian immigrants, as culturally, intellectually, morally, and biologically inferior. Despite facing these attacks, very few Eastern European Jews returned to Europe because their situation in the United States, despite the challenges they encountered, was still a marked improvement compared to their life in the Old World.

Beginning in the early 1880s, declining farm prices also prompted elements of the Populist movement to blame the perceived evils of capitalism and industrialism on Jews because of their alleged racial and religious inclination for financial exploitation and, more specifically, because of the perceived financial manipulations of Jewish financiers such as the Rothschilds.[28] Antisemitism in the United States reached its peak from the 1920s to the 1930s but had strongly diminished by the time the United States entered World War II.

"EASTERN" JEWS

Prior to the First World War, popular antipathy and disdain toward Poles, Ukrainians, Russians, and particularly Eastern Jews was deeply ingrained in Germany. The country's working-class population viewed these eastern neighbors as primitive and uneducated, and the pogroms against Jews in Russia under the tsars only served to reinforce this perception and engender a growing fear of invasion by these perceived "barbaric" easterners. A significant portion of Germans, including a notable number of educated Jews of the upper class, regarded Eastern Polish Jews as even more backward than their counterparts in other eastern states.[29]

The resentment toward Eastern Jews increased dramatically when a number of them fled to Germany to escape the pogroms during the Russian Civil War. From 1918 to 1920, a surge of mass killings decimated Jewish civilians, primarily in Ukraine, as a result of approximately 1,500 pogroms in over 1,300 localities, leading to the deaths of 50,000 to 250,000 Jews. By the 1930s, National Socialist propaganda only intensified the already existing xenophobia toward Slavs and Eastern Jews, causing many Germans, particularly among the younger population, to view them as subhuman.

THE UNITED STATES AND THE HOLOCAUST

In the 1930s, the United States and other countries in the Western Hemisphere had the potential to save numerous Jews from Hitler's Holocaust. Although the United States was not yet fully aware of the impending genocide, they were cognizant of the acts of violence and vandalism committed against Jews by Hitler's regime, particularly following *Kristallnacht* in 1938, an outrage that prompted President Franklin D. Roosevelt to issue a statement of condemnation. Despite this, public opinion was not yet moved enough to allow Jews to find refuge in the country.[30]

In May 1939, 935 refugees, almost all of them German Jews, embarked on a voyage from Hamburg on the ship named *St. Louis*. While the vessel was bound for Cuba, the majority of Jewish passengers aimed to secure safety in the United States. Although most of them had already applied for U.S. visas, their intention was to relocate from Cuba to the United States once their visas became available. However, U.S. immigration laws during that time were strictly regulated, particularly for immigration from Southern and Eastern Europe. Germany was granted a relatively generous quota, permitting up to twenty-seven thousand immigrants to be admitted annually. Despite this, the United States was much less generous in actually granting visas to German immigrants, most of whom were Jews, during the early years of the National Socialist dictatorship. Between 1933 and 1938, approximately thirty thousand German Jews emigrated to the United States, but the government issued only 30 percent of the visas that were legally available for Germans.[31]

Just prior to the departure of the *St. Louis* from Hamburg, Cuba suddenly altered its visa policy and declared that the previous admission documents would no longer be accepted, effective immediately. Jewish organizations in the United States attempted to negotiate with the Cuban government to allow the passengers in, but their efforts were unsuccessful. By early June, negotiations had broken down and the *St. Louis* was instructed to leave Cuban waters, leading it to sail toward Miami. However, U.S. officials had already announced that the ship would not be permitted to dock, leaving the *St. Louis* with no option but to return across the Atlantic Ocean. The refugees were then divided among various European countries, with only a few fortunate individuals being granted asylum in Great Britain. The rest went to the Netherlands,

Belgium, and France, all of which would later be invaded by Germany and their Jews sent to concentration camps. Tragically, 254 of the passengers on the *St. Louis* perished in the Holocaust.[32]

The "Night of Broken Glass," also known as *Kristallnacht*, was a shock to the world, and some countries, including Great Britain, took swift action to aid German Jews fleeing the National Socialist pogroms. With an estimated sixty thousand Jewish children in peril, the world looked to the United States, a nation founded by immigrants, to save thousands of these children from the brutality and persecution of the National Socialist regime. A few months later, a bipartisan bill was proposed to provide shelter to twenty thousand of these children, with thousands of American Jewish families offering to provide support and private funding covering the costs. However, the American public strongly opposed the proposal, with a Gallup poll in January 1939 showing that two out of three Americans were against bringing even ten thousand German refugee children into the country.[33]

Many people adopted an "America first" mentality when refusing refugees, believing that the country should prioritize helping its own needy and homeless citizens instead of accepting new arrivals. However, this attitude often blurred the line between "America first" and outright xenophobia. The wife of the U.S. immigration commissioner, who was also a cousin of President Roosevelt, stated that "20,000 charming children would all too soon grow into 20,000 ugly adults." The bill passed out of committee on June 30, 1939, but there was no further interest in making it a law, and it was never acted on. After World War II, attitudes toward Jews changed, and the United States and the international community recognized the importance of assisting refugees.[34]

LESSON FROM A FRANCO-GERMAN

Among the nationalist writers who are believed to have had a formative influence on Hitler's antisemitism is Paul Bötticher (1827–1891), later known as Paul de Lagarde (his mother's family was French). Lagarde's writings laid the foundations for many aspects of National Socialist dogma, in particular that of Alfred Rosenberg, the National Socialists' ideologist. Lagarde contended that Germany should create a "national" form of Christianity purged of Semitic elements and maintained that Jews were "pests and parasites" who should be destroyed "as speedily and thoroughly as possible." According to historian Timothy Ryback, Hitler left notes and markings in his personal copy of one of Lagarde's works. In an essay titled "The Current Tasks of German Politics," Lagarde anticipates the emergence of a "singular man with the abilities and energy" to unite the German peoples and calls for the "relocation of the Polish and Austrian Jews to Palestine." This latter phrase was underlined and flagged by Hitler with two bold strikes in the margin.

POST–WORLD WAR I: NEW MYTHS ABOUT THE JEWS

Prior to World War I, while Russia and Romania experienced anti-Jewish pogroms, there is no evidence of open violence against Germany's Jewish population. However, German society had a strong sense of "insiders and outsiders," with Jews often seen as the quintessential "other." Despite having had equal rights since 1871, Jews were becoming increasingly successful in business, the arts, the press, law, and medicine during the Weimar Republic (1919–1933). Although the Jewish population in Germany was relatively small and primarily from the middle class, they were blamed for controlling the economy and were subject to severe prejudice, even being excluded from certain university fields of study. In the post–World War I years, antisemitism was widespread among many judges, army officers, conservative and radical right-wing politicians, teachers, and Protestant and Catholic clergy.[35]

The term "Judeo-Bolshevism" emerged in the early twentieth century to describe a purported Jewish-Communist conspiracy. The notion was popularized by National Socialists and other far-right groups as a justification for the persecution and murder of Jews and other minority populations. The concept alleged that Jews were disproportionately represented in the leadership of the Bolshevik Revolution in Russia and that they were using Communist ideology as a guise for a Jewish plot to rule the world.

National Socialist ideology portrayed Jews as the driving force behind the spread of Bolshevism and Communism and used this to justify the persecution and extermination of Jews. Hitler's regime also spread this notion to other countries as a means of justifying Germany's actions to the public and to mobilize support. The Judeo-Bolshevik myth was used not only to demonize Jews but to cast them as a threat to the nation and global society. Taken to its extreme, the concept was used as a justification for the Holocaust. Far-right and antisemitic groups in other countries also used the Judeo-Bolshevik fantasy to advance similar ideologies.

Throughout the twentieth century, the myth of Judeo-Bolshevism, as historian Paul Hanebrink notes, loomed over Europe. Despite the AudioVolumeDownunfounded and irrational belief that Communism was a Jewish scheme to destroy European nations, fears of a Jewish Bolshevik conspiracy gained traction during the Russian Revolution and spread throughout Europe. During World War II, Fascists, National Socialists, conservative Christians, and others across Europe who were terrified by Communism viewed Jewish Bolsheviks as enemies who crossed borders to subvert order from within and introduce harmful foreign ideas. Even in the years that followed, the myth of Judeo-Bolshevism remained a potent political weapon.

Walter Laqueur attributes the widespread dissemination of the Jewish Bolshevik conspiracy theory to Alfred Rosenberg, the ideological leader of the National Socialists. Rosenberg viewed Bolshevism as a rebellion of the Jewish, Slavic, and Mongolian races against the German (Aryan) element in Russia. According to Rosenberg, the Germans were responsible for Russia's historical accomplishments and had been marginalized by the Bolsheviks, who did not act in the interest of the Russian people but instead represented the ethnic Jewish and Chinese populations.[36]

GROWING JEWISH PARANOIA IN GERMANY

Following his service in World War I, Hitler, like many others in Germany and Austria, was shocked by the defeat of the German Empire. The military high command began spreading the myth that the armed forces had not lost the war on the battlefield but rather due to a "stab in the back."[37] This was part of a series of new, frequently repeated antisemitic legends that circulated during and after the devastating loss of World War I, an unprecedented catastrophe that had claimed the lives of over three million Germans and Austrians, not to mention tens of millions of deaths worldwide. In the aftermath of the war, along with older prejudices, new stereotypes associated with the "behavior" of Jews were deliberately propagated. These myths included the following absurd contentions.[38]

- Jews had instigated World War I to bring about Europe's political and financial ruin and to leave Europe weakened and vulnerable to Jewish control.
- Jews took advantage of war's misery to increase their own wealth.
- Jews prolonged the war by leading the Bolshevik Revolution.
- Jews were responsible for the discontent behind the front and stabbed the fighting troops in the back, causing military defeat and the Democratic Socialist revolution.
- Jews in other countries dominated the post–World War I peace negotiations, while their accomplices, the domestic Jews, misled Germany into "surrender" and permanent "enslavement."
- Jews controlled the complicated and long-drawn-out finances of the reparations system to their personal advantage.
- Jews established the post–World War I constitutional democracy and employed it to weaken Germany's political strength.

A RACE, NOT A RELIGIOUS COMMUNITY

Under the guidance of Karl Mayr in the summer of 1919, Hitler was given the platform to express his antisemitic views, which until then had been rarely voiced. Unlike traditional anti-Jewish sentiment rooted in religious differences, Hitler introduced the idea that "Jewry is absolutely a race and not a religious community." He argued that Jews were a "non-German, foreign race" living among Germans and infecting Germany with their materialism. While Hitler's antisemitic opinions were not entirely new in nature, they did not align with the most prevalent form of antisemitism at the time, which was anti-Bolshevik Jew hatred, but instead were principally directed against "Jewish finance capitalism."[39] From the outset, Hitler would employ these beliefs as the foundation for his campaign against Jews, ultimately justifying the Holocaust with these xenophobic convictions.

During Germany's inflation years, when the Reichsmark's value steadily plummeted, the country became inundated with fake paper money that carried political criticism of the Weimar Republic's ineptitude. In September 1923, one-thousand-mark notes were widely distributed bearing a decidedly hateful text: *Der Jude nahm uns Silber, Gold und Speck / Und gab uns dafür den papiernen Dreck!* (The Jew took our silver, gold, and bacon in exchange for this paper filth). Ahead of the elections, another version of the same message was printed, again on fake one-thousand-mark bills, that translated as "Gold, Silver, and Bacon were once taken from us by the Jew who left us this filth. Comrades, how long do you want to let yourself be plundered and cheated by the Marxists and Jews? No votes for the Marxist and Jewish Parties: Vote List 1." The counterfeit money's message was intended to scare voters into choosing Adolf Hitler's National Socialist German Worker's Party.[40]

The National Socialists considered the creation of the Weimar Republic to be the work of the Jews and to be alien to the German Reich and even detrimental to its interests. Perceptions of Jewish conspiracy of this type found their roots in late nineteenth-century European and Russian literature such as the *Protocols of the Elders of Zion*, which portrayed the Jews as having crafted an international league that was secretly plotting to control the world.[41]

Among the accusations made against Jews, allegations of sexual misconduct were particularly harmful. Detractors have claimed that such behavior has its roots in the Old Testament, particularly through the sexual exploits of ancient Jewish kings like David and Solomon. During the Weimar Republic, however, the focus shifted to the supposed involvement of Jews in the sex trade, including brothels and the white-slave trade, as well as in the seedy world of nightclubs, cabarets, and light operetta. Furthermore, Jews were accused of propagating what was considered pornography in literature, with works by authors such as Schnitzler, Sternheim, and Wedekind being cited as examples. As a result, one of the central fictional narratives presented in National Socialist literature after 1933 was the notion of Jews being driven by insatiable lust and their desire to impregnate young Aryan women through any means of seduction, which was depicted as ritualistic.[42]

GERMANY'S JEWS IN 1933

A significant portion of Jewish Germans resided in major cities, with nearly one-third of Germany's Jewish population or an estimated 160,000 to 180,000 individuals residing in Berlin. Of the Jewish population in Germany, four out of five held German citizenship, while the remaining individuals were Polish or held citizenships of other Eastern European countries. Similar to their counterparts in Austria, the majority of Jews in Germany were well educated and had achieved financial success in professions such as law and medicine. They also pursued careers in fields such as education, the arts, the press, finance, civil service, and as shop owners, among others.

Only a few months after coming to power, the National Socialists enacted a law allowing the firing of Jewish civil servants, but President Hindenburg managed to include a clause protecting Jewish war veterans as well as those appointed by the emperor before 1914. Although the majority of Jews in Germany belonged to the middle class and held moderate to conservative political views, Hitler falsely believed that they were subversive and parasitic. Blaming the Jews for Germany's defeat in World War I, he sought revenge by commanding the SA to assault the Jews in Berlin. Jewish professionals such as judges and lawyers, and any other Jews the brownshirts could round up, were beaten with rubber truncheons, while synagogues were vandalized and Jewish-owned businesses were boycotted. By the end of June 1933, about forty Jews had been killed by the SA.[43] These overt acts of violence carried out by the National Socialists garnered significant international attention and motivated about thirty-seven thousand Jews to flee Germany in 1933 alone.[44]

NATIONAL SOCIALISM VERSUS JEWRY

Blaming the Jews for Germany's defeat in World War I was a building block that Hitler set in place in his subsequent construction of an edifice of imaginary evidence he would present to incriminate the Jews. In the 1920s and early 1930s, Germany still found itself in the throes of a major economic crisis and, according to the National Socialists, expelling the Jews was the solution to the nation's problems. In February 1920, Hitler announced his party's twenty-five-point plan, number four of which clearly predicted National Socialist intentions: "Only a national comrade can be a citizen. Only someone of German blood, regardless of faith, can be a citizen. Therefore, no Jew can be a citizen."

Though in the ensuing years Hitler's rhetoric often identified the Jews as the cause of Germany's problems, he toned down his antisemitic diatribes during the year preceding his appointment as chancellor. Again in the mid-1930s, in an aim to show himself in Germany and abroad as a man of peace, Hitler kept in check his public tirades against the Jews. This comparative moderation came to an end with the 1937 Nuremberg rallies, during which he revived his vicious Jewish threats. For the first time, he declared before a large audience that "Jewry" was intent on "exterminating" Germany's "national intelligentsia." At the 1938 Nuremberg rallies, he alleged that "the Jewish world enemy" was attempting to "annihilate the Aryan states." By the time World War II began a year later, the National Socialist regime had flooded the nation with antisemitic propaganda and legislation.[45]

"EDUCATING" GERMANY'S YOUTH

Within months of Hitler's rise to power, by April 1933, no Jewish teachers remained in Germany's public schools and universities. After segregation, however, some schools were opened for Jewish children and led by Jewish teachers, and with each passing year, more Jewish schools were constructed and more Jewish families emigrated, so that by 1938 only 27 percent of the 27,500 Jewish children in Germany attended public schools.

Within the education system, Jewish children became an object of ridicule, from both their fellow schoolmates and their teachers. They were sent to the back of the classroom to emphasize their inferiority to Aryan children.[46] Instruction on "racial purity" became compulsory in German schools, and teachers would often single out Jewish students to use as examples during "biology classes" that focused on "racial hygiene."

In Third Reich Germany, schools applied propaganda to brainwash children with National Socialist ideology. Textbooks and posters relayed to German youth the importance of racial consciousness and the premise that Jews were aliens in Germany. They reiterated the message of the racial inferiority of Jews as well as the superiority of the German peoples.[47] As outlined in the National Socialist newspaper *Der Stürmer*, the "teacher's manual" detailed the instruction of racial theory, including the topic of the so-called Jewish problem. Intermarriage between Germans and Jews was portrayed as unnatural because it did not follow the natural biological order, which does not allow for intermixing: storks mate with storks; swallows mate with swallows, and so on.[48]

The teacher's manual essentially dictated a policy of aversion to Jews. In order to make the status of the Jew as the "deadly enemy of everything German" as concrete as possible to German children, the manual suggested that pictures of Jews (who must appear ugly or distorted) be displayed on the board side by side with pictures of ideal German stereotypes. From the visual differences, other differences were inferred. "The Jews walk differently than we do. They have flat feet. They have longer arms than we do. They speak differently than we do."[49]

From denigrating the Jew to projecting him as an enemy of the German people is a short and easy step. The Jew was conveyed as an infiltrator who, once he was established in German society and had seized both political and economic power, was now set on the annihilation of the German people. In view of the ever present and imminent Jewish threat to the "unsuspecting" German population that, according to the National Socialists, had been tricked and deceived by the Jews, the Nuremberg Laws could be perceived as a reasonable act of self-defense.[50]

Germans being of Christian faith, another powerful propaganda tool for use in the classroom was the introduction of religious elements. The teacher was to propagate the idea that being Jewish is, by extension, to be a Christ-killer and, therefore, deemed criminal. In this light, Jesus is viewed as a hero who waged war against the Jews until he was ultimately killed by them. Children were provided with blatantly hateful slogans to learn and recite, such as, "Judas, the Jew, betrayed Jesus the German, to the Jews." The teacher's manual closes with a perspective of world history that denounces Jews as contributors to the destruction of major civilizations such as Egypt, Persia, and Rome.[51]

Throughout Germany, children's books were twisted in such a way as to instill hatred for Jews at a young age. These books contained disparaging and clichéd illustrations of Jewish people, who were usually depicted as stocky, with a bent posture, dark hair, an abundance of coarse body hair, dark and bulging eyes, a large crooked or bent nose, drooping eyelids, a hanging lower lip, and a heavy beard.[52]

In 1936, National Socialist organizations distributed one hundred thousand copies of a perfidious children's picture book, mainly to kindergartens and schools. Produced by Julius Streicher's *Der Stürmer* publishing house, the text, written in rhyme, displays images of strong, hardworking, clichéd "Aryan" Germans as opposed to stereotypical "ugly and evil" Jews whose only goal is to profit from the nation. The text states that the Jew's father is the devil, attempts to vilify the Jew as a profiteer and manipulator, recommends no longer buying from Jewish shops, claims that the Jews' departure from Germany is the solution, promotes a glorious image of the Hitler Youth, and claims that (we children) should love the *Führer*, fear God, and despise the Jew. The last picture in the book depicts a line of Jews on the road passing below a sign that reads "One Way Street," "Hurry, Hurry," and "The Jew is our Misfortune." The book's title, *Trau keinem Fuchs auf grüner Heid und keinem Jud bei seinem Eid* (Trust No Fox on His Green Heath and No Jew on His Oath), was a play on Martin Luther's rhyme in his 1543 anti-Judaic treatise *On the Jews and Their Lies*: "Don't trust a Jew's oath or a wolf on a green heath."[53]

In 1938 another *Der Stürmer* children's book, often actively employed in schools, was *Der Giftpilz* (The Poisonous Mushroom). The content alludes to how, just as it is difficult to tell a poisonous mushroom from an edible mushroom, it can be tough to tell a Jew apart from a Gentile. The book is

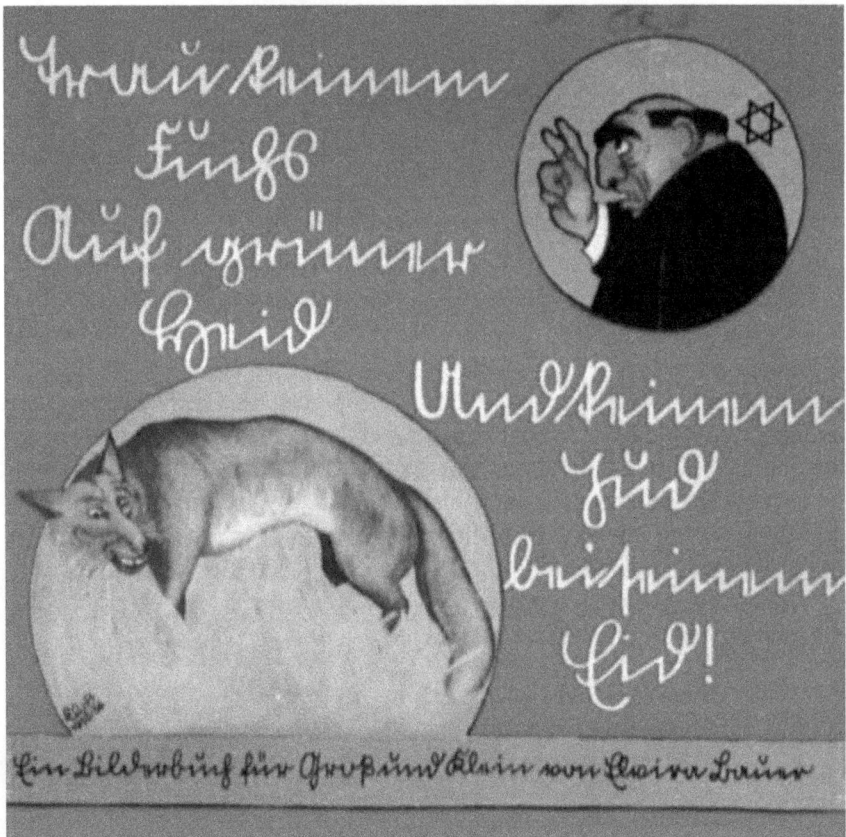

Figure 9.1.   Children's book: The Fox and the Jew (1936). *Courtesy of USHMM*

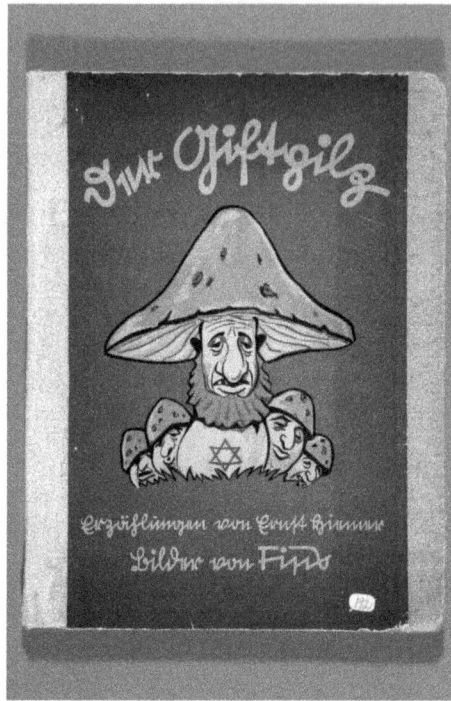

Figure 9.2.   Children's book: The Poisonous Mushroom (1938). *Courtesy of USHMM*

camouflaged as a warning to German children about the dangers purportedly posed by Jews to them personally and to German society as a whole.

In some instances, it is implied that Jews will try to molest children, Communism is led by Jews who wish to sacrifice Germany to Russia's power, wealthy Jews abuse their German servants, Jewish butchers torture animals to death, Jews kidnap Christian children to use their blood in the making of *matzohs*, the Talmud discourages Jews from performing manual labor (they should engage in trade instead), non-Jews are meant to be slaves, and Talmudic law allows Jews to cheat non-Jews and requests Jews to enslave the non-Jewish population.

In the story, the main character—a young boy called Hans—is required by his mother to learn the following poem by heart:

> A devil goes through the land,
> It's the Jew, well known to us
> as a murderer of peoples,
> a race defiler, a child's horror in all lands!
> Corrupting our youth
> stands him in good stead.

He wants all peoples dead.
Stay away from every Jew,
and happiness will come to you![54]

Der Pudelmopsdachelpinscher (The Poodle-Pug-Dachshund-Pincher) was another picture storybook written by the same author as *The Poisonous Mushroom*. Using animals and insects, Hiemer created stories in which contemptible behavior in animals and insects is applied to Jewish people. The book's title refers to a repugnant mix of breeds (races) that exemplifies the Jew as opposed to the German's pure-bred heritage. In Hiemer's book, again published by Julius Streicher, Jews are the drones of society because they live from the labor of others; like the cuckoo, they steal other peoples' homes and, like the hyaena, they prey on the wounded or weak. Other creatures, such as the locust, the bedbug, the viper, and the tapeworm, also serve to describe Jews' behavior.

The vile narrative escalates to compare the Jews to a deadly bacteria that must be eliminated before it wipes out the human race. The author's narrative concludes by exhorting young Germans, as Germany's last hope, to save a world under siege by a Jewish plague.[55] This highly repugnant work, aimed at poisoning children's impressionable young minds, was distributed in 1940, a time when the Third Reich began its unrestrained persecution of Europe's Jewish population—in Poland in particular.

The National Socialist indoctrination program's highest priority was to target Germany's young. By 1937, 97 percent of all teachers had become members of the National Socialist Teachers' Union.[56] In addition to the brainwashing of children and adolescents carried out in school, both boys and girls were required to participate in extracurricular programs of Hitler Youth from the ages of ten through eighteen, by the means of which National Socialist ideology and racism could be further instilled into these youths' minds and emotions.

Beginning in 1937, twelve elite boarding schools of the SS were in operation—three for girls and nine for boys aged fourteen to eighteen. These institutions' goal was to indoctrinate young people into National Socialist ideology above and beyond that which was taught in regular public schools. Students were carefully selected according to their physical fitness, as well as their political convictions, rather than for their intellectual strengths, and the curriculum revolved around political indoctrination as opposed to academic subjects. Many of the pupils were singled out by the SS staff as future officers.[57]

Another similar educational institution here was the network of boarding schools called the National Political Institutes of Education, or "*Napola*." These institutions operated independently from all other German secondary schools and their pupils were meant to aspire to Germany's future leadership. They were given political, administrative, and military education in the guidelines of National Socialism and were to become "efficient in body and soul for the service to the people and the state." Until the beginning of the war, the thirty-seven established *Napolas* served as strong politically and racially focused preparatory schools. During the war years, they gradually transformed their mission into training schools for future Wehrmacht and Waffen-SS.

The name *Ordensburg*, meaning "order castle" and borrowed from the historical Teutonic Order, was used to designate three castle-like educational institutions for postsecondary students who had already completed one of the Adolf Hitler schools, six months of compulsory labor-service training, two years of military service, and had chosen their profession. Reminiscent of medieval times and the valor of knighthood, these schools were designed to produce future elite National Socialist Party leaders through three to four years of rigorous physical, ideological, and racial-bias training.[58] Many of the graduates were later deployed to German-occupied territories in Eastern Europe, where they assumed high-ranking political positions. In these roles, they were responsible for expropriating the native inhabitants of those territories and resettling them with new German occupants. They were effectively fulfilling the mission that they had been trained for during their years of indoctrination: establishing and expanding the realm of the "master race."[59]

DELIVERING THE MESSAGE THROUGH THE "NEWS"

"Repeat a lie often enough and it becomes the truth," is a rule of propaganda often ascribed to Joseph Goebbels. Among psychologists, a phenomenon like this is known as the "illusion of truth" effect.[60]

The National Socialist propagandists dramatically stepped up antisemitism in Germany by raising the traditional, age-old denunciation of the Jews from a national to a global level. The new centralized high command of hate now presented its belief that the Jews were an interconnected politically active group, united on a global scale by racial bonds that transcended adherence or loyalty to individual nations. International Jewry, as the National Socialists saw it, was a formidable and self-governing entity that manipulated the world's leaders like puppets, in order to achieve their selfish and evil goals. These so-called world leader "stooges" included Franklin Roosevelt, Winston Churchill, and Joseph Stalin.[61]

The National Socialist propaganda machine was not just geared to exclude Jews from Germany but presented to the nation, and the rest of the world, the notion that the German people represented the saviors of humanity. Thanks to their bravery in confronting this "world threat" and their dedication to the noble and necessary mission of eradicating the entire world's Jewish population, the Germans would not only succeed in doing the human race a favor but should be thanked for their services. A great difference between traditional antisemitism and the National Socialists' worldview was their inculcation of an element of urgency and the need to act swiftly in the face of the imminent danger of being overcome and destroyed by world Jewry.

As already explored, expounding this "urgent" message was implemented first and foremost through racially biased education of children and young people. The press served as the next mass medium through which Hitler could establish and proliferate his National Socialist ideology. This belief was not solely one of racial hatred but emphasized the salvation of the German people from the edicts of the Versailles Treaty, as well as from the misguidance and dangers they had experienced during the fourteen topsy-turvy years of the Weimar government. The wrongs were being redressed, safety and long-lasting peace would be ensured through the rebuilding of Germany's armed forces, and the National Socialists promised long-term goals of employment, social welfare, and wealth for the nation. Above all, the pride that the German people had lost after the Great War was rapidly being restored. Plainly speaking, solving the "Jewish Question" was part of an all-inclusive package deal offered to the German people by the National Socialist Party.

As the National Socialists controlled all media in Germany and most Germans were literate, publications were their easiest instrument of mass deception. Even though Goebbels directed the Reich's Ministry of Public Enlightenment and Propaganda, it was Reich's Press Chief Otto Dietrich who worked in Hitler's office on a daily basis, relaying to his boss an account of the international news first thing each morning. Dietrich then transmitted Hitler's recommendations to the press staff in Berlin as to what altered and filtered version should be printed for the German reader. During the war years, tens of thousands of such "press directives" were passed along orally or in writing to the daily press conference in Berlin and, subsequently, to thousands of newspapers and periodicals.[62]

In a period when freedom of the press did not exist, several large National Socialist newspapers prevailed. Julius Streicher's viciously antisemitic *Der Stürmer* reached a circulation ceiling of four hundred thousand, whereas *Das Reich* rose to become the foremost journal read by Germany's political and intellectual strata. *Der Völkische Beobachter*, with a circulation of 1.4 million in 1944, was the National Socialists' principal newspaper from 1920 till the end of the war. As a prolific antisemitic writer, Goebbels produced hundreds of articles that regularly featured on the paper's front page.

VISUAL ANTISEMITIC PROPAGANDA

AudioVolumeDownThe National Socialist *Parole der Woche Wandzeitungen* (Word of the Week wall newspapers) was perhaps the most effective propaganda medium of all. This combination of text, imagery, and photographs was distributed weekly in hundreds of thousands of copies and posted in the most frequented public locations.[63] It was a unique blend of news editorial, political pamphlet, intrusive poster, and tabloid journalism aimed at shaping the opinions of Germany's society on a daily basis. In the Third Reich, one could choose not to read a paper, listen to the radio, or watch a movie, but the "Word of the Week" was an ever-present opinion-shaping onslaught that could not be avoided. Market squares, subway stations, bus stops, hospital waiting rooms, factory cafeterias, hotels, restaurants, post offices, train stations, schools, and streets were plastered with a modified version of the news, particularly during the war years, as well as the leadership's message of racial hatred.[64]

As early as 1928, National Socialists embraced antisemitic elements as components of their electoral campaigns. A 1928 electoral poster depicted a fisted arm, bearing a swastika armband, knocking down a naked red man that corresponded to their concept of a standard Jewish caricature. The text translates as "Vote List 10. Strike a blow! National Socialist German Workers' Party (swastika symbol) Hitler Movement (swastika symbol)."[65]

A 1932 electoral poster featured an industrial structure in the shape of a monumental swastika and a larger-than-life muscular man with rolled-up sleeves and Aryan features. The man looked down at a Jew who was whispering in the ear of a Marxist, among other opposing party caricatures. The text translates as "We workers have awakened. We vote for List 2, National Socialists."[66]

A poster promoting the "Aryanization" of German businesses (1936–1937) depicted a shopkeeper in the doorway of his store, kicking out a long-bearded, hat-wearing Jewish peddler. The shop front was marked *Deutsches Geschäft* (German store) and the text translates as "Out, with Jewish haggling."[67]

To advertise *Der Ewige Jude* (The Eternal Jew), a 1937 antisemitic "art" exhibition in Munich that attracted some 412,000 visitors, a poster depicted an "eastern" Jew wearing a kaftan and holding gold coins in one hand and a whip in the other.[68]

Antisemitic propaganda and the systematic persecution and mass murder of Jews greatly increased during the war years. The new archenemy became "the Jew" who, according to the media, directed "Bolshevism" and "western plutocratic" nations. The evil nemesis—world Jewry—aimed at destroying civilization, enslaving Germans among other Europeans, and ensnaring the entire world in its scheming web. A 1942 poster depicted a wealthy Jew

Figure 9.3. Propaganda poster: "The Eternal Jew" (1937). *Courtesy of USHMM*

wearing a bowler hat and peeking out craftily from behind a curtain made of the assembled flags of Great Britain, the United States, and the Soviet Union.[69]

In 1941 Goebbels seized the opportunity of an event that would even further legitimize the Reich's act of "defense" against the Jewish attacks. A self-published book written by an American Jewish theater ticket salesman in New Jersey called Theodore Kaufman and titled *Germany Must Perish* recommended the slow genocide of the entire German population through the forced sterilization of all Germans. The 104-page book also advocated the territorial dismemberment of Germany at the close of World War II, assuring that this would achieve world peace.

Though the book received relatively little attention in the United States, its very existence was used by the Third Reich as the driving force for a new campaign by which the Jews were allegedly plotting the genocide of the German people. Kaufman's single-handed attack on German wrongdoing was blown completely out of proportion by the Reich, resulting in new measures directed against Germany's Jews. All Jews were now forced to wear a yellow armband with the Star of David and the word *Jude* (Jew), while posters were pasted up on which the armband symbol was represented and which read, "Whoever wears this symbol is an enemy of our people."[70]

Figure 9.4.   Propaganda poster: "Behind Enemy Powers: the Jew" (ca. 1942). *Courtesy of USHMM*

Hitler, resolute in his paranoid belief in a Jewish conspiracy that aimed to wage a war of genocide against the supposed "innocent Germans," expressed his delusion through two posters. Produced and distributed in 1943, one of them depicts a sinister-looking Jewish man hiding behind a curtain that is being pulled aside by a muscular hand and arm, surrounded by angry fists in a landscape of flames. The poster's text reads, "The Jew: Instigator and Prolonger of the War," emphasizing the supposed truth about the true cause of the conflict. The other poster featured a giant finger pointing down accusingly at a cowering Jew in a top hat, wearing the Star of David badge, with the text, "He bears the guilt for the war!" This image aimed to place the blame for the conflict solely on the Jewish people.[71]

EASY READING AND EASY LISTENING

With a similar mission, leaflets and pamphlets also served to convey National Socialist doctrine to the masses. Widely distributed antisemitic flyers or booklets bore titles that are self-explanatory as to the nature of the content: "Why the Aryan Law" (1934), "Our Battle against Judah" (1935), "When You See This Symbol" (1941), "The Jews in World Politics" (1942), "The Jewish World Parasite" (1943), and "Germany Overcomes Jewry" (a training guide for girls of the Hitler Youth) (1944).[72] In addition, countless racially biased booklets and antisemitic articles in periodicals were published and distributed by a number of National Socialist–related organizations.

Adolf Hitler, Joseph Goebbels, Rudolf Hess, Robert Ley, and numerous *Gauleiters* exploited large gatherings, such as the Nuremberg party rallies among other mass events, to disseminate their anti-Jewish ideas through hundreds if not thousands of speeches. To easily reach an even larger audience, the radio served as an ideal medium of mass indoctrination of the German people while in the comfort of their home, in their workplace, or even in public squares where loudspeakers were set up for "special broadcasts" delivered by the leaders.

Propaganda Minister Joseph Goebbels realized the great indoctrination potential of the relatively new medium of the radio and requested the development of an affordable radio receiver, the *Volksempfänger*. It was to be mass-produced and sold at very affordable prices—even in installments—so that just about everyone in Germany would soon own one. By 1934 Germany could boast the largest number of radios per capita in the world.

In Albert Speer's last speech during the Nuremberg trials, he stated:

> Hitler's dictatorship differed in one fundamental point from all its predecessors in history. His was the first dictatorship in the present period of modern

technical development, a dictatorship which made the complete use of all technical means for domination of its own country. Through technical devices like the radio and loudspeaker, eighty million people were deprived of independent thought. It was thereby possible to subject them to the will of one man.[73]

VILIFYING THE JEW ON THE SILVER SCREEN

During the twelve years of the Third Reich, Germans were enthusiastic cinemagoers. Well over a thousand films were produced during that time, all of which were thoroughly controlled for ideological content by Goebbels's Ministry of Propaganda. Many of the movies and documentaries were commissioned or even produced by the National Socialist Party and geared to legitimize and justify the regime's actions.

In Hitler's war against what he perceived as the slayer of civilizations, an unimaginable amount of energy and resources was spent on instilling hatred for the Jew in German public opinion. For a perceived Jewish threat that represented less than 1 percent of Germany's population at the time of his accession to power, it would seem that the National Socialists' tidal wave of antisemitic propaganda was overkill. Its effectiveness, however, helped to present the war as justifiable defense measures and the expulsion—later "elimination"—of Jews as a necessary evil.

NOTES

1. Philippe Bohstrom, "Were Hebrews Ever Slaves in Ancient Egypt? Yes," *Haaretz*, March 25, 2021, https://www.haaretz.com/israel-news/2021-03-25/ty-article/were-hebrews-ever-slaves-in-ancient-egypt-yes/0000017f-f6ea-d47e-a37f-fffeebef0000.

2. Edward H. Flannery, *The Anguish of the Jews: Twenty-Three Centuries of Anti-Semitism* (New York: Macmillan, 1965).

3. Martin Goodman, *Rome and Jerusalem: The Clash of Ancient Civilizations* (London: Penguin, 2007).

4. Ibid.

5. Ibid.

6. Ibid.

7. Martin Schieber, *Nuremberg, the Medieval City: A Short Guide* (Nuremberg: Sandberg Verlag, 2009), 44.

8. Haim Beinart, *Carta's Atlas of the Jewish People in the Middle Ages* (Jerusalem: Carta, 1981).

9. Ole Benedictow, "The Black Death: The Greatest Catastrophe Ever," *History Today*, March 2005.

10. Gabriel Wilensky, "Blaming the Jews for the Black Death Plague," https:// sixmillioncrucifixions.com/blaming-the-jews-for-the-black-death-plague/.

11. Diane Zahler, *The Black Death* (Minneapolis: Twenty-First Century Books, 2009), 64.

12. Joseph Byrne, *Encyclopedia of the Black Death* (Santa Barbara, CA: ABC-CLIO, 2012), 1:15.

13. "The Black Death," JewishHistory.org, https://www.jewishhistory.org/the -black-death/.

14. Zahler, *Black Death*, 64.

15. Ibid., 13.

16. Schieber, *Nuremberg, the Medieval City*, 44.

17. Máttis Kantor, *Codex Judaica: Chronological Index of Jewish History* (New York: Zirchon Press, 2005), 203.

18. Robert S. Gottfried, *The Black Death* (New York: Free Press, 1983), 74.

19. Ibid.

20. Shlomo Simonsohn, *The Apostolic See and the Jews* (Toronto: Pontifical Institute of Mediaeval Studies, 1991), 1:1404.

21. Howard N. Lupovitch, *Jews and Judaism in World History* (London: Routledge, 2009), 92.

22. Mordecai Schreiber, *The Shengold Jewish Encyclopedia*, 4th ed. (Lanham, MD: Taylor Trade, 2011).

23. Richard Gottheil and Joseph Jacobs, "Black Death," JewishEncyclopedia.com, https://www.jewishencyclopedia.com/articles/3349-black-death.

24. "Christian-Jewish Relations: The Inquisition," Jewish Virtual Library, https:// www.jewishvirtuallibrary.org/the-inquisition.

25. Ibid.

26. "500 Years of Antisemitic Propaganda: The Katz Ehrenthal Collection," United States Holocaust Memorial Museum, https://www.ushmm.org/collections/the -museums-collections/collections-highlights/500-years-of-antisemitic-propaganda.

27. Permanent exhibit, Vienna Jewish Museum, November 2020.

28. Peter Knight, *Conspiracy Theories in American History* (Santa Barbara, CA: ABC-CLIO, 2003).

29. Evans, *Third Reich at War*, 103.

30. Dara Lind, "How America's Rejection of Jews Fleeing Nazi Germany Haunts Our Refugee Policy Today," *Vox*, January 27, 2017, https://www.vox.com/policy-and -politics/2017/1/27/14412082/refugees-history-holocaust.

31. Ibid.

32. Ibid.

33. Ibid.

34. Ibid.

35. "The Weimar Republic," FacingHistory.org, https://www.facinghistory.org/ resource-library/weimar-republic-0.

36. Walter Laqueur, *Russia and Germany: A Century of Conflict* (New Brunswick, NJ: Transaction, 1990), 33–34.

37. "Antisemitism: Why Did Hitler Hate the Jews?," AnneFrank.org, https://www
.annefrank.org/en/topics/antisemitism/why-did-hitler-hate-jews/.

38. United States Holocaust Memorial Museum, "Antisemitism in History: World
War I," Holocaust Encyclopedia, https://encyclopedia.ushmm.org/content/en/article/
antisemitism-in-history-world-war-i.

39. Weber, *Becoming Hitler*, 119–21.

40. Uli Röhm, *Das Große Buch vom Geld* (Halle: Projekte-Verlag Cornelius, 2010).

41. Norman Naimark, *Fires of Hatred* (Cambridge, MA: Harvard University Press,
2001), 59–60.

42. Kater, *Culture in Nazi Germany*, 153–54.

43. Evans, *Third Reich in Power*, 15.

44. United States Holocaust Memorial Museum, "Germany: Jewish Population in
1933," Holocaust Encyclopedia, https://encyclopedia.ushmm.org/content/en/article/
germany-jewish-population-in-1933.

45. Jeffrey Herf, *The Jewish Enemy: Nazi Propaganda during World War II and the
Holocaust* (Cambridge, MA: Belknap Press, 2006), 49.

46. Mary Mills, "Propaganda and Children during the Hitler Years," Nizkor
Project, https://web.archive.org/web/20170501233300/http://www.nizkor.org/hweb/
people/m/mills-mary/mills-00.html.

47. United States Holocaust Memorial Museum, "Antisemitism in History: Indoctrinating Youth," Holocaust Encyclopedia, https://encyclopedia.ushmm.org/content/
en/article/indoctrinating-youth.

48. Ibid.

49. Mills, "Propaganda and Children."

50. Ibid.

51. Ibid.

52. Ibid.

53. "Trau keinem Fuchs auf grüner Heid," Moopenheimers Museum, https://
moopenheimer.com/2017/03/11/trau-keinem-fuchs-auf-gruener-heid/.

54. Ernst Hiemer, *Der Giftpilz* (Nuremberg: Verlag Der Stürmer, 1938), 31.

55. Mills, "Propaganda and Children."

56. Ibid.

57. Rita Steinhardt Botwinick, *A History of the Holocaust: From Ideology to Annihilation*, 2nd ed. (Upper Saddle River, NJ: Prentice Hall, 2001), 106.

58. Lisa Pine, *Education in Nazi Germany* (Oxford: Berg, 2010).

59. Klaus Ring and Stefan Wunsch, eds., *Bestimmung Herrenmensch:
NS-Ordensburgen zwischen Faszination und Verbrechen* (Dresden: Sandstein Verlag,
2016), 288.

60. Tom Stafford, "How Liars Create the Illusion of Truth," BBC, October 26,
2016, https://www.bbc.com/future/article/20161026-how-liars-create-the-illusion
-of-truth#:~:text=Repetition%20makes%20a%20fact%20seem,to%20the%20Nazi
%20Joseph%20Goebbels.

61. Herf, *Jewish Enemy*, 7–10.

62. Ibid., 13.

63. Ibid., 12–21.

64. Ibid., 14.

65. Luckert and Bacharach, *State of Deception*, 43.

66. Ibid., 44.

67. Ibid., 68.

68. Ibid., 89.

69. Ibid., 102–103.

70. Ibid., 128–29.

71. Herf, *Jewish Enemy*, 222–23.

72. Randall Bytwerk, "Nazi and East German Propaganda: Guide Page," https://research.calvin.edu/german-propaganda-archive/.

73. "Nuremberg Trial Proceedings Volume 22," Avalon Project, Yale Law School, https://avalon.law.yale.edu/imt/08-31-46.asp.

Chapter 10

The German "People's Community"

Along with the creation of a veritable Hitler cult, National Socialism's second most effective propaganda and integration tool was the concept of the *Volksgemeinschaft* (People's Community). During the course of the First World War's attrition warfare, people of the most varied backgrounds were forced to come together, endowing them with a true sense of a "people's community." Across the political spectrum from left to right, the experience of togetherness on the battlefront continued to exert its effect during the ensuing years of the Weimar Republic in the form of the *Freikorps*, youth movements, and *völkisch* (ethnic, populist, national) groups.[1]

THE NATIONAL SOCIALIST CONCEPT
OF THE PEOPLE'S COMMUNITY

The most precise description of the National Socialist idea of the People's Community was expressed by Hitler himself: "The social unity of German people rises above classes and status, professions and denominations and all other confusion in life, regardless of class and origin, based on blood, brought together by a thousand-year life, bound by fate, for better or worse."[2]

This core component of Hitler's *Weltanschauung* was repeated again and again throughout his speeches and writings.

The National Socialists' model of *Volksgemeinschaft* presented a racially unified and organized hierarchy. It implied a mystical unity, a form of racial soul that united all Germans, including those living outside the existing confines of the Reich. Nonetheless, this soul was regarded as related to the land in the doctrine of "blood and soil," within which it was affirmed that landowner and peasant lived in organic harmony.[3]

The historical exemplification of the German people by the National Socialists consisted of an ongoing, laborious, and ever-challenged process of becoming a *Volk*—a people. The earliest tribes were brought together by one leader or another, only to eventually fall apart again. The state corpus that Charlemagne had created in his Europe-wide unification process had been gradually destroyed by the strengthening of multiple dynasties and religious denominations. The unification process had once again ignited during the second German Reich from 1871 on, only to be extinguished in 1918 due to the labor unions and political parties. Hitler viewed workers' unions as well as voters freely choosing among a democratic medley of political parties as highly dangerous forces of division that threatened the continued existence of the German people.[4]

GLEICHSCHALTUNG: SOCIAL AND POLITICAL CONFORMITY

Within months of Hitler's rise to power, measures were taken to counter the perceived dangers of a pluralistic democracy. Political parties were outlawed and crushed through police intervention, and labor unions and workers' associations were disbanded. All these multiple groups and associations were replaced by large-scale National Socialist organizations, all of which were submitted and subjected to the *Führerwille* (*Führer*'s will). On a practical level, all social and political structures were now steeped in a supposedly direct *Führer–Volk* relationship.[5] The following is a partial list of the various new organizations that served to unite the population within the vast social conformity operation and reprogramming known as *Gleichschaltung*.

The German Labor Front: The first of the National Socialists' mass organizations was the Deutsche Arbeitsfront (German Labor Front), founded in May 1933, after the storm troopers' raid on all union headquarters and the ruthless arrests of workers' union officers. Six years later, at the outbreak of the war, the Labor Front could boast some twenty million members in Germany proper and about three million more in the other lands composing "Greater Germany." The massive organization, with Robert Ley at its head, carried out press, propaganda, and welfare work and directed the activities of the *Kraft durch Freude* (Strength through Joy) program.[6]

The 168 unions that had been mercilessly dissolved were now constricted into one organization, which Hitler eventually said was "the only existing corporation." Employers, manual workers, salaried employees, and urban middle-class citizens were all herded into the Labor Front without being allowed separate associations. By the end of 1934, the remodeling of the Labor Front severed the old trade union ties and loyalties and reorganized labor entirely, thus eliminating the danger of countermoves against the regime. On the one hand, the German Labor Front was independent of the Reich's administration; on the other, it came under the complete control of the National Socialist Party. The party was eager to use the Labor Front as an instrument of its own, in order to perform any service requested by the National Socialist government.[7]

Robert Ley was not only the leader of the Labor Front but also held the title of chief of staff of the National Socialist German Workers' Party, a position fourth in rank in the party's hierarchy. From there on down, the closest affiliation between the party and the Labor Front was ensured. The "privilege" of being accepted as a member of the National Socialist Party was kept to a minimum; therefore, a vast majority of the Labor Front's members were not members of the party.

By 1939 the Labor Front counted thirty-six thousand paid officials and some two million nonpaid functionaries who offered their services in exchange for certain advantages, as well as to gain prestige. Through day-by-day conversations—and denunciations—the petty chiefs learned of workers' attitudes, behaviors, weaknesses, loyalties, family relationships, and other characteristics. In this way, the Labor Front and the party could maintain totalitarian control.[8] From 1934 on, Jews were not allowed to become members of the German Labor Front, thus excluding them from most jobs.

Having taken over the assets of dissolved labor unions, receiving dues from its members and contributions from the Reich's government, the Labor Front's financial holdings grew rapidly: by 1938 it was one of Germany's largest banking institutions, and during the war, it extended its activities throughout the occupied lands and opened branches in all their major cities. In 1937 the Labor Front trust was extended by the creation of an automobile factory, the *Volkswagenwerk* (People's Automobile Works), in which the Labor Front invested two hundred million Reichsmarks. However, the factory was soon obliged to turn out vehicles for war purposes, delaying the claims of three hundred thousand Labor Front members who had invested the two hundred million Reichsmarks in advance installment payments, in the belief that they would be entitled to the speedy acquisition of a car.[9]

The Reich's Cultural Chamber: The Reichskulturkammer (Reich's Cultural Chamber), or RKK, embodied all professions of a cultural or artistic nature, as well as culture-related businesses. Headed by the Reich's minister of public enlightenment and propaganda, Joseph Goebbels, the RKK, with its seven departments for the various arts, obliged anyone who worked in the arts to become a member. It forced its adherents to follow the principles of National Socialism and aimed at repelling "detrimental forces." These were considered to be the damaging influence of Jews in the cultural world, and the National Socialists employed the term *entartete Kunst* (degenerate art) to

Der Kdf Wagen

Figure 10.1. Propaganda poster: the "Strength through Joy" automobile. *Courtesy of Institut für Zeitgeschichte*

designate Modern and "Bolshevist" art. Jews, half-Jews, "German-blooded" citizens married to Jews, and eventually Roma and Sinti ("gypsies") were excluded from the RKK.[10] This resulted in a great number of people losing their source of livelihood.

The Reich's Food Corporation: The Reichsnährstand, a statutory corporation of German farmers, exercised legal authority over anyone involved in agricultural production and distribution. It attempted to intercede in the market for agricultural goods, using a complex system of orders, price controls, and prohibitions and establishing its authority through regional marketing associations.[11]

One of the tasks set by the Reichsnährstand was that of implementing the *Blut-und-Boden* (blood and soil) ideology. This aimed at preserving the "peasantry as the blood source of the people" and, through this, permanently ensuring the nourishment of the people. In order to achieve this, the Reichsnährstand was to promote the creation of a "new peasantry" and to counter migration into the cities.[12]

Under the legislation of the *Reichsnährstandsgesetz* (law), farmers were bound to their land as most agricultural land could not be sold.[13] The law was enacted to protect and preserve Germany's smaller hereditary estates that were no larger than 125 hectares (308 acres). Below that acreage, farmlands could "not be sold, divided, mortgaged or foreclosed upon."[14] Cartel-like marketing boards fixed prices, regulated supplies, and oversaw almost every facet of directing agricultural production on farmlands. For instance, in addition to deciding what seeds and fertilizers were to be applied to farmland, the

Reichsnährstand countered the sale of foreign food imports within Germany and monitored the payment of debts.[15]

As the scope and depth of the National Socialists' command economy escalated, food production and the rural standard of living declined. By autumn 1936, Germany began to experience critical shortages of food and consumer goods, despite spending billions of Reichsmarks on subsidies to farmers.[16] Germans were even subjected to the rationing of many major consumer goods, including produce, butter, and other consumables.[17] Beside food shortages, Germany began to encounter a loss of farm laborers, whereby up to 440,000 farmers had abandoned agriculture between 1933 and 1939.[18]

The Reichsnährstand's argument that Germany "needed" an additional seven to eight million hectares (17.3–19.8 million acres) of farmland, and that consolidation of existing farms would displace many existing farmers who would need to work new land, influenced Hitler's decision to invade the Soviet Union.[19]

The Kraft durch Freude Program: The National Socialist group called Kraft durch Freude or KdF (strength through joy), a suborganization of the German Labor Front, was created to promote the "enjoyment of life and work." Its goals also included the promotion of good health, efficiency, and team spirit in an effort to increase the nation's performance potential and, with it, economic productivity. The KdF's activities were directed at improving the work environment and providing leisure and cultural programs to workers. It was meant to bridge the class divide by allowing the "little man" access to leisure activities such as theater tickets and vacation trips—formerly reserved for the middle and upper classes.[20] Flaunting the advantages of National Socialism to the people, the KdF became the world's largest tourism operator.[21]

Large ships, such as the *Wilhelm Gustloff*, were built specially for KdF cruises. Workers and their families were also rewarded by being taken to the movies, to parks, to fitness clubs, on hikes, to sports activities, and out for concerts. Borrowing from the Italian fascist organization Dopolavoro (After Work) but extending its influence into the workplace as well, KdF rapidly developed a wide range of activities and quickly grew into one of Germany's largest organizations. According to official statistics, 2.3 million people took KdF holidays in 1934. By 1938, this figure rose to 10.3 million.[22]

Among the KdF projects, the largest was undoubtedly Prora, also known as the Colossus of Prora, a building complex on the island of Rügen on a lagoon near the Baltic Sea. Built between 1936 and 1939 as a beach resort for as many as twenty thousand holidaymakers, the propaganda jingle here was that, thanks to the National Socialists, the working class could now afford a beach holiday. It consisted of eight identical buildings along a stretch of 4.5 kilometers (2.8 mi), parallel to the beach, with the surviving structures stretching about three kilometes (1.9 mi) today. The project was neither completed nor ever used as a holiday resort.

At the outbreak of war, holiday travel ceased. Until then, KdF had sold more than forty-five million package tours and excursions.[23] By 1939, it had over seven thousand paid employees and 135,000 voluntary workers, organized into divisions covering such areas as sport, education, and tourism. The KdF also designated one or more wardens in every factory and workshop employing more than twenty people.

In the 1930s, the *Kraft-durch-Freude* program was generally regarded as an exemplary endeavor for the good of the people and as an incentive for a more productive workplace. It drew recognition even on an international level when it was awarded the 1939 Olympic Cup by the International Olympic Committee.[24] It should be noted, however, that KdF was available neither to Jews nor Sinti or Roma, once again stressing the National Socialists' divide between the German *Volk* and the *rassenfremd* (racially foreign) members of society.

The Boys and Girls of the Hitler Youth: With the intention of shaping future German adults, the National Socialist regime set about indoctrinating its most influenceable subjects: children and teenagers. In 1938 Hitler stated,

> These boys and girls enter our organizations [at] ten years of age, and often for the first time get a little fresh air; after four years of the "Young Folk" they go on to the Hitler Youth, where we have them for another four years. . . . And even if they are still not complete National Socialists, they go to Labor Service and are smoothed out there for another six, seven months. . . . And whatever class consciousness or social status might still be left . . . the *Wehrmacht* will take care of that. And when they then return after two, three or four years, so that they do not—under any circumstances—slide backwards, we immediately take them into the SA, SS, etc. And they will no longer be free their entire lives. And they are content with that.[25]

The party's ideology and organization coincided with the elitist and anti-democratic elements of the German youth movement, a collective term for a cultural and educational organization that started in 1896. The German scouts and the *Wandervogel* (literally "migratory bird," a designation for members of the German and Austrian youth movements), while essentially nonpolitical, retreated to the rustic life on the moors, heaths, and forests, where they cultivated the bonds of group life. The National Socialists' emphasis on "blood and soil," of *Volk*, nation, language, and culture, appealed to the nature of the German youth associations. The Hitler Youth took over many of the symbols and a good part of the elements that characterized the already existing German youth movement.[26] According to Walter Laqueur, the historian of the Hitler Youth movement, "National Socialism came to power as the Party of youth."

At the time of Hitler's campaigning, a large percentage of Germany's impressionable younger generation had suffered the massive health, nutritional, and material deprivation, as well as parental absence, of Central Europe during World War I and in the postwar years. This undoubtedly led to long-term effects on the personalities of these young people. Their weakened character structure likely manifested in aggression as well as in defense mechanisms like projection and displacement. The fact that inner rage could easily be mobilized by a renewed anxiety-induced trauma in adulthood is validated in the subsequent political conduct of this cohort in Germany's

Figure 10.2.   Propaganda poster: "Youth serves the Führer" (1939). All ten-year-olds join the HJ (Hitler Youth). *Deutsches Historisches Museum/BPK*

Great Depression (1929–1933), when they joined extremist paramilitary and youth organizations as well as radically motivated political parties.

The National Socialist Party already began targeting German youth in the 1920s as a receptive audience for its propaganda messages. It emphasized that the party was a movement of youth: motivated, resilient, forward look-ing, and full of hope. Millions of young Germans were won over to National Socialism not only in the classroom but thanks to extracurricular activities. In January 1933, the Hitler Youth counted approximately one hundred thousand members, but by the end of the year this figure had increased to over two mil-lion. By 1937 membership in the Hitler Youth increased to 5.4 million before becoming mandatory in 1939. The Third Reich then prohibited or dissolved competing youth organizations.[27]

The only organization that bore Hitler's name, the Hitler-Jugend (Hitler Youth), consisted of several subgroups: the Deutsches Jungvolk, boys ten to fourteen years old; the Hitler-Jugend, boys fourteen to eighteen; the Jungmädel, girls ten to fourteen; and the Bund Deutscher Mädel, girls four-teen to eighteen.

Though up until 1939 membership was not mandatory, not joining the organization was, nevertheless, frowned upon. From 1939 on, membership became compulsory and, for boys, often led to enlistment into paramilitary organizations: Hitler Youth were deployed in the navy, in aviation, for motor vehicles, and in the news. In addition, some twenty thousand volunteers came to form the fanatical SS Hitler-Jugend Armored Division.[28]

The Hitler Youth oath followed the principles of the *Volk–Führer* idealiza-tion and indoctrination: "In the presence of this blood banner which repre-sents our *Führer*, I swear to devote all my energies and my strength to the savior of our country, Adolf Hitler. I am willing and ready to give up my life for him, so help me God." This sense of allegiance, obedience, and honor shaped the mind-set of many a future soldier or member of the SS on the battlefields of World War II.

Welfare Organizations of the People's Community: Founded in 1932, the Nationalsozialistische Volkswohlfahrt (National Socialist People's Welfare) rapidly grew into the world's largest welfare organization with about eleven million members in 1938. The NSV, as it was referred to, disbanded most of the preexisting welfare groups, and those that it allowed to subsist, such as Caritas and the Red Cross, were closely monitored by the leading organiza-tion. Consistent with National Socialist ideology, the NSV was not a chari-table movement in the sense that is familiar to us but rather sought to help others help themselves so that they could become "useful and motivated" members of the People's Community. "Hopeless" or "wretched" cases were handed over to the official departments or to other welfare organizations.

The NSV saw as its mission to strengthen the People's Community through the communal spirit and a sense of solidarity: "All for one and one for all."[29]

The Hilfswerk Mutter und Kind (Mother and Child Aid Organization) was founded by the NSV in 1934 with the aim of supporting families and mothers who were racially pure and to encourage the latter to bear numerous children. The mother and child aid group's assistance included care services from the NS nursing organization, economic benefits and financial aid, help with finding a job, health promotion, rest homes for mothers, child nourishment, and the providing of kindergarten and childcare positions. Most of the Mother and Child Aid Organization's workers were volunteers: by 1939 they were half a million strong.[30]

The Compulsory Reich Labor Service: Known also as the RAD, the Reichsarbeitsdienst (Reich Labor Service) was formed in 1934 as the official National Socialist Party's work service. During Germany's depression in the late 1920s, a number of political, church, and civic groups organized work camps to help provide some employment for the numerous ex-servicemen and the staggering numbers of unemployed workers. Generally, these work camps supplied labor for various community and agricultural construction services throughout Germany and, in a general manner, helped relieve the strain of high unemployment. Even in the National Socialist Party's early years, the RAD also created a number of such camps.[31]

Service in the Reichsarbeitsdienst eventually became compulsory for all males between the ages of eighteen and twenty-five. They would first join the labor service for a period of six months before joining one of the branches of the Wehrmacht (German armed forces) for two more years. The RAD was not, however, a part of the German armed forces but an independent state organization and an auxiliary to the Wehrmacht.[32]

The RAD was not limited to men but also had many women serving in the organization. The "frontline" rank-and-file members who made up the bulk of the RAD workforce were armed with spades and used bicycles as their means of transport. Prior to World War II, the RAD participated in work projects such as the reclamation of marshland for cultivation, the building of dams, and the construction of roads.

The RAD also assisted the German armed forces during the occupation of Austria, the occupation of the Sudetenland, and the occupation of Czechoslovakia. During the summer of 1938 and up until the outbreak of World War II, some three hundred *Abteilungen* or units (a unit comprised between two and three hundred members) of the RAD participated in the construction of the massive Siegfried Line fortification along Germany's border with France. In the east, another oune hundred RAD units were enrolled in the construction of the *Ostwall* fortification line along Germany's border with Poland. As war drew nearer, in August 1939 some 115 RAD units served in East Prussia, helping with harvest work, while other RAD units served in Danzig.[33]

At the outbreak of World War II, the Reichsarbeitsdienst comprised about three hundred thousand members.[34] Some 1,050 individual units were put at the disposal of the Wehrmacht to build roads, clear obstacles, dig trenches, build airstrips, lay minefields, erect fortifications, deliver food and ammunition to the troops, and carry out any necessary support services. Serving throughout the military theater, RAD units were often encircled and forced into frontline combat, while other units were drafted directly into military service on the spot. In 1942, there were at least 427 RAD units serving on the Eastern Front. During the war years, the RAD pursued its mission of training young men prior to their service in the Wehrmacht by providing construction and agricultural work for the Reich.[35]

EIN VOLK, EIN REICH, EIN FÜHRER

Following extreme racist and authoritarian principles, the National Socialists removed individual freedoms and, in favor of the people's community, established a society that would, in theory, transcend class and religious differences. The *Führer*'s will became the foundation for all legislation: the *Führerprinzip* (*Führer* principle) dictated all facets of German life.

According to this principle, authority flowed downward from Hitler and was to be obeyed unquestioningly. All "racially pure" Germans, designated as *Volksgenossen* (people's comrades), were expected to aid those who were less fortunate and to sacrifice time, wages, and even their lives for the common good. In theory, neither lowly birth nor modest economic circumstances would be hindrances to social, military, or political advancement. NS propaganda played a decisive role in selling the myth of the People's Community to Germans, who yearned for unity, national pride, and greatness, as well as for a break with the rigid social stratification of the past. In this way, propaganda helped prepare the German public for a future defined by National Socialist ideology.

The National Socialists' emphasis on the importance of the *Volk*, the people, awakened an emotional response from a large percentage of the population. Terms such as *Volkswagen* (people's automobile), *Volkskanzler* (people's chancellor), *Volksempfänger* (people's radio), *Volkskühlschrank* (people's refrigerator), *Volkssturm* (people's army), and even *Volksgasmaske* (people's gas mask) were commonly used in everyday language.

From a historical viewpoint, the Third Reich experienced a period of solidified power during which the idea of the People's Community appealed to a large portion of the population. The economic improvement and the modest

Figure 10.3. Propaganda poster: "One People, One Empire, One Leader" (1938).
Süddeutsche Zeitung

increase in consumer options represented important factors, but more signifi-cant was the change in the general mood. The purpose of *Gleichschaltung* was to eliminate any form of opposition or dissent and establish a totalitar-ian state, in which the NS Party wielded complete control over every facet of society.

The use of associations and social organizations as instruments for educat-ing the masses was highly effective, as evidenced by the fact that a significant proportion of adult Germans were affiliated with several of these organiza-tions. The majority of Germans believed in the revival of the nation, their own upward mobility, and a brighter future for themselves and future gen-erations. Nonetheless, the propagandists knew that constant encouragement and reprogramming was necessary in order to keep the cogs of the People's Community oiled and turning.[36]

It did not take long for a large majority of Germans to believe that they were, indeed, superior to others and that the directives given by the *Führer* should be followed to the letter. Hitler's mesmerizing indoctrination of the German *Volk*—along with the threatening elements of the terror apparatus within what had soon become a police state—resulted in a vast number of citizens adopting the new "Holy Trinity" doctrine of *Ein Volk, Ein Reich, Ein Führer*: One People, One Empire, One Leader. A united *Volk* was, indeed, emerging, at the cost of those who were deemed unfit to join its ranks.

NOTES

1. Volker Dahm, "Die 'Deutsche Volksgemeinschaft' und ihre Organisationen," in *Die Tödliche Utopie*, ed. Volker Dahm et al. (Berlin: Verl. Dokumentation Obersalz-berg im Institut für Zeitgeschichte, 2008), 213.

2. Max Domarus, ed., *Hitler: Speeches and Proclamations*, vol. 3, *The Years 1939 to 1940* (Würzburg: Domarus, 1997), speech on Heldengedenktag (Heroes' Memorial Day) 1940, p. 1497.

3. Robert Cecil, *The Myth of the Master Race: Alfred Rosenberg and Nazi Ideology* (New York: Dodd, Mead & Company, 1972), 166.

4. Dahm, "Die 'Deutsche Volksgemeinschaft,'" 214.

5. Ibid., 253.

6. Ernest Hamburger, "The German Labor Front," *Monthly Labor Review* 59, no. 5 (November 1944): 932.

7. Ibid., 933.

8. Ibid., 934.

9. Ibid., 935.

10. Dahm, "Die 'Deutsche Volksgemeinschaft,'" 262–64.

11. Frieda Wunderlich, "Germany's Defense Economy and the Decay of Capital-ism," *Quarterly Journal of Economics* 52, no. 3 (May 1938): 401–30.

12. Dahm, "Die 'Deutsche Volksgemeinschaft,'" 265.

13. Raffael Scheck, *Germany, 1871–1945: A Concise History* (Oxford: Berg, 2008), 167.

14. Adam Young, "Nazism Is Socialism," *Free Market*, Mises Institute, September 1, 2001, https://mises.org/library/nazism-socialism.

15. Sheri Berman, *The Primacy of Politics: Social Democracy and the Making of Europe's Twentieth Century* (Cambridge: Cambridge University Press, 2006), 146.

16. Aly Götz, *Hitler's Beneficiaries: Plunder, Racial War, and the Nazi Welfare State* (New York: Metropolitan, 2007), 55.

17. Evans, *Third Reich in Power*, 411.

18. Martin Kitchen, *A History of Modern Germany, 1800–2000* (Malden, MA: Blackwell, 2006), 287.

19. "Food and Warfare: Marching on Their Stomachs," *Economist*, February 3, 2011.

20. Dahm, "Die 'Deutsche Volksgemeinschaft,'" 269.

21. "Wellness unterm Hakenkreuz," *Spiegel Online*, July 19, 2007, https://www.spiegel.de/geschichte/nazi-propaganda-wellness-unterm-hakenkreuz-a-948936.html.

22. T. W. Mason, *Social Policy in the Third Reich: The Working Class and the National Community* (Providence, RI: Berg, 1993), 160.

23. Hasso Spode, "Some Quantitative Aspects of 'Kraft durch Freude' Tourism," in *Europaikos tourismos kai politismos*, ed. Margerita Dritsas (Athens: Livanis, 2007), 125.

24. "The Olympic Cup," Olympic-Museum.de, https://web.archive.org/web/20060623145224/http://www.olympic-museum.de/awards/olympic_cup.htm.

25. United States Holocaust Memorial Museum, "Indoctrinating Youth," Holocaust Encyclopedia, https://encyclopedia.ushmm.org/content/en/article/indoctrinating-youth.

26. Loewenberg, "Psychohistorical Origins of the Nazi Youth Cohort," 1470.

27. United States Holocaust Memorial Museum, "Hitler Youth," Holocaust Encyclopedia, https://encyclopedia.ushmm.org/content/en/article/hitler-youth-2.

28. Dahm, "Die 'Deutsche Volksgemeinschaft,'" 273–75.

29. Ibid., 269.

30. Ibid., 271.

31. Feldgrau, "The German Reichsarbeitsdienst (Reich Labor Service)," https://www.feldgrau.com/WW2-German-National-Work-Service-Reichsarbeitsdienst/.

32. Ibid.

33. Ibid.

34. Dahm, "Die 'Deutsche Volksgemeinschaft,'" 277.

35. Feldgrau, "German Reichsarbeitsdienst."

36. Norbert Frei, permanent exhibit, Topography of Terror Documentation Centre, Berlin, December 7, 2022.

Chapter 11

Racial Hygiene for the Master Race

Hitler and the National Socialists held the view that a person's worth was not determined by their individual qualities but rather by their membership in a specific racial group. This ideology placed great importance on preserving racial purity, as any form of interbreeding between different races was believed to lead to the decline and eventual degeneration of that group. This would result in the gradual loss of the group's unique characteristics and traits, as well as its ability to protect itself, ultimately leading to its own demise.

THE "BLOOD COMMUNITY"

The National Socialist concept of a *Blutsgemeinschaft* (blood community) was that a *Volk* was a living organism established according to certain laws. This *Volkskörper* (figuratively, racial corpus) embodied not only those living at the time but also the previous and subsequent generations, and should be preserved by way of self-affirmation and procreation. This notion implied that a *Volk* was, above all, a union of people of the same "blood"—of a consistently similar genetic makeup.[1]

The ideas behind classic Social Darwinism included fixed stereotypes, both positive and negative, of ethnic group appearance, behavior, and culture. These identity groups were supposedly unalterable and found their roots in biological inheritance. To National Socialists, those in Europe belonging to the group of "inferior" or "weaker" races included mainly, though not exclusively, Jews, Sinti and Roma, and Slavs.

"NORDICISM"

The definitions of *Volk* and "race" were not the same: these two were believed to have been identical only in prehistoric times. The National Socialist racial education did not consider the German *Volk* to be *reinrassig* (racially pure) but a blend of European races in which a Phalian-Nordic racial portion dominated. "Northern blood" was viewed as possessing characteristics of the highest quality, and the Aryan race embodied the top-quality European races (as did their offshoots living outside the boundaries of Germany).

According to the National Socialists, the racial standard of the German *Volk* was no longer at its peak, and it was urgent that measures of racial hygiene be urgently implemented. On the one hand, elements of a foreign race or inferior genotype were to be eliminated, and on the other, a healthy genetic makeup was to be promoted and proliferated thanks to the application of racial policies, in particular the "northern blood" measure (*Aufnordung*, or encouragement of northern elements to dominate the race).[2]

Hitler combined the National Socialists' concept of *Volk* with a Social Darwinist belief that peoples were subjected to a constant existential struggle in which the "strong" (healthy, good) hold their own while the "weak" (sick, inferior) perish. The "perpetual fundamental law," namely, the selection of the strong and the eradication of the weak, was in Hitler's opinion cruel but rational and wise because it ensured the preservation and higher development of both *Volk* and species. In his view, any humanitarian efforts to escape this merciless law of nature and to preserve the weak at the expense of the strong would lead to the demise of that *Volk* and, finally, of the entire human species.[3]

"APPLIED BIOLOGY"

Hitler's deputy Rudolf Hess claimed that National Socialism was "applied biology." To this effect, a politically extreme, antisemitic interpretation of eugenics influenced the course of state policy. Public health programs to monitor reproduction and marriage aimed at improving the *Volkskörper*, or ethnic body, by removing biologically threatening genes from the *Volk*. Hitler's dictatorial regime, assisted by its totalitarian police and terror apparatus, stifled possible criticism of National Socialist eugenics and those who believed in individual human rights. Once all educational and cultural institutions, as well as the media, came under NS control, racial eugenics pervaded German society and institutions, especially in schoolchildren's education.[4]

In one of Plato's best-known literary works, *The Republic*, he wrote about producing a superior society by procreating high-class people among each other and by discouraging coupling between the lower classes. He also suggested a variety of mating rules to help create an optimal society. In the same vein, National Socialists believed that people inherited mental illness, criminal tendencies, and even poverty and that these preconditions could be bred out of the gene pool.[5]

The origin of the pseudoscience of eugenics can be traced back to the late nineteenth century when Francis Galton, a cousin of Charles Darwin, sought to improve humankind through the increased propagation of the British elite. His concept did not gain much support in Great Britain but was more widely embraced in the United States, where eugenics made its first official appearance through marriage laws. In 1896, Connecticut made it illegal for people with epilepsy or who were "feeble-minded" to marry. In 1903, the American Breeder's Association was created to study eugenics, and in 1911 John Harvey Kellogg, the cereal tycoon, organized the Race Betterment Foundation and established a "pedigree registry." The foundation hosted national conferences on eugenics in 1914, 1915, and 1928.[6]

As the concept of eugenics took hold in the United States, prominent citizens, scientists, and socialists championed the cause and established the Eugenics Record Office. The office tracked families and their genetic traits, claiming most people considered unfit were immigrants, minorities, or the poor. Elements of the philosophy were enshrined as national policy by forced sterilization and segregation laws, as well as marriage restrictions, enacted in twenty-seven states. Eventually, eugenics practitioners coercively sterilized about sixty thousand Americans, forbade the marriage of thousands, forcibly segregated thousands in "colonies," and persecuted untold numbers in ways that are still being researched.[7]

The National Socialist version of eugenics and racial biology was taught as early as primary school. Series of classroom posters, as well as picture books of stereotypes, provided illustrated aids on its key aspects, showing in simple pictures the urgency of the Jewish threat, the danger presented by the mixing of races, how the pure breed will always prevail, and that mixed breeds must be eliminated. In September 1935, the Blood Protection Law was announced in Nuremberg, by which marriage or sexual relations between Jews and non-Jewish Germans became criminal offenses.

Within a short time, the regime took biological segregation a step further by privately considering the "complete emigration" of all Jews in Germany as a goal. Following Germany's annexation of Austria in March, Adolf Eichmann coordinated the forced emigration of tens of thousands of Austrian Jews. In the same year, the National Socialist regime's attacks on German and Austrian Jews, as well as Jewish property, known as the *Kristallnacht*, "Night of Broken Glass," convinced many Jews remaining in the Reich that emigration was their only chance of survival.[8]

Das deutsche Gesicht

1. Nordische Kernrasse

2. Fälisch-nordische Kernrasse

3. Westischer Einschlag

Figure 11.1.   Eugenics poster in schools: "The German Face." *Courtesy of USHMM*

STERILIZATION AND EUTHANASIA PROGRAMS

Already in the first year of Hitler's dictatorship, the Law for the Prevention of Progeny with Hereditary Diseases was enacted. This law applied to those who were diagnosed with any of nine conditions: hereditary feeble-mindedness, schizophrenia, manic-depressive disorder, hereditary epilepsy, Huntington's chorea, hereditary blindness, hereditary deafness, severe physical deformity, and chronic alcoholism. Further targets were the roughly thirty thousand Roma and Sinti "gypsies" as well as some five hundred offspring of African–German unions, following French occupation of the Rhineland. Posters warned the population of the danger of allowing *minderwertig* (inferior/substandard) Germans to procreate. The enforcement of this law led to an estimated 375,000–400,000 Germans experiencing the pain, terror, and mortification of being forcibly sterilized.[9]

"Those who do not work shall not eat" became a National Socialist dictum. Posters and booklets "informed" the public about how much money it was costing the taxpayers to support those afflicted with hereditary disabilities. The demeaning designation of *minderwertig* was applied, above all, to the mentally ill, mentally disabled, "asocial" citizens, and criminals.[10] It soon became legal to sterilize those deemed unfit to procreate, and the euthanizing of unfit newborns became common practice. A controversial euthanasia program, code-named T4, also became part of the National Socialists' exclusionary eugenics and of racial hygiene methods to purify the *Volk* by eliminating the unfit. To cleanse the Aryan German population, an estimated two to three hundred thousand citizens were eliminated under the guise of "mercy killing." These victims had generally been designated as being mentally ill, disabled, asocial, or simply "unfit."[11]

THE MASTER RACE

Hitler and the National Socialists believed the Nordic or Aryan race to be the *Herrenrasse* (master race) or *Herrenvolk* (master people). The NS theorist Alfred Rosenberg understood the Nordic race to have descended from Proto-Aryans, who he believed had prehistorically dwelt on the North German Plain and previously originated on the lost continent of Atlantis.[12] Hitler viewed the Germanic peoples, or Aryans, as not only superior to all other races but entitled to territorial expansion.[13]

Within months of seizing power, the National Socialist government required Germans to obtain an *Ariernachweis* (Aryan certificate) or an *Ahnenpass* (ancestors' pass): two similar documents that certified that a person was a member of the alleged Aryan race. From April 1933, the document was required from all employees and officials in the public sector, including in the field of education.[14] Later, proof of racially "pure" ancestry was required of lawyers and medical doctors, and finally it was even required in order to attend high school or get married. Usually, the lineage was investigated two generations back, and legislation required seven birth or baptism certificates or a combination of both. A *Großer Ariernachweis* (greater Aryan certificate) was required for compliance with the requirements of the *Reichserbhofgesetz* (land heritage law) and membership in the National Socialist Party. This certificate required a family pedigree reaching back to 1800 (and to 1750 for SS officers). No matter what type of certificate was applied for, the applicant had to prove that he or she had no ancestors of "Jewish or colored blood."[15]

THE WOMAN'S ROLE IN NATIONAL SOCIALISM

In a speech on September 8, 1934, Hitler proclaimed, "In my state, the mother is the most important citizen." In an attempt to reverse the trend of falling birth rates, the National Socialist regime not only encouraged racially "acceptable" couples to have as many children as possible but made it a national duty for the "racially fit." The 1935 Marital Health Law prohibited marriages between the so-called hereditarily healthy and those regarded as "genetically unfit."[16]

Another effort to encourage the increase of "pure-blooded" Germans—and counter the high number of abortions—was the Lebensborn program (literally, Fount of Life). A registered association, Lebensborn was backed by both the SS and the state with the mission of providing assistance to unmarried mothers, encouraging unmarried women to give birth anonymously at special maternity homes, and subsequently in arranging the adoption of these children by "racially pure" and "healthy" parents, above all to SS members and their families.

UNTERMENSCHEN

National Socialists defined the Slavic people, among others, as being racially inferior, non-Aryan *Untermenschen* (subhumans), and consequently a potential threat to the Aryan or Germanic master race.[17] According to the National Socialist secret "Hunger Plan" and *Generalplan Ost*, the Slavic population was to be systematically removed from Central Europe by means of expulsion, enslavement, starvation, and extermination,[18] with the exception of a

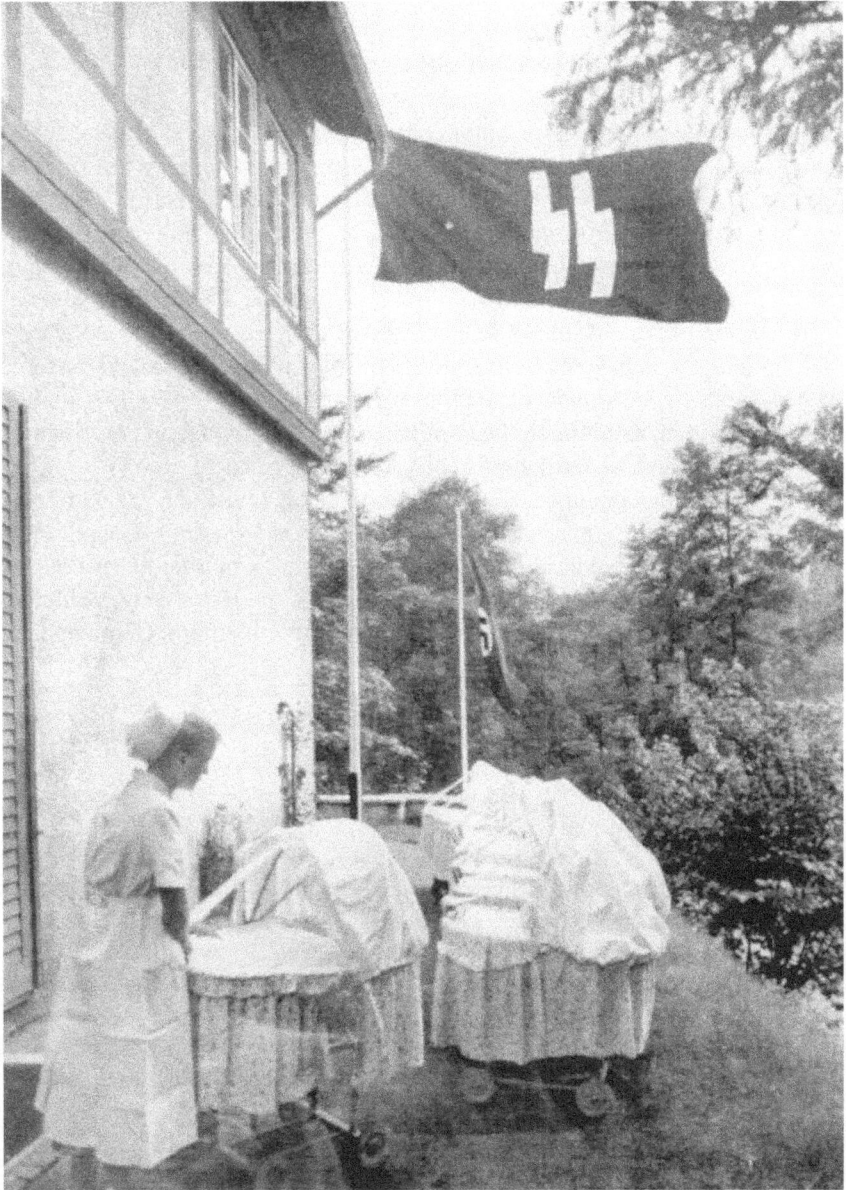

Figure 11.2.   One of the Lebensborn centers. *Bundesarchiv*

small percentage considered to be non-Slavic descendants of Germanic set-tlers and thus suitable for Germanization.[19]

HOMOSEXUALITY

During the time of the German empire, homosexuality was widely persecuted, but attitudes toward homosexual citizens became more accepting during the Weimar Republic, particularly in Berlin. This newfound tolerance, however, was abruptly reversed from 1933 onward, as the new regime claimed that homosexuals were unwilling to contribute to the strengthening of the German family and nation due to their inability to reproduce. The Gestapo and SS used the homosexuality of SA leader Ernst Röhm, among others, to justify their murders, which were also claimed to be in response to a "Röhm putsch." A widespread propaganda campaign was subsequently launched against homosexual men, resulting in the criminalization and imprisonment of nearly sixty thousand men under the guise of "preventive custody."[20]

The NS ideology of eugenics was central to its racist and genocidal policies and was used to justify unspeakable acts of cruelty and violence. The regime's implementation of eugenics ultimately led to the mass murder of millions of people—both Jews and non-Jews—and has made the terms "eugenics" and "racial hygiene" deeply associated with the horrors of Hitler's Germany.

NOTES

1. Dahm, "Die 'Deutsche Volksgemeinschaft,'" 247.

2. Ibid.

3. Ibid.

4. United States Holocaust Memorial Museum, "The Biological State: Nazi Racial Hygiene, 1933–1939," Holocaust Encyclopedia, https://encyclopedia.ushmm.org/content/en/article/the-biological-state-nazi-racial-hygiene-1933-1939.

5. "Eugenics," History.com, https://www.history.com/topics/european-history/eugenics.

6. Ibid.

7. Edwin Black, "The Horrifying American Roots of Nazi Eugenics," History News Network, September 2003, https://historynewsnetwork.org/article/1796.

8. United States Holocaust Memorial Museum, "Biological State."

9. Ibid.

10. Dieter Pohl et al., "Eugenik, 'Rassenhygiene,' Euthanasie," in Dahm, *Die Tödliche Utopie*, 402.

11. H. Faulstich, "Die Zahl der Euthanasieopfer," in *"Euthanasie" und die aktu-elle Sterbehilfe-Debatte: Die Historischen Hintergründe Medizinischer Ethik*, ed. A. Frewer and C. Eickhoff (Frankfurt am Main, Campus, 2000), 218–29.

12. Alfred Rosenberg, *The Myth of the 20th Century* (1930; Brooklyn, NY: Revisionist Press, 1982), 24–26.

13. Hitler, *Mein Kampf*.

14. Cornelia Schmitz-Berning, *Vokabular des Nationalsozialismus* (Berlin: De Gruyter, 2000), 61.

15. Isabel Heinemann, *Rasse, Siedlung, deutsches Blut* (Göttingen: Wallstein, 2003).

16. United States Holocaust Memorial Museum, "Biological State."

17. Peter Longerich, *Holocaust: The Nazi Persecution and Murder of the Jews* (Oxford: Oxford University Press, 2010), 241.

18. Timothy Snyder, *Bloodlands: Europe between Hitler and Stalin* (New York: Basic Books, 2010), 162–63.

19. Janusz Gumkowski and Kazimierz Leszczynski, *Hitler's Plans for Eastern Europe: Poland under Nazi Occupation* (Warsaw: Polonia, 1961), 7–33, 164–78.

20. Permanent exhibit, Topography of Terror Documentation Centre, Berlin, December 7, 2022.

Chapter 12

Hitler: Actor and Orator

Some maintain that Hitler never came up with a new idea and that everything he did and said was imitative of things he'd already seen, heard, or read. This may also be true of his adoption and adaptation of mass marketing a politically imbued idea, a practice commonly known as propaganda.

A HIDDEN TALENT

The first time Hitler realized he could speak and lead occurred shortly after the end of World War I while working in the army's propaganda office. At this time, as early as 1919, Hitler knew how to define political questions and, more importantly, how to seek their answers. He was becoming a man of ideas and would emerge as a political orator who possessed a remarkable grasp of political processes. The next step was to translate these ideas into policy and to learn the art of connivance and manipulation. Once he had acquired these abilities, as well as having studied German and enemy propaganda, he could weave narratives for his ideas—even if these were blatant lies or exaggerations.[1]

Hitler's very first speech for the DAP was a huge success. A leading Munich paper reported that Hitler had spoken with "rousing words" and had made a case for "the necessity to rally against the common enemy of nations"—the Jews. In these early speeches, bashing the Jews was not Hitler's only theme. He frequently expressed Pan-German views, called for the unification of Germany and Austria, and condemned the Versailles Treaty. Gradually, he shifted the DAP from purely a German workers' party to a movement promoting National Socialism.[2]

Unlike other politicians, it was Hitler's speeches that paved his way to power. Once he held the reigns, it was also his oratory that would hold the German people in his grip. During the many years and opportunities of Hitler's rabble-rousing speeches, he refined his art into producing "not a mere speech but a *Gesamtkunstwerk*, a total artwork. Hitler ravished his audiences, sensed what his listeners felt—not what they thought, but what they felt—such as frustration, anger, paranoia, xenophobia. Then he told them what to think."[3]

Hitler's longtime secretary Christa Schroeder said of her boss that he possessed the "gift of a rare magnetic power to reach people . . . a sixth sense and a clairvoyant intuition."[4] During the first six years of Hitler's stint in power, André François-Poncet, the French ambassador to Germany, had plenty of opportunities to observe him in action. He found that Hitler seemed to possess an almost psychic ability to read precisely what the crowds wanted or feared, approved or hated, believed or disbelieved, and that he knew how to play on these emotions to perfection.[5]

Early in his campaigning years, Hitler practiced gestures and expressions while standing in front of a mirror. One of his early sycophants, Ernst Hanfstaengl, likened Hitler's public mimicry to "the thrusts and parries of a fencer," "the perfect balance of a tightrope-walker," "a skilled violinist," "a really great orchestral conductor who, instead of just hammering out the downbeat, suggests the existence of hidden rhythms and meaning with the upward flick of his baton."[6]

Goebbels maintained that Hitler rehearsed entire passages as if he were an actor going on stage and that his gestures were calculated with absolute precision. Hitler ordered equipment to be installed in the speaker's podium that enabled him to adjust the lighting and indicate the perfect time for him to be photographed. So as not to have to wear glasses on stage, his speeches were typed up in large print. The size of the venues was planned in such a way that they would be overfilled.[7]

The secret lay simply in knowing how to stir up passion among the public. George Orwell aptly observed, "[Hitler] knows that human beings don't only want comfort, safety, short working hours . . . they also, at least intermittently, want struggle and self-sacrifice, not to mention drums, flags and loyalty parades."[8] Uprooting the basic precepts of Western democracy, Hitler appealed not to the mind but to the senses, to emotion rather than to reason, and he applied psychological manipulation rather than political logic.[9] This proved to be Hitler's most effective technique in mesmerizing a nation.

GERMANIZING THE *FÜHRER*

When he was but a toddler, Adolf's family moved from his birthplace, the Austrian border town of Braunau am Inn, to the Lower Bavarian town of Passau, where Adolf spent two-and-a-half years during a determinative phase

Figure 12.1. Hitler the actor rehearsing in front of a mirror (1933). *AKG Images*

of language acquisition.[10] The family then returned to Austria when Adolf was five, and he subsequently attended school near Linz.[11] In Mein Kampf, Hitler states, "The German of my youth was the dialect spoken in Lower Bavaria; I did not wish to forget it nor to learn Viennese slang."[12] Though Hitler may have been exposed to one of the Bavarian dialects at a young age, there is a strong likelihood that, despite his later claim, the dialect he spoke at home was also fashioned by his Austrian parents' native parlance as much as by the Upper Austrian vernacular of his peers during the course of his school years. The fact is that, during World War I, Lieutenant Fritz Wiedemann, Hitler's superior, noted of him, "What I noticed first was his unmilitary manner and his slight Austrian accent."[13]

From April to November 1932, during his airplane electoral campaign *Hitler über Deutschland* (Hitler over Germany), it appears that Hitler sought to define and refine the way he sounded to his audience. In secret, he took diction classes from a well-known opera singer, Paul Stieber-Walter, also known as Paul Devrient. The reason for the tuition was not only to seek help with his overstrained vocal cords but, more importantly, to be viewed as a transregional statesman who could be clearly understood by all Germans. Hitler never achieved a consistency in his staged accent: his enunciation altered depending on factors such as stress or excitement, and it also changed over a period of time. Experts' research has proven that Hitler purposely integrated his contrived manner of speech into his theatrical stage play of deception and manipulation.[14]

EARLY MODELS FOR THE REICH

In Hitler's own words, during his five and a half years as a struggling artist in Vienna, two antisemitic politicians, Vienna's mayor Karl Lueger and Georg von Schönerer, leader of the Pan-German Party in Austria, used certain tools of political indoctrination to consolidate their views and goals. Hitler later employed these same tools through his own party members. One of these tools was the use of von Schönerer's posters, which were extensively displayed in shop windows. Von Schönerer was referred to as the *"Führer"* or leader, members used the *"Heil"* greeting, and the party's newspapers were distributed to the public at taverns.[15]

Mass meetings, military-style wear, and pseudoreligious trappings, along with affiliated groups for women, teachers, and youth as well as the distribution of antisemitic children's books to schools, were the models for what Hitler would later implement in his Third Reich. In addition, these Austrian politicians' policy of violence and oppression toward Jews was later adopted into Hitler's noxious mix.[16]

Hitler's next model came from the political left: he noted the tactics of the powerful Social Democratic parties in both Austria and Germany. He grudgingly admired their skills in successfully appealing to large segments of the population through populous festivals, mass meetings and demonstrations, as well as parades—all with the effect of stimulating workers' pride and intimidating political opponents. Hitler believed that "to destroy Marxism" the National Socialist Party would have to create a propaganda machine and its own terror organization.[17]

But it was, above all, his participation in World War I that helped to shape Hitler's ideas on propaganda. In *Mein Kampf*, he notes the expertise of the enemy's propagandists. In contrast to Germany's propaganda, he felt that U.S. and British propagandists had successfully made their point, making use of simple and emotional content. Hitler admired the Allies' skill in demonizing the Germans as terrifying invaders whose goal was to destroy civilization (the Allies' use of the term "Hun" to designate the German enemy conjured up images of the "barbarian hordes" that emerged out of Central Asia to threaten Christianity and western civilization during the late Roman Empire).[18]

THE MASTER ORATOR

In *Mein Kampf*, Hitler ascertained that, as a means of exploiting the dynamics of crowd psychology, mass meetings were "the only way to exert a truly effective . . . influence on large sections of the people." However, to reiterate what was suggested earlier, Hitler did not produce anything new: the ideas he put forth were not his own but borrowed from several other right-wing groups. The originality resided solely in the way Hitler presented these ideas: "how he said something rather than what he said."[19]

In order to set the National Socialist Party apart from the myriad political parties struggling for notice in Berlin, the party determined to market Hitler as a person rather than to simply promote its party name. Hitler's personal photographer, Heinrich Hoffmann, took numerous photographs of Hitler in his studio, practicing countless poses and facial expressions, to help the politician prepare for his public appearances. Posters of Hitler and his personal public speeches greatly helped to promote this new image.

The speaker presented himself before his large audiences in carefully staged and choreographed performances. Martial music would begin the ceremony and then a warm-up speaker would build up the anticipation for Hitler's appearance. Once on stage, Hitler began slowly and evenly, gradually working up to an impassioned crescendo, accompanied by theatrical gestures. After the speech, he immediately left the stage to the sound of music. His exit was geared to preserving the magic of the performer and his work. Hitler did not believe in remaining in the room after the speech was over because this would only lead to a sense of anticlimax.[20]

Through countless speeches delivered to the most diverse audiences, Hitler increased his oratory proficiencies, aiming to tailor his discourses to listeners' particular backgrounds and interests. Whether he chose to wear a business suit or the party uniform and armband, or whether he spoke in a conversational or more strident tone of voice, depended on his assessment of the audience.[21]

Hitler often arrived at a meeting armed with a prewritten text or notes that he could refer to. However, more often than not, after appraising the crowd, he abandoned the context of the prepared speech and launched into a tirade that, according to his listeners, wholly captured their attention. People would comment later that Hitler had read their minds, had expressed their personal views or concerns or had spoken directly to them. The *Führer* had plenty of opportunity to hone his oratory skills long before he seized power. By the time he held complete control of the government, he would aim his rhetoric at enchanting and deceiving the German nation. Hitler eventually made show of an astonishing ability in being able to "read" an audience and in manipulating a crowd. The world of politics had found Hitler, not the other way around.[22]

NOTES

1. Weber, *Becoming Hitler*, 96.
2. Ibid., 157.
3. Spotts, *Hitler and the Power of Aesthetics*, 45.
4. Schroeder, *Er war mein Chef*, 283.
5. André François-Poncet, *Souvenirs d'une Ambassade à Berlin 1931–1938* (Paris: Flammarion, 1946), 354.
6. Toland, *Adolf Hitler*, 129.
7. Karlheinz Schmeer, *Die Regie des Öffentlichen Lebens im Dritten Reich* (Munich: Pohl, 1956), 123.
8. Sonia Orwell and Ian Angus, eds., *The Collected Essays, Journalism and Letters of George Orwell* (Harmondsworth, UK: Penguin, 1968), 2:29.
9. Spotts, *Hitler and the Power of Aesthetics*, 44.
10. Gustav Keller, *Der Schüler Adolf Hitler: die Geschichte eines lebenslangen Amoklaufs* (Berline: Lit, 2010), 15.
11. Hitler, *Mein Kampf*, trans. Manheim, 6.
12. Peter Ernst, "Adolf Hitlers 'österreichisches Deutsch,'" *Zeitschrift für Mitteleuropäische Germanistik* 3, no. 1 (2013): 29–44.
13. Toland, *Adolf Hitler*, 61.
14. Ernst, "Adolf Hitlers 'österreichisches Deutsch.'"
15. Ian Kershaw, *Hitler, 1889–1936: Hubris* (London: Penguin, 1999), 34–35.

16. John Weiss, *Ideology of Death* (Chicago: Ivan R. Dee, 1996), 168, 187.

17. Luckert and Bachrach, *State of Deception*, 14.

18. Ibid.

19. Kershaw, *Hitler, 1889–1936*, 133.

20. Ernst Hanfstaengl, *The Unknown Hitler* (London: Gibson Square, 2005), 75.

21. Speer, *Inside the Third Reich*, 44.

22. Spotts, *Hitler and the Power of Aesthetics*, 7.

Chapter 13

Hitler in "His" Mountains

Hitler's inaugural visit to the alpine haven of Obersalzberg above Berchtesgaden in 1923 was merely the prelude to a succession of return trips, culminating in his designation of the area as his permanent residence. From a strategic perspective, Hitler recognized the benefits of aligning himself with a fabled locale in Germany's resplendent mountain realm, resulting in a favorable impact on his public image.

With the aid of the National Socialist Party's propagandists, Berchtesgaden was extensively publicized as Hitler's *Wahlheimat* or "chosen homeland," affording him the sense of belonging in Germany that, as an Austrian, he had lacked. The tight association with a distinguished and well-known region in Germany significantly improved Hitler's political acceptability as a representative of the German people.

Despite his Austrian heritage, Hitler made a concerted effort to immerse himself in the cultural fabric of the Bavarian Alps, evidenced by his attire in traditional Bavarian clothing while being photographed at Obersalzberg, as well as his attempts to emulate a Germanic speaking style. By doing so, Hitler sought to establish himself as a rightful member of the Bavarian Alps community.

OBERSALZBERG: PERSONALIZING HITLER

In 1923—already years before Hitler's election in 1933—curious admirers and supporters flocked to Obersalzberg to catch a glimpse of the politician who had become a popular media focus in Germany. Many waited for hours on the terrace of the neighboring Hotel zum Türken that overlooked Hitler's country home, Haus Wachenfeld (later renamed the Berghof).

Following his election, the number of admirers surged, increasing by a factor of ten. Scores of individuals congregated along the perimeter of the *Führer*'s property, which was enclosed by barbed-wire-topped fencing,

Figure 13.1.   Hitler's residence and HQ, the Berghof in Berchtesgaden. *Süddeutsche Zeitung*

hoping for a glimpse of the newly elected leader. Resourceful locals even peddled stones that Hitler had previously stood on as objects of veneration for the devout. By July of that same year, Himmler, in his capacity as political police commander of Bavaria, imposed limitations on the public's ability to access Obersalzberg. Guardhouses were erected and manned along the access routes that wound up from the valley, rendering visits to the *Führer*'s abode high in the Alps akin to a "papal audience."

AudioVolumeUp

At these well-disciplined events that, in time, began to resemble a religious pilgrimage, thousands of German citizens crowded the road in front of Hitler's home or marched by while raising their outstretched right arm in what became known as the National Socialist salute. Hitler's assistant, Martin Bormann, ordered a tree to be planted at the end of Hitler's driveway so as to provide shade for the *Führer*, who allegedly could not stand the heat. To Hitler, these hour-long events provided an opportunity for the German people to experience their proximity to the *Führer* "in faithful veneration" and "boundless love."[1]

National Socialist propaganda artfully made use of his home, the Berghof at Obersalzberg, to bestow qualities upon Hitler that would legitimize his leadership: Hitler the solitary visionary, the great statesman, and the chancellor of the people. Obersalzberg's idyllic alpine setting was particularly well suited to creating an image of Hitler's private life that showcased him as intrinsically connected to his subjects. The *Führer* was presented as a people's man, a leader defending and nurturing the *Volk*: he was one of them, living modestly, in harmony with nature, devoted to and caring for the simple people, for children and animals. This was achieved especially through the purportedly truthful medium of photography—the camera "cannot lie"—which supposedly reproduced an authentic image of Hitler in the illustrated press and in books, magazines, and cigarette picture albums sold by the millions.[2]

MERCHANDIZING HITLER

Hitler soon took center stage in a growing "Hitler cult" that was commandeered by companies selling photos, paintings, and busts of the *Führer*. Hitler's image, as well as that of his home at Obersalzberg, took its place among the national symbols. As such, Hitler merchandizing included the widespread sale of postcards, collectible plates, and cushion covers, among numerous other mediums displaying either Hitler's image or that of his country home.[3]

Adolf Hitler the "gentleman farmer," as well as his "friends and colleagues" such as Heinrich Himmler, Hermann Goering, Albert Speer, or Martin Bormann, among others, who all had homes in the area, soon became hotly sought-after subjects in photo booklets. Hitler's acolyte, chief photographer Heinrich Hoffmann, published his photographs of the Obersalzberg leaders in special editions or collectible sticker photo albums titled *Hitler, Away from It All* and *Hitler, Like No-One Knows Him* or *Hitler in His Mountains*.[4] The Bavarian image of Hitler as an amenable, approachable, and exemplary neighbor, as well as the illusionary role of *Volkskanzler* (chancellor of the people), stood in contrast to the image of Hitler in Berlin, where he personified the irreproachable and superhuman leader (*Führer*) and chancellor of the Reich—the German Empire.

THE COUNTRY GENTLEMAN

In the years leading up to the war, Hitler's gentrified image was used strategically and effectively, not only within the Reich but abroad as well, with the intention of distancing the dictator from his brutal antisemitic policies. The callous image of the xenophobic agitator of the masses was given a makeover by fostering the impression of a new, sophisticated persona that emerged in carefully crafted domestic surroundings. Like a bull in a china shop, the

Hitler myth presented the *Führer* amid silk curtains and porcelain vases, intimating an internal world that was both cultivated and peaceful.[5]

Hitler's interior decorator, Gerdy Troost, played a significant part in creating the impression of her client being a man of good taste, sophistication, and culture. Influenced by British design reform movements, Troost favored quality of materials and craftsmanship over showy display. Hitler's propagandists borrowed the mountain backdrops of Germany's literary and artistic movements, such as Romanticism, to "mythologize the *Führer* as a mystic leader who immersed himself in—and embodied—the terrible yet magnificent forces of nature." Even after the onset of war, the misleading imagery of an off-duty Hitler playing with dogs and children took a long time to blur.[6]

Falling for the National Socialists' propaganda, English-language journalists promoted a distorted perception of Hitler by penning flattering accounts of the gentlemanly statesman, in spite of the obvious realities. In 1937 the *New York Times Magazine* published a front-page article on Adolf Hitler's serene mountain retreat where, "surrounded by Alpine peaks, Germany's leader communed with nature, contemplated the Reich and indulged his sweet tooth for chocolate."[7]

In truth, the Berghof served as a second seat of power and a platform for international politics and decision making. Hitler regularly held meetings with numerous representatives from various departments and ministries of the Third Reich at his Obersalzberg estate. He also hosted over forty foreign politicians and dignitaries at the property, including Mussolini, Chamberlain, kings and queens, as well as foreign ministers and ambassadors from around the world. Many of these meetings brought about significant national and international implications and played a major role in Hitler's decision-making process. In fact, it was at the Berghof that the wheels of World War II were set in motion.

In November 1938, just weeks after Hitler's takeover of the Czech Sudetenland and the same month as the *Reichskristallnacht* pogroms, *Homes and Gardens* featured an article titled "Hitler's Mountain Home" in which the author praised the *Führer*'s taste and depicted his private life as one of refinement, gentle repasts, and congenial friendships. *Life*, *Vogue*, and other widely circulated publications in the United States, Great Britain, and other countries similarly catered to readers' curiosity by offering them glossy photo-essays on Hitler's residence.[8]

The outbreak of war broke any spell that non-German people may have fallen under regarding Hitler as a peace-loving, gracious country squire at home in "his" mountains, where he lived well over a quarter of his time in power. Though citizens of other nations may have been quick to acknowledge they had been duped by such imagery, the Third Reich's effective and constantly revised propaganda campaign targeted Germany's residents in such a way that a majority of Germans accepted the war as a positive step in their *Führer*'s master plan.

NOTES

1. Albert Feiber et al., in Dahm, *Die Tödliche Utopie*, 64.

2. Ibid., 67.

3. Ibid.

4. Ibid.

5. Despina Stratigakos, "Hitler at Home: How the Nazi PR Machine Remade the Führer's Domestic Image and Duped the World," *Conversation*, September 21, 2015, https://theconversation.com/hitler-at-home-how-the-nazi-pr-machine-remade -the-fuhrers-domestic-image-and-duped-the-world-47077.

6. Ibid.

7. Ibid.

8. Ibid.

Chapter 14

Mass Events and the
Art of Propaganda

Political marketing—propaganda—assumed multiple forms during Hitler's campaigning years. Yet once he was in power, Hitler turned his own administrative leadership into an art form. When Hitler was tried for treason in 1924, he stated that political leadership should be regarded not as *Staatswissenschaft* but as *Staatskunst* (not as political science but as statecraft/state art).[1] In his notes, Hitler scrawled, "You cannot educate for politics—politics is not science—but—art." Hitler did, indeed, adopt the practice of politics-as-an-art and even once described himself as "the greatest actor in Europe."[2]

According to the journalist Joachim Fest, the first part of the "show" was choreographed with bands, marches, banners, and singing "to build up the suspense and make the speech seem like an annunciation."[3] When it came time for Hitler to speak, he would stand mute, contemplative, and then begin quietly—even hesitantly—and, gradually, the dramatic torrent of words would flow forth, eventually reaching a tremendous crescendo while he shrieked in a high-pitched voice. Hardly surprising that Hitler's performances were nothing like an improvised and random rabble-rousing tirade but rather were likened to a symphonic work.

TIMING IS EVERYTHING

Hitler would never have reached his position of power had it not been for the timing of his campaigning. His words sowed seeds on fertile ground as the Germans were experiencing historically low morale. In the aftermath of World War I, the German (and Austrian) people's national pride had suffered a devastating blow. Economic disaster, astronomic reparation payments to be made, widespread unemployment, laughable military defense, as well as a chronically unstable and ever-changing government—all these factors must have led the German people to feel like they were trapped in a leaky ship on a stormy sea at night, without a captain or even a rudder. Hardly surprising that in the 1920s a great number of Germans were hoping for a savior in their time of need. It just so happened that Hitler was looking for a following: by the most unfortunate stroke of fate, they found one another.

Striving to win over the two-thirds of the German population whose vote he did not receive at the most recent elections, the first speech Hitler made as chancellor on February 1, 1933, was a radio broadcast to the nation. As in so many subsequent speeches, he alternated hopes with fears, affirmed his position as leader, and shared his concern to pursue Germany's cultural, religious, and political heritage. Purposely avoiding any antisemitism, Hitler aimed at highlighting a broad platform that a majority of Germans could relate to. He assured the people that Christianity would be "the basis of our moral code" and promoted the defense of the family, the forging of ethnic and political unity, and teaching Germany's youth to respect "our great past."[4] For the next years of his reign of terror, Hitler's refined form of propaganda would result in seducing, deceiving, and manipulating the German people through a message of national unity and the restoration of national pride.

Making use of the press and the radio, Hitler lamented the fourteen years of "Marxism that had ruined Germany" during the period of the Weimar Republic and warned of the disastrous dangers of communism. In order to gain full control of the media, Hitler employed emergency constitutional powers to control the press and to enable authorities to ban political meetings and marches.[5]

Nationwide, a great number of publishing houses and newspapers were purchased, though many of a nonpolitical nature were left alone, provided they "self-censor" the content of their publications. The printing presses of outlawed parties were either destroyed or confiscated and put to use by the National Socialist publications, and within the framework of Germany's "Aryanization," Jewish-owned publishing houses were taken over. Of these, Ullstein was the largest in Europe, with a staff of some ten thousand. The family was first forced off its board and, a year later, coerced into selling its assets. A new law required journalists and editors to provide evidence of being "racially pure" and expected them to follow the guidelines established by Goebbels's Ministry of Public Enlightenment and Propaganda.[6]

In 1933 the National Socialists also took control of the radio as a further means of shaping the public's opinion through the repeated dissemination of carefully selected information, half-truths, and other propagandic brainwashing. Eugen Hadomovsky, head of the Propaganda Ministry's Broadcasting Department, said, "We radio people are marchers. We think of ourselves as the SA of propaganda. We march freely through the streets and enter every single house, so that the powerful current of National Socialist political and

Figure 14.1. Advertisement for the radio: "The whole of Germany listens to the Führer with the 'people's receiver'" *Bundesarchiv*

cultural ideals flows into each member of the nation. To work for the radio means: to work for the Party and the *Führer*."[7]

The party commissioned inexpensively made radios for the masses. Called *Volksempfänger* (people's receivers), these were not only affordable to every family but widely advertised so that soon Germany's radio audience became second only to the United States. Radios were installed in factories, restaurants, schools, and offices. Major announcements or the leaders' speeches were broadcast through loudspeakers in public squares. The aim was to bring about "community listening," destroy individuality, and reinforce patriotism and unity among German citizens.

Using the spoken and written word as a "cleansing tool," as well as through the widespread dissemination of the visual panoply of Hitler photos, busts, and paintings, the National Socialists gradually forced a larger portion of the nation to view the new regime in a positive way. Added to the press and pictorial propaganda, the monumental events that took place several times a year greatly contributed to creating and ensuring the *Führer* myth, as well as the concept of the *Volksgemeinschaft* (People's Community), a nearly sacred bond that united the "leader" and his "people." A sign of allegiance and belonging to the People's Community was the now infamous upraised-arm salute. Those who refused to practice it publicly were considered to stand in opposition to the *Führer* and National Socialism and, consequently, risked reprisals.[8]

The Führer myth promoted the idea that Hitler was a great statesman and a near-messianic figurehead chosen by destiny to lead the German people out of depression and despair toward a glorious future that, thanks to the rebuilding of the nation's military defenses, would guarantee peace and security. The importance of the Volksgemeinschaft concept as a central propaganda tool has often been overlooked by postwar historians. However, it served to create a common bond between the working and middle classes in Germany, and it provided people with an increased sense of purpose, pride, and patriotism.

THE NEW MESSIAH

Many people claimed that Hitler's artistic talents were akin to those of a magician, whose rhetorical tricks had a mesmerizing effect on his listeners. Rather than relying on logical persuasion, he induced a state of intoxication that unleashed primal emotions. Beyond his alleged magical abilities, Hitler aspired to present himself as a spiritual figure, a savior. Drawing on the traditions of the Catholic Church from his youth, Hitler developed a pseudo-religious agenda that incorporated ceremonies, sermons, and rituals aimed at subconsciously captivating his audience.

One of the core elements of the mass events was the honoring of the dead. As early as 1926, in the staging of mass memorial events, Hitler solemnly presented the *Blutfahne*, the so-called Blood Flag, in memory of the National Socialist "martyrs." Standing beside a flagbearer, Hitler solemnly clutched a fold of the Blood Flag and touched it to the flags of each new group's flags in a gesture of "sanctification."[9]

Hitler had two motives for orchestrating his most unforgettable events at night. First, the darkness allowed the planners to manipulate controlled lighting effects—the flickering flames of torches, the blaze emanating from colossal braziers, as well as the illuminating spotlights and pyrotechnics created an otherworldly and captivating ambiance. Second, Hitler maintained that during daylight hours individuals possessed the fortitude to resist new concepts, but at night they were more susceptible to yielding to the commanding influence of a stronger will.[10] In *Mein Kampf*, Hitler announced that his intent was to "destroy the freedom of the will" of his audience and induce a state comparable to religious exaltation.[11]

Hitler made use of his skill in propaganda and theatrics in the overall "show" production that he applied to mass events. Playing the producer or stage manager, he combined color, sound, music, and a message to create the overall event. Acting as a painter, he decorated cities with colossal banners or deployed SS and other organizations in their black, brown, or red-brown uniforms. Just like a composer, he commissioned bands and large choruses. Planning like an architect, he arranged blocks of thousands of people into precise geometric formations.[12] Impersonating a demigod, he orchestrated the entire event in such a way that a simple word from the *Führer* could set one hundred thousand people in motion or immobilize them in an instant. Each individual existed only within the collectivity of the mass of which Hitler was the master. Such awe-inducing, yet menacing, events served as an ominous affirmation of Hitler's early slogan: "One People, One Reich, One *Führer*."

"THE GREATEST SHOW ON EARTH"

Though parades and rallies marked Hitler and the National Socialists' agenda as early as the 1920s, the first monumental-scale Nuremberg party rally was organized in 1933, the year he seized power. Hitler gave every detail of each event his personal attention, be it the program of parades, festivals, dedications, commemorations, march-by salutes, or torchlight processions. He appointed himself producer, director, stage designer, and lead actor.[13]

Attending the 1934 Nuremberg party rallies, the World War II author William Shirer noted,

Figure 14.2.   Nuremberg party rally at the Luitpoldhain. *Courtesy of USHMM / Richard Freimark*

Figure 14.3.   Nuremberg party rally at the Zeppelin Field. *Courtesy of Dokumentationszentrum Reichsparteitagsgelände DZ-Ph 0239-01*

I'm beginning to comprehend, I think, some of the reasons for Hitler's astounding success. Borrowing a chapter from the Roman [Catholic] church, he's restoring pageantry and color and mysticism to the drab lives of twentieth-century Germans. [The show] had something of the mysticism and religious fervor of an Easter or Christian Mass in a great Catholic cathedral. . . . You have to go through one of these to understand Hitler's hold on the people.[14]

The longtime French ambassador to Germany, André François-Poncet, described the party rally experience as hypnotic and said that "many people returned home seduced and conquered, ready to collaborate, failing to perceive the sinister reality hidden behind the false pomp."[15]

American architect Philip Johnson perceived the risk of succumbing to the enchantment of these events. Of the 1938 Nuremberg rallies, he said, "Like the Ring [of Wagner's *Niebelungen*], even if you were at first indifferent, you were at last overcome, and if you were a believer to begin with, the effect was even more staggering. Even the Americans who were there—no special friends of the Nazis—were carried away by it all."[16] All too few Germans at the time were aware of how Hitler had managed to master the dramatic arts in such a way as to exercise psychological manipulation and mind control over the hundreds of thousands in his audience.

Those who did not—or could not—attend were bombarded with the reviews and replays of these events in the press and in the cinema. Leni Riefenstahl directed three films about the Nuremberg party rallies, which, along with her filming of the Berlin Olympics, *Olympia* (1938), resulted in worldwide attention and acclaim. Still today, these are widely credited as the most effective, and technically innovative, propaganda films ever made.

A FULL CALENDAR

In addition to the rallies at Nuremberg, Hitler created an annual calendar of "hallowed rites" as a pretext to staging mass events. Through the Bureau of Festivals, Leisure, and Celebrations, a carefully organized series of political spectacles was offered throughout the year. Among them were Heroes' Day, the National Festival of the German People, and the Rally in Honor of the German Farmers. This last event, which took on the character of a thanksgiving celebration, was attended by over a million people in 1937. These monumental events included all sorts of festivities and attractions ranging from music, dances, and the inevitable speeches to military parades, fireworks, airplane flybys, and banner-toting zeppelins.

Essentially, such large gatherings under Hitler's leadership were meant to celebrate the "unity" of the people based on "blood and soil" and to serve as a further means for the *Führer* to consolidate his hold on the German people. Among the fourteen National Socialist observances, Hitler's birthday on April 20 was the most important. On the eve of the "big day," newly appointed party functionaries formally professed their obedience to the *Führer* and masses of ten-year-old children were solemnly inducted into the Hitler Youth while swearing an oath of loyalty to their leader.[17]

The cycle of National Socialist holidays was often staged at locations named *Thingplatz* or *Thingstätte*, which resembled Greek-inspired outdoor amphitheaters built for such meetings and performances. *Thing* (pronounced "ting") is an old Germanic word meaning a gathering of people or a legal assembly. Of the four hundred *Thing* sites that were planned, some fifty were built between 1933 and 1939 and ranged in size between one thousand and two hundred thousand seats. Whenever possible, the sites were to be built in a natural setting, incorporating rocks, trees, bodies of water, ruins, and hills of some historical or legendary significance.[18]

As outdoor, immersive, multidisciplinary theaters, *Thing* sites were also venues for propagandist plays. As set out in a 1934 speech by Reich drama advisor Rainer Schlösser, the objective was "a drama that intensifies historical events to create a mythical, universal, unambiguous reality beyond reality." The shows were to be choric and to involve the audience as an expression of the *Volkgemeinschaft*. Above all, spectators were meant to identify with the National Socialist cultural revolution that they depicted.

Germany's weather often dampened the appeal of such large-scale cultural gatherings, and audience enthusiasm waned for the action-poor *Thing* plays. From 1935 on, these theaters were renamed *Feierstätten* (celebration sites) or *Freilichtbühnen* (open-air theaters), and they were used for performances of conventional plays and folk festivals such as those celebrating the summer solstice.

The methodical dissemination of National Socialist "beliefs" and "ideals" through meticulously crafted propaganda yielded an astounding and rapid impact. Through the written medium, straightforward yet frequently defamatory street posters, radio transmissions that reached the homes of nearly all Germans, and the spectacular grandiosity of Hitler's mass rallies, a successful campaign of indoctrination occurred not only among those Germans who had initially elected Hitler but also among a considerable number of his erstwhile adversaries. The National Socialists' well-oiled propaganda machine advanced mercilessly through all segments of German society, effectively fogging people's better judgment and systematically sowing seeds of discrimination and hate.

NOTES

1. Eberhard Jäckel and Axel Kuhn, eds., *Sämtliche Aufzeichnungen: 1905–1924* (Stuttgart: Deutsche Verlags-Anstalt, 1980), 1190.

2. Lutz Schwerin von Krosigk, *Es Geschah in Deutschland* (Tübingen: Wunderlich, 1951), 220.

3. Joachim Fest, *Hitler: Eine Biographie* (Berlin: Ullstein, 1998), 150.

4. Luckert and Bachrach, *State of Deception*, 63.

5. David Welch, *The Third Reich* (London: Routledge, 1993), 18.

6. Luckert and Bachrach, *State of Deception*, 66–68.

7. Inge Marssolek and Adelheid von Saldern, eds., *Zuhören und Gehörtwerden I: Radio im Nationalsozialismus* (Tübingen: Edition Diskord, 1998), 50.

8. Luckert and Bachrach, *State of Deception*, 75.

9. Jean-Denis Lepage, *An Illustrated Dictionary of the Third Reich* (Jefferson, NC: McFarland, 2013), 22.

10. Spotts, *Hitler and the Power of Aesthetics*, 53.

11. Hitler, *Mein Kampf*, 474–75.

12. Spotts, *Hitler and the Power of Aesthetics*, 54.

13. Ibid., 58.

14. William L. Shirer, *Berlin Diary* (New York: Penguin, 1941), 15, 19.

15. François-Poncet, *Souvenirs d'une Ambassade à Berlin*, 268.

16. Franz Schulze, *Philip Johnson: Life and Work* (New York: Alfred A. Knopf, 1994), 133–34.

17. Spotts, *Hitler and the Power of Aesthetics*, 100–101.

18. Rainer Stommer, *Die Inszenierte Volksgemeinschaft: Die "Thing-Bewegung" im Dritten Reich* (Marburg: Jonas, 1985).

Chapter 15

Third Reich Cinema

INDOCTRINATION THROUGH ENTERTAINMENT

In his early twenties, at a movie theater in Vienna, Hitler made the realization that this relatively new but fast-growing medium could be used for propaganda purposes: "This is the way to found a new party," he told his friend Hanisch. On February 2, 1933, two days after his appointment as chancellor, Hitler viewed the première of *Morgenrot* (Dawn), a film about a submarine commander and his crew during World War I. The film centered on themes of German honor and sacrifice as well as the glory of dying for the country.[1] This same veneration for fallen heroes of World War I, as well as for those who sacrificed themselves for the National Socialist cause during the Munich Beer Hall Putsch in November 1923, became a significant focus of National Socialist events and theatrics.

THE MOST IMPORTANT OF THE ARTS

In March 1933, Goebbels, minister of public enlightenment and propaganda, addressed representatives of the German film industry for the first time. Stating that "of all the arts, film is for us the most important," he brought up the example of the film *Battleship Potemkin*, adding, "It is a marvelously well-made film. . . . This is a film which could turn anyone with no firm ideological convictions into a Bolshevik. Which means that a work of art can very well accommodate a political alignment, and that even the most obnoxious attitude can be communicated if it is expressed through the medium of an outstanding work of art." Goebbels went on to sum up that the National Socialists' rise to power had brought about a turning point in

173

filmmaking: from then on "the only possible art is one which is rooted in the soil of National Socialism."[2]

Though Hitler wished to exploit the film industry for blatantly obvious propaganda purposes, Goebbels favored a more deviant method. Of the estimated 1,150 feature films produced during Hitler's regime, though they all were politically tainted, only about one in six were works of pure propaganda. Movies made during the Third Reich avoided a realistic portrayal of everyday life: the National Socialist salute, for instance—part and parcel of the regime's grand-scale events and a sign of praise and submission on the part of spectators—never appeared in feature films. The aim was to manipulate people without being shown the direction in which they were being led.[3] In the following section are just a few examples of the themes used in what has been described as the cinema's darkest hour.

SHAPING PUBLIC OPINION: THE SILVER SCREEN AS PROPAGANDA TOOL

The following is a sampling of some of the many films created to emotionally shape public opinion in the guise of entertainment.

The film *Refugees* (1933) relates how a group of Volga German refugees persecuted by the Bolsheviks is rescued by a blond, athletic leader-stereotype who passionately devotes himself to the "true Germany." This quarrelling group of people who wish to return to the "fatherland" eventually form a united community through the strength and authority of the leader.[4]

Operation Michael (1937) glorifies the deeds of a father-figure World War I general who strongly brings to mind Paul von Hindenburg. The story underlines death and sacrifice and manages to avoid reminding the viewer that Germany actually lost World War I.[5]

DIII 88 (1939) demonstrates the "spirit of front-line pilots in WWI" as a model and inspiration for Goering's Luftwaffe. The hero's sacrifice for his comrades and country in the line of duty would "never be forgotten" and his "spirit would live on in hundreds, in thousands of men."[6]

Shown in the United States as *Our Flag Leads Us Forward*, *Hitlerjunge Quex* (1933) tells the story of a poor boy raised in a communist environment who dreams of joining the Hitler Youth. Goebbels reflected on the film as follows: "If *Hitlerjunge Quex* represents the first large-scale attempt to depict the ideas and world of National Socialism with the art of cinema, then one must say that this attempt, given the possibilities of modern technology, is a full-fledged success." By January 1934, it had been viewed by a million spectators.[7]

Pour le Mérite (1938) endorses Germany's illegal rearmament and portrays the former Weimar Republic as a democratic quagmire in which no decent person could survive.[8]

Erbkrank (The Hereditary Defective) (1936) was one of six movies produced from 1935 to 1937 by the National Socialist Office of Racial Policy to demonize people in Germany diagnosed with mental illness and mental retardation. The goal was to win public support for the T4 euthanasia program, which was then in the works. This film, as well as the others, included original footage of patients in German psychiatric wards. Adolf Hitler reportedly liked the film so much that he encouraged the production of the full-length film *Victims of the Past: The Sin against Blood and Race* (1937).[9]

Inflammatory antisemitic films produced by the Third Reich's exclusionary regime were intended to justify actions such as the escalating persecution and vilification of the Jewish population, their obligation to identify themselves by displaying the yellow star, and the open attack on synagogues and Jewish businesses in 1938.[10]

Robert and Bertram (1939) is a musical farce and the first major National Socialist antisemitic film. It relates the tale of two nineteenth-century vagabonds who rob a Jewish banker and his friend to help a girl being forced to marry another Jew. Jews are portrayed here as clumsy, dull, greedy, and lecherous.

Linen from Ireland (1939) "demonstrates" how Jewish textile company owners are sabotaging the German linen industry by buying linen from Ireland instead of having it produced in "the fatherland." The film also attacks Britain, with whom Germany was at war by the time of the film's release.

The Rothschilds (1940) portrays the role of the Rothschild family during the Napoleonic wars. The plot revolves around the financial scheming of the Jewish banking family, which is depicted as making use of its "international" business connections to successfully speculate on the outcome of the Napoleonic Battle of Waterloo. In the end, the Rothschilds gain power and influence in England among the ruling "plutocrats."

Jud Süss (Süss, the Jew) (1940) tells how Joseph "Süss" Oppenheimer, a court Jew in eighteenth-century Germany, corrupts a local prince while despoiling the land of its wealth. Made at the behest of Joseph Goebbels, *Jud Süss* is probably the most notorious and successful piece of antisemitic film propaganda produced in National Socialist Germany and was viewed by twenty million people.

Der Ewige Jude (The Eternal Jew) (1940) is a pseudodocumentary that includes Jews filmed in Poland. Its most scandalous sequences compare Jews to rats that transmit contagious disease, overcrowd the continent, and horde precious resources. In one scene, "typical Eastern" Polish Jews have their beards shaved off to "unmask" them as looking identical to "Western-looking" Jews such as those living in Germany. The film ends with Hitler's infamous January 30, 1939, "prophesy" speech in which he foresees, "If international Jewish financiers inside and outside Europe should succeed in plunging the nations once more into a world war, then the result will not be . . . the victory of Jewry but the annihilation of the Jewish race in Europe."

The reason for the invasion of Poland and the war in general is "explained" in *Feinde* (Enemies) (1940), in which the prologue states

> Humanity will never forget the untold suffering of the German people in Poland, for whom the whole of the postwar period was a time of unceasing victimization. Deprived of their political rights, economically exploited, terrorized and dispossessed—this was their fate of the years. Then in 1939 the British guarantee to Poland precipitated the Polish massacres. Tens of thousands of innocent Germans were deported under the threat of horrible torture. 60,000 were slaughtered like cattle.[11]

Heimkehr (Homecoming) (1941) tells the story about the return to the fatherland of a group of German-speaking people who have lived under the oppression and brutality of the Poles. This German minority would have been exterminated had Hitler not "come to the rescue" by creating an empire in which there was room for every German.[12]

Hitler's love-hate relationship with England can be followed step-by-step through films such as the World War I settings of *Ein Mann will nach Deutschland* (A Man Wants to go to Germany) (1934) and *Die Ritter von Deutsch-Ostafrika* (The Riders of German East Africa) (1934), both portraying the British—though the enemy—as a brave and chivalrous opponent. In a bid to ensure an alliance with Great Britain, *Der Höhere Befehl* (The Higher Command) (1935) highlights historical German-British relations.

Moving toward an antagonistic stance is the 1936 film *Verräter* (Traitor), exposing the British secret service as the main opponent of Germany's rearmament. A twist, however, is that the storyline makes a clear distinction between the British patriot who is spying on behalf of his country and his German counterparts who betray theirs. *Kitty und die Weltkonferenz* (Kitty and the World Conference) (1939) portrays a British envoy as master of every finesse in the political game—English were, after all, "Aryans" as well.

Both *Der Fuchs von Glenarvon* (The Fox of Glenarvon) (1940) and *Mein Leben für Irland* (My Life for Ireland) (1941) glorify the Irish struggle for freedom from British oppression. Anti-British propaganda grew harsher with *Ohm Krüger* (Uncle Krüger) (1941), which attempts to prove that "Britain is the brutal enemy of any kind of order or civilization." The 1943 movie *Germanin* takes place in Africa and aims at showing the British colonialists as arrogant and ruthless and, ultimately, unfit for colonial power—as opposed to a German professor dedicated to providing the indigenous Africans with a wonder drug (Germanin) to cure sleeping sickness.[13]

Der Grosse König (The Great King) and *Die Entlassung* (The Dismissal), both released in 1942, portray historic leaders of the German people: Frederick the Great and Otto von Bismarck, respectively. According to the actor Emil Jannings, who played Bismarck, both these great figureheads were projections of Hitler: "In fact these three names [Hitler being the third] represent the same historical situation—one man against the world."[14]

Commissioned by Goebbels as early as 1943, one of the last films of the Third Reich, *Kolberg*, was released in 1945. It was intended as a war-glorifying propaganda piece to bolster the will of the German population to resist the Allies. It tells the story of the defense of the besieged fortress town of Kolberg, Pomerania, against French troops between April and July 1807, during the Napoleonic Wars. The speeches in the film are in part verbatim quotations from statements made by Goebbels and other propagandists at *Volkssturm* (Germany's last-ditch civilian army) rallies held while the movie was being shot.[15]

MISREPRESENTING WORLD WAR II

Right from the outset, Hitler propagated the notion that Germany was besieged by countless adversaries and that the German people were destined to engage in an unceasing struggle against those who sought to deny the nation its rightful *Lebensraum* or "living space." An exemplary instance of Third Reich war propaganda was the content showcased in the war newsreel compendium *Sieg im Westen* (Victory in the West) (1941), which was produced by the German Army High Command rather than Goebbels's Ministry of Propaganda. The depicted battle is fraught with challenges, as Germany's foes are portrayed as being "antipeace," thereby necessitating their complete annihilation. The film is organized to convey a range of themes from the regime's perspective, and the prologue underscores the NS account of European history and the genesis of World War II.

First, the film touts the "strategic planning and daring of the operation" with the aid of animated maps aimed at praising the leadership's genius. The second aim is to portray the superiority of German weaponry, with a strong focus on tank warfare. This is achieved with depictions of the *Blitzkrieg* in the Low Countries and France (May 10–June 22, 1940). The third theme is a spotlight on the valor of the unknown men of the assault battalions. The film's underlying message, however, is to reveal "the values for which [Germany] is fighting today: *Führer*, People, Nation." Its ultimate aim was to convince the German people, as well as the rest of the world, of Germany's superiority in arms and in overall war strategy. Though actual footage was used in the making of the film, including of French prisoners of war,[16] the blood-and-grit reality of war was never shown. That heavy fighting implies human casualties—soldiers either killed or wounded in action (and returning home as invalids)—was something the audience was not supposed to become aware of.[17]

From 1940 on, Goebbels personally supervised the production of the newsreels that made ingenious use of music and editing for propaganda purposes. At the beginning of the war, newsreels averaged eleven minutes in length, but due to their popularity and the success they had in achieving the desired manipulative effect, their length soon increased to thirty-three minutes. These newsreels were distributed to thirty-four countries in a total of twenty-nine languages and attracted a weekly audience of twenty million. Incorporating footage from the front, the newsreels' impact was such that the spectators were not given the opportunity to ask questions about the truths that were being systematically suppressed. As German defeats increased, the newsreel reports were systematically delayed: though the Allies were already on German soil, newsreel maps still showed foreign place names.[18]

Following September 1, 1939, the NS regime deemed that German culture should primarily serve the various branches of the war effort. This was to occur within the context of a dynamic interplay among the events of the war, the collective mood of the people, and the propaganda efforts of Joseph Goebbels, who sought to maintain the fighting spirit of the population and to ensure compliance with the demands of the regime, even if it was only a superficial conformity.[19]

LENI RIEFENSTAHL SPOTLIGHTS THE "MESSIAH"

Hitler personally chose the title of the only documentary film in which he played the leading part: *Triumph of the Will* (*Triumph des Willens* in German). Filmed at the Nuremberg party rallies by Leni Riefenstahl in 1934, this 114-minute-long documentary aimed at portraying the *Führer* as a new Siegfried and his devotees as extras in a monumental Wagner opera, an anonymous populous mass totally subjugated to his control. In the prologue, Hitler's plane descends from the clouds like a "messiah" to the masses awaiting salvation.[20] The commentary enthusiastically announces, "On 5 September, 1934, twenty years after the outbreak of the World War, sixteen years after the beginning of the German suffering, nineteen months after the German rebirth, Adolf Hitler flew once again to Nuremberg to hold a military display over his stalwarts."

During the four days of the 1934 Nuremberg rallies, attended by over seven hundred thousand spectators, Riefenstahl reproduced excerpts of National Socialist leaders' speeches, interspersed with footage of massed SA and SS troops and public reaction. The film's dominant theme is the return of Germany as a great power, with Hitler as the leader who will restore glory to the nation. Riefenstahl's techniques—such as moving cameras, aerial photography, the use of long-focus lenses to create a distorted perspective, and her revolutionary approach to the use of music and cinematography—have earned *Triumph of the Will* recognition as one of the greatest propaganda films in history. Riefenstahl helped to stage the scenes, directing and rehearsing some of them at least fifty times. For this, Riefenstahl won several awards, not only in Germany but also in the United States, France, Sweden, and other countries. The film was popular in the Third Reich and has continued to influence films, documentaries, and commercials to this day.[21]

The National Socialist Party actually began producing propaganda films as early as 1927, six years before Hitler's escalation to power. The films focused on the Nuremberg party rallies and were given titles such as *A Symphony of the Will to Fight* (1927) and *The Nuremberg Rally of the NSDAP* (1929).

Leni Riefenstahl's first propaganda film, titled *Der Sieg des Glaubens* (The Victory of Faith) (1933), recounts the fifth party rally, which likewise took place in Nuremberg and was similar in style and content to her later *Triumph of the Will*. The film is of some historic interest because it shows Adolf Hitler and Ernst Röhm on close and intimate terms, before the latter was shot on Hitler's orders during the "Night of the Long Knives" on July 1, 1934. As Hitler then attempted to delete Röhm from German history, all known copies of the film were destroyed, and the picture was considered lost until a copy turned up in the 1980s in East Germany.

Tag der Freiheit: Unsere Wehrmacht (Day of Freedom: Our Armed Forces) (1935), the third documentary directed by Leni Riefenstahl, highlights the seventh party rally, again in Nuremberg, with a strong focus on the resurrected German military forces. The camera follows German soldiers in their early morning preparations in their tent town and then as they march singing to the vast parade grounds. There they stage a mock battle involving infantry, cavalry, aircraft, flak guns, and the first public appearance of Germany's new tank—in fact, prohibited by the Versailles Treaty—before Hitler and thousands of spectators. In addition to Hitler's appearances throughout the film, Goering, Hess, and Himmler also have their part to play. The film ends with a montage of NS flags to the tune of the *Deutschlandlied*, the national anthem, and a scene of German fighter planes flying overhead in a swastika formation.

The first documentary feature film of Olympic Games ever made was *Olympia* (1938), written, directed, and produced by Riefenstahl, who covered the 1936 Summer Olympics held in Berlin. The film was released in two parts: the first was called *Fest der Völker* (Festival of Nations) and the second *Die Götter des Stadions* (The Gods of the Stadium). Numerous advanced and groundbreaking filming techniques were employed that, later, became industry standards. These included novel camera angles, smash cuts, extreme close-ups, and setting up tracking shot rails within the bleachers. Riefenstahl placed cameras in numerous positions on the stadium field, as well as in the grandstands. She sent off automatic cameras under balloons with instructions on how to return the film and, for the first time ever, made use of an underwater camera, a sensational innovation at the time. The camera followed divers through the air and, as soon as they hit the water, the cameraman dived down with them, all the while changing focus and aperture.[22]

Though the techniques employed are still widely admired, the film remains controversial due to its political context. Nevertheless, *Olympia* features on many lists of the greatest films of all time. The British *Daily Telegraph* recognized the film as "even more technically dazzling" than *Triumph of the Will*,[23] and the *Times* described the film as "visually ravishing."[24]

Olympia won a number of prestigious awards but fell from grace, particularly in the United States, when in November 1938 news of the *Kristallnacht* pogrom against the Jews in Germany was announced to the world. At the time, Riefenstahl, who was touring the United States to promote her film, was immediately asked to leave the country.[25]

The Third Reich's Ministry of Public Enlightenment and Propaganda selectively chose film themes that the regime wanted to present to both an informed and a credulous audience, in a contrived manner. The ministry's cadre of experts in indoctrination and brainwashing strategically targeted German viewers with the promise of entertainment—a brief respite from everyday life—as a means of injecting both subliminal and often overt propaganda into the public's psyche and emotions. The totalitarian regime's exploitation of mass media serves as a stark reminder of the crucial importance of a nation's right to freedom of information, which the German people were denied during Hitler's twelve-year tenure in power.

NOTES

1. Erwin Leiser, *Nazi Cinema* (New York: Macmillan, 1974), 20.
2. Ibid., 10–11.
3. Ibid., 12.
4. Ibid., 29.
5. Ibid., 30–31.
6. Ibid., 32.

7. Eric Rentschler, *Ministry of Illusion: Nazi Cinema and Its Afterlife* (Cambridge, MA: Harvard University Press, 1996), 55–56.

8. Leiser, *Nazi Cinema*, 52.

9. Robert N. Proctor, *Racial Hygiene: Medicine under the Nazis* (Cambridge, MA: Harvard University Press), 358.

10. Leiser, *Nazi Cinema*, 75.

11. Ibid., 69.

12. Ibid.

13. Ibid., 95–103.

14. Ibid., 112.

15. Ibid., 122–23.

16. Bruce Allen Watson, *Exit Rommel: The Tunisian Campaign, 1942–43* (Mechanicsburg, PA: Stackpole Books, 2007), 166.

17. Leiser, *Nazi Cinema*, 57–59.

18. Ibid., 60–61.

19. Kater, *Culture in Nazi Germany*, 172.

20. Ibid., 25.

21. David B. Hinton, "'Triumph of the Will': Document or Artifice?," *Cinema Journal* 15 (1975), 48–57.

22. Erik Barnouw, *Documentary: A History of the Non-fiction Film* (Oxford: Oxford University Press, 1993), 108–109.

23. "Leni Riefenstahl (obituary)," *Daily Telegraph*, September 9, 2003.

24. "Leni Riefenstahl (obituary)," *Times* (London), September 10, 2003.

25. Frank Stern, "Screening Politics: Cinema and Intervention," *Georgetown Journal of International Affairs* 1, no. 2 (2000): 65–73.

Chapter 16

Volk ohne Raum and Other Justifications for War

Shortly after ascending to power, Hitler eliminated the majority of the traditional national holidays, and those that he retained were modified to suit his purposes. The long-standing Day of National Mourning, which paid tribute to fallen soldiers, was renamed Heroes' Day and ultimately transformed into a glorification of military might. Throughout Germany, the occasion was commemorated with parades, torchlit processions, and self-aggrandizing speeches. It was during these ceremonies that Hitler announced significant political decisions or events, such as the repudiation of the Versailles Treaty's restrictions on German armament, the German occupation of the Rhineland, or the annexation of Austria. During the war years, the once somber observance no longer honored the war dead but instead exalted military heroism.[1]

Hitler and Goebbels did not invent propaganda: the word itself was coined by the Catholic Church to describe its efforts to discredit Protestant teachings in the 1600s.[2] Over the years, almost every nation has used propaganda to unite its people in times of war. During World War I, for example, both sides disseminated propaganda, but the National Socialist regime was known to have implemented propaganda as a key element of government control even before Germany instigated World War II.

PREPPING THE GERMANS FOR CONFLICT

Following the National Socialist takeover in early 1933, rearmament became a crucial aim in German national policy. Hitler hoped to reach this goal without provoking preventive military intervention by France, Great Britain, or the nations on Germany's eastern borders: Poland and Czechoslovakia. The regime was also careful in not needlessly alarming the German population, already anxious about the prospects of their country going back to war. The specter of the previous world war, and the seven million German casualties resulting from that conflict, still haunted the German people. Throughout the 1930s, Hitler depicted Germany as a victimized nation, held in bondage by the chains of the 1919 Versailles Treaty and deprived of the right of national self-determination.[3]

In preparation for the invasion of Poland that would set in motion the Second World War, the NS regime launched an aggressive media campaign with the aim of gaining the German public's support for a war that few Germans desired.[4] The remilitarization of the Rhineland in 1936 and the bloodless takeover of Austria and the Czech lands in 1938 had taken place with neither a fight nor reprisals from the Allied Powers. Germany's National Socialist propaganda machine employed the press in a widescale "exposure" of alleged "Polish atrocities," citing actual or purported discrimination and violence suffered by Germans residing in Poland. Media went on to condemn the Poles for "warmongering" and "chauvinism" and criticized Great Britain for its pledge to come to Poland's aid in the event of an attack.[5]

In April 1938, in response to President Roosevelt's plea to Hitler that he refrain from attacking individual nations, the *Führer* presented himself as a man of peace whose only aim was to reverse the alleged injustices suffered by Germany due to the harsh sanctions of the Treaty of Versailles. He maintained that he was not attempting to start a war but merely to redress wrongs and defend Germany's national interest in the same way as Great Britain, France, or the United States implemented their own foreign policies. The problem in Europe, Hitler asserted, was not German aggression but the nation's encircle-ment by potential adversaries who opposed Hitler's reasonable revisions to the territorial provisions of the Versailles Treaty.[6]

A WAR ON ONLY ONE FRONT: THE MOLOTOV-RIBBENTROP PACT

Also known as the Hitler-Stalin Pact, the Molotov-Ribbentrop Pact was a nonaggression treaty signed between the Soviet Union and Nazi Germany on August 23, 1939. The treaty included a secret protocol that divided Eastern Europe into spheres of influence, with the Soviet Union gaining control of parts of Poland, Finland, Estonia, Latvia, and Lithuania and Germany gaining control of the rest.

The pact was named after Soviet Foreign Minister Vyacheslav Molotov and German Foreign Minister Joachim von Ribbentrop, who signed the treaty. The pact came as a surprise to many, as the Soviet Union and Germany were previously bitter rivals and had been on opposite sides during the Spanish Civil War. The pact was intended to buy time for the Soviet Union to prepare for a possible war with Germany and to prevent Germany from having to fight on two fronts if Germany invaded Poland as well as Western Europe.

THE POLISH "AGGRESSION"

Just days before Germany's invasion of Poland, the German press escalated Hitler's Polish defamation program with newspaper headlines such as "All Poland Is in a War Fever," "Terror by Poles [against ethnic Germans] Grows Day by Day," and "Poland Rejects Negotiations." A German newsreel on August 23, 1939, depicted ethnic German families fleeing their homes in Poland for the safety of German refugee camps and also "revealed" Poland's territorial ambitions toward Germany.

The perfidious trigger of World War II was the German ruse of staging a border incident that would make Germans—and the rest of the world—believe that Poland had attacked first. On the night of August 31, 1939, members of the SS, dressed in Polish military uniforms, "attacked" a German radio station at Gleiwitz in Silesia.[7] Along with over twenty similar incidents, the assault was manufactured by Germany as a casus belli to justify the invasion of Poland, which began the next morning.

In Hitler's announcement the next day, he did not mention the Gleiwitz radio tower incident but grouped all provocations staged by the SS as a purported Polish assault on Germany and informed Germans of his decision to send troops into Poland in response to the Polish "incursions" into the Reich. The press was told not to mention the term "war" but to report that German troops had beaten back Polish attacks, again stressing that Germany was the victim of aggression.[8] In fact, Hitler left the burden of actually "declaring war" to Poland's allies: on September 3, 1939, the German media was able to report that, "unprovoked," Great Britain and France had declared war on Germany.

Adolf Hitler viewed the invasion and devastation of Poland as the beginning of his merciless plan for geographical expansion in pursuit of "living space in the east." Poland served as a testing ground for National Socialist policies regarding race and population, where hundreds of thousands of Polish farmers were forcibly removed with the objective of establishing a German-style district, known as a *Reichsgau*, inhabited and cultivated by "ethnic German settlers."[9]

A WAR OF EXTERMINATION

The invasion force included SS mobile units, the *Einsatzgruppen* (task forces), that were given the mission of identifying, arresting, imprisoning, or killing teachers, journalists, and other members of Poland's intellectual class. Deemed to present a source of danger to German occupation, tens of thousands of Poles were murdered. The German press once again played up stories about new "Polish atrocities," reporting that tens of thousands of ethnic Germans had been killed by Poles. In September 1939 German newsreels showed ethnic German farms supposedly torched by Poles while columns of Polish Jews, according to the narrator, "incited a war of extermination against the German people." Recognizing the convincing power of photography as irrefutable proof, representatives of the German press encouraged foreign reporters to view and photograph the corpses of slaughtered ethnic Germans, all the while photographing and filming their colleagues.[10]

To sustain the rekindled and intensifying hostilities with neighboring countries at the start of the war, the NS regime unleashed an abundance of wartime propaganda. This propaganda aimed to portray Germany's actions as legitimate and defensible at every turn. One element was the rectification of injustices perpetrated against Germany by its adversaries, while another was the notion that Germany was acting exclusively in self-preservation. An important element used in National Socialist war propaganda was depicting adversaries as a "morally reprehensible, [an] evil enemy that aimed to destroy civilization, enslave Germans and other Europeans, and envelop the globe in its conspiratorial web." National Socialist propagandists portrayed "international Jewry" as directing Bolshevism and western plutocratic democracies (ruled by the wealthy few and aimed at attaining world domination).[11]

Such stereotypical depictions of a perceived enemy were common among right-wing politicians even prior to the Third Reich. However, they were now updated and upscaled by the National Socialists to describe "the Jew" as a warmonger, a progenitor of genocide, and a purportedly "deadly threat" to Germans. Eradicating the "Jewish enemy" became an objective inseparable from winning the war.[12]

CENSORED REPORTING

On the same day as Germany's invasion of Poland, the NS regime issued a special decree by which it became a criminal offence to listen to foreign radio broadcasts. During the Second World War, the radio became a far-reaching tool for the shaping of Germans' views and public support of the war. The same applied to the other belligerent powers: by 1939 some 250 million people worldwide were listening to the battleground of a war of words.[13] The British BBC, Radio Moscow, Radio Bari, and Radio Berlin built powerful transmitters to broadcast to large audiences in tens of languages. Though many of these stations—Radio Luxembourg in particular—were taken over by Germany in the course of its invasions, the BBC estimated that in 1944 as many as fifteen million Germans, at the risk of up to two years' imprisonment or even death, were tuning in to its broadcasts on a daily basis.[14]

During the war, in an effort to better influence and manipulate public opinion, Goebbels amalgamated Germany's various newsreel companies into one, the Deutsche Wochenschau (German Weekly Show). He personally oversaw each newsreel's editing so as to present the material in the manner best suited to gaining German—and world—sympathy for a "righteous and justified" war. The distribution of newsreels to movie theaters eventually grew to two thousand, while versions appeared in thirty-six languages.[15] Thanks to mobile cinema trucks, Germans living in rural areas were exposed to the weekly newsreels' content as well.[16]

Surprisingly, Hitler achieved his highest popularity during the first couple of years of World War II while Germany secured rapid military conquests. These victories against Germany's perceived attackers reinforced the myth of Hitler's invincibility and unbeatable military strategy. Propaganda images showed him dressed in a modest military tunic—a common soldier who, through his own merits, had risen to become one of the greatest warlords. This was the man who had raised Germany out of the humiliation imposed by the Treaty of Versailles, restored national pride and honor, and defended the *Volk* against its warmongering neighbors.[17] Newspapers, newsreels, and documentary-style films showcased the victorious German armed forces and columns of enemy prisoners of war and their destroyed armament, but nowhere were wounded or dead German soldiers to be seen.

However, it's also important to note that not all Germans supported the war, and there were certainly pockets of resistance and opposition to the NS regime and the decision to go to war. People with different political beliefs, Jews, and other minority groups were particularly targeted by the government and were not allowed to express their opinion.

A WAR ON TWO FRONTS

Barely two years after agreeing to Germany's nonaggression pact with the Soviet Union, Hitler rescinded the agreement and decided to attack Russia. The goal of this invasion was allegedly twofold: on the one hand, it was a fight against Communism and its spread across the globe; on the other, it was a means of "regaining" lost territory—a bid for more *Lebensraum*.

On June 22, 1941, at dawn on the shortest night of the year, a behemoth artillery barrage lined up along the Russian border, with some three million German soldiers about to invade the Soviet Union along a front of over one thousand miles. Backed up by an additional half million troops from Romania, among other German allied nations, they stormed into Russia at numerous points between Finland and the Black Sea with 3,600 tanks, 600,000 motorized vehicles, and 700,000 field guns. Assisted by well over one thousand aircraft, the assembled armed forces represented, at the time, the largest invasion force in history.

THE STRUGGLE AGAINST COMMUNISM

National Socialism viewed Communism as a major threat to its ideology and to the German nation. Hitler believed that Communism was a Jewish-led and Jewish-financed movement that aimed to destroy the traditional social and economic order in Germany and Europe. He saw Communism as a direct challenge to his own ideology of National Socialism, which emphasized the importance of the nation, race, and the state.

In practical terms, the National Socialists used their opposition to Communism as a pretext for the persecution of Jews, other minorities, and political opponents. They also used it as a justification for the invasion of the Soviet Union, with the idea of destroying the "Bolshevik menace" and creating additional *Lebensraum* for German people.

VOLK OHNE RAUM

In Hitler's view, the Aryan (hence German) race was superior to other races, and so seizing territory from "inferior" or less deserving peoples was justified. Following the loss of territory in the aftermath of World War I, Hitler launched the concept of *Ein Volk ohne Raum*—"a people without space" (or living space)—as a political slogan and an honorable objective for a crusade.

Already in the Middle Ages, the drawbacks of overpopulation in the German states resulted in an ongoing flow of Germanic peoples into Eastern Europe. By the twentieth century, however, German general opinion began to regard the eastern territories and their boundless natural resources as "wasted" on "racially inferior" peoples, such as Slavs and Jews. The danger of accepting the notion that Germans were, and had always been, superior to the peoples in the east was that they began viewing those lands as their

Figure 16.1. Propaganda poster: "Greater Germany: Yes!" *Bundesarchiv*

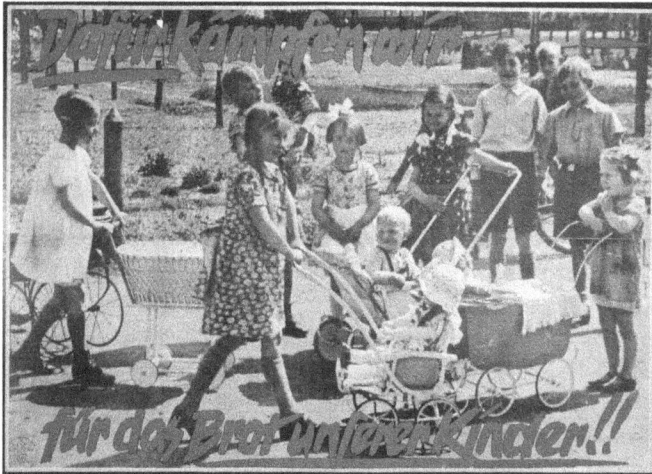

Figure 16.2. Propaganda poster: "This is what we are fighting for: to feed our children!" *Courtesy of USHMM*

birthright. An inaccurate historical view of the German role in the east during the ancient and medieval periods led expansionists to claim the importance of German "history" in Eastern Europe and to contend that these regions were actually lost German lands.[18]

During World War I, Germany achieved its goal of acquiring *Lebensraum* as far east as Minsk and established a military dictatorship set on exploiting and altering the landscape. The subsequent German defeat in the Great War brought about the loss of all its overseas colonies as well as the eastern military "kingdom" known as *Ober Ost*. Post–World War I Germans were still persuaded that their salvation awaited in the east. Hitler lamented that "the German people is today even less in a position than in the years of peace to feed itself from its own land and territory." In 1936, he excitedly alluded to the "incalculable raw materials" in the Urals, the "rich forests" of Siberia, and the "incalculable farmlands" of Ukraine.[19]

To the Germans, Eastern Europe was their "Manifest Destiny," and Hitler and his associates drew direct comparisons to the American expansion west. In the course of one of his famous "table talks," Hitler stated, "There's only one duty: to Germanize this country [Russia] by the immigration of Germans and to look upon the natives as Redskins."[20]

Hitler's intention was to seize and settle vast territories in Eastern Europe as a colony and a new breadbasket for the German people. National Socialist propaganda's justification of this takeover was based on the premise that Germanic culture had once dominated the eastern realm, and as a result, Germans were justified in reoccupying this eastern demesne in its entirety. In order to increase Germany's *Lebensraum* in the east, though, roughly thirty million Slavic inhabitants of those states would have to be starved to death.[21]

Years of consistent propaganda doubtlessly reshaped the average German citizen's opinion regarding the justification for war and possible territorial gain. Despite the bombardment of news reports and newsreels throughout the war years, Germans were not shown the suffering, mutilation, and death of their own soldiers: the war would claim the lives of 4.3 million members of the Wehrmacht.

Nor was the German public shown the barbaric scenes of mass murder of Eastern Europeans, be they Jews or non-Jews. In fact the majority of the German *Volk* was generally unaware of the crimes against humanity being carried out by their own relatives or of the genocide taking place in Poland, the Soviet Union, and other eastern states. In just a few years, the Third Reich was able to fully control the media and to remodel and distort the German people's *Weltanschauung*. The swift and total success of the Reich's propaganda campaign should give us pause and serve as a warning for us to form our political views and choose our governmental representatives with care.

NOTES

1. Spotts, *Hitler and the Power of Aesthetics*, 100.

2. Barbara Diggs-Brown, *Strategic Public Relations: An Audience-Focused Practice* (Belmont, CA: Wadsworth Cengage Learning, 2012), 48.

3. United States Holocaust Memorial Museum, "Deceiving the Public," Holocaust Encyclopedia, https://encyclopedia.ushmm.org/content/en/article/deceiving-the-public.

4. William L Shirer, *This Is Berlin: Radio Broadcasts from Nazi Germany* (Woodstock, NY: Overlook Press, 1999), 58–60.

5. Helmut Sündermann, *Tagesparolen: Deutsche Presseweisungen 1939–1945; Hitlers Propaganda und Kriegsführung* (Leoni am Starnberger See, Germany: Druffel-Verlag, 1973), 40.

6. Herf, *Jewish Enemy*, 48.

7. Alexander G. Hardy, *Hitler's Secret Weapon: The "Managed" Press and Propaganda Machine of Nazi Germany* (New York: Vantage Press, 1967), 123–34.

8. Gerhard L. Weinberg, *A World at Arms: A Global History of World War II* (Cambridge: Cambridge University Press, 1994), 33–49.

9. Permanent exhibit, Topography of Terror Documentation Centre, Berlin, December 7, 2022.

10. Luckert and Bachrach, *State of Deception*, 104–105.

11. Ibid., 101–103.

12. Ibid., 102.

13. Irving Settel, *A Pictorial History of Radio* (New York: Grosset & Dunlap, 1967), 30–31.

14. Eric A. Johnson, *Nazi Terror: The Gestapo, Jews and Ordinary Germans* (New York: Basic Books, 1999), 325, 566.

15. Kay Hoffmann, "'Nationalsozialistischer Realismus' und Film-Krieg: am Beispiel der 'Deutschen Wochenschau,'" in *Das Dritte Reich und der Film*, ed. Harro Segeberg (Munich: Wilhelm Fink, 2004), 162, 151–78.

16. Luckert and Bachrach, *State of Deception*, 111.

17. Ibid., 111–12.

18. United States Holocaust Memorial Museum, "Lebensraum," Holocaust Encyclopedia, https://encyclopedia.ushmm.org/content/en/article/lebensraum.

19. Ibid.

20. Ibid.

21. Ibid.

Chapter 17

One Crown for Two Empires

HITLER AND THE FIRST REICH

The National Socialists' widespread use of propaganda to gain approval and ensure compliance is familiar to us. Few are those, however, who realize that the terminology "Third Reich" as well as "Thousand-Year Reich" were effective elements of Hitler's bid for recognition as the builder of an empire, rather than merely the promoter of a political agenda.

THE ROMAN EMPIRE

The early Roman emperors saw it their duty to the gods to assume responsibility for the respect and propagation of pagan religion. However, beginning with the conversion to Christianity of Roman Emperor Constantine I, who ruled from 306 to 337, the majority of Roman emperors who followed both defended and expanded the Christian faith. To this effect, each emperor's role was to enforce doctrine, root out heresy, and uphold ecclesiastical unity.

After the death of Julius Nepos in 480 and the fall of the Roman Empire, the title "emperor" became defunct in Western Europe, which led the barbarian kingdoms to acknowledge the authority of the eastern emperor, at least nominally. Both the title and the relationship between the emperor and the church persevered in the Eastern Roman Empire throughout the medieval period, and the ecumenical councils of the fifth to eighth centuries were convened by the eastern Roman emperors.[1]

In 797, the Eastern emperor, Constantine VI, was deposed and replaced by his mother, Irene. The papacy, which up until this point had continued to recognize the rulers in Constantinople as Roman emperors, regarded the imperial throne as vacant since, in their opinion, a woman could not rule the empire.[2]

CHARLEMAGNE'S LEGACY

For this reason, Charlemagne was crowned emperor of the Romans (*Imperator Romanorum*) by Pope Leo III as the successor of Constantine VI. Thus began the long history of the Holy Roman Empire on Christmas Day of the year 800, a symbolic and convenient date to be remembered throughout the centuries to come. The new empire was named after the defunct Roman Empire in a medieval notion of *translatio imperii* (transfer of rule), which invests supreme power in a single ruler. The act was also considered a *renovatio Romanorum imperii* (renewal of the Roman Empire), a revival of the Western Roman Empire.

By the time Charlemagne received this great honor, he had become king of the Franks and the Lombards and conquered vast parts of Western and Central Europe as well as Northern Italy. By the power of the sword, Charlemagne, also known as emperor of the west, united a number of peoples within his vast empire—notably, the Saxons and Bavarians—but at the same time he rooted out paganism throughout his territories. He also expanded a reform program of the church that helped to strengthen its power, advance the skills and moral quality of the clergy, standardize liturgical practices, and improve the basic tenets of faith and morals.

Disappointingly, Charlemagne's three grandsons split his Europe-wide "Carolingian" empire into three realm that came to be known as West, Middle, and East Francia (Francia = land of the Franks). East Francia was first ruled by a member of Charlemagne's bloodline, but eventually, the lords of East Francia—namely, Saxon, Franconian, Bavarian, and Swabian nobles—no longer followed the tradition of electing someone from the Carolingian dynasty as a king to rule over them: on November 10, 911, they elected one of their own as the new king.

Among this early line of German rulers, a certain Otto won a decisive victory over the Magyars in the Battle of Lechfeld, and in 951 he came to the aid of Adelaide, the widowed queen of Italy, defeating her enemies. He then married her and, by so doing, took control of Italy. As a result, Otto I was crowned German-Roman Emperor by the pope in 962, and from then on, the affairs of the German kingdom became closely intertwined with those of Italy and the papacy. Otto's coronation as emperor resulted in designating German kings as successors to the former empire of Charlemagne and is considered the official beginning of the First German Reich.

THE HOLY ROMAN EMPIRE OF THE GERMAN NATION

The term *sacrum* (i.e., "holy" in the sense of "consecrated"), in connection with the medieval Roman Empire, was used from 1157 on, during the reign of Frederick I "Barbarossa." The term was added to reflect Frederick's ambition to dominate Italy and the papacy. Later, in a decree following the 1512 Diet of Cologne, the name was officially changed to Holy Roman Empire of the German Nation (in German, *Heiliges Römisches Reich Deutscher Nation*).

In the last centuries of the Holy Roman Empire, its territories resembled a piecemeal union of territories, with the Kingdom of Germany at its center and surrounded by its other components, such as the Kingdom of Italy and the Kingdom of Burgundy. For much of its history, the Holy Roman Empire consisted of a vast patchwork of hundreds of entities of varying sizes that included principalities, duchies, counties, free imperial cities, and other domains.

The territories administered by the Holy Roman Empire in terms of present-day nations included Germany (except Southern Schleswig), Austria (except Burgenland), the Czech Republic, Switzerland and Liechtenstein, the Netherlands, Belgium, Luxembourg, and Slovenia (except Prekmurje), along with vast parts of eastern France (mainly Artois, Alsace, Franche-Comté, French Flanders, Savoy, and Lorraine), northern Italy (principally Lombardy, Piedmont, Emilia-Romagna, Tuscany, Trentino, and South Tyrol), and western Poland (predominantly Silesia, Pomerania, and Neumark).

By the Golden Bull edict of 1356, the Holy Roman Empire's electoral council was set at seven "princes" (three archbishops and four secular princes). This electoral system remained unchanged until 1648, when the settlement of the Thirty Years' War required the addition of a new elector to maintain the precarious balance between Protestant and Catholic factions in the empire. Yet another elector was added in 1690, and the entire college was reshuffled in 1803, a mere three years before the empire's dissolution.

WANDERING EMPERORS

A prospective emperor had first to be elected "King of the Romans." Following this selection, the king could theoretically claim the title of emperor only after being crowned by the pope. In many cases, this took several years as the king was often held up by other tasks: frequently, he first had to resolve conflicts in rebellious northern Italy, or found himself in a quarrel with the pope himself. Later emperors dispensed with the papal coronation altogether, being content with the styling "emperor-elect"; in fact, the last emperor to be crowned by a pope was Charles V in 1530.

The Holy Roman Emperors possessed no permanent capital city, and they traveled from town to town to administrate their far-reaching territories. In the late Middle Ages, Nuremberg ranked as the "most distinguished, best located city of the realm," and the town was thus chosen as the site of numerous imperial diets (meetings of the deliberative body of the Holy Roman Empire). In 1356 Emperor Charles IV designated Nuremberg as the town where every newly elected emperor was obliged to summon his first imperial diet. In this way, Nuremberg became one of the main centers of the empire, in addition to Frankfurt, where the kings were elected, and Aachen (Aix-la-Chapelle), where they were crowned.

Most of the emperors paid numerous visits to Nuremberg: Ludwig IV "the Bavarian" resided there seventy-four times and Charles IV fifty-two times. In 1423, Sigismund gave the very precious Imperial Regalia into the keeping of the city, a mark of exceptional trust. The Habsburgs Friedrich III and his son Maximilian I were the last emperors to reside for longer periods in the castle and city.

Their successor Charles V broke with the tradition of emperors holding their first imperial diet in Nuremberg. Because of epidemics raging in Nuremberg, he relocated his first imperial diet to Worms and did not visit Nuremberg until 1541, on his way to the Regensburg Diet. Nuremberg's acceptance of the Reformation in 1524 alienated the Protestant city from the Catholic emperors, and in 1663, after the Thirty Years' War, the imperial diet was relocated permanently to Regensburg.

Following Charlemagne's successors' rule (the Carolingian line), other ruling houses acquired the position, such as the Ottonians, Saliens, Hohenstaufens, the House of Luxembourg, the Bavarian Wittelsbachs, and the Austrian Habsburgs or the House of Habsburg-Lorraine. After 1438, the emperors were sourced solely from the house of Habsburg and Habsburg-Lorraine, with the brief exception of Charles VII, who was a Wittelsbach.

The gradual end of the Holy Roman Empire approached in several stages. The medieval idea of unifying all Christendom into a single political entity, of which the church and the empire were the leading institutions, began to lose its luster. The Swiss Confederation, which had already established near independence in 1499, as well as the Northern Netherlands, left the empire. The Peace of Westphalia in 1648, which ended the Thirty Years' War, gave the territories almost complete sovereignty. Eventually, the Holy Roman Empire weakened into a powerless entity, existing in name only.

The Habsburg emperors instead focused on consolidating their own estates in Austria and elsewhere. Throughout the eighteenth century, the Habsburgs became embroiled in various European conflicts, such as the War of the

Spanish Succession, the War of the Polish Succession, and the War of the Austrian Succession. Consequently, German dualism between Austria and Prussia dominated the empire's history after 1740.

The Holy Roman Empire formally went into dormancy on August 6, 1806, when the Holy Roman Emperor Francis II (from 1804, Emperor Francis I of Austria) abdicated following his military defeat by the French under Napoleon. Symbolically, the Holy Roman Empire was born with the crowning of Charlemagne as emperor of the Romans in the year 800 and expired one thousand years later in 1806. Hitler exploited the long-lived history of the Holy Roman Empire—the First Reich—as a propaganda catchphrase, not only claiming tenure of the "Third Reich" but touting another "Thousand-Year Reich" of Germanic power and glory.

For clarity's sake, the "Second Reich" was the German Empire or the Imperial State of Germany that existed from the unification of Germany in 1871 until the abdication of Emperor Wilhelm II in 1918 at the close of World War I.

THE PRICELESS IMPERIAL REGALIA: THE RIGHT TO RULE

The Imperial Regalia and imperial relics are of various origins and date from the eighth to the fourteenth centuries. They consisted of twenty-eight objects that were safeguarded in Nuremberg for 350 years, plus three items kept in Aachen, the city of the emperors' coronation. Components of this secular treasure, as well as religious relics, were used as props during the crowning of the Holy Roman Emperor and as a symbolic affirmation of both his worldly and "holy" authority. Until the fifteenth century, the Imperial Regalia enjoyed no firm depository and sometimes accompanied the emperor on his journeys through the empire. As conflicts often arose regarding the legitimacy of the rule, it was essential for the emperor to physically possess the regalia. Some repositories, such as imperial castles or well-guarded towns of reliable governance, were used on occasion until Emperor Sigismund honored Nuremberg by permanently entrusting the city with the imperial treasure.

The most significant symbols of worldly power were the tenth-century octagonal crown (supposedly commissioned by Otto I), the scepter, the orb, the imperial sword, and the so-called Sabre of Charlemagne. The most precious religious relic was undoubtedly the Holy Lance, allegedly the spear that the Roman soldier Longinus thrust into Jesus's side while he agonized on the cross. Other holy relics included St. Stephen's purse, a piece of the Crucifixion cross, a fragment of Jesus's manger, a scrap of the tablecloth of the Last Supper, and other artefacts associated with saints in Jesus's time and later. The third part of the Imperial Regalia consisted of the coronation robe and other richly decorated vestments worn during the emperor's coronation.

In medieval times, royal authority was closely associated with the concept of divine justification, *Gottesgnadentum*, the divine right of kings, or, so to speak, the right to rule by the grace of God. In this manner, the Imperial Regalia stood for the connection between secular and divine authority but, at the same time, represented an embodiment of that authority. The regalia guaranteed royal power greater than the emperor himself—even more than his blood and dynasty.[3] The medieval crown treasures in this collection are the only ones that have survived nearly unscathed over the centuries, thus lending them tremendous historical value and making them one of the most precious treasure collections in existence.

SYMBOLS OF DIVINE POWER

The imperial crown's unusual octagonal form mimics the characteristic shape of Aachen cathedral, Charlemagne's resting place, where between 936 and 1531 many German kings and queens were crowned, among them Holy Roman Emperors. This element contributes to making this crown so unique as, according to Christian numeric symbolism, the number eight stands for the concept of salvation, the process of humankind's redemption through the Christian God. The crown's very shape, therefore, is a reminder of its sacred connotations.[4] Historic baptistries, principally in Italy, are eight sided, clearly a symbol of salvation through the act of baptism.

The stone plates forming the sides of the crown follow a strict numerical pattern. The number of stones at the front and the rear of the crown each equal twelve. In all, the sides contain 120 precious stones and 240 pearls, both of which are multiples of twelve. In the Christian tradition, twelve is a sacred number as it stands for the twelve tribes of Israel and, naturally, for the twelve apostles. As a consequence, the number twelve also stands for the propagation of faith and the Christian church itself.[5]

Of the four enameled plates, three bear the images of Old Testament figureheads: King Solomon, King David, and King Hezekiah with the prophet Isaiah, thus lending the object even more symbolic weight through the additional context of the ancient world. Inscriptions held by these kings of old explain their connection with the king who bears this crown: they refer to God's grace, righteousness, wisdom, and long life.[6] It is safe to assume that this crown was unmistakably to be viewed not only as a secular symbol of power but as a holy artifact as well.

The symbol of the imperial orb follows a tradition that dates back to antiquity: the ball represents the earth and thus world domination. The cross atop the globe represents Christ as ruler of the cosmos—the emperor is his representative. The scepter has long been considered a symbol of earthly power among rulers, but in Greek antiquity, it was viewed more like a staff— a (shepherd's) staff is also a symbol of leadership.

The Holy Lance spearhead is inlaid with a long nail, allegedly one of the nails from Jesus Christ's cross. It was thought that this "lance of Longinus," supposedly used during the Crucifixion, was presented to Charlemagne by Pope Hadrian I. A golden cuff hides a break in the spear's blade and is inscribed with the words "Lance and Nail of the Lord." As the foremost of the imperial insignia, it ranked above the crown. The power of invincibility was ascribed to it, which was thought to have given Emperor Otto I his victory over the Hungarians and the Slavs.[7]

Another major component of the Imperial Regalia is the so-called Coronation Evangeliar, produced at Charlemagne's court in Aachen in 794. At his coronation, the new "king of the west," Charlemagne, swore the oath on this Gospel—his fingers touching the first pages of this book. This act alone lent both historic and symbolic value to this beautifully gold-bound Gospel manuscript, some of which was written in real gold.[8]

A COVETED TREASURE

During his eastward advance, Napoleon, one of history's greatest plunderers, was eager to secure the Holy Roman Empire's Imperial Regalia. When, in 1796, Napoleon's French troops crossed the Rhine, Nuremberg's Imperial Regalia was hurriedly relocated farther east in Regensburg and then expedited on to Vienna in 1800. Similarly, the three objects comprising the Imperial Regalia in Aachen were sent to Paderborn in 1794 and reunited with the remainder of the treasure in Vienna in 1801. The transferal to Vienna was entrusted to Regensburg's imperial envoy, Baron von Hugel, who promised to return the treasure to Nuremberg and Aachen, respectively, once the danger was over. After peace was restored, however, von Hugel took advantage of the confusion regarding the Imperial Regalia's rightful ownership and sold the entire collection to the Habsburg family.[9] Furious, both the city of Nuremberg and the town of Aachen demanded that the treasures be returned—all to no avail.

During the Second German Reich (1871–1918) or *Kaiserreich*, the Hohenzollern family, beginning with Emperor Wilhelm I, strove to lend the new empire historic weight as a linear succession to the "old empire." This *Wiederauferstehung des Reiches* (resurrection of the empire) was also symbolized in the depiction of the Holy Roman Empire's slightly modified crown incorporated in the coat of arms of the Second German Empire. A good example of the crown's use as a symbol is at the *Niederwalddenkmal* near Rüdesheim overlooking the Rhine River. The impressively large monument was erected by Bismarck to commemorate Germany's unification in 1871 as well as its victory in the Franco-Prussian war. It depicts an allegoric representation of Germany—a gigantic female Germania figure—clutching the unique and historic crown.[10]

THE THIRD REICH'S "LITTLE TREASURE CHEST"

With its medieval history as an imperial city of the Holy Roman Emperors, as well as home to numerous German artists such as Albrecht Dürer, Nuremberg was promoted by Adolf Hitler and National Socialist authorities as "the most German of German cities." For propaganda purposes, they also endeavored to showcase the *Führer* as the true keeper and heroic reformer of the ancient Holy Roman Empire of the German Nation. No sooner had Hitler annexed Austria in March 1938 than the Imperial Regalia was repatriated from its Viennese stronghold back to Nuremberg.

The transfer by armored train was carried out with much fanfare and theatrics as further proof of Hitler's promise to right the wrongs that Germany had suffered in its past. It is interesting to note that Austria did not agree to transfer or "return" the Imperial Regalia to Nuremberg but, instead, to hand the treasure over to Hitler, who in turn handed these historic objects over to the city of Nuremberg.[11] This detail confirms that, in the same way that Charlemagne attempted to emulate Julius Caesar when he was crowned Roman emperor in 800, Hitler sought to align himself in the tradition of outstanding historical figures such as Charlemagne and Otto I. More importantly, Hitler was seeking to inject the Third Reich with "historical" value, thanks to the restoration to Germany of the most important symbols of power of the First German Reich.[12]

It is not by chance that, as early as 1927, Hitler chose Nuremberg as the backdrop for the National Socialist party rallies. Following the "homecoming" of Nuremberg's Imperial Regalia in 1938, National Socialist propaganda monikered it "Germany's Little Treasure Chest." A solemn ceremony was staged at Nuremberg's Gothic St. Katherine's Church—the new repository of the Imperial Regalia—during which the treasure was "handed over" by Arthur Seyss-Inquart, the National Socialist governor of the German *Ostmark* (Austria's new designation).

In his speech, Austria's governor declared,

Austria has returned, the Reich has been founded anew. In these festive hours the *Führer* in his role as unifier of the Reich, has recovered the crown and royal treasures of the Holy Roman Empire from the palace in Vienna, to be placed under the protection of Greater Germany. Today I carry out the wishes of the *Führer*, who orders the return of the insignia, which are sacred to the German people and represent German imperial dignity, coming back to the city at the heart of the empire.

In return Hitler confirmed:

In no other German city is there as strong a connection between past and present of the Great German Reich with such symbolic unity and expression as in Nuremberg, the old and new imperial city. This city, which the old German Reich deemed fit to defend the Regalia behind its walls, has regained ownership of these symbols which testify to the power and strength of the old Reich. Today Nuremberg is the city of the Party Rallies, the manifestation of German power and greatness in a new German Reich.

As the event coincided with the party rallies, the return of the regalia was exploited as that year's rally theme. The party rally's brochure featured drawings of the crown, coronation robe, and two swords of the Imperial Regalia, as well as a text suggestive of the association of the old and the new Reich.[13]

A few months into World War II, the Imperial Regalia was packed into twenty crates and deposited in a former beer cellar, the tunnels of which led deep into the safety of the rock below Nuremberg's imperial castle, extending over nine hundred square meters (9,700 ft²). Coincidentally, the emperors' treasure was stored alongside two works by Nuremberg's Albrecht Dürer: a portrait of Charlemagne and one of Emperor Sigismund in the Holy Roman Emperor's coronation dress.[14]

At war's end, when the U.S. armed forces assumed control of Nuremberg, Captain J. C. Thomson, a fine arts and archives officer (one of the Monuments Men), was tasked with the responsibility of retrieving and cataloguing the artwork stowed away by the Third Reich administration. Working alongside Dr. Troche, the preservationist at Nuremberg's Germanic Museum, he soon discovered that the core items of the Imperial Regalia had disappeared, namely, the crown, scepter, orb, and ceremonial swords—symbols of the legitimatization of the Holy Roman Emperor. It was assumed that either the SS or an NS resistance group had spirited the historically significant treasure away.[15]

A few weeks later, U.S. headquarters in Frankfurt commissioned U.S. officer Walter Horn with the investigation into the disappearance of the artefacts. Two factors aided tremendously in the search: first of all, Walter Horn was born and raised in Germany and was thus a native speaker, and second, during the course of his art and history studies in Heidelberg and Berlin, it just so

Figure 17.1. Poster at the 1938 Nuremberg party rallies announcing the return of the First Reich's Imperial Regalia to Nuremberg

happened that Horn and Dr. Troche of Nuremberg's Germanic Museum had been fellow students and friends.[16]

After several weeks of investigation and the questioning of suspects, Walter Horn obtained a confession from one of the perpetrators, Nuremberg's air-raid shelter director. He, along with the mayor and a city engineer, had transferred the five missing objects to a different shelter in the old town, where they were concealed thirty-some meters (about 100 ft) below ground, behind two feet of brick and concrete.[17]

Despite all the efforts made by Nuremberg's administration to preserve the Imperial Regalia, the care of which the city had been entrusted with by the Holy Roman Empire for 350 years, it was decided that this treasure of extraordinary value—both monetarily and historically speaking—would not remain in "Germany's Little Treasure Chest." The Allied Control Board in Berlin conceded to the request of the new Austrian government to have the Imperial Regalia returned to Vienna. This decision followed the guidelines laid down for all objects of value retrieved by the Monuments Men: to return all cultural treasures to their respective prewar locations.[18]

Today, the near legendary collection known as the Imperial Regalia of the Holy Roman Empire, perhaps the most precious historical legacy in the world, is displayed at the Hofburg Palace's treasury in Vienna. Duplicates of the crown, orb, and scepter can be viewed at Nuremberg's Fembo Haus Museum.

NOTES

1. Jeffrey Richards, *The Popes and the Papacy in the Early Middle Ages, 476–752* (London: Routledge & Kegan Paul, 1979), 14–16.

2. James Bryce, *The Holy Roman Empire* (1878; London: Perlego, 2013), 62–64.

3. Reinhart Staats, *Die Reichskrone: Geschichte und Bedeutung eines europäischen Symbols* (Kiel, Germany: Ludwig, 2006), 49.

4. Heinz Meyer and Rudolf Suntrup, eds., *Lexikon der mittelalterlichen Zahlenbedeutungen* (Munich: Fink, 1987), 565.

5. Ibid., 620.

6. Rudolf Distelberger and Manfred Leithe-Jasper, *The Kunsthistorisches Museum Vienna: The Imperial and Ecclestiastical Treasury* (Munich: Beck, 2019), 49.

7. Ibid., 51.

8. Ibid., 55.

9. Sydney Kirkpatrick, *Hitler's Holy Relics* (New York: Simon & Schuster, 2011).

10. Dagmar Paulus, "From Charlemagne to Hitler: The Imperial Crown of the Holy Roman Empire and Its Symbolism," University College London, 2016, https://cpb-eu-w2.wpmucdn.com/blogs.bristol.ac.uk/dist/c/332/files/2016/01/Paulus-2017-From-Charlemagne-to-Hitler.pdf.

11. Peter Heigl, *The Imperial Regalia in the Nazi Bunker* (Nuremberg: Edition Mola-Mola, 2005), 39.

12. Ibid., 13–14.

13. Ibid.

14. Ibid., 45–46.

15. Ibid., 49.

16. Ibid.
17. Heigl, *Imperial Regalia in the Nazi Bunker*, 51.
18. Ibid., 63.

PART III

State of Terror

Chapter 18

Policing the Reich

FROM DEMOCRACY TO DICTATORSHIP

Following Hitler's appointment as chancellor on January 30, 1933, and just a few days after the Reichstag fire some weeks later, the National Socialists' paramilitary organizations—the SS and the SA—unleashed an extensive campaign of violence against the Communist Party and any left-wingers, trade unionists, the Social Democratic Party, and the Center Party. Thousands of Communists and Social Democrats were arrested and jailed. In March and April, some forty to fifty thousand political foes were taken into *Schutzhaft*, so-called protective custody. The SA and SS routinely publicly humiliated, beat up, and tortured political opponents, and they looted, vandalized, or destroyed left-wing parties' offices and property.[1]

Prior to the next elections on March 5, 1933, the National Socialist paramilitary organizations implemented terror, repression, and propaganda across the land and "monitored" the voting process. In Prussia, for example, Hermann Göring ordered some fifty thousand members of the SS, SA, and the *Stahlhelm* to monitor the votes. However, despite having waged a campaign of terror against their opponents, the National Socialists gleaned just under 44 percent of the votes. Two weeks after the election, Hitler succeeded in passing an Enabling Act, which effectively provided him with dictatorial powers.[2] Bemoaning the disastrous results of the Weimar Republic's multiparty government, Hitler's objective was to remove all political opposition and to create a one-party government.

By the end of May, approximately five hundred members of the municipal administration and seventy mayors were expelled from office, and violence spread to include nonleftist political figures as well. On June 26, Heinrich Himmler, the head of Bavaria's political police and the leader of the SS, gave orders to place all Reichstag (parliamentary) and state assembly representatives of the Bavarian People's Party in "protective custody." On July 14, 1933, Hitler's regime passed legislation to outlaw all political parties, other than the National Socialist Party, and to forbid the creation of any new political party. By this point, just months after Hitler's seizure of power, all of Germany's parties had either been shut down or ordered to dissolve themselves.[3]

THE TERROR APPARATUS

The National Socialists' terror apparatus comprised five individual organizations whose common denominator was the use of violence. First and foremost was the Schutzstaffel (protection squad), known as the SS, which formed the system's main pillar with regard to administration, personnel, and ideology. Second came the police, then the Reichsicherheitsdienst (Security Service of the Reichsführer-SS), also known as RSD or simply SD, followed by the concentration camp system and the department of justice.[4]

This flexible and coordinated machinery served varying purposes over the years and adapted itself to missions that can be categorized into three phases. In its first phase, the terror apparatus's principal aim was to ensure the regime's rule by eliminating political opponents. It also worked at transforming police organizations into an effective instrument of the state's authority and of Hitler's personal dictatorship.[5]

Having achieved its first aims by 1936–1937, the organizations' next mission was to ready the terror apparatus for going to war and to prepare the German *Volksgemeinschaft* to this effect. During the war itself, the terror apparatus experienced a widening of its field of operations and a multiplication of its functions. It now was tasked with securing the home front as well as occupied territories from sabotage, resistance activities, and disloyalty. As German troops advanced into Poland and the Soviet Union, the terror organizations carried out attacks on individuals and groups, with the aim of depopulating large areas for the subsequent relocation of German farmers.[6]

THE RAPID RISE OF THE SS

Actually a subdivision of the National Socialist Party, the SS was officially a registered association. It had begun with a small guard unit known as the *Saal-Schutz* (hall security) comprised of NS volunteers to ensure security for party meetings in Munich. Hitler wanted this small guard unit to remain separate from the "suspect mass" of the party, including its paramilitary Sturmabteilung (Storm Battalion), commonly known as the SA, which he did not trust.[7] In May 1923 the group was renamed *Stosstrupp* (shock troop), and in 1925, Heinrich Himmler joined the unit, which had by then been reformed and given its final name, Schutzstaffel. From 1929 to 1945, under Himmler's authority, the SS grew from a tiny paramilitary formation in the final years of the Weimar Republic to one of the most powerful organizations in Third Reich Germany.

The organization comprised two principal groups: the Allgemeine SS (General SS) and Waffen-SS (Armed SS). The Allgemeine SS was tasked with enforcing the National Socialists' racial program as well as general policing, whereas the Waffen-SS was made up of combat units within Germany's armed forces. A third constituent of the SS, was the SS-Totenkopfverbände (Death's Head Units),[8] which ran the concentration and extermination camps. Other subdivisions of the SS included the Gestapo (Secret State Police) and the Sicherheitsdienst (Security Service). These were in charge of detecting actual or potential enemies of the National Socialist state, the elimination of any opposition, monitoring the German people for their commitment to National Socialist precepts, and providing domestic and foreign intelligence.

The SS grew rapidly in size and power thanks to its sole loyalty to Hitler, as opposed to the SA, which was viewed as partly independent and a possible threat to Hitler's authority over the party.[9] Already by the end of 1933, the membership in the SS reached 209,000.[10] Under Himmler's authority, the SS organization continued to amass greater power as ever more state and party functions were allocated to its jurisdiction. Eventually, the SS became answerable only to the *Führer*, a development typical of the organizational structure of the entire NS regime, in which legal norms were supplanted by actions undertaken according to the *Führerprinzip* (leader's principle), the premises of which was that Hitler's will was above the law.[11]

Although Hitler wielded absolute authority, it was Heinrich Himmler who held the official responsibility for the regime's terror organizations. His ascent to power commenced with his designation as leader of the SS in 1929, followed by his appointment as commander of the Bavarian political police in 1933. In 1936, he ascended to the position of German chief of police, and subsequently to minister of the interior in 1943. As the overseer of all of the Third Reich's policing entities, Himmler was ultimately accountable as one of the principal architects of the regime's ruthless campaign of persecution and extermination targeting both Jews and non-Jews.

SS MEMBERS: QUALIFICATIONS AND TRAINING

The SS motto, "*Meine Ehre Heisst Treue*" (My honor is loyalty), was engraved on the men's dress daggers and on their uniform belt buckles. Each new member of the SS was sworn in with the following oath: "I vow to you, Adolf Hitler, as *Führer* and Chancellor of the German Reich, loyalty and bravery. I vow to you and to the leaders that you set for me absolute allegiance until death. So help me God."

Himmler envisioned the SS not only to serve as an elite military force but also to set an example as the embodiment of racial purity. Recruits were subject to strict physical requirements and genealogical investigation before acceptance. Enlistees in the Leibstandarte, Hitler's personal bodyguard unit, had to be between twenty-three and thirty-five years of age, be at least one meter, eighty centimeters (5'11") in height, and be of German blood and with no criminal record or history of alcoholism. The racial requirements for SS members were based on evidence of Aryan heritage dating back to 1800, for officers to 1750.

Contrary to the SA, which was part of the defense organizations, Himmler required members of the SS to fit the mold of northern Germanic features, an elite within a company of chosen men who incorporated the heroic "ideal." Viewed as an order of men of superior class backgrounds—emulating Germany's old aristocracy—the SS attracted many members for this reason. Those who joined were often military officers, freelancers who had lost their source of income due to the economic crisis, or members of the German nobility. SS members were expected to marry by a certain age; however, the prospective partner first had to be certified and approved as "racially pure and hereditarily healthy." SS members and their wives were required to break their confessional ties with the church and to adopt a National Socialist ideological worldview.[12]

An "ancestry cult" of the SS was not limited to the organization's own research into Germanic prehistory through a study group called *Ahnenerbe* (ancestral heritage) but also encompassed pseudoreligious rituals, consecrations, and the use of cult objects such as the "dagger of honor," the skull ring, and the *Julleuchte* (yule lantern). These activities and items were meant to create a substitute religion and new mystical rites for these men and, at the same time, lend the order a quasi-esoteric aura.[13] The *Julleuchte* was an object that played an important role in the process of adaptation from Christian to a nonreligious ritual. It was used primarily during *Julfest* (Yuletide celebration), which SS members held at the end of the year, in lieu of Christmas. Himmler gave all married SS men yule lanterns as gifts—each came with an accompanying certificate claiming it was a replica of a piece "from the early history of our people." In fact, these lanterns were an exact imitation of Swedish candleholders from around 1800.[14]

In an effort to professionalize their officers, the SS founded a leadership school in 1934; the first one was located in the Bavarian town of Bad Tölz, a second school in Braunschweig, and others were created soon after. Himmler employed experienced military veterans and skilled officers to build a training regimen that became the foundation for the Waffen-SS.[15] In 1937, Himmler rechristened the leadership schools Junker (pronounced "Younker") Schools in honor of the landowning *Junker* aristocracy that once dominated the Prussian military.

The schools aimed to train and mold the next generation of leadership within the SS: cadets were taught to become adaptable officers who could perform any task assigned to them, be it in a police role, at a concentration camp, as part of a fighting unit, or within the greater SS organization.[16] Personality coaching was emphasized, which meant that future SS leaders and officers were shaped, above all else, by a National Socialist *Weltanschauung*. Education at the Junker Schools was aimed at communicating a sense of racial superiority, creating a bond to other dependable like-minded men, ruthlessness, and a toughness that concurred with the value system of the SS. Throughout their training, cadets were continuously monitored for their "ideological reliability."[17]

Part of the SS members' worldview education consisted of learning about Nordic runes.[18] The jagged, lightning-bolt double *S* insignia of the SS was one of such runes called *Sig* drawn from Guido von List's Armanen Order. In ancient Norse and Germanic rune lore, the *Sig* rune signified the sun: its Elder Futhark reconstructed name was *sowilo*, "sun"; Younger Futhark name was *sól*, "sun"; and Anglo-Saxon Futhorc name was *sigel*, "sun" (Elder and Younger Futhark represent two forms of the old German/Norse alphabet, known as runes, and the Futhorc is the old English runic alphabet). Guido von List changed the name to mean "victory" (*Sieg* in German). In National Socialist Germany, *Sig* or the *Siegesrune* (rune of victory) was the most recognizable and widely used symbol after the swastika. The SS rune insignia with two oblique *Sig* runes was created in 1933 by the penniless graphic designer Walter Heck, who received two and a half Reichsmarks for the rights to this design.[19]

THE BROWNSHIRTS

Hitler founded the Sturmabteilung (Storm Detachment), also known as the SA, in Munich in 1921, drawing its initial membership from various thuggish individuals who had aligned themselves with the budding National Socialist

Figure 18.1. Ideological training: teaching ancient runes to SS members (1934). *Süddeutsche Zeitung*

movement. Many of the early recruits were former members of the *Freikorps* (a volunteer militia group), armed opportunistic factions, and ex-soldiers who had engaged in street battles with leftist groups in the nascent days of the Weimar Republic. Sporting brown uniforms, similar to the fashion of Mussolini's Fascist Blackshirts in Italy, the SA was charged with safeguarding party members at meetings, participating in National Socialist marches, and physically assaulting political adversaries.

Provisionally in disarray after the failure of Hitler's Munich Putsch in 1923, the SA was restructured in 1925 and rapidly resumed its violent activities, intimidating voters in national and local elections. From January 1931, it was led by Ernst Röhm, who embraced radical anticapitalist ideas and dreamed of turning the SA into Germany's main military force. Under Röhm, SA membership swelled with the ranks of the Great Depression's unemployed, growing to four hundred thousand by 1932 and possibly to two million—twenty times the size of Germany's legally authorized army—by the time Hitler came to power in 1933.[20]

In the early days of the National Socialist government, the SA engaged in unbridled street violence against those who opposed the National Socialists. However, it was regarded with suspicion by the regular army and influential industrialists, both groups whose support Hitler was striving to obtain. Despite Hitler's objections, Röhm persisted in advocating for a "second National Socialist revolution" of a socialist nature, and he sought to merge the regular army with the SA under his personal leadership. On June 30, 1934, a day later referred to as "the Night of the Long Knives," Hitler ordered the SS to carry out a "blood purge" of the SA leadership. Röhm and numerous SA leaders were summarily executed. In the wake of this event, the SA's strength significantly diminished, and it no longer played a major political role in the regime. From 1939 onward, the SA was relegated to training all able-bodied men for home guard units.[21]

THE FORCE OF THE POLICE

When Himmler was appointed *Reichsführer* SS and chief of the German police in 1936, the police, still formally organized as a federal entity, was assimilated into the Reich. Himmler held sway over the Reich's three police forces: Ordnungspolizei (Orpo), "regular police"; Sicherheitspolizei (Sipo), "security police"; and Sicherheitsdienst (SD), "security service."

In 1939 the Sipo and SD were merged to form the Reichssicherheitshauptamt (RSHA), Reich's Main Security Bureau.

When the National Socialists came to power, a good portion of the police force grew wary of the party's objectives. National Socialist protests and violence, particularly in the last years of the Weimar Republic, had been rebellious, and the police had carried out thorough and repeated investigations of both the National Socialists and the Communists. Despite the National Socialists' history of public agitation, Adolf Hitler professed his respect for law and order and promised to uphold traditional German values. The police and other conservatives looked forward to the widening of police power resulting from a strong centralized state, welcomed the end of factional politics, and agreed to end democracy.[22]

The NS regime lessened the workload and challenges that the police had faced during the Weimar Republic. By censoring the press, Hitler's regime shielded the police force from public disapproval. With the banning of the Communist Party, as well as other factions, street brawls had been eradicated. Police manpower was widely extended thanks to the integration of the National Socialists' paramilitary organizations as an auxiliary police force.

The new regime centralized and fully funded the police to better control criminal gangs and to ensure state security. The NS state increased staff and training and went about updating police equipment. The Third Reich's policies granted the police departments unprecedented liberties regarding arrests, incarceration, and the treatment of prisoners. Police officers could now take "preventive action," that is, make arrests without any evidence required for a conviction in court, and detainees had no recourse to legal representation.[23]

Through centralized authority and the assimilation of the SS and its organizations within the police departments' infrastructure, the NS leadership seized complete control of the once traditional police and transformed it into an instrument of state repression and, eventually, of genocide.[24]

GESTAPO: THE SECRET STATE POLICE

Though officially an organ of the Reich's Home Office or Department of the Interior, the Geheime Staatspolizei or Gestapo, created in April 1933, was a special agency that defined its own tasks and jurisdiction. The Gestapo served as an instrument of the *Führer*'s authority and, pledging unwavering loyalty to Hitler, carried out his orders regardless of what measures this would imply. It functioned as a normal police department as well, but often resorted to acts of terror.[25]

The Gestapo's ideological premise was to ensure the German people's "right to live," to maintain its population, and to further its existence. In practice, the organization did not attempt to monitor the entire German population but rather aimed at eliminating any political opposition and hunting down and liquidating racial minorities. To this effect, the Gestapo's two main tools were *Schutzhaft* and *Sonderbehandlung*.[26]

Schutzhaft (protective custody) was not unique to the Gestapo but was quickly adopted as their policy. Unlike the former definition of this type of confinement, by which the detained subject was to be granted protection, it was now the "people and the state" that were to be protected by imprisoning the inmate. In the beginning, protective custody was carried out in state prisons; later, however, the suspect was often interned in a concentration camp.

Sonderbehandlung (special treatment) was the code name for the administrative order to execute a prisoner. "Special treatment" was introduced and implemented against Poles by Reinhard Heydrich at the outset of the Polish campaign, in other words, during the first days of World War II. Eventually, the true meaning of *Sonderbehandlung* remained no longer a secret, so the term *Evakuierung* (evacuation) replaced it, especially in subsequent Jewish extermination operations.[27]

THE SD: TOP SECURITY

The ideological elite, according to Himmler and Heydrich, comprised of the best members from both the SS and the police force, constituted the branch known as the Sicherheitsdienst des Reichsführers-SS (Security Service of the Reich's SS Leader). This organization served as the intelligence-gathering agency for the SS and was responsible for safeguarding Hitler and other high-ranking officials. Prior to 1937, the activities of the SS and Gestapo overlapped, but they were subsequently clearly distinguished. One of the SD's primary duties was to examine international organizations and intellectual movements that were deemed adversarial, with the help of informants from all segments of society. During the war, the SD played a significant role in the elimination of Jews and other civilian groups residing in territories occupied by German forces.[28]

THE LEGAL SYSTEM

Under National Socialism, many of the freedoms enjoyed by Germans during the Weimar Republic were quickly curtailed. The party's grip on the legal system made it almost impossible to oppose the regime. Judges were compelled to pledge loyalty to Hitler and were expected to act solely in the interests of National Socialism. Lawyers were required to join the National Socialist Lawyers' Association, which subjected them to close scrutiny. The role of defense lawyers in criminal trials was significantly diminished, and standardized penalties for crimes were abolished, leaving it to local prosecutors to determine appropriate punishments for those found guilty. As an example, the number of capital crimes increased from three to forty-six. These measures reduced the number of criminal offenses by over fifty percent between 1933 and 1939. However, many convicts were not released at the end of their sentences but instead transferred to the growing number of concentration camps established by the SS.

Sondergerichte (special tribunals) were set up throughout the nation and were responsible for all offenses that fell under the provisions of the Reichstag Fire Decree or the laws regarding "acts of treachery." The main aim of these courts was to drastically shorten proceedings and to strengthen the prosecuting attorneys' powers. It was not possible to lodge an appeal against the decisions of these special tribunals. From 1938 on, any offense could legally be appointed to one of these courts. Four days after Germany's invasion of Poland a law was passed, the *Volksschädlingsverordnung* (ordinance on antisocial parasites), by which any offense, no matter how petty, could legally be punishable by death. During the war years, the number of "special courts" increased from twenty-six to seventy-four.[29]

The Reich's entire terror apparatus, from the police to the Gestapo, was also reinforced by a vast network of informants and collaborators, who were encouraged to report on their neighbors, friends, and even family members if they were suspected of opposing the regime. Overall, the policing organizations in Germany played a central role in the NS dictatorship's efforts to control and terrorize the population, and it eventually became a key tool in the Reich's campaign of genocide and ethnic cleansing during the Holocaust.

NOTES

1. United States Holocaust Memorial Museum, "Nazi Political Violence in 1933," Holocaust Encyclopedia, https://encyclopedia.ushmm.org/content/en/article/nazi-political-violence-in-1933.
2. Evans, *Coming of the Reich*, 317–39.
3. United States Holocaust Memorial Museum, "Nazi Political Violence in 1933."
4. Volker Dahm, "Der Terror- und Vernichtungsapparat," in Dahm, *Die Tödliche Utopie*, 322.
5. Ibid.
6. Ibid.
7. Chris McNab, *The SS, 1923–1945* (London: Amber Books, 2009), 14–16.
8. Ibid., 137.
9. Shelley Baranowski, *Nazi Empire: German Colonialism and Imperialism from Bismarck to Hitler* (Cambridge: Cambridge University Press, 2010), 196–97.
10. Christian Zentner and Friedemann Bedürftig, *The Encyclopedia of the Third Reich* (New York: Macmillan, 1991), 901.
11. Ibid., 903.
12. Dahm, "Der Terror- und Vernichtungsapparat," 279–80.
13. Ibid., 280.
14. Wulff E. Brebeck, Matthias Goldmann, and Kreismuseum Wewelsburg, *Endtime Warriors: Ideology and Terror of the SS* (Berlin: Deutscher Kunstverlag, 2015), 147.
15. Adrian Gilbert, *Waffen-SS: Hitler's Army at War* (New York: Da Capo Press, 2019), 21–22.
16. Adrian Weale, *Army of Evil: A History of the SS* (New York: New American Library, 2012), 206–207.
17. André Mineau, *SS Thinking and the Holocaust* (Amsterdam: Rodopi, 2011), 29.
18. Dahm, "Der Terror- und Vernichtungsapparat," 328.
19. "Norse Rune Symbols and the Third Reich," The Viking Rune, https://www.vikingrune.com/2009/07/norse-runic-third-reich-symbols/.
20. "SA: Nazi Organization," *Encyclopaedia Britannica*, July 15, 2020, https://www.britannica.com/topic/SA-Nazi-organization.
21. Ibid.
22. United States Holocaust Memorial Museum, "German Police in the Nazi State," Holocaust Encyclopedia, https://encyclopedia.ushmm.org/content/en/article/german-police-in-the-nazi-state.
23. Ibid.

24. Ibid.
25. Dahm, "Der Terror- und Vernichtungsapparat," 336–37.
26. Ibid.
27. Ibid., 338–39.
28. Ibid., 344–45.
29. Ibid., 360.

Chapter 19

Persecution ·

When discussing Hitler's leadership of Germany, our primary association tends to point to both war and the ignominious concentration camp system. History, however, shows us that concentration camps existed long before Hitler came to power and were not conceived in Germany. Perhaps the reason the stigma still remains today is that at no time in human history, apart from the former Soviet Union's less documented Gulag internment system, did a concentration camp network develop in such vast proportions.

THE DARK PAGES OF HISTORY: FORCED LABOR, PERSECUTION, DEPORTATION, AND GENOCIDE

Throughout history, humanity has witnessed numerous cases of minority groups being subjected to forced exile, massacre, or genocide. From the sacking of Carthage in 146 BCE by the Roman Empire to the Ottoman Empire, nineteenth-century America, seventeenth-century Ireland, and medieval Sicily, mass extermination has taken place in different parts of the world. The twentieth century saw numerous instances of persecution, forced deportation, and genocide on a global scale.

The National Socialist regime led by Hitler has been held responsible for the widespread use of slave labor, particularly within the concentration camp system in Germany and in occupied territories. However, the practice of forced labor is not limited to National Socialist Germany. The term "slave" originates from "Slav," a member of the Slavic people, and the Romans exploited Slavic captives as slaves in the slave markets. Following the invasion of Poland in 1939, the existing German concentration camp system grew dramatically with the influx of Slavic prisoners.

Slave labor has been a harsh reality since ancient times and prevalent across the world. Imperial powers have often forced it on minority groups, as seen in ancient Mesopotamia. Slavery was a major social institution in Egypt,

Greece, Rome, and China and was widely accepted by the religions of the time. The Byzantine Empire relied on forced labor for over a millennium as the backbone of its economic system in the Mediterranean.

From the 1400s, European ships transported enslaved Africans to Europe. The colonization of North and South America intensified the slave trade, with slaves being traded for manufactured goods in Africa and then sold to the colonists in the Americas, mainly for use in agriculture. The cycle continued with the return of tobacco, sugar, cotton, cocoa, and rum to Europe.[1] The American colonies relied entirely on the unpaid labor provided by slaves. In the twentieth century, Belgium, China, Cambodia, and the Soviet Union sanctioned the use of slave labor on occasion.

The term "concentration camp" was first used to refer to the *reconcentrados* set up by the Spanish military in Cuba during the Ten Years' War.[2] In 1896, General Valeriano Weyler of Spain initiated the first wave of the Spanish "Reconcentration Policy," sending thousands of Cubans to concentration camps. Rural populations were required to move to designated camps located in fortified towns, and those who did not comply within eight days were shot. There the housing conditions were untenable, food was scarce, and disease and famine soon swept through the camps. By 1898, one-third of Cuba's population had been forcibly interned, resulting in over four hundred thousand deaths.[3]

The use of concentration camps can also be seen in the "zones of protection" established by the United States during the U.S.-Philippine War[4] and by the British for the internment of Afrikaans-speaking Boers and Black Africans.[5] The Soviet Union's gulags and Maoist China's Laogai were responsible for the mistreatment, exploitation, and death of millions in the twentieth century.[6]

TYPES OF GERMAN CONCENTRATION CAMPS AND THE INSTITUTIONS OF THE HOLOCAUST

Though every camp that operated during the Third Reich could be held accountable for causing deaths, the general term "concentration camp" can be somewhat misleading and easily confused with other types of camps or institutions of internment, persecution, and murder.

In Germany a concentration camp was a place of imprisonment and punishment initially created to isolate and "reeducate" political opponents of the Reich. Eventually, these camps were used to take in so-called asocials, such as beggars, the "work-shy," and certain classifications of small-time or repeat criminals. Forced labor, harsh discipline, and breaking the will of the prisoners hallmarked such camps. Contrary to the general public's belief, Jews represented a minority of the detainees in the Germany-based camps until the last couple of years of the war. Though gas chambers were built at some concentration camps on German soil—especially during the war years—they were used principally for the murder of weakened inmates rather than for systematic extermination.[7]

The implementation of ghettos was, in fact, the first wide-scale method of "concentrating" or "herding together" Europe's Jewish community prior to their final expatriation to an undefined location (the Polish region of Lublin and the island of Madagascar were mentioned in some documents). The first ghettos were created in Polish cities, starting in 1939, and later Theresienstadt was established in Bohemia, while a series of temporary ghettos was set up in Hungary. Such ghettos served as centers of preselection of those victims that German officials either sent to forced labor camps or to be exterminated.[8]

Transit camps were large holding centers in countries other than the Soviet Union or Poland, in which Jews were already isolated in ghettos. These camps usually came under direct German administration, though the transit camp in Drancy, near Paris, was administrated by the local regime. It is note-worthy that, up until their occupation by German troops, Italy and Hungary refused to extradite their Jewish community, whereas some other countries willingly cooperated, such as Croatia (responsible for the deaths of tens of thousands at the Jasenovac Camp) and Romania (accountable for at least one hundred thousand deaths at makeshift ghettos and camps when they occupied the Transnistrian region of Ukraine).[9]

The genocide of the Jewish people did not begin in death camps. The large-scale murder of Jews, as well as of Red Army officers and Communist officials, took place through mass shootings carried out by the Einsatzgruppen (SS paramilitary death squads) in Lithuania, Latvia, Belarus, and Ukraine. By the end of 1941, these special task forces had decimated over one million people in the eastern territories—so many victims that the SS began to worry about the psychological repercussions these atrocities could have on their perpetrators. As a result, they introduced the implementation of systematic killing with specially equipped gas vans, as well as through the creation of death camps.[10]

Death camps, or extermination camps, were designed and operated specifi-cally for that purpose and were purposefully located in Poland, far from the German population. Four camps (Kulmhof, Belzec, Sobibor, and Treblinka) were established solely for the purpose of liquidating people—principally Polish Jews. Also located in Poland, Majdanek-Lublin functioned as both a forced labor and an extermination camp, and the already existing forced labor and transit camp of Auschwitz was expanded to serve as an extermination camp as well. Two more killing centers existed in the east: Maly Trostenets in Belarus and Sajmiste in Serbia. Janowska Camp in Ukraine was not equipped with gas chambers but was responsible for the extermination of between one and two hundred thousand Jews.[11]

Six euthanasia centers were created in Germany and one in Austria to annihilate Germans with disabilities, in which some seventy thousand non-Jewish men, women, and children also met their deaths. Parallel to the euthanasia program in the Reich, SS units targeted Polish mental institutions in 1941, simply shooting all the patients, and for the rest of the war implemented a euthanasia policy in hospitals and institutions throughout German-occupied lands.[12]

"PROTECTIVE CUSTODY" AND THE ESTABLISHMENT OF THE GERMAN CAMP SYSTEM

Although the majority of German voters had supported candidates from opposing parties, Hitler's National Socialists proceeded to target and arrest leaders and activists from these parties. With the support of SA, SS, and *Stahlhelm* members, the National Socialists used force to pursue and apprehend leading members of the Communist Party, the Social Democratic Party, trade union leaders, and left-wing intellectuals. By April 1933, approximately fifty thousand individuals had been arrested, and over one hundred thousand men and women were placed in protective custody that year alone. As state prisons became overcrowded, around eighty-five makeshift concentration camps were established nationwide to isolate and intimidate Hitler's political opponents.[13]

As the temporary concentration camps, housed in prisons, empty factories, schools, or military barracks, were overflowing, Heinrich Himmler—at the time, head of Bavaria's political police force—established a central concentration camp in a disused World War I ammunition factory. This first official camp, located a few kilometers outside of Dachau, a historic old town not far from Munich, opened its gates on March 22, 1933. Though the Dachau Concentration Camp officially fell under the jurisdiction of Bavarian state administration, its running operations in reality lay entirely in the hands of the SS. Himmler replaced the camp commander with a friend of his, Theodor Eicke, who later made an infamous name for himself in the camp system's extensive eastern expansion in German-occupied territories.[14]

Contrary to the south, the Prussian (northern German) concentration camps were established by the state government authorities and employed civilian directors responsible for the camps' administration and supply. Guard duty was allotted to the police force or members of the SS or the SA auxiliary police. Apart from Dachau, the main camps in Germany at that time were Oranienburg near Berlin, Kislau in the region of Baden, Moringen near

Hannover, Sachsenburg near the city of Chemnitz, and Columbia-Haus at Berlin-Tempelhof.[15]

On Hitler's forty-fifth birthday, April 20, 1934, Göring handed over directorship of the Prussian Gestapo to Heinrich Himmler. By so doing, Himmler succeeded in becoming the sole commander of the entire German political police force. In turn, he promoted Theodor Eicke to general inspector of concentration camps as well as head of the SS guard units. Now transferred to Berlin, Eicke was tasked with restructuring all the camps following the Dachau model. Over time, large numbers of political prisoners were released from the various camps. From fifty thousand in April 1933, the figure dropped to twenty-two thousand in October of the same year and nine thousand in April 1934. Most of the original makeshift or temporary camps were disbanded until only about three thousand detainees were still incarcerated in concentration camps at the end of 1934.[16]

ALTERING THE ENEMY STEREOTYPE

Though the concentration camps had been built supposedly to reeducate and reintegrate tens of thousands of German citizens, by mid-1935 the total number of inmates stood at a mere 4,700—only slightly above the all-time low figure of three thousand a few months before. Now that the Reich's political foes had been subdued through acts of terror and violence, Himmler and Heydrich issued directives to look for additional categories of prisoners.

As a first measure, the state police transferred detained Communist Party officials from the state prisons to concentration camps. In October 1935, Himmler brought the subject of Germany's "asocial" citizens to Hitler's attention. This was the first time the notion of "protecting" the *Volksgemeinschaft* (People's Community) through the internment of so-called *Volksschädlinge* (those harmful to the people) was introduced to the general public.[17] The term *Volksschädling* is a "pest" metaphor that was first used in various contexts at the beginning of the twentieth century. It gained usage as a term for people who were characterized as "harmful elements" because of their nonconformist behavior, usually with the intention to degrade them as vermin and to dehumanize them. From 1930 on, the term was also used for alleged traitors to the nation or to the "common good of the country."

The new "enemies" of the people were henceforth to include "degenerates" in mind or body, those living off of society as selfish "parasites," "subhumans" incapable of integrating into the community such as beggars, homeless, vagrants, "gypsies," prostitutes and pimps, alcoholics, homosexuals, and those who "avoided" a working job. These categories, among others, such as Jehovah's Witnesses, applied to an extremely eclectic grouping of citizens whose lifestyle or behavior deviated somewhat from the accepted social norm. However, the police force enjoyed every legal right to send anyone it considered to be unfit to remain in society to a concentration camp. Being "asocial" was viewed as a precursor to criminality, and from the police's perspective, incarceration was arguably a preventive measure in fighting crime. They regarded criminality not as a result of the perpetrator frequenting a criminal entourage but rather as a product of defective or criminal genes. Thus criminal "prevention" entailed the "eradication" of the "born" criminal and of "criminal clans."[18]

WOMEN IN THE CONCENTRATION CAMP SYSTEM

Right from the beginning in 1933, women were by no means spared persecution and camp imprisonment. Forerunners to the infamous Ravensbrück women's concentration camp, the Moringen women's "protective custody" camp and the Lichtenburg women's concentration camp, were instituted for female prisoners in the early years of the NS regime.[19] In 1938, 40 percent of the women detained at the Lichtenburg concentration camp were categorized as "antisocial preventive detention prisoners," and in May 1939, 974 women were transferred to Ravensbrück—among them 388 Jehovah's Witnesses. Over the following years, Ravensbrück became the largest women's concentration camp in the Reich with a total of some 120,000 women passing through its ominous gates, tens of thousands of whom did not survive.[20]

THE CONCENTRATION CAMPS IN THE PRESS

From the early beginnings, Dachau—as the first official state camp—was a focus of the press. National Socialist propaganda depicted the camp system as an institution where the prisoners lived in extremely humane conditions. Here they were to learn ethics and the value of work, as well as to be reeducated with the aim of learning how to better integrate into society. In many cases, however, the camp authorities sought to portray camp inmates as repulsive, degenerate individuals who were better removed from German society. National Socialist propaganda attempted to portray many inmates as human "bastards" who were racially "inferior," professional criminals, or enemies of the "people." An essential part of the camps' image was the publicizing of camp "tours" for German and foreign delegations. The aim of these tours was, first, to show off an orderly, clean, and modern establishment and, second, to convince the visitors of the racial or social "inferiority" of the prisoners.[21]

CAMP LIFE

The German concentration camp network became an integral part of National Socialist repression. Through it, the authorities could remove citizens' personal freedoms while evading legal procedures. The camps made use of barbaric torture practices and could liquidate the state's opponents practically without a trace. Himmler's Gestapo would not have been able to grow into the terror organization that it became without the camps' gruesome reputation. Upon arrival, in an effort to break their personalities, prisoners were immediately subjected to brutal ill-treatment and the threat of unspeakable forms of punishment, or even death, which loomed over the inmates throughout each and every day.[22]

The daily routine in most camps customarily began between 4:00 and 4:30 in the morning (in some camps one hour later in winter), when prisoners were awoken in their barracks. Inmates were allotted thirty to forty-five minutes to use the toilet, get dressed, make their beds, clean the barracks, and have breakfast. In many camps, toilet and washing facilities (where there was usually only dirty water and no soap or toilet paper) were shared by up to two thousand prisoners. Those who did not finish these tasks within the set time faced mistreatment. Prisoners then had to line up for the morning roll call on the *Appellplatz*, a routine registration of all prisoners in the camp (including those who had died in the night or those that were ill). Inmates were counted twice: any discrepancies resulted in a recount. Sometimes morning roll call could take hours, often in extreme weather conditions. Those that collapsed or who missed roll call faced beatings, torture, or execution.[23]

Following roll call, prisoners set off for work, usually on foot. The type of work varied from camp to camp but often consisted of factory work, road construction, or labor in stone quarries.

In later years, in many of the camps, with the aim of reducing the amount of time walking and increasing the amount of time working, lunch was brought to the prisoners' work places. Work typically finished at approximately five or six o'clock in the evening or at sundown in winter. Prisoners were then marched back to the camp to participate in the evening roll call. Those who had died during the day were also brought out to the roll call to be counted. This, again, could take hours in the event of inaccuracies. After the evening roll call was completed and the evening soup consumed, prisoners were sent back to their barracks, where they had "free time." Some prisoners used this period to barter between each other for additional food or to repair their clothing. Others, exhausted, simply retired to their beds.[24]

Upon arrival at most camps, prisoners were stripped of their own civilian clothing and made to wear a blue striped uniform, though this was not always the case. Men were issued a cap, trousers, and jacket, whereas women wore a dress or skirt with a jacket and a kerchief for their head. Some uniforms, especially those of higher-ranking prisoners such as *Kapos* included pockets. These were very useful for hiding extra rations or concealing handy luxuries such as cutlery. Footwear usually consisted of wooden or leather clogs. As socks were not supplied, many prisoners suffered sores from rubbing—a normally benign occurrence that could become very dangerous in the poor and unhygienic conditions of most of the camps.[25]

Prisoners' clothing was typically inadequate for the conditions in which they were expected to work and live. In general, uniforms displayed each prisoner's number, stitched onto the front left-hand side of the uniform, as well as a triangle to show the category of prisoner to which they had been classified. Jews wore two yellow triangles forming the Star of David, political prisoners wore red triangles, Roma and Sinti wore brown triangles (although they were also sometimes classed as "asocials," a category that was represented by black triangles), homosexuals wore pink triangles, and Jehovah's Witnesses wore purple triangles.[26]

Between 1933 and 1939, prisoners in concentration camps were provided with a simple breakfast consisting of bread or porridge, served with tea or ersatz coffee, in tin bowls and mugs. Lunch usually consisted of vegetable soup, occasionally accompanied by bread, and dinner might consist of more soup or, in some of the earlier camps, bread and cheese. However, after the outbreak of war in January 1940, the food rations for camp inmates were significantly reduced. Portion sizes were smaller, less nutritious, and provided only twice a day, resulting in an average daily intake of no more than 1,300 calories.[27]

CAMP SECURITY AND DISCIPLINARY MEASURES

For the training of its younger or new members, starting in 1934, the SS founded Leadership Schools in which experienced military veterans and qualified officers provided a training regimen that became the foundation for the Waffen-SS.[28] The schools' objective was to instruct and mold future generations of SS leaders, with cadets trained to carry out any task assigned to them, be it in the police force, guarding a concentration camp, on the battlefield, or in administration.[29] The intense SS training also instilled in the young men a sense of racial superiority, ruthlessness, and toughness in carrying out their duty: they swore utter loyalty and obedience to the *Führer* in the enforcement of the September 15, 1935, Law for the Protection of German Blood and German Honor.

Figure 19.1. Prisoners in the quarry at Flossenbürg Concentration Camp (1942). *Copyright Niederländisches Institut für Kriegdokumentation Courtesy of Flossenbürg Memorial*

Adjacent to the prototypical Dachau Camp was the garrison area, where SS leaders and guards received ideological indoctrination and were put through military drills. The fundamental precepts of the guards' training was hatred and intolerance of all political opponents of the Reich, as well as rabid racism and antisemitism. In the early years, the SS members of other camps attended Dachau's "school of violence."[30]

Camp detainees were not monitored and brutalized solely by members of the SS. Additionally, some inmates, called *Kapos* (also spelled *Capo*, from the Italian for "head" or "chief"), were assigned by the SS guards to supervise forced labor or carry out administrative tasks. This "prisoner self-administration" minimized costs by allowing camps to function with fewer SS personnel.

The camps were encircled by tall barriers, which consisted of high-voltage electric wires and barbed-wire fencing. A broad section leading up to the fence was designated as off-limits for prisoners. Anyone who breached this no-man's-land was at risk of being shot by the guards positioned in nearby watchtowers. Additionally, some camps were surrounded by a deep concrete moat. The unbearable living conditions in the camps drove many prisoners to despair and suicide. Some prisoners ran toward the fence, where they met their demise through gunfire or electrocution.

Most camps included a prison within the prison: a block of cells for the purpose of carrying out interrogation, punishment, and torture as well as to place prisoners in solitary confinement. Penal torture included being tied to a trestle and receiving around twenty-five blows with a heavy "bullwhip" or detention in a concrete cubicle in which, due to its narrow and confining space, the prisoner was forced to stand for up to seventy-two hours. The most sadistic form of punishment was the so-called pole hanging or medieval *strappado*, wherein the victim's hands were tied behind his back and he was suspended by a rope attached to the wrists, typically resulting in dislocated the victim's shoulders. Weights were sometimes added to the body to intensify the effect and increase the pain, or dogs were set on the unfortunate inmate to tear and pull at his legs.

TARGETING THE JEWS IN GERMANY

In the wake of Germany's defeat in World War I, the National Socialists, as well as other right-wing nationalist parties and organizations, spread the myth that Germany's internal enemies—Social Democrats, liberals, pacifists, and Jews—had "stabbed the country in the back" just as Germany was on the verge of military victory. A few years later, the Reich Federation of Jewish Front Soldiers called for an end to anti-Jewish propaganda and, through a poster campaign, reminded the nation that twelve thousand Jews died fighting in World War I. The month Hitler came to power (January 1933), there were an estimated 523,000 Jews living in Germany. With a total population of some sixty-seven million, Jews represented about 0.75 percent of the entire population. Foreseeing problems ahead, some thirty-seen thousand Jews emigrated that same year.[31]

Having slammed the door behind him on his native Austria seven years earlier at the age twenty-four, Adolf Hitler had arrived in Munich with a very different experience of Jewish presence and population percentages. At that time, the Jewish population in Munich was only eleven thousand, a large proportion of which had recently immigrated into Germany from the east due to numerous Russian pogroms against the Jews there.[32] Indeed, Munich's population approached six hundred thousand, some 1.8 percent of whom were Jews. The Austrian capital Hitler had left behind had a Jewish population of 175,000, or 8.6 percent of the city's population. The Vienna that Hitler had known for several years had elected an antisemitic mayor, Karl Lueger, whose charismatic leadership Hitler admired. The mayor's use of violence and fear to intimidate political opponents and Jews provided a model for the future *Führer*.[33]

Eighty percent of the Jews in Germany possessed German citizenship, the remainder Polish. For the most part, German Jews were well-integrated and widely accepted members of society. They held positions in government, education, and the medical and legal professions; many were farmers, property owners, jewelers, and shopkeepers.

The National Socialist Party's twenty-five-point program, published in Munich on February 24, 1920, stated in points four and five, "Only someone of German blood, regardless of faith, can be a citizen. Therefore, no Jew can be a citizen. Whoever is not a citizen shall be able to live only as a guest in Germany and must be subject to legislation for foreigners." However, in the latter years of Hitler's campaigning and prior to his appointment as German chancellor, he and his fellow NS agitators temporarily subdued their previously vehement accusation and vilification of the Jews. Once in power, the National Socialists' principal foes had been the party's political opponents. With that danger taken care of through banning, intimidation, and violence, the regime now turned its eyes once again toward the *Judenfrage*, the "Jewish question."

In September 1935, the passing of the Nuremberg "blood laws" put into effect the racial regulations of the NS Party's twenty-five-point program published fifteen years earlier. German Jews were now barred from Reich citizenship and prohibited from marrying or having sexual relations with persons of "German or related blood." Additional ordinances disenfranchised Jews and deprived them of most political rights.

These laws did not define a Jew as a person with specific religious beliefs but rather as anyone who had three or four Jewish grandparents, regardless of whether that individual identified himself or herself as a Jew or belonged to the Jewish religious community. Many Germans who had not practiced Judaism found themselves trapped in the jaws of the National Socialist monster: even those whose Jewish grandparents had converted to Christianity were still classified as Jews. The same laws were soon applied to other minority groups, such as "gypsies" or "African Germans" and their offspring.[34] Breaking these laws was punishable by incarceration in a prison or, more likely, a concentration camp.

In the wake of the National Socialists' seizure of power in 1933, as well as the 1935 Nuremberg Laws and the *Kristallnacht* pogroms of 1938, vast numbers of German and Austrian Jews abandoned their respective homelands. Of Germany's half million Jews, about 346,000 had emigrated by 1941, though many of them were later captured in German-occupied lands.[35] In 1938, Austria counted a Jewish population of about 192,000, the overwhelming majority living in Vienna, the capital, an important center of Jewish culture, Zionism, and education. Between 1938 and 1940, 117,000 Jews emigrated from Austria.[36]

From 1936 on, the main drive for filling Germany's concentration camps was twofold: first, to provide free labor for the Third Reich's monumental building projects, and second, to work in the armament industry. Apart from politically prominent Jewish persons, Jews were not interned in Germany's camps in any significant numbers until 1938. Percentage-wise, the Jewish population of Austria (4 percent) was five times that of the Jewish presence in Germany (less than 0.8 percent). Following Germany's annexation of Austria in March 1938, thousands of Austrian Jewish prisoners were transported to Germany's concentration camps to supply forced labor. The pogroms against Jews in both Germany and Austria in November of the same year resulted in transports of thousands more Jewish victims to the German and Austrian camps. Within the camp hierarchy, the Kapos (most often German criminals) formed the upper crust, and at the very bottom of the ladder, Jewish detainees received the worst treatment and the most abuse.

DISEASE, MEDICAL FACILITIES, AND MEDICAL EXPERIMENTS

Due to overcrowding, weather exposure, and malnutrition, disease could easily propagate in the camps. Countless were affected by or died of dysentery, tuberculosis, typhus, and phlegmon (cell tissue infection). The camp doctors barely intervened to help sick prisoners, and prisoners who were medical doctors were not allowed to work in the infirmary.[37] Essentially, the medical team was only present to help those who were likely to recover and return to work and to expedite the deaths of those whom they deemed would remain unfit for work.

Many camps conducted brutal experiments on human subjects, often resulting in fatalities, even on those who were healthy. The military officials were particularly interested in malaria treatments, biochemical and sulfanilamide experiments, as well as research for aeronautics and marine distress. Harmful experiments were also carried out to simulate the effects of high altitude, hypothermia, and seawater consumption.[38] Subjects were intentionally wounded and reinfected multiple times to test the efficacy of various drugs. Some experiments also focused on mass sterilization techniques, while others studied the treatment of hepatitis and other diseases. Additionally, prisoners classified as homosexual were forcefully sterilized or castrated.[39] Jews, Roma, and Sinti were often selected as test subjects for these inhumane and barbaric experiments, although there were exceptions to this pattern.

CAMP EXPANSION DURING THE WAR

Between 1933 and 1945, the camp system in Germany greatly expanded to include hundreds of annex camps or subcamps where prisoners were sent to work in factories—often connected to the armament industry—to repair bombed railroads and bridges, or to work on farms. As Germany invaded neighboring nations, Polish, Czech, Soviet, and other prisoners of war and civilian "undesirables" began to pour into the camps located in Germany, in many cases outnumbering the German inmates. In the course of Germany's occupation of extensive parts of Europe, ghettos for Jews and prisoner-of-war camps were established abroad. While mass extermination by shooting took place in the Soviet Union starting in the autumn of 1941, plans for the elimination of Europe's entire Jewish population were only discussed—not yet implemented—by the leadership of the Third Reich.[40]

HITLER'S EMIGRATION PLANS FOR THE JEWISH POPULATION

When referring to his plans for the Jews, Hitler frequently employed the German word *Vernichtung*, which can be understood as "destruction," "abolishment," or "extermination." Depending on the chronology and context, in some cases Hitler's schemes aimed to eliminate the Jews' capacity to control their destiny. Sometimes he referred to the abolishment of the presence of Jews in Germany (and eventually in Europe), and at other times he clearly spoke of the actual genocide of Jewish men, women, and children.

Some historians are of the opinion that up until mid-1941, Hitler's use of the term *Vernichtung* suggested the destruction of the European Jewish community through forced emigration, as the word was interchangeably employed with *Verbannung* (banishment) and *Entfernung* (removal). Starting from the autumn of 1941, however, Hitler's use of the word *Vernichtung* or even *Ausrottung* (extermination) unambiguously implied physical extermination. Even the term *Endlösung* (Final Solution) carried varying connotations to the NS leaders, depending on the time period. The historian Christian Gerlach insists that, up until Germany's invasion of the Soviet Union, the term *Endlösung* did not imply the immediate liquidation of the Jews.

The original goal of the National Socialist regime was to compel the Jewish community to relocate to Palestine, which was perceived as a distant and economically disadvantaged region under British control. Hitler viewed Palestine as an ideal destination due to his belief that the British would prevent the creation of a Jewish state there. To facilitate Jewish emigration, the National Socialist government signed the Haavara Agreement in August 1933 with the Anglo-Palestine Bank and the German Zionist Union. Around sixty thousand German Jews migrated to Palestine between 1933 and 1938, but at a high price as they were required to forfeit half of their assets to Germany. The program ultimately lost momentum, as most German Jews had no interest in relocating to the Middle East or adopting Zionism, and the program was unsuitable for poor or working-class Jews. In the late 1930s, the British terminated the initiative due to increasing Arab resistance.[41]

After Germany's annexation of Austria, seizure of the Sudetenland in 1938, and subsequent control over the "Czech Protectorate," the Third Reich gained vast territories and resources as well as more than 334,000 new Jewish residents, equivalent to around 60 percent of the Jewish population in Germany when Hitler acceded to power five years earlier. In an effort to stimulate their emigration, Jews were subjected to cruel treatment, and approximately forty thousand Austrian Jews managed to flee. Unfortunately, many Jews were unable to leave due to a lack of available destinations. Palestine was no longer a feasible option, and immigration quotas from the German Reich were stringently enforced in countries such as the United States, Canada, South Africa, Great Britain, and Australia. In July 1938, the League of Nations convened an emergency conference in Evian, France, bringing together representatives from twenty-five nations and various relief organizations. Despite these efforts, the conference failed, as no country, regardless of size, expressed a willingness to admit significant numbers of Jewish refugees.

The French colony of Madagascar continued to be viewed as a feasible option, and by 1939 Hjalmar Schacht, the president of the Reichsbank, devised a plan to deport the remaining Jewish population from the Reich, approximately six hundred thousand individuals, to the disease-ridden island. According to the malicious strategy, Germany would incur no expenses for the extradition, as Jewish assets would remain in the country and bolster the national economy. However, the scheme failed to materialize for two primary reasons: first, the transportation of such a large number of individuals would have to pass through hostile sea lanes, and second, there was a lack of support from Zionist organizations and the world Jewish community.

During the summer of 1940, after the inclusion of Polish Jews, among others, into the growing Reich, Reinhard Heydrich and Adolf Eichmann updated a report proposing the relocation of interned Jews, totaling about four million people, to a Jewish "reservation" on Madagascar. This strategy became an integral part of the genocidal "Final Solution to the Jewish Question," with Madagascar once again chosen as European Jews' final destination, transformed into a German protectorate governed by a German police governor. The island's swampy terrain and high prevalence of malaria would have made life exceedingly difficult for Europeans, and the combination of tropical diseases, police brutality, and scarce resources would most likely have resulted in the deaths of the Jewish settlers, effectively turning the area into a colossal death camp.[42]

NOTES

1. Kevin Bales and Becky Cornell, *Slavery Today* (Toronto: Groundwork Books, 2008), 27–28.

2. Andrea Pitzer, "Concentration Camps Existed Long before Auschwitz," *Smithsonian*, November 2, 2017, https://www.smithsonianmag.com/history/concentration -camps-existed-long-before-Auschwitz-180967049/.

3. Donald H. Dyal, *Historical Dictionary of the Spanish American War* (Westport, CT: Greenwood Press, 1996); G. J. A. O'Toole, *The Spanish War: An American Epic* (New York: W. W. Norton, 1984).

4. Sean Braswell, "The Concentration Camps of America's Forgotten War," OZY. com, August 22, 2017, http://www.ozy.com/flashback/the-concentration-camps-of -americas-forgotten-war/80333/.

5. André Wessels, *A Century of Postgraduate Anglo-Boer War (1899–1902) Studies* (Bloemfontein: Sun Press, 2010), 32.

6. Simon Sebag Montefiore, *Stalin: The Court of the Red Tsar* (London: Folio Society, 2003), 643; Jung Chang and Jon Halliday, *Mao: The Unknown Story* (New York: Anchor Books, 2005), 338.

7. Martin Winstone, *The Holocaust Sites of Europe: An Historical Guide* (London: I. B. Tauris, 2011), 3.

8. Ibid., 6.

9. Ibid., 4–5.

10. Ibid., 5.

11. Ibid., 4.

12. Ibid., 8–9.

13. Dahm, "Der Terror- und Vernichtungsapparat," 304–305.

14. Ibid., 305.

15. Ibid.

16. Ibid., 306.

17. Ibid., 311.

18. Ibid., 347.

19. Alyn Bessmann and Insa Eschebach, eds., *The Ravensbrück Women's Concentration Camp: History and Memory* (Berlin: Metropol, 2013), 24.

20. Ibid., 28.

21. *The Dachau Concentration Camp, 1933 to 1945* (Dachau: Comité International de Dachau, 2005), 65–66.

22. Ibid., 17.

23. Wiener Holocaust Library, "Daily Routines," The Holocaust Explained, https: //www.theholocaustexplained.org/the-camps/ss-concentration-camp-system/daily -routines/.

24. Ibid.

25. Ibid.

26. Ibid.

27. Ibid.

28. Gilbert, *Waffen-SS*, 21–22.

29. Weale, *Army of Evil*, 206–207.

30. *Dachau Concentration Camp*, 93.

31. Luckert and Bachrach, *State of Deception*.

32. Museum of Beit Hatfutsot, "The Jewish Community of Munich," Open Databases Project, n.d.

33. Aristotle Kallis, *Nazi Propaganda and the Second World War* (Basingstoke, UK: Palgrave Macmillan, 2005).

34. Unites States Holocaust Memorial Museum, "The Nuremberg Race Laws," Holocaust Encyclopedia, https://encyclopedia.ushmm.org/content/en/article/the-nuremberg-race-laws.

35. Dieter Pohl et al., "Rassenpolitik, Judenverfolgung, Völkermord," in Dahm, *Die Tödliche Utopie*, 376.

36. Unites States Holocaust Memorial Museum, "Austria," Holocaust Encyclopedia, https://encyclopedia.ushmm.org/content/en/article/austria.

37. *Dachau Concentration Camp*, 120.

38. Ibid., 182–85.

39. Günter Morsch and Astrid Ley, eds., *Sachsenhausen Concentration Camp 1936–1945: Events and Developments* (Berlin: Metropol, 2006).

40. Pohl et al., "Rassenpolitik, Judenverfolgung, Völkermord," 434.

41. Norman Naimark, *Fires of Hatred* (Cambridge, MA: Harvard University Press, 2001), 64–65.

42. Ibid., 44.

Chapter 20

Extermination

After the invasion of Poland, all Polish Jews and non-Jews over the age of twelve residing in the German-occupied regions of Poland designated as the "General Government" were compelled to undertake forced labor.[1] An estimated twelve million forced laborers, mainly from Eastern Europe, were employed in the armament sector in Germany during the war.[2] The German demand for slave labor escalated to the point that in a campaign called the *Heu-Aktion* (hay operation), children were sometimes abducted for work assignments. Over two thousand German corporations reaped the benefits of forced labor during the National Socialist regime, many of which are still globally recognizable brands today.[3]

A large number of Jews who did not manage to escape Austria in 1938 were expatriated to occupied Poland and to other destinations in German-occupied Eastern Europe such as Minsk, Riga, and Lodz, and to ghettos in the Lublin region of Poland. Most Jews sent to Minsk and Riga were shot by detachments of the paramilitary death squads known as *Einsatzgruppen* shortly after arrival. Others found themselves interned in the numerous forced labor camps or, worse yet, in extermination camps. Over fifteen thousand Viennese Jews were deported to Theresienstadt in Bohemia, and thousands more ended up in work camps in Germany.[4]

THE "JEWISH THREAT" OR THREATENING THE JEWS?

In response to what Hitler termed "propagandistic objections" regarding his party's antisemitism and mistreatment of the German Jewish population, he menaced the Jews in general with mass extermination if they stirred international criticism of Germany's efforts in claiming its justifiable domination over Europe: "I have very often been a prophet in my life and have mostly been laughed at," he declared. "I will again be a prophet today: If international Jewry in and outside of Europe should succeed in driving the peoples

232

once more into a World War, then the result will not be the Bolshevization of the earth and therewith the victory of the Jews, but it will mean the destruction of the Jewish race in Europe."[5]

FROM DEPORTATION TO EXTERMINATION

The invasion of the Soviet Union by Germany in June 1941 marked a significant change in policy regarding the Jewish populations of Europe. The invasion not only aimed to forcibly remove unwanted residents from areas that Hitler deemed part of Germany's *Lebensraum* in Poland, Ukraine, and Crimea but also resulted in the manifestation of mass extermination plans. Richard Heydrich was charged with either directing the Jews to the malarial swamps of Siberia or relocating them to the harsh Arctic regions of Russia. This malevolent agenda marked the transition from ethnic cleansing to systematic genocide.

INDOCTRINATING *EINSATZGRUPPEN*
AND ORDINARY SOLDIERS

The Commissar Order, passed down by Wilhelm Keitel, who was in charge of the Combined Armed Forces Supreme Command, directed the Wehrmacht to execute any Soviet political commissars captured among troops. These commissars were believed to be enforcing the ideology of "Judeo-Bolshevism" in the military and were seen as the "originators of barbaric, Asiatic methods of fighting." Years of National Socialist indoctrination had led soldiers, particularly their officers and commanders, to view the conflict as a racial one. The extensive propaganda campaign had convinced them that they were fighting against Jewish Bolshevism and World Jewry, and that their role was to protect the very existence of the German people.[6]

German advances were also hindered by enemy "partisan" units that were responsible for harassing German forces, sabotaging supply lines and communication networks, and gathering intelligence. Partisan fighters would often engage in guerrilla warfare, making sudden attacks on German forces and then disappearing back into the countryside. The partisans played an important role in disrupting German operations and were instrumental in helping the Soviet army push back the German advance. One of the Commissar Order campaign slogans was "The Jew is a partisan, and the partisan is the Jew."[7] The Jews were portrayed as a significant security threat and subjected to violence by both the SS and regular army personnel. This systematic killing of Jews not only impacted the rational thought but also the irrational beliefs of German soldiers fighting at the front, who justified such murders on the basis of the misguided conviction that Jews were saboteurs and hence an enemy of the fatherland.

National Socialist ideology comingled the Soviet brute and the Jewish fiend into a shared image of evil. Unlike the Germans' attacks on France or Great Britain, their invasion of Soviet lands was regarded as a war of survival against the threat of perceived international Bolshevism and an international Jewish conspiracy. In the soldiers' minds, this was mankind's opportunity and obligation to rid the world, once and for all, of the "Jewish-Bolshevik" demons. Wehrmacht soldiers were brainwashed into believing that the enemy encountered in the east was not a fellow soldier but an *Untermensch* (subhuman) and the source of all evil. A pamphlet distributed to the ordinary troops affirmed, "Anyone who has ever looked at the face of a red Commissar knows what the Bolsheviks are like. . . . We would insult the animals if we described these mostly Jewish men as beasts. They are the embodiment of the Satanic and insane hatred against the whole of noble humanity. The shape of these commissars reveals to us the rebellion of the *Untermenschen* against noble blood."[8]

The indoctrination was successful as the Wehrmacht alone can be held accountable directly or indirectly for the murder of between one and one and a half million victims.[9] Before an official decision was made to carry out the genocide of Europe's Jews, mass killings of Jews in Belorussia, Ukraine, Lithuania, and Galicia during the summer of 1941 set the stage for the acceptance of the industrialized and officially sanctioned extermination of Jews.[10]

In addition to the military forces, four SS units were formed to implement the Commissar Order. These units consisted of around six thousand personnel who were dispatched to follow the army into Russia, along with small groups of SS and police forces, which added up to a total of approximately twelve thousand men. The volunteers for these units were mainly drawn from lower-middle-class former Free Corps or SA members who were subjected to intense ideological indoctrination by the SS with the purpose of reinforcing their already existing biases against Slavs and Jews. The primary targets of these task forces were the communist intelligentsia and Jewish leadership, but they often killed any Jews they encountered, leading to the indiscriminate killing of both men and women as well as children. As a result, the number of victims increased significantly, with one brigade alone responsible for the murder of around twenty-five thousand Jews within a month.[11]

By December 1941, Hitler decided to once and for all "deal with the Jewish question" and gave Himmler and his Stormtroopers the green light to liquidate the Jews. Goebbels reviewed Hitler's orders as follows:

As far as the Jewish question is concerned, the *Führer* has decided to clear the table of the matter. He had prophesied to the Jews that if they once again bring about a world war, they would experience their destruction. Those were no mere phrases. World war has come, the destruction of the Jews is the necessary consequence. This question should be looked at without any sentimentality. We are not here to take pity on the Jews, but only to have sympathy for the German people. If the German people has again sacrificed in the Eastern campaign at present 160,000 dead, so the originator of this bloody conflict should have to pay with their lives for it.[12]

The statement in question likely pertains to the pivotal decision to implement the systematic annihilation of Jews and other minority groups during World War II, which is now recognized as the Holocaust or the Shoah. The war in Europe served as a pretext for the genocide, enabling the National Socialists to carry out their strategy of mass murder, which included the extermination of Jews, Gypsies, Poles, and other Slavic peoples as well as people with disabilities or chronic illnesses. On January 20, 1942, the director of the Reich Security Main Office, Richard Heydrich, hosted a meeting at a villa on Lake Wannsee near Berlin to ensure cooperation among various government departments in executing the Final Solution, which involved exterminating Europe's Jews through industrialized methods like gassing, forced labor, and starvation. During this meeting, state officials were made aware of the systematic plan for carrying out the genocide.[13]

The Wannsee Conference, a seminal moment in the history of the Holocaust, highlights the distinction between the Jewish Holocaust and other instances of persecution, ethnic cleansing, or genocide throughout history. History has showcased multiple examples of persecution, exploitation, expropriation, internment, pogroms, or extermination, which usually resulted from an outburst of hatred against a minority and an escalation of group violence such as the genocide of the Armenians in the late 1800s and early twentieth century or that of the Herero and Namaqua people in South West Africa in 1904–1908.[14]

The Holocaust exposed the National Socialist regime's systematic, industrialized, and highly efficient plan for carrying out the premeditated murder of millions of people. Unlike other cases of ethnic cleansing, the NS genocide was based on the creation of a fictitious "antirace" of "infectious" Jews through propaganda. The German population was encouraged to yearn for the global eradication of Jews, and Hitler aimed to hunt down every single Jew, regardless of their location. The extent of hatred generated by Hitler's propaganda was unparalleled and constituted a type of *Rassenwahn*, or racial madness, that transformed persecution into extermination.

THE EXTERMINATION CAMPS

In 1942 and 1943, the weapons industry and war machine were in such high need of supplies that forced labor camps increased exponentially throughout large parts of Europe. Despite the high death quota at these camps and factories, the aim was not to kill the inmates but to exploit their work potential to a maximum.[15] The inmates who died from exhaustion, malnutrition, or disease were viewed simply as one of the risks, or costs, of the detention policy.

However, somewhat earlier—between 1941 and 1942—within the framework of the diabolical "Final Solution" plan, as many Jews as possible who were living in Eastern Europe were to be eliminated within a short time frame. Adolf Eichmann was responsible for the deportation of Jews from Germany and from territories annexed or occupied by Germany to ghettos, concentration camps, and extermination camps.[16] Apart from the *Einsatztruppen*'s shooting operations aimed at annihilating entire Jewish communities, the SS and police introduced mobile gas vans. These paneled trucks had exhaust pipes reconfigured to pump poisonous carbon monoxide gas into sealed spaces, killing those locked within. Up until the first half of 1944, the German terror apparatus, aided by the armed forces, decimated between one and one and a half million Jews in shooting operations or in gas vans in the occupied Soviet Union.[17]

In October 1941, Himmler had ordered the regional SS and Police Chief General Odilo Globocnik to elaborate a plan to methodically kill all Jews residing in the German-controlled Polish territories. In 1942, this project was code-named Operation Reinhard, a reference to Reinhard Heydrich, who had been authorized to direct the implementation of the Final Solution but who was assassinated by Czech agents in May 1942 in Prague. Globocnik's goals were to "resettle" (i.e., to kill) the Polish Jews, to exploit the skilled or manual labor of some Polish Jews before killing them, to secure the personal property of the Jews (clothing, currency, jewelry, and other possessions), and to identify and secure alleged hidden and immovable assets such as factories, apartments, and land.[18]

To carry out the genocide of up to two million Jews, Globocnik ordered the creation of three killing centers in German-occupied Poland: Belzec, Sobibor, and Treblinka II. He and his staff implemented the mass murder of up to 1,700,000 Jews in these Operation Reinhard killing centers and in shooting operations throughout the Polish General Government territory. The majority of victims were Polish Jews, although German, Austrian, Czech, Dutch, French, Yugoslav, and Greek Jews were also murdered at the Reinhard killing centers.[19]

The first official extermination camp, called Kulmhof in German or Chełmno in Polish, was located about fifty kilometers (31 mi) north of Lodz, next to the village of Chelmno nad Nere. The camp was especially created to carry out mass murder and, parallel to Operation Reinhard, was in use from December 1941 to March 1943, and again in June and July 1944.[20] At the very least, 152,000 people were murdered at Kulmhof, making it the fifth deadliest extermination camp after Sobibor, Belzec, Treblinka, and Auschwitz.[21]

Majdanek Camp, also known as Maidanek or Lublin-Majdanek, was established near the city of Lublin in Poland. It served a dual purpose as a forced labor camp and an extermination camp, receiving prisoners from nearly thirty different countries. The majority of the inmates were Polish citizens, including Jews, with additional prisoners hailing from the Soviet Union and Czechoslovakia. Alongside Poles and Jews, Russians, Belarusians, and Ukrainians made up the largest groups of inmates, with a small percentage of prisoners representing other nationalities, such as French and Germans. Due to the appalling living conditions, executions, and murders in gas chambers, of an estimated 150,000 prisoners who were sent to Majdanek, eighty thousand people were killed, according to the most recent research. The largest group of victims was Jews, with around sixty thousand killed, followed by Poles, Belarusians, Ukrainians, and Russians. To conceal evidence of these crimes, the corpses of those who died or were killed were burned in pyres or in the crematorium.[22]

Auschwitz, located in the part of occupied Poland directly annexed by the Third Reich, was the largest of the German concentration and extermination camps. It began operating in May 1940 as a camp for Polish prisoners and eventually included three camp zones: the main camp (Auschwitz I), Birkenau Camp (Auschwitz II), and Monowitz Camp, as well as external camps (Auschwitz III). Experimentation in mass executions at Auschwitz began in 1941, and from March 1942, Jews from all parts of Europe were herded there for "selection": either to be sent straight into the gas chambers or into forced labor. Even among those who were "lucky" enough to work—rather than be gassed with Zyklon B—very few survived. Over a million people perished in the nightmare that was Auschwitz.[23]

DID THE WORLD KNOW WHAT WAS GOING ON?

During the summer of 1941, British intelligence intercepted classified German radio transmissions that reported organized mass murders in Lithuania, Latvia, and later Ukraine. Soviet Russia also supplied reports of the horrific crimes being committed on the front. On August 14, 1941, Winston Churchill informed the public as follows:

Figure 20.1. Jewish families wait at the selection ramp at the Auschwitz-Birkenau Concentration Camp. *Courtesy of Auschwitz Memorial*

Figure 20.2. Auschwitz gas chamber and crematorium (1943). *Courtesy of Auschwitz Memorial*

> As [Hitler's] armies advance, whole districts are being exterminated. Scores of thousands, literally scores of thousands of executions in cold blood, are being perpetrated by the German police troops upon the Russian patriots who defend their native soil. . . . And this is but the beginning. Famine and pestilence have yet to follow in the bloody ruts of Hitler's tanks. We are in the presence of a crime without a name.

In the spring of 1942, additional evidence of heinous crimes against humanity emerged when American journalists, who had been stranded in Germany after the United States entered the war, were exchanged for Axis nationals trapped in the United States. These journalists recounted the mass killing of approximately four hundred thousand Jews in the Baltic states. As Poland fell to Germany, its leaders established a temporary government in exile in Britain. In June 1942, they received a confidential report from occupied Poland confirming that the Germans were carrying out executions of Jews across the country. This report was widely covered by newspapers around the world, with headlines proclaiming the Jewish death toll to be in the millions.[24]

Citing atrocity reports dating back to World War I that were later proven to be fabricated, American and other international journalists were very cautious regarding accusations of genocide. Their reports did not receive front-page attention, and the writers were careful not to accentuate claims of atrocities. Nonetheless, on December 13, 1942, Edward R. Murrow of CBS Radio openly reported, "Millions of human beings, most of them Jews, are being gathered up with ruthless efficiency and murdered. The phrase 'concentration camps' is obsolete, as out of date as economic sanctions or non-recognition. It is now possible only to speak of extermination camps." Four days later, the governments of the United States, Britain, and the Soviet Union released a joint statement that "the German authorities, not content with denying to persons of the Jewish race in all the territories over which their barbarous rule has been extended the most elementary human rights, are now carrying into effect Hitler's oft-repeated intention to exterminate the Jewish people of Europe."[25]

The Allies were of the opinion that the best way to help the Jews' plight was to win the war, and they warned the German leaders that they would be held responsible for their crimes. Tragically, the war was not won for another two and a half years, during which time the mass murder relentlessly continued.

DEATH MARCHES

As Germany's military defeat steadily neared, the Allied armies closed in on the known NS forced labor camps and extermination camps: the Soviets approached from the east, while the British, French, and Americans advanced from the west. The SS frantically attempted to move the prisoners out of the camps and away from the respective fronts in order to continue to employ them as slave labor. Many of these relocations began or ended with long stretches covered on foot in the winter of 1944–1945, which came to be known as "death marches." Camp inmates were forced to walk great distances in freezing cold, with little or no food, water, or rest. Those who fell behind were shot. Nine days before the Soviets arrived at Auschwitz, the guards marched some sixty thousand prisoners out of the camp toward various destinations such as Gliwice or Wodzislaw Slaski, a town fifty-five kilometers (35 mi) away, where the inmates were crammed into freight trains headed for other camps. Roughly one-quarter of the prisoners died before ever reaching their destination.

Some marches were implemented simply as a means of killing large groups of prisoners before the arrival of the Allied troops. During one such march, seven thousand Jewish prisoners, six thousand of them women, were moved from camps in the Danzig region, bordered on the north by the Baltic Sea. On the ten-day march, seven hundred were killed, and those still alive when the prisoners reached the shores of the sea were driven into the water and executed.

Nearly fifty thousand prisoners, mostly Jews, were evacuated from the Stutthof camp system in northern Poland. Roughly five thousand prisoners from Stutthof subcamps were marched up to the Baltic Sea coast, where they were forced into the water and gunned down. Though others were taken away on more circuitous routes, over twenty-five thousand of the prisoners from Stutthof—one out of two—perished during the evacuation.

As American forces approached, the SS initiated a mass evacuation of prisoners from the Buchenwald concentration camp and its external camps. Close to thirty thousand prisoners were forced to flee the advancing U.S. troops on death marches, during which about one-third died.[26]

The SS also evacuated countless other camps in much the same manner—on death marches that sometimes lasted weeks. Sadly, an estimated 250,000 people died due to the appalling conditions they faced either through marching on foot or being overcrowded into freight cars just before their liberation by Allied forces.[27]

LIBERATING THE CAMPS

During the spring of 1944, the SS transported a great number of the eastern territories' prisoners to concentration camps farther west. Soviet troops arrived at Majdanek during the night of July 22–23 and found it to have remained intact: this was, in fact, the first major concentration camp to be liberated. Soviet officials requested that journalists should inspect the camp to witness firsthand the atrocities that had taken place there. In the summer of 1944, the Soviets seized the Belzec, Sobibor, and Treblinka mass-murder compounds. The Germans had already disassembled these camps in 1943, once most of Poland's Jews had been liquidated.[28]

As Allied troops advanced across Europe from both the east and the west, they came across hundreds of thousands of concentration camp captives. Large numbers of these prisoners had been lucky enough to survive forced marches from camps in occupied Poland into Germany. Unfortunately, most all the prisoners were suffering from starvation or disease.[29]

When the Soviets liberated Auschwitz, the largest killing compound and concentration camp, in January 1945, the camp leaders had forced most of the prisoners to march. Left behind were some seven thousand emaciated prisoners still alive, which provided more than sufficient evidence of mass murder in Auschwitz. Though the SS had demolished most of the camp warehouses, the Soviet soldiers still found plenty of personal items that had belonged to the victims: hundreds of thousands of men's suits, more than eight hundred thousand women's outfits, thousands of suitcases, and more than fourteen thousand pounds of human hair. In the months to come, the

Soviet forces liberated more camps in the Baltic region and in Poland as well as the Stutthof, Sachsenhausen, and Ravensbrück concentration camps in Germany.[30]

U.S. troops liberated the Buchenwald concentration camp near Weimar, Germany, on April 11, 1945, with some twenty thousand prisoners. They also liberated the large forced labor camps of Dora-Mittelbau, Flossenbürg, Dachau, and Mauthausen, as well as their corresponding subcamps.[31]

British armed forces liberated camps in northern Germany, including Neuengamme and Bergen-Belsen. In the latter camp, about sixty thousand prisoners, the majority of whom were in critical condition because of a typhus epidemic, were still alive. Regrettably, over ten thousand of them died from the effects of malnutrition or disease within a few weeks of liberation.[32]

The SS's attempts to move camp inmates from the east to camps in Germany during the war's final months led to horrendous overcrowding, exacerbating the already dire conditions in these facilities. Consequently, Allied liberators encountered unimaginable conditions in Germany's concentration camps, where countless bodies lay in decaying heaps. Only with the discovery of these camps could the world comprehend the full reality of the barbaric cruelty and unspeakable massacres that had occurred. The handful of prisoners who had survived the abuse, forced labor, and malnutrition were mere living skeletons, many too weak to even move. Rampant disease posed an ever-present danger, necessitating the burning down of many of the camps to curb the spread of epidemics. Survivors of the camps, although grateful for

Figure 20.3.   U.S. Senator Alben Barkley visits Buchenwald Concentration Camp (April 24, 1945)

having escaped death, had to confront a long and arduous path to recovery, both physically and mentally.[33]

On October 7, 1943, Joseph Goebbels wrote about the Final Solution in his diary:

> Regarding the Jewish question, he [Himmler] gives us a blunt and straightforward image. He is convinced that we can solve the Jewish issue in the whole of Europe by the end of this year. He advocates the most radical and toughest solution, which is to wipe out the Jews with kith and kin. Of course this is a brutal, but also an effective solution. We are the ones who must assume the responsibility that this issue is dealt with once and for all in our time. Future generations will surely no longer dare to deal with this problem with the courage and the obsession with which we can still do it today.[34]

In the operations carried out to implement the final Solution, the Third Reich's terror apparatus murdered approximately six million Jews—two-thirds of the Jews living in Europe in 1939.[35] In addition to the Holocaust, Hitler and his regime launched a war that proved to be the deadliest military conflict in history. It is estimated that a total of seventy to eighty-five million people perished, which was at that time about 3 percent of the world population, estimated at 2.3 billion.[36]

CONCENTRATION CAMP MEMORIAL SITES

Numerous former concentration camp memorial sites, as well as some former euthanasia centers, are open to the public in Germany and neighboring countries. Each of these victim sites documents that particular establishment's history and horrors and is often complemented by an interpretive center. More information about camp memorial sites in Germany is provided in this book's last chapter.

NOTES

1. Diemut Majer, *"Non-Germans" under the Third Reich: The Nazi Judicial and Administrative System in Germany and Occupied Eastern Europe with Special Regard to Occupied Poland, 1939–1945* (Baltimore, MD: Johns Hopkins University Press, 2003).

2. Michael Marek, "Final Compensation Pending for Former Nazi Forced Labourers," *Deutsche Welle*, October 17, 2005.

3. American Jewish Committee, "Comprehensive List of German Companies That Used Slave or Forced Labour during World War II Released," December 7, 1999.

4. United States Holocaust Memorial Museum, "Austria."

5. Speech to the Reichstag on January 30, 1939, in Max Domanus, ed., *Hitler: Reden und Proklamationen 1932–1945* (Munich: Süddeutscher Verlag, 1963), 2:1058.

6. Evans, *Third Reich at War*, 175–76.

7. Hannes Heer, "Killing Fields: The Wehrmacht and the Holocaust in Belorussia, 1941–1942," *Holocaust and Genocide Studies* 11, no. 1 (1997): 79–101.

8. Omer Bartov, *Murder in Our Midst* (Oxford: Oxford University Press, 1996), 83.

9. Omer Bartov, *Hitler's Army* (Oxford: Oxford University Press, 1992), 83–92.

10. Naimark, *Fires of Hatred*, 77.

11. Dahm, *Die Tödliche Utopie*, 382.

12. Elke Fröhlich, ed., *Die Tagebücher von Joseph Goebbels*, pt. 2, vol. 2 (Munich: Sauer, 1995), 498–99.

13. Naimark, *Fires of Hatred*, 79–80.

14. Ibid., 226.

15. Pohl et al., "Rassenpolitik, Judenverfolgung, Völkermord," 453.

16. Ibid., 445.

17. United States Holocaust Memorial Museum, "Gassing Operations," Holocaust Encyclopedia, https://encyclopedia.ushmm.org/content/en/article/gassing-operations.

18. United States Holocaust Memorial Museum, "Operation Reinhard," Holocaust Encyclopedia, https://encyclopedia.ushmm.org/content/en/article/operation-reinhard-einsatz-reinhard.

19. Ibid.

20. United States Holocaust Memorial Museum, "Chelmno," Holocaust Encyclopedia, https://encyclopedia.ushmm.org/content/en/article/chelmno.

21. "Jewish Survivors of Chelmno Camp Testify at Trial of Guards," Jewish Telegraphic Agency Archive, January 22, 1963, https://www.jta.org/archive/jewish-survivors-of-chelmno-camp-testify-at-trial-of-guards.

22. Majdanek Camp website, https://www.majdanek.eu/en.

23. Pohl et al., "Rassenpolitik, Judenverfolgung, Völkermord," 449.

24. Facing History & Ourselves, "Holocaust and Human Behavior," https://www.facinghistory.org/resource-library/holocaust-human-behavior.

25. Ibid.

26. United States Holocaust Memorial Museum, "Death Marches," Holocaust Encyclopedia, https://encyclopedia.ushmm.org/content/en/article/death-marches.

27. Wiener Holocaust Museum, "Death Marches," The Holocaust Explained, https://www.theholocaustexplained.org/death-marches/.

28. United States Holocaust Memorial Museum, "Liberation of Nazi Camps," Holocaust Encyclopedia, https://encyclopedia.ushmm.org/content/en/article/liberation-of-nazi-camps.

29. Ibid.

30. Ibid.

31. Ibid.

32. Ibid.

33. Ibid.

34. Pohl et al., "Rassenpolitik, Judenverfolgung, Völkermord," 450.

35. United States Holocaust Memorial Museum, "'Final Solution': In Depth," Holocaust Encyclopedia, https://encyclopedia.ushmm.org/content/en/article/final -solution-in-depth.

36. U.S. Census Bureau, "Historical Estimates of World Population," https:// www.census.gov/data/tables/time-series/demo/international-programs/historical-est -worldpop.html.

Chapter 21

Resisting the Reich

At the time of the National Socialist takeover, a majority of German electors had cast their votes for other political parties such as the Social Democratic, Communist, or Center Party.[1] This leads us to understand that a strong sentiment of disapproval of Hitler and the National Socialist Party rapidly manifested in Germany. As the ideas and changes that the regime brought with it were gradually implemented, either new adherents joined the opposition or those who had initially expressed reservations about the party were seduced to join the rest of Hitler's followers. The bulk of Germans either adapted to, went along with, or actively supported National Socialism.

During its short existence of fourteen years (1919–1933) the Weimar Republic had experienced constant change and turmoil, and its political administration had been stigmatized by the humiliation of the Versailles Treaty and the economic abyss of the Great Depression. In light of the number of changes in the nature and leadership of Germany's government up until Hitler's appointment as chancellor in January 1933, those who had not given their approval of the new man in office were not concerned about his nomination: they thought it unlikely he would remain in power for long and resolved to shift their plans for rebellion to the back burner. Within months of Hitler's establishment at the helm of the Reich, opposition to the new order became limited due to the danger involved in opposition and the repression of dissenting voices, as well as the growing support for Hitler and the National Socialist Party.

TORN BETWEEN HOPE AND FEAR

Between 1933 and 1939, about half a million Germans fled the country for fear of political or racial persecution, while some went underground.[2] In the regime's early years, opposition and resistance groups were composed of disparate political and ideological strands representing various classes

of German society that were seldom able to work together.[3] With the support of German emigrant operatives in neighboring countries, some of these
groups carried out anti–National Socialist propaganda campaigns through the
distribution of literature and other acts of protest and opposition.[4] Political
opponents of Hitler's regime, to avoid detection, dissimulated their messages
in banal looking pamphlets such as *Die Kunst des Selbstrasierens* (The Art
of Shaving).[5]

Distinct groups such as the leftist political parties, the Bavarian mon-
archists, student movements, Jehovah's Witnesses, Habsburg supporters,
church-led opposition, and other organizations attempted to motivate their
fellow countrymen to stand up to the regime but were, however, systematically shut down, imprisoned, and often murdered by the Gestapo. Some of
the individual Germans who opposed the regime, including intellectuals,
artists, and ordinary citizens, spoke out or participated in occasional acts of
resistance. Not only were German and Austrian resistance efforts targeted by
the Reich's terror apparatus, but activists ran the constant risk of betrayal by
those who had been successfully indoctrinated by Hitler's persona, premises,
and promises.

Indeed, Hitler's regime became widely accepted by and to a great extent
popular with the German people, not only throughout the prewar period but
even during the first two years of World War II. The disappointments and
political weaknesses of the Weimar Republic had discredited democracy in
the eyes of most Germans. Hitler's seeming success in reestablishing full
employment after the devastations of the Great Depression and his bloodless foreign policy triumphs such as the remilitarization of the Rhineland in
1936 and the *Anschluss* of Austria in 1938 were applauded both nationally
and internationally.[6]

OPPOSITION FROM THE CHURCHES

As institutions, neither the Catholic nor the Protestant churches were in a
position to directly oppose the regime, yet it was thanks to the clergy that
the first measures of German opposition to the policies of the Third Reich
emerged. A great number of clergymen attempted to resist the regime's efforts
to infringe on ecclesiastical autonomy, and a few expressed broader misgiv-
ings about the new order.[7] Several priests, such as the Jesuits Alfred Delp
and Augustin Rösch, as well as the Lutheran preacher Dietrich Bonhoeffer,
worked successfully within the clandestine German resistance. The Protestant
pastor Martin Niemöller (founder of the Confessing Church) and the Catholic
Bishop Clemens August Graf von Galen (who denounced the National

Socialists' practice of euthanasia) upheld the principles of human rights and justice as the indispensable pillars of a political system.[8]

Historian Ian Kershaw sums it up by stating that the churches "engaged in a bitter war of attrition with the regime, receiving the demonstrative backing of millions of churchgoers. Applause for Church leaders whenever they appeared in public, swollen attendances at events such as Corpus Christi Day processions, and packed church services were outward signs of the struggle . . . especially of the Catholic Church against Nazi oppression." Though the church ultimately was unable to shield its youth organizations and schools, it was somewhat successful in mobilizing public opinion to alter government policies.[9]

JEHOVAH'S WITNESSES PROTESTS

Between 1936 and 1938, Jehovah's Witnesses in Germany staged a series of significant acts of resistance. When Hitler came to power, this religious community, with about twenty-five thousand members, was labeled as a "Jewish-Internationalist" group and banned due to its refusal to serve in the military and bear arms. Despite the ban, the organization was able to continue operating illegally. In late 1936, Jehovah's Witnesses distributed a resolution protesting their community's persecution, leading to a nationwide rally with no prior notice. This was a propaganda victory for the group and was followed by another successful demonstration the following summer, a feat unmatched by any other banned organization.[10]

THE RED ORCHESTRA

In the mid-1930s, a group of friends including Arvid Harnack (a senior executive at the Reich Ministry of Economics) and his wife, Mildred, as well as Harro Schulze-Boysen (an employee at the Reich Ministry of Aviation) and his wife, Libertas, formed friendship and study circles in Berlin. Over time, their personal contacts led to the formation of seven resistance circles in 1940–1941 made up of over 150 individuals from diverse backgrounds and ideologies, including students, artists, journalists, and civil servants, many of whom were women.

They fought against National Socialism through various means, including discussions on political and artistic issues, assistance to persecuted people, and documentation of National Socialist crimes. They also spread their message to the public by distributing leaflets and posting notes and reached out to like-minded individuals in other parts of Germany.

Harnack and Schulze-Boysen also relayed intelligence to the Soviet Union, and the group increased its political education efforts by distributing leaflets and letters. In 1942, the Gestapo discovered their resistance organization and labeled it a Soviet espionage group, "Red Orchestra," leading to investigations and trials for treason. By late 1942, death sentences were passed, and over fifty members of the Red Orchestra were executed.[11]

THE KREISAU CIRCLE

Starting in 1940, a group of individuals with diverse social backgrounds and ideological beliefs, united in opposition to the regime, held regular meetings in Berlin, Munich, and the Kreisau Estate in Silesia. The Kreisau Circle, as it came to be called, was led by friends Helmuth James Graf von Moltke and Peter Graf Yorck von Wartenburg and consisted of Christians of different denominations, Social Democrats, conservatives, and liberals who came together to establish common ground through respectful discourse.

Their goal was to develop a comprehensive plan for a new political, social, and intellectual framework that could be implemented after the fall of the Third Reich. Through conferences, discussions, and memos, they aimed to create a new foundation for human relations and state governance, exploring issues such as governmental structure, limitations on state power, the economy, education, and the role of the church. A crucial objective for them was to secure Germany's position in a new postwar European order. The Kreisau Circle had a significant impact on the ideas of those opposed to the National Socialist state and who sought to take action. Some members of the circle even participated in plans to assassinate Hitler. Many members were sentenced to death by the People's Court due to their connections to the failed July 20, 1944, coup. A few members of the Kreisau Circle survived and went on to shape postwar Germany.[12]

RESISTANCE DURING WORLD WAR II

The initial triumphs of the German military in 1939 and 1940 were met with widespread jubilation. However, as the war progressed and German cities were devastated by Allied air raids, the regime's reputation was damaged, resulting in an increase in dissent toward the war. Open acts of defiance or resistance were rare, and collective opposition was nearly impossible to organize. The political opposition, especially the Social Democratic and Communist Parties, had already been crushed by the Gestapo years prior, leaving most of their leaders dead, imprisoned, or in exile.

As a measure of precaution, the Gestapo arrested and detained many former Communist functionaries prior to the Russian invasion in order to avoid
the possible formation of resistance bands. Despite these safeguards, several
Communist resistance groups surfaced in cities with a large labor presence,
such as in the east or in the Ruhr region. With the support of exiled party
members abroad, these rebellious units managed to distribute leaflets urging
opposition to the regime and encouraging acts of sabotage. A result was the
success of a small group of young Jewish Communists in blowing up part of
an anti-Soviet exhibition organized by Goebbels. The outcome of their brave
revolt was the arrest of thirty of their members and the subsequent execution
of fifteen.

THE WHITE ROSE

The student resistance movement called the Weisse Rose (White Rose) was
created in Munich by the siblings Sophie and Hans Scholl, along with a few
fellow students and a professor. The White Rose group was motivated by
ethical, moral, and religious considerations, and its members supported and
took in individuals of the most varied backgrounds. Starting in June 1942, the
group conducted an anonymous leaflet and graffiti campaign that called for
active opposition to the National Socialist regime.

When the defeat at Stalingrad was officially announced, the White Rose
distributed their sixth—and last—leaflet. The tone of this writing, authored
by Hans Scholl and two others, was decidedly patriotic. Headed "Fellow
students!," it announced that the "day of reckoning" had come for "the most
contemptible tyrant our people has ever endured. . . . The dead of Stalingrad
adjure us!"[13] The text of this sixth leaflet was smuggled out of Germany to
the United Kingdom by Helmuth James Graf von Moltke, a German law-
yer and member of the Kreisau Circle. In July 1943, copies were dropped
over Germany by Allied planes, retitled "The Manifesto of the Students
of Munich."

By this means, the efforts and message of the White Rose became widely
known in Germany during the last couple of years of the war, but as with
other attempts at resistance, they did not result in any large-scale opposition
to Hitler's regime. The White Rose's core group was arrested by the Gestapo
in February 1943, and following a show trial, Sophie and Hans Scholl were
guillotined.[14] As the blade was about to drop, Hans Scholl purportedly cried
out, *"Es lebe die Freiheit"* (long live freedom).[15]

THE ROSENSTRASSE PROTEST

In the period from February 27 to March 6, 1943, a group of roughly two hundred Germans who were not of Jewish descent, mainly women, congregated outside a Jewish community building situated on Rosenstrasse in Berlin. Inside the building, approximately two thousand Jews, mainly men who were married to non-Jewish partners and their sons, had been taken into custody by the police. The non-Jewish relatives of those who were detained were worried that their loved ones would be sent to the east, as had happened to seven thousand Jews in the recent past.

The police repeatedly ordered the crowd to disperse, but the demonstrators immediately returned and eventually maintained a continuous presence, taking turns throughout the day and night to demonstrate their resolve to get answers and to draw attention to the outrage. Such a demonstration was unheard of in Hitler's Germany, where only official parades and public events were allowed, and despite media censorship, news of the revolt spread by word of mouth throughout the country and eventually leaked out to the international media.[16]

According to accounts, the Reich's Security Office had issued a decree that exempted Jewish partners of mixed marriages from being deported. The reason for the Gestapo's detention of the men and boys in the Rosenstrasse community center was purportedly to process their papers and verify their identities and statuses. After this "registration," the plan was to release them back to their homes but to have them replace deported Jews in factories and facilities in and around Berlin that had lost much of their forced labor. As a result, the Gestapo's operation in late February 1943 came to be known as the "Factory Action" after the war.

Other sources claim that the Rosenstrasse detainees were indeed going to be deported to Auschwitz but that on March 6, 1943, Goebbels, in his capacity as the *Gauleiter* of Berlin, ordered all of the men imprisoned at Rosenstrasse to be released, stating, "I will commission the security police not to continue the Jewish evacuations in a systematic manner during such a critical time [a reference to the defeat in the Battle of Stalingrad]. We want to rather spare that for ourselves until after a few weeks; then we can carry it out that much more thoroughly."[17]

By March 11, all the Rosenstrasse Jewish detainees were free with the exception of twenty-five who had already been shipped off to Auschwitz in the early part of the roundup but were promptly repatriated so as to avoid public dissent.

The brave women who risked their freedom and their lives by demanding the liberation of their Jewish husbands serve as an example of peaceful

German resistance to the National Socialist regime of terror. The German historian Konrad Kwiet intimates that "the successful outcome of this late protest suggests that if similar actions at an earlier stage had been carried out throughout Germany, they might have halted the increasingly destructive course of the German anti-Jewish policy."

ASSASSINATION ATTEMPTS

Though the outbreak of World War II was viewed with enthusiasm by a large portion of the German population, approval for a new conflict was not unanimous: the horrendous death toll and ensuing economic disaster of the First World War still loomed over Germany like an apocalyptic shadow. While the old "elite," the conservative military figures still present from World War I or the Weimar Republic days, plotted to remove Hitler, there was very little they managed to achieve. Allegedly, however, no less than forty-two unsuccessful assassination attempts were planned or carried out against Hitler before and during the war.

Just two months into the war, in November 1939, Georg Elser, a carpenter from Württemberg, laid a plan to assassinate Hitler. He read in the newspapers that Hitler would be speaking at a party meeting on November 8 at Munich's *Bürgerbräukeller*, the beer hall where Hitler had staged the Beer Hall Putsch on the same date in 1923. Elser stole explosives from his workplace with which to build a powerful time bomb and, for more than a month, managed to remain inside the beer hall after hours each night, hollowing out a pillar behind the speaker's rostrum in order to place the bomb inside.

On the night of November 7, Elser set the timer and fled toward the Swiss border. Unexpectedly, Hitler delivered a much shorter speech than usual and left the *Bürgerbräukeller* thirteen minutes before the bomb exploded, killing seven people and injuring dozens. Had Hitler still been speaking, the bomb would have most likely killed him. Elser was arrested at the border and sent to the Sachsenhausen Concentration Camp. In 1945 he was transferred to the Dachau Concentration Camp, where he was executed two weeks before the camp's liberation.

A second assassination attempt was carried out by high-ranking members of the military while Hitler was returning from his easternmost headquarters, FHQ Wehrwolf, near Vinnitsa in Ukraine, to the Wolfsschanze (Wolf's Lair) in East Prussia. On March 13, 1943, a bomb was smuggled onto Hitler's plane. The bomb was disguised as a box for two bottles of Cointreau. The fuse was set so that Hitler's plane was expected to explode about thirty minutes later, near Minsk, close enough to the front to be attributed to Soviet fighters. Probably due to the cold, the detonator's percussion cap did not go off, and Hitler again escaped certain death.

Some days later, on March 21, 1943, when Hitler was visiting an exhibition of captured Soviet weaponry in Berlin, Colonel Rudolf Christoph Freiherr von Gersdorff was scheduled to explain some exhibits. He had secretly volunteered to carry out a suicide bombing using the same bomb that had failed to go off on the plane, concealed on his person. Unfortunately, the only new chemical fuse he could acquire was a ten-minute fuse. Again Hitler departed ahead of schedule after hurrying through the exhibition much faster than the scheduled thirty minutes. Gersdorff managed to dash to a bathroom to defuse the bomb and save his own life.

On November 9, 1943, a member of the elite Infantry Regiment 9, Axel von dem Bussche, volunteered to kill Hitler with hand grenades. This was to take place during a presentation of new winter uniforms, but the train carrying the goods was destroyed by an Allied air raid in Berlin, and the event had to be postponed. A second presentation planned for December at the Wolf's Lair had to be canceled on short notice because, at the last minute, Hitler decided to travel to Berchtesgaden instead.

On February 11, 1943, another young officer, Ewald-Heinrich von Kleist, attempted to assassinate Hitler in the same manner that von dem Bussche had intended. Again, Hitler canceled the event that would have allowed Kleist to approach him.

On March 11, 1944, Cavalry Officer Eberhard von Breitenbuch volunteered for an assassination attempt at the Berghof in Berchtesgaden. Armed with a Browning pistol concealed in his pocket, he was, however, unable to carry out the plan because guards would not allow him into the conference room with the *Führer*.

One of the leading instigators of the preceding assassination attempts was Henning von Tresckow, second general staff officer of Army Group A under Gerd von Rundstedt. In 1943 Tresckow met Colonel Claus Schenk Graf von Stauffenberg for the first time. Severely wounded in North Africa, Stauffenberg was a devout Catholic, a political conservative, and a zealous German nationalist with a taste for philosophy. At first, he had favored the new regime but soon became disillusioned. By 1942 he shared the widespread opinion among Wehrmacht officers that Germany was headed for disaster and that Hitler must be toppled. Initially, his religious scruples had prevented him from coming to the conclusion that assassination was the correct way to achieve this. Following Stalingrad, however, he concluded that not assassinating Hitler would represent an even greater moral evil.

Starting in late 1943, it became increasing challenging to approach Hitler, who spent most of his time either at the Wolf's Lair in East Prussia or at his home, the Berghof, in Berchtesgaden. On July 1, 1944, Stauffenberg was appointed chief-of-staff to General Fromm at the Reserve Army headquarters in Berlin, a post that would enable him to attend Hitler's military conferences, both in East Prussia and in Berchtesgaden, and provide him with the opportunity to assassinate the *Führer*.

After two aborted attempts to shoot Hitler at his Berghof residence and carrying a bomb around in a briefcase to several official meetings, Stauffenberg flew back to the Wolf's Lair on July 20, 1944, for another one of Hitler's military briefings, again with a bomb in his briefcase.

Stauffenberg, having previously activated the timer on the bomb, set his briefcase down, under the table around which Hitler and over twenty officers were seated or standing. Ten minutes later, Stauffenberg made an excuse to leave the room, shortly after which the bomb exploded, demolishing the conference room. Several officers were killed but not Hitler, who apparently was protected from the detonation by the heavy table leg. The reprisal was fierce, with the arrest of some five thousand people suspected of having played a part in the conspiracy against Hitler. Of these, some two hundred—including Stauffenberg—were executed.

It can be established that opposition or resistance to the National Socialist regime in Germany during Hitler's dictatorship was limited due to the dangers it posed to those who spoke out against the government. Despite the repression, many German individuals and groups risked their lives to speak out or to fight for their ideals and for the freedom of their fellow citizens, regardless of origin, race, or creed.

NOTES

1. Das Deutsche Reich, "Reichstagswahl November 1932," https://gonschior.de/weimar/Deutschland/index.htm.

2. Hartmut Mehringer et al., "Widerstand und Emigration," in Dahm, *Die Tödliche Utopie*, 467.

3. Anton Gill, *An Honourable Defeat: A History of the German Resistance to Hitler* (New York: H. Holt, 1994), 2.

4. Mehringer et al., "Widerstand und Emigration," 491.

5. Ibid., 494.

6. Shirer, *Rise and Fall of the Third Reich*.

7. Theodore S. Hamerow, *On the Road to the Wolf's Lair: German Resistance to Hitler* (Cambridge, MA: Belknap Press, 1997), 133.

8. Ibid., 288–89.

9. Kershaw, *Hitler*, 210–11.

10. Mehringer et al., "Widerstand und Emigration," 473.

11. "Red Orchestra," Gedenkstätte Deutscher Widerstand, https://www.gdw-berlin.de/en/recess/topics/14-the-red-orchestra/.

12. Ibid.

13. Jacob G. Hornberger, "Holocaust Resistance: The White Rose—a Lesson in Dissent," Jewish Virtual Library, https://www.jewishvirtuallibrary.org/the-white-rose-a-lesson-in-dissent.

14. Richard Hanser, *A Noble Treason* (San Francisco: Ignatius Press, 2012).

15. Inge Scholl, *The White Rose: Munich, 1942–1943* (Middletown, CT: Wesleyan University Press, 2011).

16. United States Holocaust Memorial Museum, "The Rosenstrasse Demonstration, 1943," Holocaust Encyclopedia, https://encyclopedia.ushmm.org/content/en/article/the-rosenstrasse-demonstration-1943.

17. Nathan Stoltzfus, *Resistance of the Heart* (New York: W. W. Norton, 1996), 245.

PART IV

Additional Perspectives

Chapter 22

Hitler's Secret Book

THE UNPUBLISHED SEQUEL TO *MEIN KAMPF*

In the course of the four years during which Hitler was forbidden to speak in public, he continued to express his worldviews by dictating two more manuscripts of his memoirs and opinions while sojourning at Obersalzberg above Berchtesgaden.

It is astonishing how few people today—even World War II history buffs—have heard about, let alone read, Hitler's unpublished sequel to the infamous *Mein Kampf*. Historians and scientific researchers on Hitler's sphere of influence and the National Socialist period widely fail to study, or refer to, the important source of historically valuable information divulged in *Hitlers Zweites Buch* (Hitler's Second Book), at one time referred to as "Hitler's Secret Book."

Mein Kampf, on the other hand, has been referenced countless times as a source of Hitler's *Weltanschauung* in hundreds of books and articles. To better understand Hitler's foreign policy, war plans, and persecution of the Jews, among other topics, his "secret" or unknown and unpublished book sheds light on the politician's early worldview, dictated in 1928, five years before seizing power, and a decade before the inception of World War II.

For clarity's sake, this "Second Book" should not be confused with Hitler's "Volume 2" of *Mein Kampf*. There is the general assumption that, in Landsberg Prison, Adolf Hitler wrote the entire memoir "Four and a Half Years (of Struggle) against Lies, Stupidity, and Cowardice," the title of which was later shortened to *Mein Kampf* (My Struggle). It is true that the first volume was, indeed, dictated to his secretary Rudolf Hess in 1924, but the second volume was dictated in Berchtesgaden in 1925 following his early release from prison. These two volumes were later merged and published as *Mein Kampf* by Max Amann of Eher-Verlag as a single two-part book: volume

1 titled "A Reckoning" and volume 2 "The National Socialist Movement." However, the unpublished manuscript of Hitler's "Second Book" discussed below was dictated to a typist in June and July 1928 and is wholly separate from *Mein Kampf*.

THE DISCOVERY OF "HITLER'S SECRET BOOK"

Referred to in the 1960s as "Hitler's Secret Book," the manuscript was located in the late 1950s by the renowned historian Gerhard Weinberg, a German-born American military historian noted for his studies of National Socialist Germany and World War II. Weinberg has penned a dozen or more books related to these topics, as well as numerous articles for renowned magazines and scientific journals. He was elected president of the German Studies Association in 1996, has been a fellow of the American Council of Learned Societies, and was a Fulbright professor at the University of Bonn, a Guggenheim Fellow, and a Shapiro Senior Scholar in Residence at the U.S. Holocaust Memorial Museum, among many other such honors.[1]

In 2009, Weinberg was chosen as the recipient of the $100,000 Pritzker Military Library Literature Award for lifetime excellence in military writing, and in 2011 he was awarded the Samuel Eliot Morison Prize, a lifetime achievement award given by the Society for Military History. The listing of Weinberg's accomplishments and reputation has been included with the aim of validating the authenticity of the manuscript in question: Hitler's unpublished book.

The actual document dictated by Adolf Hitler in 1928, but never published during his lifetime, was hidden away in a cache of confiscated German records in Alexandria, Virginia, until it was located by Gerhard Weinberg in 1958. Though the manuscript was subsequently published in Germany by the Institute for Contemporary History in Munich in 1961, the work titled *Hitlers Zweites Buch: Ein Dokument aus dem Jahr 1928* (Hitler's Second Book: A Document from the Year 1928) sold out quickly and was not published in Germany again until 1995, when it reappeared as part of a series titled Hitlers Reden, Schriften, Anordnungen (Hitler's Speeches, Writings, Directives), edited by the same institute.

In 2006, Weinberg edited an English-language version of the original text, translated by Krista Smith and published by Enigma Books, an edition that included Weinberg's thought-provoking introduction to the historical document. It is a shame, however, that *Hitler's Second Book* is out of print today, as it contains some highly interesting statements regarding the future *Führer*'s views on Great Britain and the United States, as well as on the choice of allies he had in mind for the new Germany. As early as 1928, Hitler came to the

HITLERS
ZWEITES
BUCH

EIN DOKUMENT
AUS DEM JAHR
1928

HERAUSGEGEBEN VOM INSTITUT FÜR ZEITGESCHICHTE

Figure 22.1.   Cover page of Hitler's Second Book, published 1961

conclusion that Germany would need to prepare for war with the United States, a plan that helps us understand why, already in 1937, he ordered the development of intercontinental bombers and long-haul super-battleships.[2]

Having stated that the English-language book is no longer available, there still exist limited copies of a Bramhall House (New York) edition reprinted in 1986 with introductions by notable historians William Shire and Telford Taylor. Apparently, a pirated version is in circulation, mostly as an electronic book, that is the result of an untrustworthy translation and is allegedly published by a right-wing editor.

AUTHENTICATING THE MANUSCRIPT

Knowing that a purported diary of Adolf Hitler was exposed as a fake,[3] that false Hitler quotes have been in circulation, and that works of art attributed to Hitler were revealed as forgeries, it is essential to validate the authenticity of Weinberg's astonishing 1958 discovery. The historian had followed a lead from a 1949 book written by Albert Zoller, a French officer who carried out the interrogations of Hitler's secretary Christa Schroeder and whose report made mention of an unpublished book on foreign policy dictated by Hitler. The second mention of the manuscript came from Hitler himself when he said, "In 1925 I wrote in Mein Kampf (and also in an unpublished work) that world Jewry saw in Japan an opponent beyond its reach."[4]

Meanwhile, thanks to Josef Berg,[5] a colleague of Hitler's publisher Max Amann, the Institute of Contemporary History in Munich also got wind of the alleged existence of another book. Berg claimed that Hitler had dictated the manuscript to Amann and that, in addition to the copy in the publisher's safe, a second copy had been stored at Obersalzberg. Both claims would be confirmed with the discovery of the manuscript. Weinberg located the document among files that U.S. authorities were in the process of microfilming: the book in question had been laid aside and erroneously thought to be simply a draft of *Mein Kampf.* Along with the long sought-after manuscript was the confiscation memo proving that an American officer had obtained it from Hitler's publisher, Eher-Verlag, in May 1945, after the book was handed over by Josef Berg with the claim that it was a work written by Hitler more than fifteen years earlier.[6]

When the 1961 German-language publication was released in Germany, Albert Speer noted in his diary that he remembered that Hitler, at the time of the construction of the Berghof in the mid-1930s, had "accepted a hundred-thousand-mark advance" from Eher-Verlag "for a manuscript that he—for reasons of foreign policy—did not yet wish to see published."[7]

Also, a letter dated June 26, 1928, signed by Hitler's personal secretary Rudolf Hess in Hitler's chancellery in Munich, responded to someone's request for an appointment with Hitler as follows: "Herr Hitler is likely to be in Berlin for several days at the beginning of July. A visit . . . can hardly be considered earlier, as Herr Hitler will probably be away from Munich until his trip to Berlin, in order to write his book."[8] In addition, Weinberg also compared passages in the original manuscript that correspond to events that took place in 1928.[9]

WHY WAS THE BOOK KEPT SECRET?

Weinberg suggests that Amann likely advised against publishing Hitler's second book due to the poor sales of *Mein Kampf* in 1928, with only 3,015 copies sold. Additionally, the financial struggles of the National Socialist Party at the time, including the forced cancellation of their annual rally for lack of funds, would have made it unwise to invest in a new book that could compete with *Mein Kampf*.[10] Furthermore, the political and economic developments of 1929 would have required extensive revisions to the original manuscript, which Hitler did not have time for.[11] Speer also cited "foreign policy reasons" for Hitler's failure to publish his 1928 manuscript. The blatant proposition of a new war to acquire vast territories in Eastern Europe and the constantly repeated disavowal of the 1914 borders as the goal of German policy could have led Hitler, especially in the first years after his rise to power, to view the publication of his "foreign policy position" as inopportune.[12]

HITLER'S 1928 MANUSCRIPT: CONTENT AND EXCERPTS

The "Second Book" by Hitler, with its focus on foreign policy, serves as a crucial source of insight into the period when Hitler was still vying for power. It offers an unfiltered view of his ideology and subsequent policies as leader of the Third Reich. In an effort to highlight the most significant and revealing discussions contained in the 238 pages of the manuscript, this text provides section titles for thematic organization. It's important to note that the book was never edited after its initial dictation, and the English translation will feature any original errors or omissions.

THE ONGOING FIGHT FOR BREAD AND LAND

In chapter 1, Hitler's first line states that "politics is history in the making. History itself represents the progression of a people's struggle for survival."[13] He explains that the instinct of self-preservation

> corresponds to the two most powerful motivations in life: hunger and love. While the . . . satisfaction of the eternal hunger guarantees self-preservation, the gratification of love secures its furtherance. In truth, these two impulses are the rulers of life. . . . The laws that apply to the individual are the same for a society: a people is a collectivity of more or less equal people who need to fight for their self-preservation and continuity.[14]

Hitler elaborates on the creation of the planet and, finally, the appearance of humans who eventually form "families, tribes, peoples, states."[15] Humans fight off animals—and each other—in the pursuit of self-preservation. Politics, he maintains, "is the art of the implementation of this struggle."[16]

The next discussion raises the argument that war is dangerous because it "leads to a racial selection within a people; this means a disproportionate destruction of the best elements."[17] The most courageous, idealistic, valorous, and strong men of the nation are willing to sacrifice their lives on the battlefield "for the benefit of the community," in contrast to "those pathetic egoists who see the preservation of their own strictly personal existence as the highest duty of this life. The hero dies, the criminal . . . survives."[18] Hitler concludes this thought by stating that war should only be considered as a means to preserve this existence.

A peaceful society, he argues, will eventually weaken: rather than fight for their bread, they will be content with less bread or leave their homeland in search of better conditions. "The farm boy who emigrated to America 150 years ago was the most determined and boldest in his village."[19] As a consequence, migration from Germany will in the long run deprive the nation of its "best bloodline" and reduce its population. Hitler sums up by stating, "Fundamentally peaceful policy becomes a scourge for the people."[20]

In chapter 2 Hitler states that "the most secure basis for the existence of a people has always been its own territory and land."[21] However the growth of a healthy population must be proportionate to the nation's *Lebensraum* (living space). He proceeds to endorse a policy of invasion for the acquisition of additional territory to feed the population. He says,

> The human life lost on the battlefield will automatically be replaced many times over. Thus, from the distress of war grows the bread of freedom. The sword breaks the path for the plow, and if one wishes to speak of human rights, then

in this one case war has served the highest right: it gave land to a people that wishes to cultivate it industriously and honestly and which can in the future provide daily sustenance for its children.[22]

In his argument, Hitler does not mention the rights of those from whom the Germans are stealing the land. He then describes the dangers of international trade and commerce and concludes that a population and its *Lebensraum* must be in a healthy proportion to each other, but to achieve that, a people needs weapons because "land acquisition is always linked to the use of force."[23]

GERMANY'S ARMED FORCES AND RACIAL SUPERIORITY

In the same chapter, Hitler uses the example of the subjugation of 350,000 Helots through the greater strength of only six thousand Spartans due to their "racial superiority." Here he reveals his views on eugenics and child euthanasia in order to breed these alleged supermen whose

> racial superiority . . . was the result of systematic racial preservation, so we see in the Spartan state the first racialist state. The abandonment of sick, frail, deformed children—in other words, their destruction—demonstrated greater human dignity and was in reality a thousand times more humane than the pathetic insanity of our time, which attempts to preserve the lives of the sickest subjects—at any price—while taking the lives of a hundred thousand healthy children through a decrease in the birth rate or through abortifacient agents, subsequently breeding a race of degenerates burdened with illness.[24]

In chapter 3 Hitler claims that the "handing over of our weapons" as ordered by the Versailles Treaty was insignificant—"weapons can rust."[25] The significant issue was the destruction of the German army, he maintains. Hitler praises the military as a time-honored product of the German people:

> The German army at the turn of the century was still the greatest organization in the world and its effectiveness was more than beneficial for our German people. The breeding ground of German discipline, German efficiency, even disposition, open courage, bold recklessness, tenacious perseverance, and unyielding honesty. The sense of honor of an entire profession gradually and imperceptibly became the common property of an entire people.[26]

He also boasts about the social equality of the German armed forces, in which the meritorious, and not only the rich or titled, can become officers and leaders.

Hitler goes on to maintain that Germany has been unarmed many times throughout history but that "our real defenselessness lies in our pacifist-democratic contamination, as well as in the internationalism that destroys and poisons our people's most significant sources of strength."[27] He claims that "the source of a people's entire power lies not in its store of weapons or its army organization, but in its inner quality—represented by the racial significance or racial value of a people, by the presence of superior individual personal qualities, and by a healthy attitude toward the idea of self-preservation."[28] He continues by arguing that "all peoples are not the same" and that their values and culture "provide a benchmark for the overall valuation of a people." He concludes this racial assertion by stating, "The higher the racial worth of a people, the greater its overall value, [through] which, in conflict and in the struggle with other peoples, it must then mobilize for the benefit of its life."[29]

THE *FÜHRER* PRINCIPLE

In chapter 4 Hitler examines the value of learning from history and suggests forcing the acquired values and way of life on the German people—whether they agree with them or not.

> Thus, for those who feel called to educate a people, it is their task to learn from history and to apply their knowledge practically, without regard to the understanding, comprehension, ignorance, or even repudiation of the masses. The greatness of a man is all the more significant the greater his courage to use his superior insight—in opposition to the generally prevailing but ruinous view—to lead to overall victory. The National Socialist movement would have no right to consider itself a truly great phenomenon in the life of the German people if it did not summon the courage [to] learn from the experiences of the past and impose on the German people the laws of life that it represents, despite all opposition.[30]

PRAISE FOR BISMARCK

Chapter 6 includes a brief history lesson in which Hitler praises Otto von Bismarck for his successes in the Franco-Prussian War of 1870–1871. Approvingly, he reiterates, "A large number of German states that were previously only loosely allied with each other—and historically were not infrequently hostile to each other—were united into one Reich. . . . A province of the old Holy German Empire, lost 170 years earlier (which had been definitively annexed by France in a brief theft), came back to the motherland [now known as Alsace Lorraine]."[31] However, Hitler strongly lamented Germany viewing these new subjects as citizens of the Reich: "It was problematic that this state included [over three] million Poles and [figures unknown] from Alsace and Lorraine who had become French. This conformed neither to the idea of a nation state nor to that of an ethnic state."[32]

HATRED FOR THE POLES

Hitler sees no chance of including Polish people in the Germany nation and recommends their "removal":

[The nation-state] would also have to instill German thoughts in these people, through [their] education and life, and turn them into bearers of these ideas. This was weakly attempted, possibly never seriously desired, and in reality the opposite was achieved. The ethnic state, in contrast, could under absolutely no circumstances annex Poles with the intention of turning them into Germans one day. It would instead have to decide either to isolate these alien racial elements in order to prevent the repeated contamination of one's own people's blood, or it would have to immediately remove them entirely, transferring the land and territory that thus became free to members of one's own ethnic community.[33]

LESSONS FROM WORLD WAR I
AND EXPANSIONIST AIMS

Chapter 7 includes a detailed criticism of the Triple Alliance—the secret 1882 agreement between Germany, Austria-Hungary, and Italy. Though Otto von Bismarck was the principal architect of the alliance, Italy's aim was mostly to gain support against France shortly after losing its North African ambitions to the French. Hitler bemoans Germany having been "pushed into the war" and views the alliance as follows:

But the benefits of the Triple Alliance lay exclusively on the Austrian side. Due to determining factors in the policies of the individual states, only Austria could ever be the beneficiary of this alliance. . . . It was a defensive alliance, which, according to the provisions of the agreement, was at most only intended to secure the maintenance of the status quo. Because of the impossibility of sustaining their people, Germany and Italy were forced to adopt an offensive policy.[34] . . . In reality, the advantages of the alliance with Austria lay all on Austria's side, while Germany had to bear all the disadvantages. And they were not few.[35]

He also laments how, due to this alliance, Germany took all the undue blame for having initiated World War I.

Still recalling Germany's expansionist failures in the Great War, Hitler advocates vast enlargement for Germany:

> however, only through a territorial policy in Europe could the population resettled there, be preserved for our people including their military utilization. An additional 500,000 square kilometers of land in Europe can provide millions of German farmers with new homesteads, and can add to the strength of the German people millions of soldiers available for the decisive moment. The only area in Europe that could be considered for such a territorial policy was Russia. The sparsely populated western areas bordering Germany (which had already once welcomed German colonizers as bearers of culture) also came into consideration for the new European territorial policy of the German nation.[36]

Though Hitler explicitly refers to the rape of Russian land, to give an idea of Hitler's goal of acquiring half a million square kilometers of territory for the resettling of German farmers, France was roughly that size in 1928 or, to offer an example on Germany's eastern borders, Poland and Czechoslovakia together corresponded more or less to the landmass that Hitler coveted.

In chapter 8 Hitler expresses his views on the disasters of the Great War:

> The only war aim that would have been worthy of these enormous casualties would have been to promise the German troops that so many hundreds of thousands of square kilometers of land would be allotted to the frontline soldiers as property or made available for colonization by Germans. In that way, the war would also immediately have lost the character of an imperial undertaking and would instead have become a matter of concern to the German people. Because ultimately, the German soldiers did not really shed their blood so that the Poles could obtain a state. . . . In 1918 we thus stood at the conclusion of a completely pointless and aimless waste of the most valuable German blood.[37] Once again, our people offered up infinite heroism, courage in the face of sacrifice—yes, courage in the face of death—and willingness to accept responsibility, and nevertheless had to leave the battlefield defeated and weakened. Victorious in a thousand battles and engagements, yet still conquered by the losers in the end.[38]

He also repeats the widely propagated lie about Germany's forced surrender:

> On November 11, 1918, in the forest of Compiègne, the armistice agreement was signed. For this, fate had destined a man who had been one of the chief culprits in the disintegration of our people. Matthias Erzberger, representative of the Center Party—and, according to various claims, the illegitimate son of a maid and a Jewish employer—was the German negotiator who then also signed his name to a document which, unless one assumes a deliberate intent to destroy

Germany, appears incomprehensible in light of the four and a half years of heroism demonstrated by our people.[39]

Erzberger's opponents circulated the fabricated contention that he was part Jewish,[40] an untruth that was widely repeated in the post–World War I era.

The chapter also includes a dramatically formulated critique of Germany's surrender at the end of the war:

> People should not speak of national honor, particularly in today's Germany, and people should not attempt to give the impression that national honor can [again] be preserved through any sort of outwardly directed rhetorical barking. No, that cannot be done—because it no longer exists at all. And it has by no means disappeared because we lost the war or because the French occupied Alsace-Lorraine, the Poles stole Upper Silesia or the Italians took South Tyrol. No, our national honor is gone because the German people, in the most difficult time of its struggle for survival, demonstrated a lack of conviction, shameless servility, and cringing, groveling tail-wagging that can only be called shameless. Because we gave in pathetically without being forced to do so, because the leadership of this people, against historical truth and its own knowledge, assumed the war guilt—yes, burdened our entire people with it.[41]

Interestingly, Hitler vents his anger more at the so-called November Criminals—the politicians who negotiated and signed the 1918 Armistice— than at the World War I enemies of the Reich:

> Anyone who today wants to act in the name of German honor must first announce the most relentless fight against the intolerable defilers of German honor. But those are not our former opponents; rather, they are the representatives of the November crime. That collection [of] Marxist, democratic-pacifist, and Centrist traitors that pushed our people into its current state of powerlessness. Upbraiding one-time enemies in the name of national honor while acknowledging as gentlemen the dishonorable allies of these enemies in our own midst—that fits with the national dignity of this current so-called national bourgeoisie. I admit most frankly that I could reconcile myself with every one of those old enemies, but that my hate for the traitors in our own ranks is unforgiving and will remain. What the enemies did to us is serious and humiliating for us, but the sins committed by the men of the November crime—that is the most dishonorable, dastardly crime of all time. By attempting to bring about circumstances that will someday force these creatures to accountability, I am helping to restore German honor.[42]

GERMAN EMIGRATION TO THE UNITED STATES

Chapter 9 begins with Hitler deploring the fact that so many Germans were forced to emigrate due to lack of space. In particular he mentions those who lived in the United States (referred to as the American Union):

> under no circumstances will they be able to participate any longer in the motherland's struggle with destiny in any significant way, nor in the cultural development of their people. Whatever the Germans in North America achieve specifically, it will not be credited to the German people, but is forfeited to the body of culture of the American Union. Here the Germans really are only the cultural fertilizer for other peoples everywhere. Yes, in reality the greatness of these peoples, to a high degree, is not infrequently [attributable] to achievements contributed by Germans.[43]

However, Hitler already sees German emigrants to English-speaking countries as a lost cause: "But because the German people does not consist of Jews, the [Germans?] in Anglo-Saxon countries in particular will, unfortunately, nevertheless become progressively more anglicized. They will presumably also become spiritually and intellectually lost to our people in the same way that their practical work achievements are already lost to our people."[44]

RETURN OF GERMAN LANDS THROUGH WAR

Conversely, Hitler sees hope for those Germans still residing near the borders of the Reich, though their regions' return to the Reich would come only at the cost of war: "But with regard to the fate of those Germans who were forcibly cut off from the German body politic through the Great War and the peace treaties, it must be said that their fate and their future is a question of politically regaining the power of the motherland. Lost territories are not regained through protest campaigns but by a victorious sword."[45]

HITLER'S PRAISE FOR THE UNITED STATES

Though Hitler expresses next to no hope for Germany's success in international trade, he begrudgingly cites America's successes:

> in addition to all the European states that are struggling for the world market as export nations, the American Union is now also the stiffest competitor in many areas. The size and wealth of its internal market permits production levels and thus production facilities that decrease the cost of the product to such a

degree that, despite the enormous wages, underselling [by Germany] no longer seems at all possible. The development of the automotive industry can serve as a cautionary example here. It is not only that we Germans, for example, despite our ludicrous wages, are not in a position to export successfully against the American competition even to a small degree; [at the same time?] we must watch how American vehicles are proliferating even in our own country.[46] This is only possible because the size of the internal American market and its wealth of buying power and also, again, raw materials guarantee the American automobile industry internal sales figures that alone permit production methods that would simply be impossible in Europe due to the lack of internal sales opportunities. At issue is the general motorization of the world—a matter of immeasurable future significance. For the American Union, in any case, today's automobile industry leads all other industries."[47]

Once again praising the United States, this time Hitler weaves his views of "racial superiority" into the picture and regrets the emigration of the Nordic peoples from Europe:

This gradual removal of the Nordic element within our people leads to a lowering of our overall racial quality and thus to a weakening of our technical, cultural, and also political productive forces. The consequences of this weakening will be particularly grave for the future because now a state is appearing as an active participant in world history which for centuries, as a true European colony, obtained through the emigration of Europe's best Nordic forces, which has now, facilitated by the commonality of the original blood, formed these forces into a new national community of the highest racial quality.[48]

"It is not by chance," he continues,

that the American Union is the state in which by far the greatest number of bold, sometimes unbelievably so, inventions are currently taking place. Compared to old Europe, which has lost an infinite amount of its best blood through war and emigration, the American nation appears as a young, racially select people. Just as the achievements of a thousand degenerate Levanters[49] in Europe—say, on Crete—cannot equate with the achievements of a thousand racially much superior Germans or Englishmen, the achievements of a thousand racially questionable Europeans cannot equate with the capabilities of a thousand racially first-rate Americans.[50]

Hitler perceives the United States as being a "Nordic-Germanic state and not at all a mishmash of peoples"[51] and commends the United States for having implemented a strict immigration quota: "the American Union itself, motivated by the theories of its own racial researchers, established specific criteria for immigration."[52] "By making an immigrant's ability to set foot on

American soil dependent on specific racial requirements on the one hand as well as a certain level of physical health of the individual himself . . . [53] Scandinavians," he continues, "then Englishmen and finally Germans are allocated the largest contingents. Romanians and Slavs very limited; Japanese and Chinese one would rather exclude altogether."[54]

GERMANY'S MILITARY VULNERABILITY
AND FUTURE ALLIES

In chapter 11 Hitler examines Germany's vulnerable situation in the event of attack: "Germany is currently encircled by three power factors or power groups. England, Russia, and France are currently Germany's militarily most threatening neighbors. . . . Germany lies wedged between these states, with completely open borders."[55] He worries about the great length as well as the lack of natural obstacles along Germany's border with France and points out that much of this zone includes Germany's principle industrial area and that fighting over it could lead to the destruction of the nation's resources.[56] He mentions that Germany's second largest industrial region, Saxony, would be endangered should Czechoslovakia join the fray.[57] If Poland were involved as well, he adds, Germany would be open to attack along that border, a mere 175 kilometers (109 mi) from the capital, Berlin.[58]

Hitler drives the point home by claiming, "France comes into question as the most dangerous enemy because, thanks to its alliances, it is in a position to be able to threaten almost all of Germany with airplanes within an hour of the outbreak of a conflict. Germany's military counteraction against the application of this weapon is, all things considered, currently nil."[59] Russia's alliance with France in World War I makes Hitler cautious:

> there are still well-intentioned national men who believe in all seriousness that we must enter into an association with Russia. Considered even from a purely military perspective, such an idea is unfeasible or disastrous for Germany. Just as prior to 1914, today we can also always assume it to be absolutely certain that in every conflict in which Germany will become entangled—regardless of the reasons and regardless of the causes—France will always be our enemy. Whatever European combinations may appear in the future, France will always cooperate with the anti-German ones.[60]

He maintains that France's possession of Alsace-Lorraine does not, in any way, satisfy its long-term intentions and that its hopes are "still the conquering of the Rhine border; [and] the tearing up of Germany into individual states, as loosely attached to one another as possible." Hitler also ascertains that "actually, France has never taken part in a coalition that would also have advanced German interests in any way. In the last three hundred years, up to 1870, Germany has been attacked by France twenty-nine times."[61]

As was his custom, Hitler pitches racial slurs into his attack on the French in no uncertain terms

French nationalist chauvinism has removed itself so far from ethnic viewpoints that in order to satisfy a pure urge for power the French allow their own blood to be niggerized [*sic*] just to be able to maintain the numerical character of a "Grandnation" [*sic*]. France will thus also be a perpetual international trouble-maker until a decisive and thorough instruction of this people is undertaken one day. For the rest, no one has characterized the character of French vanity better than Schopenhauer with his dictum: Africa has its monkeys and Europe its French.[62]

Hitler's ongoing obsession with a perceived "Jewish-capitalist Bolshevik Russia" and its imminent threat to Germany is made clear in his claim that "any European coalition that does not mean tying down France is automatically prohibited for Germany."

The belief in a German-Russian understanding is fanciful as long as a government that is preoccupied with the sole effort to transmit the Bolshevist poison to Germany rules in Russia. Thus, when communist elements agitate for a German-Russian alliance, this is then natural. They justly hope that in doing so, they can bring Bolshevism to Germany itself. But it is incomprehensible when nationalist Germans believe that they can arrive at an understanding with a state whose highest interest includes the destruction of precisely this nationalist Germany. It goes without saying that if such an alliance were to materialize today, its result would be the complete dominance of Judaism in Germany, just as in Russia.[63]

He also issues a warning: "So if a German-Russian alliance were one day to have to stand the test of reality—and there are no alliances without thoughts of war—then Germany would be exposed to the concentric attacks of all of western Europe without being able to mount any serious resistance of its own."[64] Hitler closes chapter 11 with a glimpse of his future actions: "For Germany, a future alliance with Russia has no sense . . . the goal of German foreign policy . . . in the one and only place possible: [acquiring] space in the East."[65]

BRITISH "WORLD COLONIZATION" AS A MODEL

In chapter 14, in defense of his own expansionist ambitions, Hitler expresses his admiration for British racial attributes and Britain's world colonization. "The pride of the English today," he observes,

> is no different than the pride of the ancient Romans. It is mistaken to believe that world empires owed their origin to chance or that at least the events that determined their development were random historical incidents that always turned out well for a people. Ancient Rome, just like England today, owed its greatness to the correctness of Moltke's dictum that "in the long run luck is only with the competent." This competence of a people, however, does not lie in its racial worth alone, but also in the capability and skillfulness with which this worth is employed. A world empire of the magnitude of ancient Rome or current Great Britain is always the result of marrying the highest genetic quality with the clearest political objective. The objective of today's England is determined by the quality of the Anglo-Saxon people itself and the insular location. It was part of the Anglo-Saxon people's character to pursue space. Inevitably, this drive could only find its fulfillment outside today's Europe.[66]

In his final discourse, chapter 16, Hitler concludes that, despite the fact that Germany and Italy fought on opposing fronts in World War I, a future alliance should be welcome for both parties: "A nationally aware Germany and an equally proud Italy will one day—through their sincere, mutual friendship, based on common interests—also be able to heal the wounds left by the Great War." And again: "Only a National Socialist Germany will find the way to an ultimate understanding with fascist Italy and definitively eliminate the danger of military conflict between the two peoples." He also adds Great Britain into his planned alliance: "So if one examines Germany's foreign policy options more closely, then only two states actually remain as potential valuable allies for the future: Italy and England. Italy's relationship with England itself is already a good one today."[67]

Broadening his scope of allies, he adds: "Spain and Hungary can also already be assigned to this community of interests today—if only quietly.[68] . . . In the distant future, one could then perhaps imagine a new association of nations—composed of individual states of superior national quality—that could then perhaps challenge the imminent overpowering of the world by the American Union."[69]

HITLER'S WAR AGAINST INTERNATIONAL JEWRY

In the final statements and arguments of his two-hundred-and-some pages on domestic and foreign policy, Hitler returns to his ongoing obsession with the "Jewish Question":

> The war against Germany was waged by a most powerful international coalition in which only some of the states could have had a direct interest in the destruction of Germany. . . . The power that initiated this enormous war propaganda campaign was international Jewry.[70] The Jews, although they are a people whose core is not entirely uniform in terms of race, are nevertheless a people with certain essential particularities that distinguish it from all other peoples living on the earth.
>
> Judaism is not a religious community; rather, the religious ties between the Jews are in reality the current national constitution of the Jewish people. The Jew has never had his own territorially defined state like the Aryan states. Nonetheless, his religious community is a real state because it ensures the preservation, propagation, and future of the Jewish people. . . . The fact that no territorial boundaries underlie the Jewish state—as is the case with Aryan states—is associated with the fact that the essence of the Jewish people lacks the productive forces to build and sustain a territorial state.[71]

Here Hitler brings in the National Socialist ideology of "blood and soil," in contrast to the purported values of his "enemy":

> But here the struggle for survival takes various forms, corresponding to the entirely different natures of the Aryan peoples and the Jews. The basis of the Aryans' struggle for survival is the land, which is cultivated by them and which now provides the general basis for an economy that, in an internal cycle, satisfies their own requirements through the productive forces of their own people. The Jewish people, because of its lack of productive capabilities, cannot carry out the territorially conceived formation of a state; instead, it needs the labor and creative activities of other nations to support its own existence. The existence of the Jew himself thus becomes a parasitic existence within the life of other peoples.[72]

Hitler proceeds to demonize the Jew as an apocalyptic force that threatens every nation on earth:

> The ultimate goal of the Jewish struggle for survival is the enslavement of productively active peoples. Weapons assisting him in this are the attributes of shrewdness, cleverness, cunning, disguise, and so on, which are rooted in the character of his people. They are stratagems in his fight to preserve life, just like the stratagems of other peoples in military conflict. In terms of foreign

policy, he attempts to get the peoples into restlessness, divert them from their true interests, hurl them into war with one another, and thus gradually—with the help of the power of money and propaganda become their masters. His ultimate aim is the denationalization and chaotic bastardization of the other peoples, the lowering of the racial level of the highest, and domination over this racial mush through the eradication of these peoples' intelligentsias and their replacement with the members of his own people.[73]

Hitler's final xenophobic statement on a perceived imminent threat posed by "the Jew" is that National Socialists will lead the decisive fight to save humanity from "International Jewry's" downward spiral of inevitable doom:

> The Jewish international struggle will therefore always end in bloody Bolshevization—that is to say, in truth, the destruction of the intellectual upper classes associated with the various peoples, so that he himself will be able to rise to mastery over the now leaderless humanity. In this process, stupidity, coward-ice, and wickedness play into his hands. Bastards provide him the first opening to break into a foreign ethnic community. Jewish domination always ends with the decline of all culture.[74] . . . The fiercest struggle over the victory of the Jews is currently taking place in Germany. Here it is the National Socialist movement alone that has taken up the fight against this execrable crime against humanity.[75]

It is clear that when Adolf Hitler was thirty-nine years old, five years before he came to power, he held well-defined opinions about the political, economic, and social state of the world. In "Hitler's Second Book," he expresses his intentions to impose his will on the German people, his preference for certain alliances with countries like Italy, his proposals for a war of expansion in Eastern Europe, and his plan for a National Socialist campaign against global "Jewry."

Regrettably, when he and the National Socialists rose to power in 1933, Hitler's 1928 domestic and foreign policies were, indeed, implemented. Thanks to a state-of-the-art propaganda assault on the German people, the creation of an efficient terror organization, and the prodigious remilitarization of the Reich, Hitler's twelve-year reign would generate the greatest calamity in recorded human history.

NOTES

1. "Gerhard Weinberg," PritzkerMilitary.org, https://www.pritzkermilitary.org/explore/commemorate-their-service/gerhard-weinberg-honorial.

2. Gerhard Weinberg, Foreword to *Hitler's Second Book: The Unpublished Sequel to Mein Kampf,* by Adolf Hitler (New York: Enigma Books, 2006).

3. Robert Harris, *Selling Hitler: The Story of the Hitler Diaries* (New York: Pantheon, 1986).

4. Percy Ernst Schramm, ed., *Hitlers Tischgespräche im Führerhauptquartier 1941–1942* (Stuttgart: Seewald, 1965), 178.

5. Adolf Dresler, *Geschichte des "Völkischen Beobachters" und des Zentralverlags der NSDAP* (Munich: Zentralverlag der NSDAP, 1937), 89.

6. Gerhard Weinberg, Introduction to *Hitler's Second Book: The Unpublished Sequel to Mein Kampf*, by Adolf Hitler (New York: Enigma Books, 2006).

7. Albert Speer, *Spandauer Tagebücher* (Frankfurt am Main: Ullstein, 1975), 533.

8. Rudolf Hess to the Gauleitung Hannover-Nord of the NSDAP, June 26, 1928, with notation of receipt June 28, 1928; Niedersächsischen Hauptstaatsarchiv Hannover, Des. 310 I A 19.

9. Weinberg, Introduction to *Hitler's Second Book*.

10. Oron James Hale, "Adolf Hitler: Taxpayer," *American Historical Review* 60, no. 4 (July 1955): 830–42.

11. Gerhard Weinberg, Introduction to *Hitler's Second Book*.

12. Ibid.

13. Adolf Hitler, *Hitler's Second Book: The Unpublished Sequel to Mein Kampf*, by Adolf Hitler (New York: Enigma Books, 2006), 7.

14. Ibid., 7–8.

15. Ibid., 9.

16. Ibid.

17. Ibid., 11.

18. Ibid.

19. Ibid., 13.

20. Ibid., 14.

21. Ibid., 16.

22. Ibid., 17.

23. Ibid., 27.

24. Ibid., 20.

25. Ibid., 28.

26. Ibid., 30.

27. Ibid., 30–31.

28. Ibid., 31.

29. Ibid.

30. Ibid., 38–39.

31. Ibid., 49.

32. Ibid., 49–50.

33. Ibid., 50.

34. Ibid., 73.

35. Ibid., 66.

36. Ibid., 78.

37. In World War I, 1,885,291 German soldiers were killed and 4,248,158 were wounded. See *Statistisches Jahrbuch für das Deutsche Reich 1924–25* (Berlin: Herausgegeben vom Statistischen Reichsamt. Verlag für Politik und Wirtschaft, 1925), 25.

38. Hitler, *Hitler's Second Book*, 83–84.

39. Ibid., 81.

40. See Klaus Epstein, *Matthias Erzberger and the Dilemma of German Democracy* (Princeton, NJ: Princeton University Press, 1959).

41. Hitler, *Hitler's Second Book*, 96–97.

42. Ibid., 98.

43. Ibid., 99.

44. Ibid., 100.

45. Ibid., 100–101.

46. In 1927, 35,686,000 Reichsmarks' worth of motorcycles and motor vehicles were exported from the United States to the German Reich. At that time, equivalent German goods valued at 693,000 Reichsmarks were sold in the United States. See *Statistisches Jahrbuch für das Deutsche Reich 1928* (Berlin: R. Hobbing, 1928), 327f.

47. Hitler, *Hitler's Second Book*, 106–107.

48. Ibid., 108–109.

49. Levanters = inhabitants of the Levant, the Mediterranean lands east of Italy.

50. Hitler, *Hitler's Second Book*, 109

51. Ibid., 118.

52. Ibid., 118, footnote by Weinberg: "Allusion to the May 26, 1924, Immigration Act of 1924 to limit the immigration of aliens into the United States, which regulated immigration into the U.S.A. much more tightly. The First Quota Act of May 19, 1921, had already established maximum limits for individual ethnic groups."

53. Ibid., 109

54. Ibid., 118.

55. Ibid., 136.

56. Ibid.

57. Ibid., 137

58. Ibid., 138.

59. Ibid., 139.

60. Ibid., 140.

61. Ibid., 141.

62. Ibid., 144.

63. Ibid., 144–45.

64. Ibid., 148.

65. Ibid., 153.

66. Ibid., 160–61.

67. Ibid., 229–30.

68. Ibid.

69. Ibid., 231.

70. Footnote by Weinberg: "As is generally known, the situation was precisely the opposite. To the extent that one can even speak of a 'Jewish' position in World War I, it was—due to the pogroms in Russia—more pro- than anti-German."

71. Ibid., 233.

72. Ibid., 234.
73. Ibid.
74. Ibid., 234–35.
75. Ibid., 237.

Chapter 23

Did Occultism Play a Role
in the Third Reich?

Since the 1960s, numerous trendy books penned by sensationalist writers have suggested that Hitler and the National Socialist phenomenon were products of esoteric or demonic guidance. Some have concluded that the astonishing and inexplicable rise of National Socialism in traditional and religious Germany was the doing of supernatural forces. A consistent view among some conspiracy-driven authors is that the Third Reich's leaders were actively involved in various sorts of occult practices that, according to some, even lent them otherworldly powers. We shall attempt to ascertain if there is irrefutable proof or not that occult or esoteric beliefs and activities existed among the Third Reich's tyrants.

HITLER'S PROFESSION OF FAITH

Hitler's infamous statement in *Mein Kampf*, "By defending myself against the Jew, I am fighting for the work of the Lord,"[1] reminds us that he repeatedly expressed his belief in God both in public and in private. Whether he believed in a higher being or not, "Divine Providence" and "God" became regular components of Hitler's rhetoric. As early as 1920, Hitler's twenty-five-point program for the National Socialist Party included provisions for "Positive Christianity" as the future religion of the people.[2] Ultimately, this nondenominational dogma would reveal itself to be nationalistic and antisemitic and promote the belief in a non-Jewish Jesus Christ.

Raised a Catholic and professing a faith in divine authority, Hitler referred numerous times in outbursts or speeches to a higher power: "Even today I am not ashamed to say that, overpowered by stormy enthusiasm, I fell down on my knees and thanked Heaven from an overflowing heart for granting me the good fortune of being permitted to live at this time." Or in the style of a preacher, projecting on National Socialism a divine mission:

> In this hour I would ask of the Lord God only this: that, as in the past, so in the years to come He would give His blessing to our work and our action, to our judgement and our resolution, that He will safeguard us from all false pride and from all cowardly servility, that He may grant us to find the straight path which His Providence has ordained for the German people, and that He may ever give us the courage to do the right, never to falter, never to yield before any violence, before any danger. . . . I am convinced that men who are created by God should live in accordance with the will of the Almighty. . . . If Providence had not guided us I could never have found these dizzy paths. . . . Thus it is that we National Socialists, too, have in the depths of our hearts our faith. We cannot do otherwise: no man can fashion world-history or the history of peoples unless upon his purpose and his powers there rests the blessings of this Providence.[3]

If Hitler was secretly driven by occult or arcane philosophies, he certainly confirmed the opposite. In a speech heard by hundreds of thousands delivered at the 1939 Nuremberg party rallies, he declared,

> National Socialism is not a cult-movement—a movement for worship; it is exclusively a *völkisch* political doctrine based upon racial principles. In its purpose there is no mystic cult, only the care and leadership of a people defined by a common blood-relationship. . . . We will not allow mystically-minded occult folk with a passion for exploring the secrets of the world beyond to steal into our Movement. Such folk are not National Socialists, but something else—in any case something which has nothing to do with us. At the head of our program there stands no secret surmising, but clear-cut perception and straightforward profession of belief. But since we set as the central point of this perception and of this profession of belief the maintenance and hence the security for the future of a being formed by God, we thus serve the maintenance of a divine work and fulfill a divine will—not in the secret twilight of a new house of worship, but openly before the face of the Lord. . . . Our worship is exclusively the cultivation of the natural, and for that reason, because natural, therefore God-willed. Our humility is the unconditional submission before the divine laws of existence so far as they are known to us men.[4]

THE SENSATIONALISTS

Authors in the period from around 1960 to the 1990s appeared to be engaged in a competition to craft the most sensationalized tales about Hitler and his associates, ranging from beliefs in the occult to initiation into secret mystical orders and even engaging in demonic practices. These authors bought into the alleged supernatural realm in order to explain the extraordinary success and power wielded by Hitler and his top officials, resulting in the proliferation of a rapidly expanding crypto-history of the National Socialist phenomenon. The implication was that Hitler was supported and controlled by an ultimate and esoteric force—dark powers, invisible hierarchies, unknown superiors, a magical elite, or secret societies.[5]

In *The Spear of Destiny* (1982), Trevor Ravenscroft alleges that Hitler was transfixed at the sight of the spearhead of Longinus's lance, which purportedly pierced Jesus's side at the Crucifixion. Seeing this relic for the first time at Vienna's Treasury Museum, Hitler supposedly discovered he was chosen for a great political mission. However, according to the notable archeologist Keith Fitzpatrick-Matthews, Trevor Ravenscroft's source of such affirmations—including Hitler supposedly being an occultist—was through Ravenscroft's séances with a dead man named Walter Stein.[6]

In *Gods and Beasts: The Nazis and the Occult* (1977), Dusty Sklar lists a multitude of pseudosciences that circulated as an undercurrent in pre-Hitler Germany, but with regard to proving Hitler's supposed occult interests, she refers to Ravenscroft and other questionable sources and can evidence no proven direct connections of the *Führer* to such beliefs.

According to J. P. Holding, in the 1974 book *The Occult and the Third Reich*, Jean-Michel Angebert (actually the pseudonym for two authors) makes use of imagination and storytelling more than proven facts.[7] Holding also lays bare the fanciful and far-fetched surmising of Gerald Suster, a devotee of the occultist Alister Crowley, in his three books *The Occult Messiah* (1981), *Hitler and the Age of Horus* (1981), and *Hitler: Black Magician* (1996).[8]

HITLER'S ALLEGED THREE ESOTERIC MENTORS

One thing that Guido von List, Jörg Lanz von Liebenfels, and Rudolf von Sebottendorff had in common is that they were born "commoners," yet later in their lives, all three styled themselves with the aristocratic "von" as part of their name pedigree. Another common link was that all three became deeply involved in the development and dissemination of esoteric, Pan-German, pagan, theosophical, *völkisch*, antisemitic, or anti-Catholic beliefs. Above all, many authors have suggested that one or all of these men influenced Hitler's worldview or, in some way, National Socialism.

It should be kept in mind, however, that the occult revival of the late 1800s and early 1900s was the intellectual sideline of only a few, not a mainstream phenomenon, and was a reaction to the reign of materialism and industrialization of the time. Occultism in Germany was in fact an import from the

American Theosophical Society and the work of its founder, the adventuress and occultist Helena Blavatsky.[9]

GUIDO VON LIST

The Austrian occultist Guido von List (1848–1919) was the first popular writer to combine *völkisch* (nationalist, racist) ideas with occultism and theosophy. He claimed that the ancient Teutons (North Germans/Danish) had followed a gnostic religion that involved initiation into the mysteries of nature. He called this religion Wotanism, a type of early shamanism, and began studying and interpreting ancient runes. The religion that List interpreted from these various elements was to be implemented as the faith of a new Pan-German realm. He distinguished between the exoteric (Wotanist) and the esoteric (Armanist) types of religious systems. The Armanen, according to List, were ancient priest-kings. He also affirmed that the swastika was a holy Aryan symbol and that it had developed from the "fire-whisk" from which the creator had swirled the cosmos into being.[10]

There is no evidence that Hitler read the works of Guido von List, yet the similarity between the occultist's precepts and some of those associated with National Socialism appear to be more than coincidental. List's blueprint for the new Pan-German empire required the brutal subjugation of "non-Aryans to their Aryan masters in a highly structured hierarchical state." To qualify for education or posts in civil service, racial purity had to be proven. The Ario-German people would rule over the slave castes of non-Aryans, follow strict racial-marital laws, and only the pure-blooded would be allowed citizenship. These guidelines, published in 1911, read like the first draft of the National Socialists' 1935 racial purity laws, the so-called Nuremberg Laws.[11]

Guido von List also developed a detailed conspiracy theory that attempted to prove that Christianity had played a negative and destructive role in the history of the Ario-Germanic race.[12] Such concepts were later widely disseminated by the National Socialists' ideologist, Alfred Rosenberg, one of the key developers of the new "Positive Christianity."[13]

LANZ VON LIEBENFELS

In his youth, Jörg Lanz von Liebenfels (1874–1954) joined the Cistercian monks near Vienna until an "enlightenment" that resulted from his discovery of a Knight Templar's tombstone. After leaving the order, he began developing racial theories and embraced the notion of a strange prehistoric world of godlike Aryan supermen whose spiritual duty it was to carry out a sacrificial extermination of the submen, the "Apelings."[14] Influenced by social Darwinism, Lanz described the blue-eyed, blond-haired race as the good principle and various dark races or "Mediterraneanoids" as the evil principle. Lanz developed a system of belief that he termed "Ariosophy," similar in substance to his contemporary occultist Guido von List's "Armanen" principles. He also founded a new chivalrous organization that he called the Order of the New Templars and, with the financial support of his Viennese friends, purchased a castle as its headquarters.

Lanz advocated brood mothers in eugenic convents, served by pure-blooded Aryan males. The racist occultist recommended using "racial inferiors" as beasts of burden, deporting them to Madagascar, and incinerating them as a sacrifice to God. Here again, the National Socialist regime's employment of Jews, Slavs, and others as slave labor or incinerating them in crematoria and plans for deporting the Jews to Madagascar, as well as the psychopathy of the Holocaust, were foretold by Lanz's xenophobic suggestions.[15]

Beginning in 1905, Lanz von Liebenfels, based in Vienna, began publishing a periodical titled *Ostara* (named after the pagan goddess of spring), a journal in which he and other like-minded occultists, Pan-Germanists, anti-semitists, and followers of Guido von List could express their views. Basic themes included racial somatology, antifeminism, antiparliamentarianism, and the spiritual differences between the "light" and the "dark" races in all aspects of society. One of the 1906 issues, written by Harald Grävell van Jostenoode, crusaded for the return of the Holy Roman Empire's Imperial Regalia from Austria to Germany, an act that was carried out by Hitler as soon as he annexed Austria to the German Reich.[16]

The British historian Nicholas Goodrick-Clarke defends in detail the sources from which he affirms that Hitler not only was an avid reader of *Ostara*'s sexist, racist, and occult-imbued content but also kept a collection of at least fifty of these scurrilous pamphlets. Whether the down-and-out artist read *Ostara* or not, many similarities exist in the respective opinions of Hitler and Liebenfels. Both men saw the world as divided between light-skinned Aryan heroes and dark-skinned "apelings," and they both stressed the high value of marriage but viewed women ambivalently.[17]

RUDOLF VON SEBOTTENDORFF

The Germanenorden was founded in Berlin in 1912 by Theodor Fritsch and several leading occultists connected to the Guido von List Society and the High Armanen Order. The rituals of the order were influenced by theories about the Aryan race, Freemasonry, and the operas of Richard Wagner. The Germanenorden's principal aims were the monitoring of the Jews and their activities, the dissemination of antisemitic materials, propagating *völkisch* ideology, and offering assistance to its members. The order's roots were undeniably planted in Guido von List's Ariosophy, and its symbol was a curved swastika superimposed on a cross.[18] These elements would all be emulated during the course of Hitler's Third Reich.

The adventurer and world traveler Rudolf von Sebottendorf (1875–1945) became so interested in the Germanenorden that, in 1917, he founded the Bavarian branch of the order. With the help of Walter Neuhaus, an occultist fascinated by astrology, chiromancy, and the mystical ideologies of secret cults, Sebottendorf attracted some 1,500 members to the new Germanenorden division within a year. Meetings of the order's brethren took place in the posh rooms of Munich's grand Vier Jahreszeiten Hotel, with as many as three hundred members attending on a regular basis. To avoid drawing attention from socialist or prorepublican activists, the order disguised itself as the "Thule Society," the moniker alluding to the ancient name of Iceland, supposedly the outpost of Germanic refugees according to Guido von List. The Thule Society's symbol was a dagger superimposed on a shining swastika sun wheel.[19]

In 1918, Sebottendorf purchased a newspaper, the *Beobachter* (Observer) and renamed it the *Münchner Beobachter und Sportblatt* (Munich Observer and Sports Page), with the intent of propagating the Thule Society's anti-semitic views and doctrine. Two years later, the paper belonged in part to an early supporter of Hitler's and eventually slid into the hands of Anton Drexler, chairman of the Deutsche Arbeiter Partei (German Workers' Party), the precursor to Hitler's National Socialist German Workers' Party. The newspaper's shares were transferred to Adolf Hitler in 1921, and the paper was eventually renamed the *Völkischer Beobachter*, the party's main propaganda newspaper.[20]

CONCLUSIONS

Neither the occultist Germanenorden nor Sebottendorf's Thule Society could claim to have served as blueprints for National Socialist doctrine, but some of Hitler's earliest supporters, as listed in chapter 5, were either members of or associated with the Thule Society. The "mystical" and racist organization did, however, help shape Hitler's future ideological structures, even if only through the swastika symbol and having provided a newspaper for his party's propaganda.

Although Hitler was given a variety of books on occultism, he did not display any interest in Germany's pagan and Nordic cults. Instead, his concept of Aryanism was influenced by the Greek and Roman tradition. According to those who knew him well, Hitler was an avid reader, but he did not read materials on the occult—instead, he extensively read books on history, particularly military history.[21]

Though the various abovementioned authors and lecturers on the mishmash of occultism, runology, racial issues, astrology, the supernatural, and knightly orders may have exerted minor influence on some of the Third Reich's leaders, there is no proof that any of them practiced any form of occultism. A sole common theme expressed by the three occultists mentioned—pro-Aryan racism—was mirrored in the dogma of the National Socialist spearheads. The use of the *Sig* rune to designate the SS and the adoption of the swastika symbol as the National Socialists' logo have little to do with occultism, and there is no evidence of any of the Reich's leaders having been members of cults or secret societies or carried out searches for ancient secrets or artifacts. Though much has been insinuated regarding Hitler's possible connection to mystical, occult, or dark forces, it is wise to scrutinize and question such authors' references and source material.

NOTES

1. Hitler, *Mein Kampf*, 25.
2. Laurence Rees, *The Dark Charisma of Adolf Hitler* (New York: Pantheon Books, 2012), 135.
3. Speech at the Reichstag, February 20, 1938, in Baynes, *Speeches of Adolf Hitler, April 1922–August 1939*, 410.
4. Speech delivered at Nuremberg, September 6, 1938, in Adolf Hitler, *My New Order* (New York: Reynal & Hitchcock, 1941), 500.
5. Nicholas Goodrick-Clarke, *The Occult Roots of Nazism* (London: Tauris Parke, 2004), 218.
6. Keith Fitzpatrick-Matthews, "'The Spear of Destiny': Hitler, the Hapsburgs and the Holy Grail," *Bad Archaeology*, December 30 2012, https://badarchaeology.wordpress.com/2012/12/30/the-spear-of-destiny-hitler-the-hapsburgs-and-the-holy-grail/.
7. J. P. Holding, *Hitler's Christianity* (n.p.: Tekton, 2013), ebook, chap. 2.
8. Ibid.
9. Goodrick-Clarke, *Occult Roots of Nazism*, 18.
10. Ibid., 33–52.
11. Ibid., 64.
12. Ibid., 68.
13. Cecil, *Myth of the Master Race*, 85–92.
14. Goodrick-Clarke, *Occult Roots of Nazism*, 90
15. Ibid., 97.

16. Ibid., 194–95.
17. Ibid., 196–97.
18. Ibid., 123–34.
19. Ibid., 142–44.
20. Ibid., 146–47.
21. Weber, *Becoming Hitler*, 246–48.

Chapter 24

Religion in the Reich

THE BATTLE OF THE TWO CROSSES

As an Austrian, Hitler was raised in a typically Catholic household—however, he was anything but the ideal Christian. Just like Himmler, he understood the necessity of attracting votes and that the early marketing of the National Socialist Party must target the religious morality of the predominantly Christian German population. Hitler even states in *Mein Kampf*, "By defending myself against the Jew, I am fighting for the Lord's work."[1] A basis of the party's ideology was its "crusade" of fighting the Jews, and Hitler aimed at presenting himself as a defender of Christianity. Anyone familiar with Hitler's speeches and writings can confirm that he frequently incorporated the terms "God," "Spirit," and "Divine Providence" in his oratory. He was, after all, addressing a people whose social tradition was deeply rooted in Christianity.

THE NATIONAL SOCIALISTS' "POSITIVE CHRISTIANITY"

In 1920 Hitler stated in the National Socialist Party's twenty-five-point platform, "The Party as such stands for a *Positive Christianity*, without binding itself denominationally to a particular confession." "Nondenominational," the term could be widely reinterpreted. The new National Socialist idea of Positive Christianity allayed the fears of Germany's Christian majority by indicating that the movement was not anti-Christian.[2] The roots of Positive Christianity lead back to the nineteenth century and excessive German nationalism coupled with a strong reaction to ultramontanism (the clerical political conception within the Catholic Church that places strong emphasis on the powers and infallibility of the pope). Though not officially a proponent of Positive Christianity, Ignaz von Döllinger was a famed nineteenth-century Bavarian theologian whose views were widely discussed, acclaimed, or protested throughout Western Europe. He claimed that "God had given Germans, in particular, the world historical task of reinterpreting Catholic theology for the dawning modern age," and he called on German Catholics to "shed the yoke of ultramontanism and to assume their predestined role as "teachers of all the nations."[3]

A later promoter of Positive Christianity was another Bavarian Catholic, Franz Schrönghamer Heimdal, who published *Das Kommende Reich* (The Coming Reich) in 1918. The work charted a detailed plan for the "ecumenical yet distinctly Catholic-oriented spiritual rebuilding of Germany," and he differentiated the purity of Christ and his true followers from the alleged immorality of the Jewish-capitalistic spirit. While Heimdal did not conceal his Catholic convictions, the future Reich that he proposed was to be interconfessional. However, both Catholics and Protestants would be bonded in a "racial community [*Volksgemeinschaft*] of the same blood, the same law and the same morals," maintained through "race-based eugenic measures."[4] Soon after, Heimdal produced two more flamingly antisemitic works, *The Antichrist* and *Judas, the World Enemy*, and he joined the National Socialist Party in 1920.

The three main principles of National Socialist Positive Christianity are clearly defined in Heimdal's *The Coming Reich*, namely, an expurgated publication of the Bible, a non-Jewish Jesus, and orthopraxy as opposed to orthodoxy.[5] Advocates of Positive Christianity contended that traditional Christianity emphasized the passive rather than the active aspects of Christ's life, highlighting his miraculous birth, his suffering, his sacrifice on the cross and other-worldly redemption. Positive Christianity aimed to replace this doctrine with a "positive" focus on Jesus as an active preacher, organizer, and fighter who opposed the institutionalized Judaism of his day. Positive Christianity's chief divergences from mainstream Christianity were the following:[6]

- Rejection of the Jewish-written parts of the Bible (including the entire Old Testament)
- Claiming Aryan origins and non-Jewishness for Christ based on the argument that the population of Galilee was racially distinct from that of Judea
- Promotion of national unity to overcome confessional differences, eliminating Catholicism and uniting Protestantism into a single unitary positive Christian church
- Encouragement of followers to support the creation of an Aryan homeland

Hitler defined the non-Jewish Christ of Positive Christianity in a statement made at the founding of the Rosenheim party office in 1921: "I can imagine Christ as nothing other than blond and with blue eyes, the devil however only with a Jewish grimace."[7] In a 1922 speech Hitler called Jesus "the true God" and also "our greatest Aryan leader."[8]

Positive Christianity's premise that Jesus Christ was not Jewish was based on the notions of the British racially biased author, Houston Stewart Chamberlain, who exercised a strong influence on both Hitler and the Reich's ideologist, Alfred Rosenberg. Chamberlain argued that Jesus was a member of an Indo-European, Nordic enclave in ancient Galilee and struggled against Judaism. Rosenberg quoted Dr. Emil Jung, referring to statements by the Syrian Christian preacher Ephraem (fourth century): "Jesus's mother was a Danaite woman (that is, someone born in Dan), and he had a Latin as father. Ephraem sees this to be not dishonorable and adds: 'Jesus thus derived his ancestry from two of the greatest and most famous nations, namely, from the Syrians on the maternal side and from the Romans on the paternal.'"[9]

THE GERMAN CHURCHES

At the time of Hitler's takeover, in addition to a minority of 3.5 percent nondemonitational "believers in God," about 95 percent of Germans were Christians, of which roughly one-third were Catholic and two-thirds Protestant. It may surprise some that in Germany and Austria the church is funded through public taxing, which are compulsory if a member wishes to be part of the church community and enjoy the rites of baptism, communion, marriage, extreme unction, funeral, and burial.

Both Adolf Hitler and Joseph Goebbels had stopped attending Catholic mass or going to confession long before 1933 and became increasingly anti-Christian, but neither of the two Third Reich leaders officially "left the church" and neither of them refused to pay his church taxes.[10] The remaining religious minorities, such as Jehovah's Witnesses, Bahá'í, and the Seventh-Day Adventist Church, all disappeared from Germany, while astrologers, healers, fortune tellers, and practitioners of witchcraft were banned as well. Though Jewish persecution began in small ways as soon as the National Socialist regime was established, Jews were allowed to practice their faith until the catastrophic *Reichskristallnacht* in November 1938, when 267 synagogues were destroyed by rioters in Germany, Austria, and Sudetenland.[11]

During the 1930s, the predominant Protestant church in Germany was known as the German Evangelical Church, which included the three major theological traditions that had originated from the Reformation: Lutheran, Reformed, and United. This church saw itself as a crucial pillar of German culture and society, grounded in a theological tradition of loyalty to the state. In the aftermath of Germany's defeat and humiliation in World War I, during the 1920s a movement called the Deutsche Christen (German Christians) emerged within the German Evangelical Church, which embraced several National Socialist principles. When the National Socialists came to power, this movement advocated for the establishment of a national "Reich Church" and supported a version of Christianity that aligned with NS ideology.[12]

In opposition to the German Christians and their Reich Church, a countermovement developed called the Bekennende Kirche (Confessing Church) that professed "allegiance to God and scripture, not to a worldly *Führer*." Both the Confessing Church and the German Christians remained part of the German Evangelical Church, which resulted in major conflict within German Protestantism. The regime took advantage of this struggle to implement its fight against the church and Christianity. Some members of the Confessing Church have gone down in history, such as the theologian Dietrich Bonhoeffer, executed for his role in the conspiracy to overthrow the regime, and Pastor Martin Niemöller, who spent seven years in concentration camps for his criticisms of Hitler.[13]

Once Hitler came to power in 1933, he assured the nation that "the rights of churches will not be restricted, nor will their relationship to the state be changed."[14] In fact, his personal contempt of Christianity never came to the public's attention.[15] That same year, the Reich Concordat was signed, a treaty that guaranteed the rights of the Roman Catholic Church in Germany. However, the concordat required all clergy to abstain from becoming active in and for political parties. Essentially, the Third Reich's intention was to reduce the church's influence by restricting its organizations to purely religious activities.[16]

The National Socialists' Positive Christianity statement of 1920 might have been welcomed by many church leaders but was, nonetheless, brazenly antisemitic:

> We demand the freedom of all religious confessions in the state, insofar as they do not jeopardize the state's existence or conflict with the manners and moral sentiments of the Germanic race. The Party as such upholds the point of view of a positive Christianity without binding itself to any one confession. It combats the Jewish-materialistic spirit at home and abroad and is convinced that a permanent recovery of our people can only be achieved from within, on the basis of the common good before individual good.

The Concordat helped to appease the Catholic leadership in Germany and abroad, but to Hitler the agreement was simply a means of putting an end to the Catholic Church's "meddling in politics."[17] Hitler's plan for the Reich

Church was that "once that leadership was established, political control could then be applied to make the whole Church an instrument of the National Socialist Party."[18] After political power was stripped from both the Catholic and Protestant churches in Germany, National Socialist ideology could be forced on the nation.

Hitler, however, was not the National Socialist regime's sole influencer. Similarly to Hitler, Heinrich Himmler was raised a Catholic and identified with this faith at least until 1924, when he began to doubt Christianity.[19] Himmler was interested in works that touched on the occult, as well as Teutonic and old German mythology that promoted the notion of the Aryan race's superiority.[20] He became increasingly anti-Christian, to the point where he aimed at restoring Germany to its pagan and mythological roots, free of Christianity, by any means necessary.[21] As head of the SS, Himmler imposed these beliefs on the organization, a conviction that escalated in open attacks on the church. Himmler, with Hitler's approval, spearheaded a radical and aggressive policy toward the church and its clergy that increased in intensity into the war years.[22]

In public speeches, Hitler portrayed himself and his National Socialist movement as faithful Christians.[23] In 1928 Hitler said in a speech, "We tolerate no one in our ranks who attacks the ideas of Christianity . . . in fact our movement is Christian."[24] However, Propaganda Minister Joseph Goebbels saw an "insoluble opposition" between the Christian and National Socialist worldviews,[25] and Heinrich Himmler considered the main task of his SS organization as becoming the vanguard in overcoming Christianity and restoring a "Germanic" way of living.[26] Hitler's right-hand man and spokesman for the *Führer* Martin Bormann advised government officials in 1941 that "National Socialism and Christianity are irreconcilable."[27] According to Goebbels's diaries, Hitler hated Christianity. In an April 8, 1941, entry, he wrote of Hitler, "He hates Christianity, because it has crippled all that is noble in humanity."[28] It is known that Hitler admired the ancient Greeks' religion and their bright and open temples, as compared to dark and enclosed medieval Christian cathedrals.

HITLER'S CLAIMS OF PEACEFUL
DEALINGS WITH THE CHURCH

Hitler delivered the following speech at the Reichstag on January 30, 1939:

We are indeed perhaps better able than other generations to realize the full meaning of those pious words "What a change by the grace of God." Among the accusations which are directed against Germany in the so-called democracies, is the charge that the National Socialist State is hostile to religion. In answer to that charge I should like to make before the German people the following solemn declaration: 1. No one in Germany has in the past been persecuted because of his religious views, nor will anyone in the future be so persecuted. 2. The National Socialist State since 30th January 1933, from public monies derived from taxation through the organs of the State, has placed at the disposal of both Churches the following sums:

In the fiscal year 1933 130 million Reichsmark

In the fiscal year 1934 170 million Reichsmark

In the fiscal year 1935 250 million Reichsmark

In the fiscal year 1936 320 million Reichsmark

In the fiscal year 1937 400 million Reichsmark

In the fiscal year 1938 500 million Reichsmark

In addition to this there has been paid over some 85 million Reichsmark each year from contributions of the separate States, and some 7 million Reichsmark from contributions of the parishes and parish associations. . . . Further, the Church in the National Socialist State is in many ways favored in regard to taxation and for gifts, legacies, etc., it enjoys immunity from taxation. . . . It is therefore, to put it mildly, effrontery when, especially foreign politicians, make bold to speak of hostility to religion in the Third Reich. But if it be true that the German Churches regard this position as intolerable, the National Socialist State is at any time ready to undertake a clear separation between Church and State as is already the case in France, America and other countries, I would allow myself only one question: "What contributions during the same period have France, England or the United States made through the State from the public funds?"

History tells us different: at the time Hitler made such claims that no one had been persecuted because of his religious views, countless members of the Protestant and Catholic faiths, as well as Jehovah's Witnesses, had been imprisoned or killed.

In the same speech Hitler affirmed,

This State has only once intervened in the internal regulation of the Churches, that is when I myself in 1933 endeavored to unite the weak and divided Protestant Churches of the different States into one great and powerful Evangelical Church of the Reich. That attempt failed through the opposition of the bishops of some States; it was therefore abandoned. For it is in the last resort not our task to defend or even to strengthen the Evangelical Church through violence against its own representatives. . . . But on one point it is well that there should be no uncertainty: the German priest as servant of God we shall protect, the priest as political enemy of the German State we shall destroy.

CONTROLLING THE CHURCH

Immediately after the party gained power, churches and monasteries became targets, as did clergy-led schools such as those run by Jesuits. In order to de-Christianize the Reich, all clergymen were closely monitored for any signs of opposition to National Socialist ideology, resulting in roughly a third of German priests facing some form of retaliation. The persecution was particularly severe in the annexed Polish regions, where the church was systematically dismantled and many priests were either killed, deported, or forced to flee. Of the 2,720 clerics from Germany and occupied territories imprisoned at the special "priest barracks" in Dachau, 2,579 (94.88 percent) were Catholic and 209 were Protestant. These numbers do not account for the number of church leaders interned in other concentration camps, nor how many were murdered by Hitler's regime.

According to the author Richard Overy, Hitler believed that all religions were now decadent—in Europe it was the "collapse of Christianity that we are now experiencing"—and the reason for the crisis was science. Hitler, like Stalin, took a very modern view of the incompatibility of religious and scientific explanation. At any rate, Hitler knew in 1933 that he could not instantly remove the centuries-old religious beliefs and foundations of a nation whose inhabitants innately identified themselves as Christians. He would not reveal his violently anticlerical views to those sixty-seven million Germans whose trust and support he needed to gain. Instead, the *Führer* would focus on restoring the nation to its former glory while carrying out an unprecedented deployment of both propaganda and terror. All the while, he and his ideology marketers implemented a seductive campaign of Hitler worship that incorporated both Christian and pagan symbols and ideals.

PRESENTING THE SAVIOR

A dramatic campaigning era poster of Hitler greets—and distresses—visitors as they enter the informative Documentation Center at Obersalzberg in Berchtesgaden. Adolf Hitler, wearing a brown uniform, seems to advance out of the picture toward the viewer as he leads an army of SA men. He, just like the brownshirts he is leading, holds aloft a large swastika banner in his upraised right hand (in the style of a holy crusade or the divine calling of Joan of Arc) while his left hand is clenched into a fist that suggests anger and a readiness to fight. The *Führer*'s fist draws attention to the Iron Cross medal pinned to his chest as proof of both his experience as a war veteran and a soldier decorated for acts of bravery.

Hitler's facial expression is one of determination and resolve, and his gaze is fixed into the eyes of the beholder. Taking this political message to a different dimension, a well-known, symbolic Catholic composition blatantly stands out above Hitler's head: a bird hovers with outstretched wings while rays of sunlight stream down upon the "chosen one." To Christians this symbology unmistakably represents the Holy Spirit and is often portrayed above Jesus Christ's head: here the unspoken and subliminal message proclaims this man to be the Messiah of the German people in their hour of need. The poster simply states, "Es Lebe Deutschland" (long live Germany).

The story of National Socialist Germany is, in essence, a tale of confrontation between two saviors and two "crosses" (in German the swastika is called a *Hakenkreuz*, a "hooked cross"). With time, the church was obliged to choose, for in the end, only one cross could prevail.[29]

Viewed from the German people's perspective, Adolf Hitler's achievements, in the briefest time period, bordered on the miraculous. Among other political triumphs, Hitler the new "Savior," unfettered by the restrictions of a democracy, appeared to accomplish the following:[30]

1. Rebuild Germany's ruined economy.
2. Remove the shame of Germany's World War I defeat by reclaiming the Rhineland and abrogating the Versailles Treaty's edicts.
3. Provide culture and vacations for millions of working-class Germans.
4. Build training schools for the unskilled and decrease unemployment from six million to just three hundred thousand.
5. Successfully reduce crime to a minimum.
6. Build autobahns and promise ordinary Germans an affordable car.
7. Restore national pride and make Germans believe they could achieve greatness once again.

Hitler, an avid reader of Nietzsche's works, was familiar with the statement from his book *The Antichrist*: "I call Christianity the one great curse, the one enormous and innermost perversion, the one moral blemish of mankind. . . . I regard Christianity as the most seductive lie that has yet existed." Hitler was so taken with the writings of Nietzsche—the man who claimed that "the churches were tombs and sepulchers of God"—that he gifted a copy of the author's work to his friend and Italian counterpart Benito Mussolini.[31]

THE *FÜHRER* PRINCIPLE AND THE *FÜHRER* CULT

The *Führerprinzip* (leader principle) set the fundamental basis of political authority in the Third Reich's governmental structure. This principle can be best explained to mean that the *Führer*'s word stood above all written law and that governmental procedures, resolutions, and agencies were compelled to implement the will of the *Führer*.

Nationwide image campaigns were launched that presented Hitler like an idol to the masses. The propaganda media included posters of Hitler's image against a backdrop of huge crowds and the words *"Führer wir Folgen Dir! Alle sagen Ja!"* (*Führer* we follow you! Everyone says yes!). In National Socialist Germany, the Hitler cult was ever-present and distributed in over-whelming proportions.[32] The regime did not aim at achieving legitimacy and public consensus through democratic institutions and procedures, but rather it put in motion common experiences and emotions that would create a clear relationship between the leader and the *Volk*. This leadership cult mirrors the Christian premise that Jesus Christ is the shepherd of humanity. Like his sheep, the believers trust and follow this leadership for the protection, suste-nance, and guidance that he will provide.

Similarly to the depiction of Jesus Christ in homes and in churches, Hitler's image loomed omnipresent. His portrait was reproduced on postcards, post-age stamps, coins, and banknotes, displayed in schools, public buildings, and on billboards. Mass-produced plaster or bronze busts were to be placed in private homes, and copies of *Mein Kampf* were gifted to newlyweds. Songs praising the *Führer* were performed by young and old alike, and oaths of unfailing allegiance to the *Führer* were taken by members of the Hitler Youth, the military, the SS, and most regime-controlled organizations. "Divine Providence" had given Hitler to Germany, he claimed, and history shows that he would use his allegedly God-given authority to serve as the shepherd and savior of the German people.

The *Führer* cult's most striking ritualization was achieved in the staging of annual feast days and celebrations during which the *Führer* played the main role. In a parody of Christian "holy" days, a series of nationwide feast days dotted the National Socialists' yearly calendar. January 30 marked the "Day of the Seizure of Power." After the "Party's Founding Day" on February 24, the *Volkstrauertag* (People's Day of Mourning) for the dead of World War I was held in March, as well as the *Verpflichtung der Jugend* (Youth's Declaration of Commitment). Hitler's birthday on April 20 became a national holiday and was followed by massive military parades on May 1.

Following Mother's Day came the pagan-like lighting of fires for the Summer Solstice, amid much fanfare and marches provided by the Hitler

Youth and SS. The main event was the weeklong Nuremberg party rallies, attended by hundreds of thousands of compliant members of the People's Community. After the pagan-inspired ceremonies of the massive autumn thanksgiving festivals came the November 9 Memorial Day. This solemn commemoration was performed to honor the "fallen martyrs of the Movement," in other words, the rioters who died during Munich's Beer Hall Putsch. The year's calendar of celebrations ended with Christmas, though this Christian holiday was celebrated in a number of new ways as the years passed.[33]

THE BLOOD BANNER AND HONORING THE DEAD

The *Blutfahne* (Blood Flag) became a much revered symbol of National Socialists. During the November 1923 Beer Hall Putsch in Munich, police opened fire on the protesters as they marched through the streets, resulting in sixteen deaths among the National Socialist rioters. The flagbearer Heinrich Trambauer was hit and dropped the flag, whereupon Andreas Bauriedl, an SA man marching alongside the flag, was killed and fell onto it, staining the flag with his blood.[34] The Blood Flag was presented to Hitler following his release from Landsberg prison, and he had it fitted to a new staff and finial; just below the finial, a silver dedication sleeve was added that bore the names of the sixteen dead participants in the putsch.[35]

At the second party congress at Weimar in 1926, Hitler ceremonially conferred the flag on Joseph Berchtold, head of the SS at the time.[36] From then on the flag was regarded as a sacred relic by the National Socialist Party and carried by SS-*Sturmbannführer* Jakob Grimminger at various ceremonies and events.

The Blood Flag played a significant role in the grand and theatrical displays of the National Socialist Party at their annual Nuremberg rallies. The location chosen for these events, the *Luipoldshain* parkland outside of Nuremberg, had originally been built to commemorate the First World War's military victims in Weimar Republic times. However, the National Socialist regime appropriated the site to stage massive ceremonies, not to commemorate the victims of the Great War but to glorify the sixteen "martyrs" of Munich. The park was destroyed to accommodate up to 150,000 SA and SS men standing in formation beneath towering swastika banners reaching up to twenty-four meters (78 ft) in height.[37]

In this colossal Roman-era setting, Hitler, reminiscent of a high priest, ceremoniously touched new National Socialist organizations' banners with the Blood Flag, thereby "sanctifying" them.[38] These pseudoreligious theatrics were staged as part of a solemn ceremony called the *Fahnenweihe* (flag

Figure 24.1. Hitler dedicating standards during the Blood Flag Ceremony at a Nuremberg rally (1935). *Courtesy of USHMM*

consecration). When it was not in use, the Blood Flag was kept at the National Socialist Party headquarters in Munich, known as the "Brown House," watched over by an SS guard of honor.

If the dead putsch participants were now the new saints, then their flag had become a "holy relic." The press reports and speeches related to such pseudo-religious events echoed the rhetoric of the faith with terms such as "sacrifice," "martyrs," "resurrection," and "holy place of pilgrimage." The new saints had sacrificed themselves for Hitler as a "sacred duty" to the cause, and the notion of devotion and loyalty to the *Führer* as "savior" of the German people was reinforced by rhetoric and spectacle. In addition to the religious concepts of conversion, hope, and faith, Hitler aimed the theatrics at reinforcing a sense of unity, of belonging to the same "church."[39] Referring to the National Socialists' violent beginnings with the Beer Hall Putsch, Hitler described the spilled blood as "baptismal water for the Reich."[40]

Two *Ehrentempel* (honor temples) were constructed in austere neo-Greek style near the party headquarters and Hitler's office building at Königsplatz in Munich. These structures "enshrined" the remains of the sixteen activists killed in the 1923 Beer Hall Putsch.

CHRISTIAN SYMBOLS IN THIRD
REICH PROPAGANDA

Starting with the Catholic cult of the Virgin Mary as Mother of God, honoring motherhood is one of western Christian culture's oldest traditions. An *Ehrenkreuz der deutschen Mutter* (cross of honor of the German mother) was awarded to ethnic German women as a medal for having mothered numerous children. In 1939 alone, some three million women received this award, also simply known as the *Mutterkreuz* (mother's cross).

The medal was shaped like the Marian Cross of the Teutonic Knights (*Marinenkreuz der Deutschen Ritterorden*), an order also known as the Order of Brothers of the German House of Saint Mary in Jerusalem[41] and viewed by National Socialists as a historical bulwark of German presence and domination in the Balkans. This design of the Marian Cross is a type of "cross *pattée*," in which the arms are narrower at the center and flare out to become broader at the perimeter. In the middle, against a sunburst background, a swastika reminds us that Hitler and the National Socialists were the patrons of this award. The Christian cross—to all Germans a deep-rooted symbol of salvation—is combined here with the National Socialists' hooked cross or "twisted cross," as it is sometimes monikered.

In western society, we record years starting with year zero as a rough estimation of when Jesus Christ was born. The National Socialists began introducing the notion of Hitler's ascent to power in January 1933 as "year zero." The year 1938, for instance, would be referred to as the "fifth year" of Adolf Hitler's new calendar. Here again we find Hitler being portrayed as the (new) savior.

"Heil Hitler!" was a salute adopted by the party in the 1930s as a gesture of obedience to Adolf Hitler and to glorify the German nation (later also the German war effort). According to historian Ian Kershaw, the salute was mandatory for civilians but mostly optional for military personnel, who retained the traditional military salute. Though the adjective *heilig* means "holy," the word *heil* in German signifies health or wholeness on the one hand but also a salutation expressing salvation or asking for pardon on the other. The English equivalent "hail" is familiar to us, mainly associated with the Roman Catholic Church in the Hail Mary (Latin, Ave Maria), a traditional prayer of praise for the Blessed Virgin Mary. In this context, the salutation *"Heil Hitler"* resembles a proclamation of humility and praise for the *Führer* as more than a political or military leader—a spiritual savior, redeemer, or messiah.

The German Wehrmacht's crushing defeat in the battle to win Stalingrad came as a shock to the German people, who had been constantly assured of the nation's victories. A poster was produced depicting a ruined fortification perched atop a rock, over which flutters a tattered and torn swastika flag. Emerging from a sunburst, a large right hand with raised thumb, index finger, and middle finger folded annular and little finger makes the Christian sign of benediction, a gesture associated with Jesus Christ, a pope, or a high priest. The text *"Führer befiehl, wir folgen!"* (*Führer* commanded, we follow!) comes from a National Socialist song but is employed here to associate the hand of benediction with Hitler's own command: another marriage of Christian symbology with National Socialist propaganda.

THE HOOKED CROSS: SYMBOL OF TERROR?

To most people today, the Third Reich's symbol and logo, the swastika or *Hakenkreuz*, is indissociably linked to Hitler's regime of terror. Its history, however, is ancient, and the pictogram was traditionally associated with positive elements.

According to the *Encyclopedia Britannica*, the word "swastika" is of Sanskrit origin and was an ancient symbol used in Indian religions such as Hinduism, Buddhism, and Jainism. In Hinduism, the symbol with arms pointing clockwise (卐) is called *swastika*, symbolizing *surya*, "sun," and prosperity and good luck, while the counterclockwise symbol (卍) is called *sauvastika*, symbolizing night or tantric aspects of Kali, who in Hinduism is the goddess of time and is synonymous with doomsday and death. A Greek gold disk with swastikas (at the Otago Museum) and a first-century Roman floor mosaic featuring a swastika (at the Antiquities Museum in Parma, Italy) bear witness to the symbol in Europe's classic cultures.

In Great Britain the common moniker associated to the swastika from Anglo-Saxon times was *fylfot*, a name that may have originated from the Anglo-Saxon *fower fot*, meaning "four-footed" or "many-footed."[42] The word *fylfot* is Scandinavian and is a compound of the Old Norse *fiǫl-*, equivalent to the Anglo-Saxon *fela* and German *viel*, "many," and *fótr*, "foot": the many-footed figure.[43]

Over the centuries, the swastika has been used as a symbol of good fortune or protection in Norway, Sweden, Denmark, Finland, Iceland, Ireland, France, Poland, Latvia, Russia, and Spain. As a favored symbol of the Navajo and prior to the 1930s, the swastika was used in the United States in countless architectural features and decorations, as well as in the choice of logos for numerous companies and associations.

Collectors have identified more than 1,400 different swastika-design coins, souvenir or merchant-trade tokens, and watch fobs, distributed mostly by local retail and service businesses in the United States. The tokens that can be dated range from 1885 to 1939, with a few later exceptions. About

57 percent have the swastika symbol facing to the left, 43 percent to the right. Most promise good luck or feature additional symbols such as a horseshoe, four-leaf clover, rabbit's foot, wishbone, or keys.[44] In 1925, Coca-Cola made a lucky watch fob in the shape of a swastika with right-facing arms and the slogan, "Drink Coca-Cola—five cents in bottles."

Following World War I, several far-right nationalist movements appropriated the swastika as their emblem. As a symbol, it began to represent a racially "pure" state. Among other such secret or exclusive organizations, the German Thule Society elected to use a stylized swastika as its symbol. Though himself not a member, Hitler's friend and mentor Dietrich Eckart was associated with the Thule Society and was likely the person who suggested its use as the visual symbol that became the icon of the new party.

When the National Socialists took control of Germany, the inferences of the swastika forever changed. In *Mein Kampf*, Adolf Hitler wrote, "I myself, meanwhile, after innumerable attempts, had laid down a final form; a flag with a red background, a white disk, and a black swastika in the middle. After long trials I also found a definite proportion between the size of the flag and the size of the white disk, as well as the shape and thickness of the swastika."[45]

The color arrangement of the National Socialist flag deliberately mirrored the colors of the flag of Imperial Germany (1871–1918), the "Second Reich," a period that still inspired those Germans who were disappointed by the state's floundering attempts at democracy during the Weimar Republic. The imperial flag's color combination with the swastika resulted in a striking logo, a visual pictogram that became permanently linked with Hitler and his National Socialist Party. The majority of German political parties had no political insignia; the Communist Party and the National Socialist Party were exceptions.[46]

The ancient *Hakenkreuz* or swastika was exploited as a recognizable trademark in the framework of National Socialist propaganda, appearing on not only flags but election posters, armbands, medallions, and badges for the military and all party organizations. This powerful symbol aimed at eliciting pride among Aryans, but the "jagged cross" or "twisted cross" also struck terror into Jews and all those who were considered enemies of Hitler's Germany.[47]

Today, in Germany and throughout Europe, any public display of National Socialist symbols, even on the Internet, is prohibited by law under threat of criminal prosecution. In the United States, however, it is still legal to exhibit National Socialist symbols and propaganda because of the country's laws protecting free speech.[48]

Hitler and his Third Reich leaders knew and used the authority of pseudoreligious solemnity and ritual. Apart from an easily recognizable emblem, the swastika banner and the monumental shows of power at large-scale events, including the use of the swastika-emblazoned Blood Flag, were implemented by the dictatorship as a confirmation of political change, a respect for "ancient" German tradition, a promise of strong leadership, and of the dawning of a new era in which the German people were to regain their lost sense of pride and unity. History has shown us that, ultimately, behind the pomp, show, and promises of the National Socialist regime, in Hitler's hands the swastika came to symbolize destruction and death.

THE RELIGION OF THE FUTURE

Alfred Rosenberg, whom Hitler appointed as chief ideologist for the Third Reich, played a major role in the development of the Positive Christianity movement, which he continued to develop despite the strong disapproval of both Rome and the Protestant church.[49] Rosenberg regarded Positive Christianity as a transitional faith, and in the midst of the regime's shattered efforts to control Protestantism through the agency of the pro-Nationalist German Christians, he, along with other radical leaders such as Robert Ley and Baldur von Schirach, promoted the neopagan German Faith Movement, which more completely rejected the Judeo-Christian concepts of God.[50]

During the war years, the paganist Rosenberg outlined a plan for Germany's future religion that would necessitate the "expulsion of the foreign Christian religions," replace the Holy Bible with *Mein Kampf*, and substitute the Christian cross with the "twisted cross" (the swastika) in nazified churches.[51] The National Socialists' war on the German church infrastructure and Christianity as a whole was indeed a "battle of the two crosses."

A statement of the time summed up Hitler's hold on the German population: "People are no longer a mass of individuals—a formless, artless mass. Now they form a union, moved by a will and communal feeling. They learn to move in formations or to stand still, as if molded by an invisible hand."[52] It is clear from history that the act of destroying one's fellow humans can occur swiftly and easily, as evidenced by Hitler's Holocaust. However, attempting to change the religious convictions of an entire nation is a much more daunting and time-consuming task, requiring an extraordinary amount of audacity. Hitler and the National Socialists may have seen this challenge in the same light as the mission of the Christian church, which took centuries to win people over to the teachings of Jesus Christ and the principles of Christianity throughout western civilization. Hitler may have envisioned himself not only as the founder of a new "Thousand-Year Reich" and savior of the German people, but also as the messiah of a new world religion free from Christ, the Bible, and Jews, which would be remembered for centuries to come.

NOTES

1. Hitler, *Mein Kampf*, 25.

2. Rees, *Dark Charisma of Adolf Hitler*, 135.

3. Holding, *Hitler's Christianity*, ebook, chap. 1.

4. Derek Hastings, *Catholicism and the Roots of Nazism* (Oxford: Oxford University Press, 2010), 2.

5. Holding, *Hitler's Christianity*, ebook, chap. 1.

6. Richard Steigmann-Gall, *The Holy Reich: Nazi Conceptions of Christianity, 1919–1945* (Cambridge: Cambridge University Press, 2003), 13–51.

7. Ibid., 37.

8. Ibid., 27.

9. Rosenberg, *Myth of the Twentieth Century*, 76.

10. Steigmann-Gall, *Holy Reich*, xv.

11. United States Holocaust Memorial Museum, "Kristallnacht."

12. United States Holocaust Memorial Museum, "The German Churches and the Nazi State," Holocaust Encyclopedia, https://encyclopedia.ushmm.org/content/en/article/the-german-churches-and-the-nazi-state.

13. Ibid.

14. Christopher Tatara, "Hitler, Himmler, and Christianity in the Early Third Reich," *Constructing the Past* 14, no. 1 (2013): article 10.

15. J. S. Conway, "Between Cross and Swastika: The Position of German Catholicism," in *A Mosaic of Victims: Non-Jews Persecuted and Murdered by the Nazis*, ed. Michael Berenbaum (London: I. B. Turus, 1990), 181.

16. Frank J. Coppa, ed., *Controversial Concordats* (Washington, DC: Catholic University of America Press, 1999), 143.

17. Ernst Christian Helmreich, *German Churches under Hitler: Background, Struggle, and Epilogue* (Detroit: Wayne State University Press, 1979), 150–51.

18. J. S. Conway, *The Nazi Persecution of the Churches* (Vancouver: Regent College Publishing, 1997), 34.

19. R. Manvell and H. Fraenkel, *Heinrich Himmler: The Sinister Life of the Head of the SS and Gestapo* (London: W. Heinemann, 1965), 9.

20. Peter Longerich, *Heinrich Himmler*, trans. J. Noakes and L. Sharpe (Oxford: Oxford University Press, 2012), 77.

21. Ibid., 267.

22. Tatara, "Hitler, Himmler, and Christianity."

23. Baynes, *Speeches of Adolf Hitler, April 1922–August 1939*, 1:19–20.

24. Steigmann-Gall, *Holy Reich*, 60–61.

25. Kershaw, *Hitler*, 381–82.

26. Longerich, *Heinrich Himmler*, 265.

27. Shirer, *Rise and Fall of the Third Reich*, 240.

28. Joseph Goebbles, *The Goebbels Diaries, 1939–1941*, trans. Fred Taylor (London: Hamish Hamilton, 1982), 304–305.

29. Erwin Lutzer, *Hitler's Cross: How the Cross Was Used to Promote the Nazi Agenda* (Chicago: Moody, 2016), 71.

30. Ibid., 20.

31. Ibid., 34.

32. Hans Günter Hockerts et al., "Führermythos und Führerkult," in Dahm, *Die Tödliche Utopie*, 189.

33. Ibid., 194.

34. Hilmar Hoffmann, *The Triumph of Propaganda: Film and National Socialism, 1933–1945* (Providence, RI: Berghahn Books, 1995), 1:20–22.

35. Ibid., 1:194.

36. Ibid., 1:20–22.

37. Alexander Schmidt et al., *Das Reichsparteigelände in Nürnberg* (Nuremberg: Sandberg, 2005), 17–26.

38. Lepage, *Illustrated Dictionary of the Third Reich*, 22.

39. Spotts, *Hitler and the Power of Aesthetics*, 105–106.

40. Karlheinz Schmeer, *Die Regie des Öffentlichen Lebens im Dritten Reich* (Munich: Pohl, 1956), 104.

41. Peter Van Duren, *Orders of Knighthood and of Merit* (Gerrards Cross, UK: Colin Smythe, 1995), 212.

42. Robert Philips Greg, "Meaning and Origin of Fylfot and Swastika," *Archaeologia* 48, no. 2 (1885): 298.

43. Ibid.

44. Gary Patterson, *United States Swastika 1907–1936* (Manchester, NJ: self-published, 2000).

45. United States Holocaust Memorial Museum, "The History of the Swastika," Holocaust Encyclopedia, https://encyclopedia.ushmm.org/content/en/article/history-of-the-swastika.

46. Ibid.

47. Ibid.

48. Ibid.

49. "Nuremberg Trial Defendants: Alfred Rosenberg," Jewish Virtual Library, https://www.jewishvirtuallibrary.org/nuremberg-trial-defendants-alfred-rosenberg.

50. Pierre Ayçoberry, *The Social History of the Third Reich* (New York: New Press, 1999), 191.

51. Shirer, *Rise and Fall of the Third Reich*, 240.

52. Werner Hager, *Das Innere Reich: Bauwerke im Dritten Reich* (Munich: Albert Langen Georg Müller Verlag, 1937), 1:7.

Chapter 25

The Third Reich: A New Rome?

A NEW ROME?

Though Hitler much admired the Greeks and their civilization, his veneration for the Roman Empire waxed far greater. The ancient Romans' grandeur
and imperial might deeply impressed Hitler, in particular their monumental
architecture as witnessed by Rome's Colosseum, the Baths of Caracalla, the
Pantheon, and Hadrian's tomb.

Perhaps there was more to Hitler's reverence for the magnificence of Rome
than its famed culture and architecture. Hitler vaunted his Reich as a thousand-year empire. Some three hundred years after the fall of the thousand-year
Roman Empire, Charlemagne was selected and crowned by Pope Leo III as
the successor of Roman Emperor Constantine VI. The "transfer of rule," as it
was named, implied jurisdiction of the "Holy Roman" Emperor Charlemagne
over greater parts of Europe as the revival of the Western Roman Empire,
with this time around Jesus Christ as its patron. Like its Roman predecessor,
Charlemagne's Holy Roman Empire lasted, in principle, a thousand years
(800–1806), and according to Hitler's concept, the Third Reich was to emulate the two preceding ones, both in might and in duration.

ANTIQUITY'S LESSONS

The ruins of two-thousand-year-old structures eventually gave rise to the term
"ruin value," coined by Hitler's architect Albert Speer in a 1936 publication, *Ruinenwert* (The Value of Ruins).[1] The basic concept was to showcase
the greatness of a culture long after its decline. Hitler deplored the Roman
Empire's fall and stated, "The Romans were erecting great buildings when
our forefathers were still living in mud huts . . . we were still throwing stone

hatchets and crouching around open fires when Greece and Rome had already reached the highest stage of culture."[2]

Though it is commonly accepted that fascist movements are inclined to glorify the national past of the country in which they develop, fascist regimes occasionally attempt to resurrect an even older and more illustrious past, seeking their ideological foundations in ancient Greece and Rome. This phenomenon is clearly discernible in the case of two of the most powerful and indisputably fascist regimes of all: Benito Mussolini's Italy and Adolf Hitler's Germany.[3]

The legitimization of a dictatorial or fascist leadership was also a concern for Hitler's Italian counterpart, known as *Il Duce*, who for propaganda purposes made use of ancient Rome as the historical foundation stone on which his regime could be built. The *Duce* (from the Latin *dux*, meaning "leader") spawned a propaganda campaign of *romanità* (an admiration of ancient Rome's culture and institutions) and made use of the designation "The Third Rome"—his era being touted as third to the ancient Roman Empire as well as to the Holy Roman Empire.

According to British historian Helen Roche, the similar trends toward classicism in Italy and Germany can be partially attributed to the difficulties faced in establishing stable national identities in both countries.[4] These difficulties were caused by the fragmented nature of their geography and administration and the delayed process of unification. Italy, for instance, did not attain its full unification as a kingdom until 1870, while the German states only united as components of Otto von Bismarck's German Empire in 1871. In both cases, the aftermath of World War I led to the downfall of their respective regimes, followed by the rise of a dictator in each country amid the chaos.

Roche maintains that, once fascism had gained power in Italy, the glorification of ancient Rome was part and parcel of Mussolini's rhetoric. This exaltation of antique culture assumed many forms, from the declaration of Rome's "birthday" as a national holiday (replacing the socialist May Day celebrations) to the pronouncement of a resurrection of the Roman Empire following Italy's victorious colonial exploits in Ethiopia. As time passed, Mussolini's persona was shaped into the majestic gravitas of a Roman emperor and the savior of Italy. In Tripoli he even posed on horseback, surrounded by Libyan *lictors* (magisterial attendants) in antique Roman costume and bearing *fasces* (Roman axe-shaped symbols of power).[5]

Augustus Caesar, later deified, was seen as an inspiration for Mussolini, who was often portrayed in propaganda images as a godlike figure rather than a mere mortal. Mussolini adopted what he believed were suitable "Roman" poses, such as jutting his chin forward and holding his back ramrod straight, in order to create an image of himself as a statuesque figure, much like Augustus.[6]

Il Duce's plans included the architectural transformation of the city of Rome, a huge project that required gutting entire neighborhoods to better showcase ancient Roman monuments. Further efforts in fanning the flames of ancient Rome were seen in reintroducing Latin through schoolteachers, intellectuals, and academics as "the perfect expression of the new spirit of Italian Fascism." Much pomp and ceremony were deployed in celebrating the Roman emperor's bimillenary, which represented a resolute endeavor to conflate the Age of Augustus and the Age of Mussolini in the eyes of the public.[7]

Hitler rarely traveled abroad, but he made a point of seeing Rome in May 1938 on a six-day visit. According to cultural historian Frederic Spotts, Rome was, in fact, the only city that Hitler truly admired and felt challenged to outshine. Though Mussolini was eager to display Italy's growing military might, Hitler only had eyes for the ancient sights: the Roman forum, the Circus Maximus, the Arch of Constantine, the Colosseum, and above all the Pantheon, which he considered to be the most perfect structure ever built. Hitler viewed these sites from the perspective of an architect, planning his own reproductions for Germany. Both the interior and exterior of the Pantheon would serve as examples for his Great Hall in Berlin, and Rome's Colosseum would provide a blueprint for his Nuremberg Congress Hall.[8]

MODELS OF INTIMIDATION
ARCHITECTURE FOR THE REICH

Hitler's visit to Rome left him overwhelmed. In his speeches, a recurrent theme was the long-lasting splendor of the Reich's future architecture. Hitler spoke of the "timeless significance," the "eternal value," and the "millennial legacy" of his projected structures. During the Russian campaign, he stated that "military battles are eventually forgotten. Our buildings, however, will stand. The Colosseum in Rome lasted over the ages." Wishing to emulate, or exceed, the builders of antiquity, he vowed, "I want German buildings to be viewed in a thousand years as we view Greece and Rome." Projecting the Reich's capital as the standard-bearer of imperial greatness, he was set on transforming Berlin into the world's most magnificent city. "As capital of the world," he flaunted, "Berlin will be comparable only to ancient Egypt, Babylon or Rome!"[9]

For Hitler, in like measure to Mussolini, Roman history provided an ideal outline for procuring and eternalizing imperial dominion, an element that unquestionably exercised a significant influence on the *Führer*'s own self-perception, both as an architect and as a military commander in chief. In Hitler's mind, Rome represented the perfect model for acquiring and securing

Figure 25.1. Hitler on a sightseeing tour with Mussolini in Venice (1934). *Courtesy of USHMM / Gift of Martin Shallow III*

the modern accoutrements and infrastructure of imperial power: untiring parading legions (SS), a straight and efficiently designed road network for commerce and military transport (autobahns), the colonization of Europe and Africa (the Third Reich's same intentions), and above all monumental architecture on a scale that was deliberately intended to dwarf Mussolini's "puny efforts."[10]

To Hitler, however, who also harbored a deep admiration for ancient Greece, the National Socialist image of the Aryan man generally took the form of a young Greek Adonis, as exemplified in stone in the heroic neo-Greek nudes of Third Reich sculptors such as Arno Breker or Josef Thorak.[11] This idealized demigod would reach its apogee by competing in a new Olympic Games, a direct tie between the glories of the ancient Greeks and present-day German "Aryan" athletes.

THE FAMOUS, BUT FALSE, "ROMAN SALUTE"

Though many assume that the Roman salute—raising an outstretched right arm in deference and loyalty to superiors—was adopted as the National Socialist salute, the origin is incorrect. The salute used by both German National Socialists and Italian Fascists is, surprisingly, unknown in Roman literature and was never mentioned by ancient historians of Rome: no Roman work of art exhibits a salute of this kind. The only similar, but not exact, reproduction of such a gesture in Roman and other ancient cultures generally had a significantly different function and was never identical with the modernly disseminated straight-arm salute.[12]

The culprit for this misreading of Roman ritual can probably be attributed to the French artist Jacques-Louis David. Starting with *The Oath of the Horatii* (1784), an association of the now-recognizable gesture with Roman republican and imperial culture was born.[13] The painting depicts Horatius's three sons who swear on their swords, held by their father, that they will defend Rome to the death.[14] However, the event depicted in David's painting is his own creation,[15] and during the French revolutionary period, David continued to produce paintings depicting this same gesture. In Mussolini's Italy, the symbolic value of the gesture grew in popularity, and the salute was seen to demonstrate the Fascists' "decisive spirit, firmness, seriousness, and acknowledgment and acceptance of the regime's hierarchical structure."[16]

PARALLELS

The models that characterize the Roman Empire are undisputedly mirrored in Hitler's Third "Empire": totalitarianism, quasi-deification of the leader, military conquests, detailed administrative structures, abhorrent racism, the enslavement of Jews and conquered peoples, the construction of straight long-distance roads, as well as the erection of monumental arenas for the entertainment of the masses and to pay tribute to the state's leaders.

One fundamental difference between the two regimes is that, unlike the Third Reich, the Roman Empire did not engage in a policy of genocide but rather in the assimilation and romanization of conquered peoples. Was this one of the major factors that determined the Romans' influence throughout Europe for over a millennium, whereas Hitler's Third Reich collapsed after only twelve years of terror?

NOTES

1. Jonathan Petropoulos, *Artists under Hitler: Collaboration and Survival in Nazi Germany* (New Haven, CT: Yale University Press, 2014).

2. Speer, *Inside the Third Reich*, 94.

3. Helen Roche, "Mussolini's 'Third Rome,' Hitler's Third Reich and the Allure of Antiquity: Classicizing Chronopolitics as a Remedy for Unstable National Identity?," *Fascism: Journal of Comparative Fascist Studies* 8, no. 2 (2019): 127–52.

4. Ibid.

5. Ibid.

6. Ibid.

7. Ibid.

8. Spotts, *Hitler and the Power of Aesthetics*, 322–24.

9. Ibid., 322.

10. Roche, "Mussolini's 'Third Rome.'"

11. Ibid.

12. Martin M. Winkler, *The Roman Salute: Cinema, History, Ideology* (Columbus: Ohio State University Press, 2009), 2.

13. Ibid., 55.

14. Thomas Crow, "Facing the Patriarch in Early Davidian Painting," in *Rediscovering History: Culture, Politics, and the Psyche*, ed. Michael Roth (Stanford, CA: Stanford University Press, 1994), 308.

15. Winkler, *Roman Salute*, 44.

16. Simonetta Falasca-Zamponi, *Fascist Spectacle: The Aesthetics of Power in Mussolini's Italy* (Berkeley: University of California Press, 2000), 110–13.

Chapter 26

Women in the Reich

How did the female population fare during the Third Reich? Most works on Hitler's regime and World War II spotlight the politicians, soldiers, members of the terror organizations, and other male-dominated roles or activities during Hitler's regime. Here we shall take a look at what changes were ushered into the lives of German girls and women and how they reacted to the National Socialist reformation of the nation's social values.

WOMEN IN THE WEIMAR REPUBLIC

The November Revolution of 1918 resulted in a pivotal political achievement for women, namely, the suffrage in national elections. It was hoped that this breakthrough would serve as a symbol of modern democratic values and lead to an expansion of women's rights in the future. In the subsequent year, nearly 80 percent of eligible women exercised their voting rights, and 10 percent of the newly formed National Assembly were women delegates.[1]

Despite initial expectations, the advent of World War I did not trigger a widespread surge in female labor-force participation in Germany. Nonetheless, the conflict did instigate significant transformations in the nature of women's work. During the First World War, approximately four hundred thousand women departed from domestic service and agriculture, while a slightly larger cohort assumed roles in traditionally "masculine" occupations within war-related industries, such as metalworking, machine building, and chemicals. Additionally, some women assumed provisional administrative positions in the military or civilian sectors. These changes may not have represented a seismic shift in women's employment patterns, yet they likely bolstered women's self-assurance by expanding the range of job opportunities available to them.[2]

A significant number of young war widows were faced with the arduous task of fending for themselves in an era marked by persistent job insecurity and exorbitant inflation. Those wives who had not been widowed were often encumbered by the presence of husbands who had returned home with disabilities or psychological trauma stemming from their wartime experiences. Furthermore, some women who aspired to marry and raise children were unable to do so due to a dearth of eligible male partners. This situation was largely attributable to the fact that approximately two million men, the majority of whom were aged between eighteen and thirty-four, had perished on the battlefield.[3] For many working-class women, both single and married, destitution was an everyday reality.

From 1919 to 1933, a total of 111 female representatives were elected to the Reichstag. Notably, the National Socialist Party was the sole political organization with no female MPs. With the coming of the Third Reich, the position of women in German politics was soon to be eradicated altogether.

NATIONAL SOCIALISM: A MALE PHENOMENON

According to its doctrine, the National Socialist movement insisted that politics were unequivocally a male domain, and the presence of women in parliament was viewed as a lamentable symptom of liberalism. In the 1920s, Hitler shared the widespread belief that men and women were inherently dissimilar and that women were endowed with unique attributes and obligations that rendered them unsuitable for employment outside the home, except in roles characterized by empathy and nurturing.[4] Furthermore, like many other German political leaders and religious authorities, Hitler was preoccupied with the marked decline in the country's birth rate and the attendant menace this posed to Germany's restoration as a dominant power after the conclusion of World War I.[5]

The so-called NS Party philosopher Alfred Rosenberg espoused the belief that German women ought to be "emancipated from emancipation." He argued that women should be freed from the Marxist tenet of gender parity and reinstated in their natural positions as mothers and homemakers. Rosenberg viewed feminism as an aberration incompatible with the Germanic spirit and thought it had been imported into Central Europe through the corrupting influence of the French Enlightenment. He urged German women to categorically reject the notion of sexual equality and to revert to their traditional roles as the progenitors of the population and the custodians of its biological heritage. Political affairs, accordingly, could be entrusted once more to those who possessed the knowledge necessary to act in the best interests of the state, namely, men.[6]

According to Hitler, the notion of women's emancipation was an invention of "Jewish intellectuals" and consequently inconsistent with German identity.

In Hitler's view, a genuine German subscribed to the belief that the realm of the state was the domain of men, while the arena of women was defined by their roles as wives, mothers, and caretakers of the home and family. He announced, "We do not consider it correct for the woman to interfere in the world of the man, in his main sphere. We consider it natural if these two worlds remain distinct. To the one belongs the strength of feeling, the strength of the soul. To the other belongs the strength of vision, of toughness, of decision and of the willingness to act."[7]

Goebbels expressed a similar take on womanhood in a manner that contemporary women would likely find abhorrent and reprehensible: "The mission of the woman is to be beautiful and to bring children into the world. . . . The female bird pretties herself for her mate and hatches the eggs for him. In exchange, the mate takes care of gathering the food, and stands guard and wards off the enemy." From 1933 on, National Socialist ideology referred to the required social changes as "The German Resurrection" and said that its transformation was "a male event." In the relatively modern age of the 1930s, the woman's place was—still—in the home.[8]

VOTING AND MEMBERSHIP AMONG WOMEN

Of particular interest is the fact that, in 1933, women constituted less than 6 percent of NS Party membership, representing less than 1 percent of the female population as a whole.[9] It is likely that many women who cast their ballot for the National Socialist Party in 1932 or early 1933 did so to express their opposition to alternative parties, specifically to the Communist Party of Germany and the Social Democratic Party, or possibly to express their dissatisfaction with the Weimar regime as a whole, which appeared to have yielded nothing but economic turmoil and political unrest. Additionally, some women may have held the expectation that Hitler's party would facilitate a revival of economic prosperity and help restore their husbands' jobs.[10]

WOMEN'S ORGANIZATIONS

During the ascent of the National Socialists, all preexisting women's associations were dissolved, and the NS-Frauenschaft (National Socialist Women's League, or NSF) emerged as the first official women's organization subject to centralized party monitoring. A fierce struggle ensued within the party to gain control over women's activities, a fight that culminated in the selection of Gertrud Scholtz-Klink as the leader of the NSF in February of 1934. Scholtz-Klink was specifically chosen by male party leaders due to her capacity to provide stability and unwavering compliance with the require-ments of the nascent state. As a devoted mother of four children and a fervent supporter of National Socialism, she accepted the leadership of the NSF and its subordinated mass organization, the Deutsches Frauenwerk (German Women's Bureau, or DFW), with a profound conviction that she could rees-tablish the German family as the foundation of the Third Reich.[11]

The primary objective of women's organizations during the National Socialist era was to provide guidance on domestic management and child-care, as well as to foster an appreciation of German culture. In NS propa-ganda, such domestic and cultural endeavors were reframed as the principal domains where women could facilitate the revival of the German nation through the medium of female-oriented establishments. The "new" woman was expected to acquire proficiency in domestic duties such as cooking and cleaning, attain familiarity with the regime's racial and demographic policies, and become a teacher of young children, transmitting a "healthy" German outlook and values to future generations.

Specialized branches of social assistance provided training for women to assume roles as auxiliary nurses and social workers, partly to facilitate their involvement in the implementation of the regime's family and racial policies and partly to address the anticipated shortage of skilled nurses and domestic personnel as the economy prepared itself for war. This was of paramount importance to the government, as it was unwilling to become overreliant on hospitals administered by religious orders. In the late 1930s, as the prospect of war loomed ever nearer, the German Women's Bureau also arranged broader instruction on civil defense and provided air-raid protection training.[12]

The Kraft-durch-Freude (Strength through Joy) organization was designed, in particular, to appeal to women, as they were more inclined to participate in initiatives that offered opportunities for family travel. In addition to tourism, sports constituted a significant domain of interest for the organization, and it is possible to discern here a more deliberate effort to eliminate class distinc-tions. Women's sports activities aligned well with the regime's priority of encouraging the multiplication of "healthy mothers with healthy children" in anticipation of future racial objectives. Special evening and weekend courses were also provided for women athletes, comprising pursuits such as cycling, synchronized acrobatics, folk dancing, and even marksmanship practice.[13]

The League of German Girls (Bund deutscher Mädel, or BDM) was estab-lished through the amalgamation of several local groups, and it expanded so rapidly that by 1939 it boasted an equal number of female participants as the entire NS Youth movement had male members.[14] The BDM provided young German girls with an opportunity to engage in out-of-school activities, such as physical training, competitive sports, military-style parades, and lessons in politics and racial awareness—activities that were previously reserved

Figure 26.1. Young women in sports clothing at the Community Day of the Nuremberg rallies (1938). *Bundesarchiv*

for men and boys according to a gender and education model of two separate spheres.

The requirements of BDM membership included maintaining cleanliness and an orderly appearance, and the organization's adherents were expected to develop a "tough as leather, hard as steel and swift as greyhounds" attitude, similar to their male counterparts.[15] The use of cosmetics and feminine beauty products by young girls was strictly prohibited and deemed "un-German."[16] However, the most significant aspect of the BDM was the emphasis on camaraderie among girls from different regions of Germany and diverse social classes. Ultimately, the BDM served as part of the mass indoctrination movement that was converting the German population into a united *Volk* and shaping the future women of Germany.[17]

While National Socialist social models prioritized family and home values, their youth organizations and labor service schemes led both boys and girls away from their parents. The contradiction between these ideals became more apparent during the war, as girls were expected to meet state obligations by engaging in farmwork, caring for evacuees and wounded soldiers, working in the weapons industry, and assisting in homes and schools for ethnic Germans in the occupied territories of the east.[18]

EDUCATION

Schools for German girls sought to impress upon students the values and morals of National Socialist ideology. Particularly for girls, the precepts of eugenics and racial hygiene were paramount. The dangers posed to the Aryan race by "foreign" and "tainted" blood were spelled out in regularly scheduled classes that made use of stereotyped photos and drawings of perceived enemies: Jews, Slavs, and Romani.

In 1934, the Law against Overcrowding in German Higher Education Institutions and Schools was put into effect, which limited the enrollment of female students in university studies to no more than 10 percent of the number of male graduates. Additionally, female students were prohibited from attending NS elite educational institutions such as the Adolf Hitler Schools and the Order Castles. Moreover, girls were not provided with the opportunity to learn Latin, which was an essential prerequisite for university admission.[19]

Girls were instructed in subjects such as needlework, music, foreign languages, and homecraft, which encompassed a range of skills including nursing, social work, household management, and childcare, instead of scientific and mathematical disciplines. As of April 1938, female students who managed to pass the university entrance examination, despite encountering numerous obstacles, were compelled to complete a "domestic year" prior to being permitted to attend university, assuming that the designated quota had not already been exceeded. The impact of such discriminatory policies is evident in the fact that the number of female university students decreased by more than two-thirds between 1932 and 1939. It is worth noting that this was a significant setback for women's education in Germany, as remarked on by a historian who claimed that the National Socialists had pushed back the progress of women's education by three decades.[20]

THE FEMALE IDEAL

National Socialist propaganda targeted women by urging them to embrace their traditional domestic roles as mothers and housewives, leaving the arenas of politics and employment to men. Furthermore, NS racial ideologues advocated for women to abstain from using makeup and wearing foreign styles of clothing, which were considered "decadent." Sex appeal was deemed "Jewish cosmopolitanism," and unnecessary dieting was discouraged due to its potentially adverse impact on fertility. Under the leadership of Magda Goebbels, the regime even established a German Fashion Bureau to promote and define a Germanic clothing style. Women were encouraged to engage in physical fitness activities, and smoking was strongly condemned, particularly during and after pregnancy.

In NS propaganda, the "ideal German woman" was portrayed as an individual who recognized her obligations to the race and the *Volk*, surpassing her duties to her family and herself. She was also knowledgeable in the tenets of National Socialism and willing to make sacrifices for the advancement of the movement. According to this ideology, she was deemed a "giver" rather than a "taker" of life, reflecting a fundamental biological difference between men and women. This difference was judged to be the reason why women were deemed unsuitable for military service or political involvement since politics, according to National Socialist doctrine, revolved solely around war and peace. The exclusion of women from the public sphere of politics and warfare was an integral aspect of ensuring the survival of the regime and the achievement of its expansionist and racist objectives. The success of these objectives was contingent upon women having no actual voice in the decision-making processes pertaining to life and death, which were controlled by the Third Reich's male leadership.[21]

MARRIAGE AND MOTHERHOOD

In the initial stages of the NS regime, the German female populace was encouraged to enter into marriage and bear children. This strategy served a dual purpose. First, it aimed to increase the Aryan population, and second, women were encouraged to vacate their workplaces, thus creating job opportunities for unemployed men. As a means of achieving these objectives, an extensive system of marriage loans was implemented in 1933. Eligible couples could obtain an interest-free loan of one thousand Reichsmarks, which amounted to roughly one-fifth of the average annual salary. The loan was disbursed to the husband in the form of vouchers for furniture and other household items, upon condition that the woman would relinquish her job or career to devote herself to motherhood. The loan was repayable in increments that decreased by a quarter for each child that the couple produced. Therefore, having four children would entirely repay the loan.[22] By 1939, as many as 42 percent of all marriages were supported by the plan, a trend that continued into the early years of the war.[23]

NS propaganda placed significant emphasis on promoting a "cult of motherhood," which aimed not merely to boost birth rates but to increase the number of racially desirable births. Within this framework, the "German mother" occupied a revered position in National Socialist iconography, distinct from the "racially insignificant" mother. Artistic representations and posters frequently depicted the image of a breastfeeding German mother surrounded by her robust offspring, often set in traditional rural environments, thus evoking the National Socialist idealized vision of family life.[24]

In Germany, mothers and housewives were not only provided with support through state benefits such as marriage loans but also honored on a national level. Mother's Day was officially declared a holiday for the first time, highlighting the significance of this role. In 1934, Goebbels emphasized that this occasion should not be treated as a simple "coffee-and-cake event" but rather as a day devoted to families and with a particular focus on the mother. He insisted that all churches address the theme of motherhood on this day and that theaters offer appropriate and deserving productions for families or single mothers free of charge.[25]

Upon Scholtz-Klink's appointment as leader of the NSF, one of her first undertakings was the creation of the Reich Mothers' Service (Reichsmütterdienst, or RMD). The RMD was, to a greater extent, an amalgamation of previous mothers' welfare groups that had hitherto been run by church organizations. Its mission was to endorse motherhood as a national cause of the highest importance.[26] The RMD provided goal-oriented courses in cooking, sewing, bookkeeping, pre- and postnatal childcare, and most importantly, the precepts of "racial hygiene," in other words, choosing an Aryan husband.

In a public show of the merits of bearing lots of children, starting in 1938 the *Mutterkreuz* (mother's cross) was awarded to honor "deserving" mothers: a bronze cross was given to those with four or five children, a silver one for mothers with six or seven offspring, and a gold cross for having borne eight or more children. In 1939 alone, three million German women were awarded the mother's cross.[27]

During the NS regime, the limited number of birth control centers that had been permitted to operate during the Weimar Republic were closed down, and abortion was deemed detrimental to the health of the German nation. Consequently, laws related to abortion were made stricter, with severe prison sentences imposed on individuals assisting in terminating pregnancy.

POLICING FEMALE SEXUALITY

According to the NS *Weltanschauung*, sex and marriage were viewed as ways to fulfill one's duty to the *Volksgemeinschaft* and the National Socialist state. Women who didn't marry or couldn't bear children were not only criticized

Figure 26.2.   A Happy Mother, a National Socialist Ideal, Germany, 1936. *Alamy DDYCJF*

Figure 26.3. **"Mothers' Crosses" in bronze, silver, and gold.** *Courtesy of Institute of Contemporary History Munich-Berlin*

in private but also publicly shamed for undermining the nation's well-being and accused of "racial desertion" among other offenses. Nevertheless, many couples were likely influenced by social pressures and had children immediately after getting married to avoid being noticed.

No criminal prosecutions of gay women took place in the Third Reich, as National Socialist policies on female homosexuality were established on the basis that lesbianism was not something to be punished as an individual misdemeanor and therefore did not require the intervention of the Gestapo or the courts.[28] Though gay women were not at risk of prosecution, an unknown number were likely subject to persecution as so-called asocials, an eclectic category of citizens who had committed no identifiable crime but were nonetheless taken into "protective custody" by the police—often implying temporary internment in a concentration camp.[29] In the meantime, many gay women, as well as gay men, in NS Germany undoubtedly chose to get married in order to avoid raising suspicions and, in some cases, in order to save their jobs or careers as well.

RACIAL POLICY

Other elements of the National Socialist "revolution," however, such as the antisemitic measures and the pressure to buy from "Aryan" stores only, were far less popular and less successful than anticipated. Indeed, as with the attempts to reorganize approaches to child-rearing and housekeeping along National Socialist lines discussed above, most German women in the

1930s proved resistant to attempts by the party and state to tell them where they should shop and what they should wear. Thus, reports and eyewitness accounts from various sources on the April 1933 boycott of Jewish shops indicate that the campaign was largely a failure.[30]

While numerous women were among the victims of the regime's racial and social policies, others participated as active agents in enforcing the discriminatory laws and measures implemented by men. The League of German Women Doctors was among the first women's organizations to exclude Jewish members and readily conformed to the requirements of NS *Gleichschaltung*. Furthermore, many ordinary German women aided in the ostracism of their Jewish neighbors and acquaintances from the *Volksgemeinschaft*, the national community, thereby contributing to their "social death" even before the organized violence of *Kristallnacht* in 1938.[31]

The leaders of women's organizations, in particular Gertrud Scholtz-Klink of the NSF, openly endorsed National Socialist policies aimed at sterilizing the "unfit" and "asocial" while providing additional material and financial support to "racially valuable families."[32] In March 1941 the government ordered that all Jews in the Reich, regardless of gender and with the exception only of those under fifteen and over sixty-five, should register for work—in other words, be employed in a form of forced labor within the Reich.[33]

Regarding the Holocaust, meaning the systematic deportation and mass killing of Jews in the extermination camps of occupied Poland between 1941 and 1945 and in the mass shootings of Soviet Jews carried out by the *Einsatzgruppen* after the Nazi invasion of the USSR in 1941, the participation of women in its implementation was lower than that of men. In the personnel of the death camps at Belzec, Sobibor, and Treblinka, no women were present. Nevertheless, women constituted approximately 10 percent of the guards within the entire concentration camp system, including at Auschwitz-Birkenau.[34]

WOMEN AND WORK

In line with the regime's aim to reduce unemployment, it was deemed advantageous to encourage women to leave the workforce, thereby creating employment opportunities for men. However, this approach was counterproductive as many occupations held by women, such as nursing and sewing, were traditionally perceived as feminine roles.[35] Despite the implementation of the Marriage Loan Scheme in 1933, a significant number of middle-class and working-class women continued to work in wage-based jobs in the mid-1930s. Additionally, the rearmament program, which commenced in 1936, brought a greater number of women into the workforce.

NS labor policy introduced a compulsory year of service (*Pflichtjahr*) in agriculture or household work for single women under twenty-five who intended to pursue employment in industry or various office jobs. This scheme, distinct from other labor service programs, was launched in February 1938 and revised ten months later to incorporate a greater number of women, so that in early 1938 some 77,400 girls were registered to start their *Pflichtjahr*, whereas the number increased to 1,217,000 a year later.[36]

Due to a shortage of raw materials and the demands of the rearmament program, the labor industry encountered bottlenecks. This predicament compelled the National Socialists to reconsider their belief in confining women to domestic duties. In 1936 and 1937, the government issued several decrees, including the elimination of the condition that a woman receiving a marriage loan must give up her job and not seek another. As a result, women were not only urged to take up clerical and factory jobs but could also train for white-collar professions. The German Labor Front urged employers to establish day nurseries for the children of female workers and to modify working hours to safeguard the health of women employed in industry.[37] By 1943 a total over 14.5 million girls and young women are estimated to have contributed to the German war economy in some way, performing the equivalent of about 150 million work hours per year.[38]

Figure 26.4. Propaganda poster enticing women to return to work during World War II (1941). *Alamy B3EK7C*

WOMEN IN FILM PROPAGANDA

Post-1939, the role of women in a militarized Reich became a significant topic for the German film industry, engendering conflicting perspectives. Although the earlier portrayal of women as comrades to men was continued, it underwent modifications in form. Women were also represented as receptacles for childbirth, consequently highlighting sexuality within that context.

As soldiers were increasingly perceived as men entitled to sexual pursuits beyond procreation, both male and female sexual types seeking affairs were depicted in films, usually to the benefit of men. This approach did not necessarily revive the prewar image of the vamp, as portrayed by actors like Zarah Leander, but instead focused on young unmarried and sometimes married women who were willing to yield themselves to soldiers in happy submission. The propaganda makers were cautious in this area as extramarital relationships between soldiers and German women threatened to undermine marriages and the traditional family structure.[39]

OPPOSITION AND RESISTANCE

The number of women who actively participated in politically motivated opposition and resistance groups, like the Communist Rote Kapelle or the Kreisau Circle, comprising both Christian-conservative and social democratic influence, remained small. This reinforces the idea that resistance was predominantly a male activity. According to statistics, women represented only 5 to 10 percent of those convicted of belonging to an illegal political organization in Hitler's Germany. However, in left-wing resistance groups, women played critical roles in maintaining underground networks to care for the families of imprisoned or murdered comrades, as well as to prepare for the period after the liberation from National Socialist tyranny.

A more substantial group of women who opposed the regime were those with strong religious convictions, such as various Catholic and Protestant women who considered National Socialism an "ungodly" phenomenon.[40] These women functioned as couriers for underground Communist groups and the Prague-based Sopade (Social Democratic Party in exile). They assisted in typing and distributing illegal pamphlets and provided comfort to men who had been affected by the regime's rise to power. Furthermore, they put themselves at even greater risk by allowing their homes to be used for clandestine meetings and as hiding places for political fugitives or Allied airmen on the run.

As a result, many of these women faced severe beatings, summary execution, or imprisonment in ad hoc concentration camps, often in former workhouses or disused factories, established by the Gestapo. Some women spent months or even years in such camps. The SS later established its camp for women at Ravensbrück.[41] The Gestapo often detained the wives, daughters, and sisters of suspected political opponents as hostages or for the purposes of interrogation and intimidation. Women who refused to disclose the whereabouts of their male relatives could face extended periods of solitary confinement, coupled with frequent beatings and torture.

A notably successful act of opposition to the SS was achieved by a group of German wives who demonstrated remarkable courage by mounting a week-long protest vigil despite savage threats of reprisal from the Gestapo. Their demonstration, known as the Rosenstrasse Protest, came in response to the arrest and likely deportation of their Jewish husbands, who had been apprehended during the "factory action" in Berlin on February 27, 1943.

THE RAVAGES OF WAR

As the end of the war approached, women in Germany continued to face numerous challenges. Due to conscription, a large number of male relatives were absent, with 1.9 million confirmed dead and 1.7 million taken prisoner or missing in action by the end of 1944. This resulted in an overwhelming burden being placed on women, particularly those who were raising young children or running farms and small businesses without sufficient labor or raw materials. Urban women with children and those who worked in factories were particularly affected by food shortages, often having to queue for hours before or after work to obtain essential supplies. The state's increased intervention in homes through labor conscription, rationing, and forced evacuations also caused significant resentment, especially amid rumors that wealthy women, such as the wives of senior party officials, mayors, and socialites, were allowed to evade most wartime restrictions.[42]

During the waning days of World War II and in the aftermath of the return of peace, German women residing in the eastern regions of the Reich and who were situated in areas occupied by the Red Army experienced unimaginable suffering. Reports emerged as early as October 1944 detailing the atrocities committed by inebriated Soviet soldiers against defenseless civilian women. In Nemmersdorf, East Prussia, Wehrmacht troops discovered the bodies of sixty-two German women and girls who had been raped and mutilated.

From January 1945 onward, mass rape became the most horrifying tool for terrorizing the vanquished German populations of East Prussia, Pomerania, and Silesia. The estimated number of female victims ranged from tens of thousands to two million, with the victims' ages ranging from eight to sixty-eight. Women were usually coerced to submit to their attackers "at gunpoint," with some eyewitness reports indicating that up to twenty-four officers and Red Army regulars attacked a single woman. Soviet sources confirmed these crimes. Approximately one in three women living in Berlin at the end of the war was raped by Russian soldiers, representing about half a million women.[43]

It is apparent that the Third Reich's guidelines for women would have been perceived as restrictive and demeaning to many due to the limits set on higher education and careers, as well as women's confinement in an antiquated role. On the other hand, the financial upswing, the supposed glorification of motherhood, participation in female-only organizations, military successes, and the restoration of German pride likely helped to counterbalance the regime's negative aspects, including open persecution of the country's Jews. Some historians confirm that a majority of women embraced their responsibilities as child bearers and reproducers of the Aryan race and that they came to view themselves as superior to all other peoples and races.[44]

During the postwar occupation of Germany, American and British soldiers were impressed by the hardworking attitude displayed by women as they cleared the rubble from the country's bombed-out cities in preparation for rebuilding. However, in 1945, western observers were particularly struck by the significant disparity between the number of women and men in both the eastern and western regions of Germany. For instance, the October 1946 census revealed that there were 126 females for every 100 males, with an even greater ratio of 146 females to 100 males in Berlin.[45] This resulted in post–World War II Germany becoming known as a "country of women," which would take one to two generations to correct the demographic imbalance caused by the two world wars.[46] A more challenging issue to overcome would prove to be the mixed feelings of loss, resentment, and—eventually—guilt experienced by German women.

NOTES

1. Julia Sneeringer, *Winning Women's Votes: Propaganda and Politics in Weimar Germany* (Chapel Hill: University of North Carolina Press, 2002), 10.

2. Detlev Peukert, *The Weimar Republic: The Crisis of Classical Modernity* (Harmondsworth, UK: Penguin, 1991), 277.

3. Matthew Stibbe, *Women in the Third Reich* (London: Arnold, 2003), 13.

4. Hitler, *Mein Kampf*, trans. Manheim, 400–401.

5. Ute Frevert, *Women in German History* (Oxford: Berg, 1989), 188.

6. Stibbe, *Women in the Third Reich*, 17.

7. *Frankfurter Zeitung*, September 9, 1934, in *Nazism 1919–1945: A Documentary Reader*, vol. 2, ed. Jeremy Noakes and Geoffery Pridham (Exeter: University of Exeter Press, 1998), 255–56.

8. Evans, *Third Reich in Power*, 331–32.

9. Jürgen Falter, *Hitlers Wähler* (Munich: C. H. Beck, 1991), 143.

10. Stibbe, *Women in the Third Reich*, 27.

11. Ibid., 34–35.

12. Jill Stephenson, *The Nazi Organization of Women* (London: Croom Helm, 1981), 196.

13. Stibbe, *Women in the Third Reich*, 48–49.

14. Ibid., 113.

15. Lisa Pine, *Nazi Family Policy* (Oxford: Berg, 1995), 47–58.

16. Ilse Köhn, *Mischling, Second Degree: My Childhood in Nazi Germany* (London: Penguin, 1981), 84.

17. Clifford Kirkpatrick, *Woman in Nazi Germany* (London: Jarrolds, 1939), 83.

18. Stibbe, *Women in the Third Reich*, 109.

19. Rolf Eilers, *Die Nationalsozialistische Schulpolitik* (Cologne: Westdeutscher Verlag, 1963), 18–21.

20. Stibbe, *Women in the Third Reich*, 110.

21. Kirkpatrick, *Woman in Nazi Germany*, 112–13.

22. Elizabeth Heineman, *What Difference Does a Husband Make?* (Berkeley: University of California Press, 1999), 21–26.

23. Stibbe, *Women in the Third Reich*, 44.

24. Ibid., 40–41.

25. Ibid., 41.

26. Robert A. Brady, *The Spirit and Structure of German Fascism* (New York: H. Fertig, 1937), 205.

27. Dahm, "Die 'Deutsche Volksgemeinschaft' und ihre Organisationen," 250.

28. Stibbe, *Women in the Third Reich*, 51.

29. Ibid., 52.

30. Ibid., 44.

31. Marion A. Kaplan, *Between Dignity and Despair: Jewish Life in Nazi Germany* (Oxford: Oxford University Press, 1998), 5.

32. Stibbe, *Women in the Third Reich*, 75.

33. Ibid., 97.

34. Ibid., 75–77.

35. Evans, *Third Reich in Power*, 333.

36. Stibbe, *Women in the Third Reich*, 91.

37. Evans, *Third Reich in Power*, 366–67.

38. Stibbe, *Women in the Third Reich*, 120.

39. Kater, *Culture in Nazi Germany*, 193.

40. Stibbe, *Women in the Third Reich*, 130.

41. Sybil Milton, *Women and the Holocaust* (New York: Monthly Review Press, 1984), 306.

42. Martin Kitchen, *Nazi Germany at War* (London: Longman, 1995), 143.

43. Stibbe, *Women in the Third Reich*, 165–69.

44. Ibid., 179–80.

45. Robert G. Moeller, *Protecting Motherhood* (Berkeley: University of California Press, 1993), 27.

46. Ibid., 2.

Chapter 27

The Hidden Face of Eva Braun

For almost fourteen years, Adolf Hitler shared his private life with a secret companion, Eva Anna Paula Braun. Despite being perceived as a politically disengaged and decorative addition to the dictator, modern historians have uncovered a different aspect of Hitler's partner. Eva Braun only gained public attention after her death in 1945, following her suicide alongside Hitler in a Berlin bunker.

THE PHOTOGRAPHER

Born into a middle-class family in Munich, Eva Braun was the second of three daughters born to a schoolteacher and a seamstress. As noted by German historian Heike Görtemaker, Braun had a difficult childhood and often stayed with her best friend, whose mother she referred to as "Mama." After completing her studies at a Catholic high school in Munich, Braun enrolled in a Catholic business school at the Convent of the English Sisters for a year.[1]

Starting in 1929, Eva Braun found employment with Heinrich Hoffmann,[2] who was a founding member of the party and Hitler's official photographer. Although initially employed as a shop and sales clerk, Braun quickly learned the art of photography and developing. It was during her time at the studio that she met "Herr Wolf" (Adolf Hitler), who was introduced to her. At the time, Braun was only seventeen years old, twenty-three years younger than Hitler,[3] a coincidence as Hitler's mother was also twenty-three years younger than his father.

During this period, Hitler was residing in his Munich apartment with his half niece, Geli Raubal, who was pursuing her university education. Hitler had an extremely possessive and domineering relationship with Raubal, forbidding her from socializing with friends and insisting on being close to her at all times, accompanying her or having her chaperoned on shopping trips, to the cinema, and to the opera. Historian Ian Kershaw contends that Hitler's behavior toward Geli had all the characteristics of a strong, possibly latent, sexual dependency, regardless of whether it was actively sexual or not. In September 1931, the day after Hitler and Geli had an argument, she was discovered dead in his apartment, allegedly from a self-inflicted gunshot wound to her chest, using Hitler's pistol. She was only twenty-three years old at the time.[4]

Hitler's niece's suicide caused quite a scandal, particularly in Bavaria. Conceivably fearing a loss of public approval, Hitler announced to his political activists that he lived only for politics and that he renounced a private life of his own. With the complicity of Josef Goebbels, Hitler began to construct a mythos of reclusiveness and isolation that would make him personally invulnerable. This unique self-positioning outside the common social norm would confirm Hitler's supremacy over everyone else and, as a chaste hero, help to make his messianic qualities believable.[5] Having—in the public eye— removed himself from human needs and desires, Germany's "savior" would henceforth keep any carnal relationship secret.

IN THE SHADOWS

Following Geli Raubal's death, Hitler and Eva Braun began seeing more of each other, though the exact nature of their relationship in the early years is unclear. Evocative of Geli's suicide the year before, Eva attempted suicide herself in August 1932 by shooting herself in the chest with her father's pistol. The attempt is largely viewed as not serious but rather a bid for Hitler's attention.[6] Görtemaker maintains that this event marked a turning point in their relationship and that eyewitnesses remembered Hitler "spoiling" Braun in the way one would treat a lover, and the historian Angela Lambert maintains that this was actually the time when the two became lovers.[7]

Though rarely seen, when in the public eye Braun was classified as one of Hitler's secretaries, later as a photographer. In the early years of their relationship, she divided her time between Berchtesgaden and Munich and was only occasionally present in Berlin. Braun often spent the night at Hitler's Munich apartment when he was in town[8] and in 1933 began to work as a photographer for Hoffmann.[9] This occupation allowed her to travel as a photographer for the National Socialist Party in the company of Hoffmann and Hitler's entourage.[10] Braun was also provided with her own apartment adjoining Hitler's at the new Reich Chancellery in Berlin, completed according to a design by Albert Speer,[11] of which he said, "The windows looked out onto a narrow courtyard. Here, even more than at Obersalzberg, she led a completely isolated life, stealing into the building through a side entrance and going up a rear staircase, never descending into the lower rooms, even when there were only old acquaintances in the apartment, and she was overjoyed whenever I kept her company during the long hours of waiting."[12]

In the beginning, Albert Speer noticed that Eva Braun kept her distance from Hitler's inner circle, including himself. However, as time passed and they became more acquainted, he realized that her reserved manner, which others mistook for haughtiness, was simply her feeling uncomfortable about her uncertain position in "Hitler's court."[13] According to Speer, Hess's wife, Ilse, and his own wife, Margarete, befriended Eva and regarded her as their equal. On the other hand, the wives of other high officials who resided part-time at Obersalzberg, such as Magda Goebbels, Gerda Bormann, Emmy Göring, Erna Hoffmann, and Hanni Morrell, often displayed a condescending attitude toward Eva and considered themselves socially superior to the "vulgar Munich girl."[14] Even Hitler's long-serving senior secretary, Christa Schroeder, once suggested to Hitler that Eva was unworthy of him, to which he brusquely replied, "She suits me well enough!"[15]

THE FIRST LADY

Perhaps it is partly due to Speer's opinion of Braun that popular views of the *Führer*'s companion depict a passive, unassuming, pale shadow of her overbearing master. Postwar historians have not helped either as they tended not to lend any importance to women and their roles during the Third Reich. However, according to Braun's biographer Görtemaker, the history of Eva Braun as a marginalized self-depreciating woman, unaware of Hitler's politics in the making, needs to be reviewed.[16]

Following the transformation of Hitler's Berchtesgaden residence into the magnificent Berghof estate in 1936, Eva Braun served as the primary hostess of the mountain retreat. Hitler was hardly ever alone during his time there, as he was continually surrounded by a group of about twenty to thirty leaders and their spouses, along with a handful of favored artists, movie stars, and personal physicians like Karl Brant or Theodor Morrel.[17]

From 1936 on, Eva played a central role at the Berghof enclave, where she managed both Hitler's personal life and the guests who visited. Despite facing challenges from individuals who were older, who were more sophisticated, and who often held unfavorable opinions of her, Eva was able to create a relaxed atmosphere among the guests, be they VIPs, leaders of the Third Reich, or Hitler's friends from the early days of the party. Prior to Eva's arrival, Magda Goebbels, the attractive wife of Propaganda Minister Joseph Goebbels, had been the *dame de la maison* at the Berghof. However, on more formal or official occasions, Magda would resume this role again, which caused distress for Eva.[18]

Despite any personal opinions the staff at the Berghof may have held toward Eva Braun, they were made aware that she was the mistress of the house and to be referred to as *"Chefin"* (boss) or by the more flowery *"gnädiges Fräulein"* (old-fashioned formal address, equivalent to "Gracious Miss").[19] Despite this flattering deference, Eva's role and presence at the Berghof was usually portrayed as "part of Hitler's private office," which effectively kept her existence and true position in Hitler's inner circle a secret from the majority of the German public. It was more than likely difficult for Eva to accept that her role at the Berghof and in Hitler's life was primarily sexual and domestic in nature and that she was not well regarded by many.[20]

Conversely, there are firsthand accounts that portray Eva Braun as being untouchable and impervious in her favored position with the *Führer*, in complete control of who was allowed to join the inner circle of guests at the Berghof and who was not. Many people felt the need to curry favor with her, and they worried about what Braun might say about them or think of them in front of Hitler. On one occasion, criticism of Braun resulted in her excluding the Goebbels couple from the privileged assemblies for several months until they apologized.

Albert Speer stated that Braun was the only person who would dare interrupt one of Hitler's habitual table monologues, and Speer's wife, Margarete, claimed that Braun was not shy but in fact conscious of her role and had the last say.[21] Hitler granted Eva more license than anyone else, and she was even permitted to tease him or, in some cases, to rebuke him or have the last word. She was known to good-humoredly interrupt Hitler's long speeches by suggesting doing something else: "Oh come on, Adolf, that's enough talk—let's watch a film!" Or when the night dragged on too long, she'd exclaim, "Time we all went to bed!" and Hitler would slowly rise and follow Eva upstairs.

Speer recalled how, in the presence of his table companions, Eva Braun might pertly call Hitler's attention to the fact that his tie did not match his suit or that she sometimes cheerfully referred to herself as "Mother of the Country."[22] In January 1943, as part of austerity measures imposed by "total war," Eva Braun learned of a proposed ban on "hair permanents" as well as the end of cosmetics production and, consequently, rushed to Hitler in "high indignation." Hitler advised Speer that, instead of an outright ban, he should quietly stop production of "hair dyes and other items necessary for beauty culture" and "cease the repair of apparatus for producing permanent waves."[23] Outwardly, Braun appeared to be the very model of compliance and devotion, but behind the façade, she was learning to use her hold over Hitler and on occasion knew how to manipulate the *Führer*.

In his memoirs Speer observed that, for the most part, the wives of the National Socialist top brass resisted the temptation of power far better than their respective husbands, who tended to lose themselves in their fantasy worlds. These women, he noted, looked on at the often outlandish antics of their husbands with inner reservations, such as Frau Goering, who was inclined to smile at her husband's obsession with pomp. "In the final analysis," Speer added, "Eva Braun, too, proved her inner superiority. At any rate she never used for personal ends the power which lay within her grasp."[24] Despite the Berghof circle's knowledge of Eva Braun's privileged position as the *Führer*'s "significant other," the secret of their relationship never leaked out to the public.

NOT SO NAÏVE

It is generally assumed that Eva Braun lived in an apolitical sphere, totally unaware of the National Socialists' worldview, and that she isolated herself in a childlike world of innocence. It is true that Braun was ushered away when business or political conversations took place or when cabinet ministers or other dignitaries were present.[25] Furthermore, Braun was not a member of the National Socialist Party.[26]

However, the Berghof's inner circle, over which Eva Braun covertly held sway, was fully aware of the political developments and activities of the Reich. Topics were sometimes discussed at lunch or during the long evenings over which Hitler liked to preside. These same intimates, including Braun, traveled to Vienna for Hitler's annexation victory speech. The result of Von Ribbentrop's negotiation with the Soviet Union on the nonaggression pact was long awaited by the elite gathering at the Berghof and subsequently celebrated. Also, it would have been impossible for Eva Braun not to be aware of the National Socialists' antisemitic views and repressive policy. Not only did Hitler's intimates hold thAudioVolumeUpe same radical *Weltanschauung*, but Braun, who adored the cinema, would have undoubtedly witnessed the sweeping changes in the Third Reich's propaganda-driven and often outright antisemitic movie messages.[27]

PRIVILEGES OF THE POST

In her capacity as photographer in Heinrich Hoffmann's employ, Braun took countless photographs and made movies of Hitler and the members of the inner circle at the Berghof. Even up till 1943, Hoffmann paid her extremely high prices for many of these photos that he, in turn, put to profit thanks to the publication of his popular photo books.[28] Hoffmann assembled many albums and booklets on Hitler, such as "The Hitler Nobody Knows" (1933) or "The Face of the *Führer*," publications that effectively contributed to shaping the *Führer*'s public image for political marketing and propaganda purposes. Many of the photos and film footage of the National Socialist elite relaxing at the Berghof can be attributed to Eva Braun, thus making her complicit in the Third Reich's deceptive propaganda machine

"TILL DEATH DO US PART"

During the war years, Eva Braun became increasingly confident in her role with Hitler and in her influence over him. At the same time, however, her dependence on Hitler reached the point where she told her friends that, if

Figure 27.1. Eva Braun at the Berghof with a movie camera by her side. *Age Fotostock*

he died—such as was nearly the case with the July 22, 1944, assassination attempt at the Wolf's Lair—she would kill herself. A few months later, in October, she went so far as to state this intention in her written will.

In April 1945, Braun moved to Berlin with the purpose of staying with Hitler till the end, yet supported his obstinate illusion in believing that the war could still be won. On April 22 Speer paid his last visit to Hitler at the Berlin bunker. Following hours of discussion and after Hitler had retired to his quarters, Eva Braun invited Speer to her room. Speer commented that Braun "was the only prominent candidate for death in this bunker who displayed an admirable and superior composure" and that she "radiated an almost gay serenity."

Realizing that Speer would be hungry and thirsty after his long conversation with Hitler, she ordered him some champagne, cake, and sweets and told him, "You know, it was good that you came back once more. The *Führer* had assumed you would be working against him. But your visit has proved the opposite to him. . . . Anyhow, he liked what you said to him today. He made up his mind to stay here, and I am staying with him. And you know the rest, too, of course. . . . He wanted to send me back to Munich. But I refused; I've come to end it here."[29]

A short week after her statement, in the night of April 28, Adolf Hitler married Eva Braun in a small civil ceremony in the Berlin bunker with Joseph Goebbels and Martin Bormann as witnesses. Following the ceremony, Hitler hosted a simple wedding breakfast with his new wife,[30] who was now called, legally speaking, Eva Hitler. The next day, Hitler and his wife bid their farewells to staff and members of the inner circle.[31] Later that afternoon, Eva Hitler bit into a cyanide capsule[32] and Adolf Hitler shot himself in the temple with his pistol.[33]

The fourteen years of Eva Braun's captivity as a secret bird in Hitler's "golden cage" were over. In Hitler's will, Eva's name featured first on the list of those to whom he bequeathed a monetary inheritance. Posthumously, all that Eva would receive was the world's attention on the little-known "Munich girl" who had agreed to live in the *Führer*'s shadow.

NOTES

1. Angela Lambert, *The Lost Life of Eva Braun* (New York: St. Martin's Press, 2006), 49–52.

2. Ibid., 55.

3. Heike B. Görtemaker, *Eva Braun: Life with Hitler* (New York: Alfred A. Knopf, 2011), 12–13.

4. Kershaw, *Hitler*, 219–20.

5. Heike B. Görtemaker, "Eva Braun. Leben mit Hitler—Dr. Görtemaker, 17.06.2019," Stiftung Demokratie Saarland, YouTube video, https://www.youtube.com/watch?v=v3U71FCpajM.

6. Görtemaker, *Eva Braun*, 48–51.

7. Lambert, *Lost Life of Eva Braun*, 130.

8. Görtemaker, *Eva Braun*, 81.

9. Ibid., 12.

10. Ibid., 19.

11. Ibid., 88.

12. Speer, *Inside the Third Reich*, 130.

13. Ibid., 47.

14. Lambert, *Lost Life of Eva Braun*, 228.

15. Idem., 230.

16. Görtemaker, "Eva Braun."

17. Ibid.

18. Lambert, *Lost Life of Eva Braun*, 1.

19. Ibid., 201–202.

20. Ibid., 204.

21. Speer, *Inside the Third Reich*, 100.

22. Ibid., 256.

23. Ibid., 146–47.

24. Ibid.

25. Lambert, *Lost Life of Eva Braun*, 324.

26. Ibid., 338.

27. Görtemaker, "Eva Braun."

28. Görtemaker, *Eva Braun*, 171–73.

29. Speer, *Inside the Third Reich*, 484.

30. Antony Beevor, *Berlin: The Downfall 1945* (New York: Penguin, 2002), 342–43.

31. Kershaw, *Hitler*, 954.

32. Heinz Linge, *With Hitler to the End: The Memoir of Hitler's Valet* (London: Frontline Books, 2009), 199.

33. Kershaw, *Hitler*, 955.

PART V

Dealing with Collective Guilt

Chapter 28

How Nazified Were the Germans during the Third Reich?

Decades have passed since World War II, yet still today we seek to determine the accountability of the ordinary German citizen during Hitler's regime. When thinking stereotypically about the "Nazis," most people tend to proffer an image of a nation of Hitler-idolizing, sadistic, and warmongering fanatics whose sole aim was to conquer the world and annihilate the Jews.

It is true that hundreds of thousands of average Germans readily and deliberately took part in the persecution and mass murder of innocent people. However, despite rumors of widespread killings and the genocidal goals of Hitler's regime, a vast number of Germans remained passive bystanders. The German people were not, by nature, merciless executioners, and they possessed stable personalities before Hitler came to power. In fact, Germans' family lives were remarkably similar to those of average middle-class British or American families.[1]

HOW MANY GERMANS BACKED HITLER?

The surprising fact that only one-third of German voters supported the National Socialist Party before Hitler's takeover in 1933 indicates that the majority of the nation did not endorse its political agenda. Furthermore, Hitler's ascent to power may not have been possible without the twin economic disasters of the inflation of 1923 and the Great Depression that began in 1929.[2] However, in a short amount of time, his regime managed to create the impression of having eradicated decades of deprivation, restored economic stability, established a sense of security through remilitarization, and achieved the peaceful annexation of the Rhineland, Sudetenland, and Austria. This led to the gradual acceptance or even praise of Hitler's regime by opponents of National Socialism, as national pride replaced the shame of Germany's defeat and the subsequent imposition of the Versailles Treaty.

German historian Sebastian Haffner reckoned with credibility that, by 1938, Hitler had succeeded in winning the support of "the great majority of that majority who had voted against him in 1933." The personalized focus of the regime's "successes" reflected the incessant efforts of propaganda, which had been consciously directed to creating and building up the "heroic" image of Hitler as a towering genius.[3] The *Führer* myth and *Führer* cult both played a major role in fashioning an infallible superman leader and a caring shepherd of the German flock. By early 1939, the German *Volk* were confident their shepherd would continue to lead them to greener pastures, not to war.

Despite the fact that war was one of the last things Germans wanted when Hitler came to power, and despite the *Führer* repeatedly claiming to desire peace, the National Socialists' propaganda campaign for war was highly effective. As a result, Hitler's popularity increased for the first two years of the war. As an example, at the outbreak of war, the National Socialist Party counted some 5.5 million members, but by war's end it had over 8 million. The general membership of the NS Party consisted primarily of the urban and rural lower middle classes. Some 7 percent belonged to the upper class, another 7 percent were farmers, 35 percent were industrial workers, and 51 percent were what can be labeled as middle class. At the peak of party membership toward the end of the war, 63 percent of the members were male and 37 percent female, yet the total of eight million still represented a mere 10 percent of Germany's population at the time.[4] These figures suggest that only a minority of politically active Germans actually joined the National Socialist Party.

Hitler's popularity during his time in power was significantly influenced by the disproportionate number of young people in Germany's population, a generation more predisposed to the ideology of National Socialism. In 1933, for instance, nearly one-third of the nation comprised individuals between the ages of eighteen and thirty. The National Socialists' emphasis on concepts such as "blood and soil," the unity of the *Volk*, German culture, the restoration of national pride, the promotion of ethical values, pageantry, allegiance to the flag, songs, war games, comradery, group discipline, the sanctity of sacrifice, and dedication to the nation and their father-figure *Führer* all contributed to creating a near unquestioning devotion to the "savior" of Germany's economy and society.

CONFORMING THE YOUNG

In a speech featured in the film *Triumph of the Will*, Hitler pledged that soon young people would not even be able to imagine the bygone "infection of our poisonous party system. Hitler Youth," he said, "has been consigned to us and has become ours, body and soul. They live in this proud Germany of the Swastika and will never again let it be ripped from their hearts." The ability to shape the minds and hearts of future National Socialists rested largely on the dedication of teachers to National Socialist principles, which included a perspective on human nature that emphasized race and conflict, a conviction of the absolute superiority of the Aryan race, and a communal code grounded in the concepts of *Volk* and *Führer*.[5]

Special training courses as well as camps molded the teaching body into instruments of National Socialist indoctrination. Teachers who were not entirely supportive of the new regime found that they could maintain a balance between conformity and dissent as long as they did not openly criticize Hitler or NS policies. As one former student explained it, "People floated along in a confused jumble of Christian and National Socialist attitudes."[6] Nevertheless, the prevalence of antisemitic sentiment increased, with teachers joining their students in verbally and in some instances physically assaulting Jewish children. Although only one in three or one in four teachers may have displayed fervent support for NS ideology, it was enough to create a miserable existence for those Jewish children who were ostracized as unwanted.[7]

National Socialist educators realized that their early approach to antisemitism was too extreme and subsequently adjusted to reduce overt racial hatred. Instead, they emphasized the formation of a collective consciousness in which individuals deemed to be racial outsiders were excluded. This more moderate version of *Gleichschaltung* allowed individual teachers greater flexibility to tailor their approach to their own circumstances and preferences, while still conveying the clear ethical directive to show reverence to the *Führer*, expel those deemed alien, make sacrifices for the *Volk*, and embrace challenges. Although compliant teachers may not have embodied the archetypal National Socialists advocated by party leaders in 1933, they prepared their pupils for inclusion in the Hitler Youth and for devotion to the *Volk*.[8]

Alfons Heck, a former member of the Hitler Youth, offered a firsthand account of how NS disinformation shaped moral reasoning. In 1940, when Alfons witnessed the Gestapo arresting his best friend, Heinz, along with all of the Jewish people in his village, he did not think to himself, "How awful that they're arresting Jewish people." Instead, having internalized the indoctrination about the so-called Jewish menace, he thought, "What a shame that Heinz is Jewish."[9]

GLEICHSCHALTUNG OR AUSSCHALTUNG

Though the term *Gleichschaltung* literally translates as "same-switching" or "same-shifting," it has no equivalent in English. To an electrician, the term would be understood as "phasing" or "synchronization." The closest meanings implied by the NS mind-set include a process of forcible coordination or enforced (political) conformity. On the other hand, *Ausschaltung* is the process of being switched off, disconnected, or eliminated, the fate of all those who would not or did not conform to mainstream society or the Aryan prototype.

Almost imperceptibly, while the public scarcely took notice, the government worked to align all aspects of society with the ideology and objectives of the party. This process involved the coordination and regulation of political, economic, social, and cultural institutions, including trade unions, media, education, and religious organizations, in order to ensure adherence to National Socialist principles. All organizations faced two options: either comply with *Gleichschaltung* or face dissolution.[10] Through *Gleichschaltung*, the regime aimed to eliminate any opposition or dissent and establish a totalitarian state in which the NS Party exerted complete control over all facets of society. The use of associations and societies as a means of educating the population was undoubtedly effective, as most adult Germans belonged to at least several of these organizations.[11] Those who were able to find employment, particularly young people, could take pleasure in becoming part of the community, enjoying the benefits of their work, and contributing to larger nationalist and socialist endeavors.

The National Socialist ideology fostered the objective of eradicating social and economic stratification within German society while promoting a feeling of unity and camaraderie among Germans. The government provided common individuals the chance to possess their own homes with gardens and recognized the contributions of the working class and farmers through festivities that highlighted their significance and a sense of inclusion within an elite community. The subordinate groups of the German Labor Front dedicated themselves to enhancing workers' sense of belonging and communicating the essence of their socialist vision through activities during their leisure time. Such tangible social and economic transformations enticed an increasing number of Germans to adopt National Socialism.[12]

NATIONAL SOCIALISM: A MORAL CODE

National Socialism functioned as an ideological system that met the customary roles that are attributed to such a belief structure. It provided solutions to the uncertainties that life presents, imbued purpose in the midst of randomness, and elucidated the workings of the world. In addition, it created its own framework of morality, disapproving of self-interest as unethical while extolling altruism as virtuous. By evoking a generational chain of ethnic comrades (*Volksgenossen*) to Germans' ancestors and descendants, NS ideals incorporated the individual within the collective well-being of the nation. Hitler presented National Socialism as the antidote to the feeble and effeminate Weimar Republic, offering instead a bold, masculine order. In place of religion, National Socialist culture provided an absolutist secular faith.[13] Tragically, the road to Auschwitz would be paved with the perceived unquestionable morality of these beliefs.

National Socialism offered a comprehensive system of meaning to all ethnic Germans, communicated through potent symbols and collective festivities. It taught individuals how to differentiate between allies and adversaries, genuine believers and dissenters, non-Jews and Jews, resembling a religion. Its emphasis on self-sacrifice and rejection of self-centeredness exhibited parallels to ethical teachings in other cultures. However, while international covenants advocated for universal human rights, NS public culture expressed the opposite premise: "Not every being with a human face is human."[14]

National Socialist dogma emphasized nationalism, German traditions, and militarism, and the majority of citizens either fully embraced these ideals or at the very least pledged loyalty to the new regime, resulting in overall dutiful submission by German society. No significant resistance was evident, and any opposition from the socialist and Communist factions was brutally quelched, leaving no large-scale organized opposition.[15]

WINNING OVER THE NATION BY TONING DOWN ANTISEMITISM

According to historian Claudia Koonz, by scrutinizing the popular press of Germany and four other European nations (France, Great Britain, Italy, and Romania) from 1899 to 1939, it becomes evident that before 1933 Germans were less antisemitic in their attitudes and actions toward Jews compared to their neighbors.[16] This begs the question of how ordinary Germans, who had no greater prejudice than people elsewhere in Europe, became indifferent bystanders and collaborators in acts of persecution?

Goebbels was known for his racist beliefs, but his ministry did not focus much on promoting racial hatred before 1939. For racial reeducation to be effective, it had to come from seemingly impartial sources rather than propaganda. Knowledge, rather than propaganda, had the ability to alter attitudes.[17]

In portraying himself as a symbol of virtue and champion of moral righteousness, Hitler positioned his regime as the vehicle that would reinstate ethical order.[18] Remarkably, he spoke very little about race and instead focused on three key themes in his early 1930s speeches: denouncing the Versailles victors, insulting his opponents, and discussing topics such as honor, struggle, glory, and morality.[19] He promised to revive "family, honor, and loyalty, *Volk* and *Vaterland*, culture and economy," and to restore the "eternal foundation of our morality and faith." According to Hitler, Germans' struggle was not just for themselves but for Germany, a notion of selflessness that received a resounding response of approval from the audience.[20] In fact, between the spring of 1933, shortly after his accession to leadership, and the launching of World War II, only on three occasions did Hitler vent his phobic racial hatred to the masses.[21]

BUREAUCRATIC EXCLUSION AND DEPORTATION

Instead of repeatedly verbally announcing persecution and exclusion of the Jewish population, Hitler allowed the legal system and the terror organizations to carry out the dirty work for him. The legal exclusion of Jews from the *Volksgemeinschaft* likely exerted a psychological impact on the general public by fueling a belief in Aryan supremacy, and it also served the interests of those who coveted Jewish positions and assets. Although German Jews were understandably distressed by this discrimination, there was a range of popular opinions on antisemitism, and by 1939 a consensus had formed that most Germans were unfazed by the Jews' exclusion from the "People's Community."[22]

AudioVolumeUpThe NS leaders' antisemitism was common knowledge, but a well-managed public relations strategy enabled many moderate Germans to justify their support for the National Socialist regime. They could embrace the emphasis on ethnic identity and economic revitalization while downplaying National Socialist atrocities as secondary or even trivial. Media coverage of concentration camps and mass arrests portrayed the state's actions as protective measures, and dissenting opinions were discredited as being influenced by foreign powers.[23]

On the other hand, historian Sara Gordon ascertains in her analysis of German public opinion based on German Security Service reports during the war, as well as on Allied questionnaires collected during the occupation,

It would appear that a majority of Germans supported elimination of Jews from the civil service; quotas on Jews in professions, academic institutions, and commercial fields; restrictions on intermarriage; and voluntary emigration of Jews. However, the rabid anti-Semites' demands for violent boycotts, illegal expropriation, destruction of Jewish property, pogroms, deportation, and extermination were probably rejected by a majority of Germans. They apparently wanted to restrict Jewish rights substantially, but not to annihilate Jews.[24]

Nevertheless, indifference and a willingness to tolerate the persecution of Jews—to consider it unimportant—was a defining feature of the attitude of the majority of "ordinary Germans" during the Reich.[25]

"INFORMATIONAL" BRAINWASHING

In January 1933, all Germans were considered part of the same nation. However, in the following six years, the National Socialist regime gradually expelled those whom it considered to be Jewish. Despite the initial resistance from non-Jewish shoppers and merchants who continued to frequent businesses owned by Jews, militant National Socialists felt empowered to persecute Jews. This was done through actions such as smashing windows or scrawling graffiti near Jewish homes, as well as by taunting Jews on the streets with derogatory terms like "Yid" or "Jewish Pig." Furthermore, roving gangs of NS thugs assaulted Jews and destroyed or stole their property. While most Germans did not support radical anti-Jewish measures, the NS leaders faced a dilemma as the violence that pleased their most ardent supporters turned away potential supporters who were crucial for political stability.[26] The new leaders exploited their technologically advanced media to maintain power despite irreconcilable expectations between radical and moderate supporters.

Claudia Koonz asserts, perhaps rather contentiously, that while many bystanders may have sympathized with defenseless Jews tormented by brown-shirted bullies, most Germans, like other Europeans and North Americans, saw the legal expulsion of Jews from certain aspects of public life as an adjustment to counteract the perceived special rights enjoyed by Jews in those areas. She adds that, though cultural antisemitism was prevalent among most Germans, only a minority of resolute racists approved of punishing innocent people.[27] While it is prudent to not take a stance on the motivation behind excluding or persecuting Jews, it is likely that most German adults were neither brainwashed nor terrorized. They simply complied with regulations they agreed with and found ways to evade those they opposed. Jewish

Germans who left the country relate shared memoirs revealing that both violent antisemites and courageous friends coexisted in Germany.[28]

Various media such as books, magazines, newspapers, radio, and exhibits bombarded Germans with information about the alleged Jewish threat. Academic research institutes provided false evidence of Jews' "otherness," offering an alternative source of knowledge about "Jewry." This seemingly objective evidence contributed to the expulsion of Jews from the moral community. While rational antisemitism lacked sound evidence in 1933, fraudulent research in the mid-1930s dignified by scholarly sources made Jews strangers in Germany. The majority of Germans initially deplored the destruction of Jewish property and boycotts but gradually accepted the "outsider" status of Jews as a basic fact.[29]

To effectively carry out their crimes, perpetrators needed to maintain a moral self-image despite their heinous acts. Scholarly racism aided this process in several ways. First, by dehumanizing individual Jews and labeling them as "Jewry," perpetrators could justify any action against them. Second, by projecting their own intentions onto the victims, they absolved themselves of personal responsibility. Deportation and mass murder grew to be seen as preemptive self-defense against an imagined lethal threat. Third, the focus on finding honorable methods of solving the "Jewish problem" placed the morality of the perpetrators above the suffering of the victims. Lastly, the endorsement of a stoic and unsentimental attitude steered the perpetrators away from feelings of pity.[30]

As a result of such lack of empathy, Jewish citizens of the Third Reich were systematically stripped of their dignity, their rights, and their property, and many lost their lives. Starting in late 1941, over 260 trains deported more than one thousand Jews each from Germany, with similar "purging" of Jews from Austria and annexed regions so that, by late 1943, Germany had achieved *Judenfrei* (Jew-free) status.[31] In the interests of social hygiene and spurred by the work ethic, academic persecutors did not torment or murder: they "cleansed" and "purified" the *Volksgemeinschaft*.

It would not have been difficult for Germans to acquire information about the treatment of deported Jews, as almost anyone returning from service in the east, including the military, SS, and other involved organizations, could provide details. The mass-murder process of the Holocaust occurred in different ways across Europe, and the large number of participants made it impossible to keep the operation a secret.[32] In the aftermath of the war, survivors, perpetrators, collaborators, bystanders, and their descendants held heated debates about how much ordinary Germans knew about the Final Solution. Millions of people made a conscious decision to remain willfully ignorant about the atrocities and simply chose not to inquire about these crimes.[33]

Claudia Koonz concludes that the Final Solution was neither the result of actions on the eastern front in 1941 nor the theory or implementation of a single agency. Rather, powerful groups within the government, NS Party, and SS reached a consensus for genocide within Germany during the regime's first six years of networking, theoretical debates, and factional disputes prior to the invasion of Poland in 1939.[34] Germans did not become National Socialists because of a dislike for Jews, Koonz suggests; rather, they became antisemites because of their affiliation with National Socialism.[35]

WERE THE GERMANS VIOLENT AND SADISTIC BY NATURE?

As already observed, Germany's younger generation represented a prodigious majority and force among the proponents of National Socialism, as well as membership in the SA and SS. Most had experienced the damaging effects of either World War I or the economic slump and political confusion of the Weimar Republic years—or both. Added to parental absence or partial neglect, this cohort was prone to anxiety and depression that was easily manifested in aggression against the perceived enemy responsible for their childhood or teenage troubles: the Jew.

The generation that grew up during the war era frequently exhibited either vulnerable egos or domineering egos that readily turned to violent solutions when confronted with challenges, particularly those encountered during the Great Depression. A considerable proportion of people from this group became members of paramilitary groups that existed before or during the Third Reich. Moreover, the psychological predisposition of the younger generation rendered them inclined to blindly follow an omnipotent and faultless leader, such as the *Führer*.

There is ongoing controversy among experts as to whether or not the National Socialist leaders who perpetrated the crime of genocide were aberrant and pathological. This would imply that their compliers, in particular the henchmen directly involved in torturing and killing, may also have been mentally ill. Despite such questioning, the theory of dispositional instability fails to explain the obedience of the rank and file who ran the Holocaust machine. A working example is the Majdanek death camp trial in Germany, during which neighbors of the camp staff were reportedly shocked when camp guards were arrested by the police, accused, and eventually convicted of horrific crimes. After the war, these men and women had supposedly led lives as good citizens, with no manifest signs of mental disorder.[36]

Researcher Michael Selzner concedes that attempts to explain conformity to National Socialist directives as a result of distinctive lines of personality in abnormally large numbers of Germans have failed. Instead, he maintains that, given the proper circumstances, even a small proportion of the population—10 percent for instance—possessed the psychological traits of the National Socialist perpetrator personality.[37]

Following up this line of thought—that is, the power exerted by the perpetrators over their compliers or executioners—the surprising and now well-known research of Yale University psychologist Stanley Milgram, first carried out in the 1960s, comes to mind. The experiments measured the willingness of study participants—men from a diverse range of occupations with varying levels of education—to obey an authority figure who instructed them to perform acts of cruelty conflicting with their personal conscience.

Even if we deny the adequacy of Milgram's experiment, the haunting truth remains that people obey authority, despite inner agony and personal morality. Compelling as this evidence might appear, the "simply following orders" reasoning leaves much to question. One important factor is that Milgram's model does not fully match the historical structure of the Shoah itself. These torturers and executioners were clearly more implicated than ordinary people simply doing ordinary jobs. Some of these everyday citizens became part of a killing machine while many others refused to comply.[38]

A psychological study of the question of responsibility of the compliers led the German political sociologist Stefan Immerfall to search for ways of reconciling microsocial and macrosocial factors. To address the question of how to connect individual behavior and its change over time to the evolution of a genocide system, he suggested four processes of key importance: time dynamics, disintegration, fragmentation, and entrapment.[39]

Time dynamics: Genocide evolves step-by-step and does not simply appear out of nothing. Even if Hitler was determined to exterminate Jews, there was initially no fixed "solution to the Jewish problem." The National Socialists embarked on a path of anti-Jewish policies that ultimately led to the Final Solution, but the consequences were neither conceivable nor foreseeable when the perpetrators initially came to power. The gradual escalation of anti-Jewish sentiment made it easier for the general population to comply with each single step and more difficult to refuse the next one. Harm harbors more harm, and bystanders gradually transform into potential perpetrators.[40]

Disintegration: Following their takeover, the National Socialists destroyed all opposing organizations. Add to this the threat of reprisals from the terror apparatus and surveillance, and the destruction of civil society resulted in extremely unfavorable conditions for any attempt at collective action.[41]

Fragmentation: Between 1934 and 1944, most of the German population, including those who had not voted for Hitler, did not feel imminently threatened by official repression, so long as they went with the flow. The 1938 *Kristallnacht* pogroms were not to be repeated because the regime sensed that most Germans did not like to witness acts of mass violence and public disturbance. As a consequence, visible outbursts of violence were abandoned; instead, the identification, deportation, and later destruction of Jewish and other targets became highly routinized. Jews were removed from public life in a gradual way. Many Germans had a fair idea of what might be happening in the concentration camps in Poland to which Jews were transported, but as they were removed from direct visibility, the lack of proximity paved the way for large-scale indifference.

Another aspect of fragmentation is division of labor, according to which the Holocaust was, in fact, the collective result of many smaller steps. The town official only filled out the appropriate paperwork, the trainmaster only put together train schedules, and each process was separate from the preceding one, until the victim was put to death. Routine work, not only on the organizational level but also at the level of the individual links in the chain, minimizes the inclination and the opportunity to raise moral questions.[42]

Entrapment: Even before the onset of war, many Germans were, to a certain degree, not simply passive but semiactive participants in the National Socialist system. What may have begun as mental approval of the system's positive and appealing goals became a trap once the war had fully unfolded. At this point, the number of victims was disproportionately larger than the initial target group of German Jews who should be "encouraged" to leave Germany. Drawn into the Holocaust and its brutal abuse of entire populations—principally in the occupied Eastern European territories—soldiers and civilians, perpetrators and bystanders alike, now began to fear reprisals. The Germans had good reason to assume that they might become collectively a global target of blame and revenge, depending on whether they, as individuals, had supported or resisted Hitler. This condition made it extremely difficult for Germans to distance themselves from the National Socialist regime until its final demise.[43]

WERE ALL GERMAN SOLDIERS "NAZIS"?

On the battlefield, soldiers of the German army did not greatly differ from their nemesis counterparts, the Allies. On both sides, these men were convinced they were carrying out, not only their duty to their homeland, but a higher calling. The average German soldier on the Normandy battlefield had been told that the enemy had declared war on Germany and that it was his responsibility to defend his home. But just how tainted by National Socialist principles of Aryan superiority, racial prejudice, and Hitler's infallibility were the members of the German armed forces?

In January 1933, the military played a key role in persuading President Paul von Hindenburg to dismiss Chancellor Kurt von Schleicher and appoint Hitler as chancellor instead. The armed forces had come to the conclusion that Hitler alone was capable of peacefully reaching the national consensus that would allow the creation of the *Wehrstaat* (defensive state), and thus the military leadership successfully pressured Hindenburg.[44]

As part of an effort to preserve the army's traditional semi-independence, beginning in the mid-1930s the military progressively aligned itself with National Socialist principles in a bid to persuade Hitler that, in the wave of *Gleichschaltung* (forcible coordination), it was not necessary to end the traditional military entity of a "state within a state." The unplanned result of their effort to defend the "state within a state" by "self-*Gleichschaltung*" was to ultimately weaken such a status. Meanwhile, a new generation of technocratic officers was coming to the fore, a group that was much less anxious about preserving the military "state within a state" and more set on progressively transitioning into a National Socialist *Wehrstaat*.[45]

On December 8, 1938, the OKW (Armed Forces High Command) instructed the officers of all three branches to become fully versed in National Socialist ideology and to apply the regime's values in all situations. Beginning in February 1939, pamphlets were issued that were presented as required reading in the military. The titles are self-conclusive: *Hitler's World Historical Mission, The Battle for German Living Space, Hands off Danzig!*, and *The Final Solution of the Jewish Question in the Third Reich*. The last treatise stated, "The defensive battle against Jewry will continue, even if the last Jew has left Germany. Two large and important tasks remain: firstly, the eradication of all Jewish influence, above all in the economy and in culture and, secondly, the battle against World Jewry, which tries to incite all people in the world against Germany."[46]

The renowned historian Richard Evans maintains that junior officers in the army were inclined to be particularly fanatical National Socialists, a third of them having joined the party by 1941. Buttressing the mission of the junior leaders were the National Socialist Leadership Guidance Officers, a group created with the sole purpose of indoctrinating the troops for the "war of extermination" against Soviet Russia.[47] Among higher-ranking officers as well, close to 30 percent were party members by 1941.[48]

German historian Jürgen Förster claims that the Wehrmacht followed Hitler's criminal directives during Operation Barbarossa not solely because of their sense of duty to carry out orders but because they had been convinced that the Soviet Union was run by Jews and that it was Germany's service to the world to annihilate "Judeo-Bolshevism." The majority of Wehrmacht officers sincerely believed that most Red Army commissars were Jews who embodied the Red Army's backbone and driving force. They were persuaded that the best way to win the war against the Soviet Union was to exterminate the commissars by implementing the "Commissar Order" in a move to divest the Russian soldiers of their allegedly Jewish leaders.[49]

Beginning in 1943, the inflow of officers and conscripts who had been educated chiefly within the National Socialist indoctrination system gradually intensified Hitler's politics of hatred in the army.[50] The German officer corps that originally had been dominated by the German nobility and upper classes was broken down by Hitler into a "people's officer corps." By eliminating the institutional social restrictions that had formerly stipulated who qualified to become an officer, Hitler made rank dependent on combat ability and verve, thus emboldening soldiers to fight with increased grit in an effort to improve their chances of a swift rise through the ranks. In this manner, the Wehrmacht turned into a "soldiers' community" bonded by a shared ambition, fanaticism, and crime.[51] As evidence of the above claims, it has been proven that the vast majority of Wehrmacht officers fully cooperated with the SS in murdering Jews in the Soviet Union.[52]

According to the International Committee of the Red Cross, "By its very nature, the phenomenon of war entails excesses, blunders and acts of violence going beyond military necessity." There is no such thing as a "clean" war, and even a war waged in accordance with international humanitarian law involves an unleashing of violence against persons and property with all the attendant suffering and destruction. Obviously, in such circumstances it may be difficult to draw the line between what is lawful and what is not, an act that is legitimate and one that is not, an act that is morally acceptable and one that is not.[53]

The majority of those who carried out the Holocaust willingly became agents of systematic extermination. This was due, in part, to the hardening circumstances of war and deprivation, which resulted in soldiers and paramilitary personnel being conditioned to unquestioningly follow orders and execute them mindlessly. Such individuals were accustomed to accepting and enduring hardships, including the pain and death of both themselves and their enemies. As one soldier on the eastern front noted, "One becomes cruel and without feelings. One is no longer one's self."[54]

According to the German scholar Felix Römer, members of the German armed forces did not fully embrace National Socialism uniformly but instead exhibited diverse shadings or stages and were not devoid of inconsistencies within their belief. Even social groups such as the working class, who were thought to be resistant to the appeals of National Socialism before 1933 and beyond, underwent a change of heart after joining the military and serving with loyalty while never posing a mutinous threat similar to the one that occurred in November 1918. Historian Robert Gellately states that not all Germans in uniform believed in the tales of an international Jewish conspiracy that needed to be halted, and some rejected the torrent of hateful rhetoric while still identifying with National Socialism.[55]

German men on the eastern front committed atrocities in a manner resembling hunters, lynch mobs, and serial killers rather than soldiers. Discussions about whether these perpetrators viewed their actions as a "blood sport" or a "noble cause" have taken place ever since the war crimes trials. One has to factor in that, between 1933 and 1939, those involved in racial warfare had undergone mental training in preparation for their later tasks. Prior to setting foot on Polish soil, soldiers had been indoctrinated with the core tenets of NS ideology, including reverence for the *Führer*, devotion to the *Volk*, a belief in the justice of conquest, and the existence of a Jewish peril.[56] The commander of the notorious Order Police Battalion 101 further solidified this indoctrination by claiming that the Jewish civilians that the soldiers were about to exterminate were responsible for the terrorist air raids over German cities.[57]

THE ALLIES' SECRET POW RECORDINGS

During a lecture trip to Glasgow in 2001, German military historian Sönke Neitzel learned of the existence of secretly recorded conversations of German prisoners of war. British intelligence services had covertly recorded thousands of German POWs during World War II and created protocols from passages of conversations they found significant. Neitzel collaborated with social psychologist Harald Welzer to study around fifty thousand pages of British archives and an additional one hundred thousand pages collected by the National Archives in Washington, DC. The researchers' findings, published in 2012 under the title *Soldaten: On Fighting, Killing, and Dying*, reveal the unaltered views and feelings of German soldiers fresh from the heat of the battle. Though not all Germans may have reacted to the outbreak of World War II with euphoria, some seventeen million German men let themselves be drafted in the armed forces over the course of the war.[58] These transcripts shed light on how these men perceived the ugly business of war and, in particular, what they thought about the mass murders taking place in Eastern Europe.

Plenty has been written about the sordid dimensions of the unrestrained violence and heinous war crimes committed during World War II. The authors of *Soldaten* suggest that rules are least relevant in ground combat. "Wherever soldiers take prisoners," they claim, "secure occupied territories, and battle partisans, particular forms of logic dominate. Individually perpetrated violence, such as rape or killing, becomes not only more possible but increasingly likely." The state of being at war creates a social space that is more open to violence than in peacetime.

One of the distinguishing features of World War II was the National Socialists' campaign of exterminating certain groups—an action that took place outside of the war context itself. Another damning practice of the German belligerents was their genocidal treatment of Soviet POWs. Narrative examples of these crimes can occasionally be found in the surveillance protocols, and it is likely that the vast majority of the German military, even in the western theater, was aware of these crimes. However, this knowledge—and occasional involvement—did not appear to hold much importance in the soldiers' frame of reference. They were more concerned with their own survival and comforts—or lack thereof—than to find empathy for the suffering of others, in particular of those they believed to be racially inferior.[59]

In the POWs' conversations, they rarely question their own or their colleagues' often criminal treatment of prisoners of war, the local population, or partisans (the fate of which was far worse than uniformed fighters as partisans and members of the Resistance did not fall under the prisoner-of-war regulations of the Hague Convention). "The soldiers do not think to question their behavior," the authors write. "Their task is to take care of the necessities: 'work,' 'extreme measures' and 'retribution.' They focus on achieving results, not finding reasons."[60]

This unquestioning willingness to be part of a larger picture can be found in the context of those active in the Holocaust itself: at each level of the implementation of this genocide, from marksmen to camp doctors who decided which unfortunate prisoner would die immediately and which detainee would be forced to work, the perpetrators were more concerned with methods of killing than with justifying its necessity.[61]

In a rare instance of obtaining source material from an executioner in Czechoslovakia, the unwitting former henchman described to a colleague his experience of murdering Jews as follows:

> At the barracks, it was a treadmill. They came from one side, and there was a column of maybe 500 or 600 men. They came in through the gate and went up to the firing range. There they were killed, picked up and brought away, and then the next six would come. At first you said, great, better than doing normal duty, but after a couple of days you would have preferred normal duty. It took a toll on your nerves. . . . But orders were orders.[62]

Members of the German armed forces carried out acts that they never would have been either capable of—or allowed—under normal circumstances. Particularly in the eastern theater of war, these soldiers experienced what it felt like to commit murder without the fear of consequences, to exercise total power over their victims, and to do something completely out of the ordinary, a monstrous deed, yet remain free from any possible reprisals or punishment.

Violence of this kind needs neither a motive nor a reason: it is its own motivation.[63] According to the authors of *Soldaten,*

> The trope of sacrifice, too, allowed Germans to kill without feeling guilty. Ideologists of annihilation like Himmler or practitioners like Rudolf Höss [Auschwitz Camp commander, not Hitler's crony Rudolf Hess] continually stressed that destroying human lives was an unpleasant "task" that ran contrary to "humane" instincts. But the ability to overcome such scruples was seen as a measure of one's character. It was the coupling of murder and morality—the realization that unpleasant acts were necessary and the will to carry out those acts in defiance of feelings of human sympathy—that allowed the perpetrators of genocide to see themselves as "respectable" people, as people whose hearts, in Höss's words, were not bad.[64]

Not all soldiers displayed such complete indifference, and in fact a large number condemned the mass killing of Soviet POWs as "a downright disgusting bit of work," "dreadful," or "ghastly business." One soldier stated that the war was a point of cultural shame and the greatest crime in human history. Upon hearing about a Russian village's entire male population being executed following someone shooting at the occupying German troops from a house, a sergeant in a POW camp exclaimed, "Why do we do all these things? It's not right."[65] Another soldier stated that his fellow soldiers had given Germany a bad name for decades to come, and another, upon hearing about a mass execution in the Soviet Union, declared, "I tell you. If that's the way things are, I'll stop being German. I don't want to be German anymore."[66]

In general, however, members of the military preferred to consider unpleasant acts as not their affair but the "business" of the omnipresent *Führer* and his high command. On the whole, the soldiers did not form individual opinions of the National Socialist state, Hitler's dictatorship, or even the persecution of Jews.[67] In some instances, however, soldiers repeated the myths that had been told them when they were younger, such as in this account of a nineteen-year-old sailor: "I know what the Jews did. About 1928 or 1929 they carried off the women and raped them and cut them up and the blood—I know of many cases—every Sunday in their synagogues they sacrificed human blood, Christian blood."[68]

But even die-hard National Socialists often expressed empathy toward Jews they had personally known and were dismayed at the "scandalous treatment" of the Jewish minority by a "cultured people." Another opined, "I was always against the persecution of the Jews, too. One should have been able to exile the Jews but one shouldn't have treated them like that." One POW warned, "It will be a disgrace being a German after the war. We'll be as much hated as the Jews were." "The greatest mistake was the expulsion of the Jews," seconded another. "That and, particularly, the inhuman treatment," added a third.[69]

Refusing orders, displaying cowardice, or deserting the armed forces were hardly options, as such offenses entailed execution. During the course of World War II, some twenty thousand German soldiers were handed down the death sentence. By comparison, only 146 American soldiers were put to death, but an estimated 150,000 Soviet military were executed by their own courts during that time.[70]

How can we evaluate the German soldier's mind-set and behavior during World War II? The experts who authored *Soldaten* sum up their findings in several points. Their extreme behavior and near religious trust in the *Führer*, as well as "temporally specific contexts of perception," affected the perspective, interpretation, and actions of soldiers. In addition, "role models and the desire to set a good example" probably influenced the men's behavior more than other factors. Their "soldierliness," as it was perceived and implemented as a group, determined and dictated their individual actions.[71] It was the military's social environments that compelled the armed forces to act in a certain manner, rather than an ideological mission, such as fighting against a perceived "global Jewish conspiracy" or a "Bolshevik genetic inferiority."[72]

The soldiers' widely diverse and sometimes diametrically opposed views of the war were rarely echoed in their actions. In battle, most soldiers behaved in a similar manner, "regardless of whether they were Protestants or Catholics, Nazis or regime critics, Prussians or Austrians, university graduates or uneducated people." The *Soldaten* authors conclude, "The decisive factor in the atrocities . . . was a general realignment from a civilian to a wartime frame of reference. . . . Within this context, soldiers could murder Jews without being anti-Semites and fight fanatically for the fatherland without being committed National Socialists."[73]

The evidence has demonstrated that German soldiers were motivated by a dual sense of duty: to safeguard their homeland and families, as well as to obliterate the enemy in order to prevent a potential invasion and the perceived corruption of Germany. These soldiers had been subject to rigorous ongoing indoctrination in National Socialist principles and lived in fear of the death penalty for any hint of defeatism, noncompliance, or desertion. Consequently, many soldiers who may have been kind and compassionate civilians at home mindlessly followed the example of their violent comrades.

It is reasonable to assert that the German military, much like the civilian population, was repeatedly exposed to highly effective NS programming. A majority in the armed forces were young people who were educated under the misguidance of National Socialist dogma. However, it remains a challenge to determine the degree to which each individual succumbed to such NS indoctrination and how many still allowed their innate moral codes to prevail.

NOTES

1. Berit Brogaard, "Group Hatred in Nazi Germany: 80 Years Later," *Psychology Today*, July 1, 2018.

2. Robert Gellately, *Hitler's True Believers: How Ordinary People Became Nazis* (Oxford: Oxford University Press, 2020), 316.

3. Ian Kershaw, "The Führer Myth: How Hitler Won over the German People," *Spiegel International*, January 30, 2008.

4. Chris McNab, *Hitler's Masterplan: The Essential Facts and Figures for Hitler's Third Reich* (London: Amber, 2011).

5. Claudia Koonz, *The Nazi Conscience* (Cambridge, MA: Belknap Press, 2003), 131.

6. Melita Maschmann, *Account Rendered: A Dossier on My Former Self* (London: Abelard-Schumann, 1965), 31.

7. Koonz, *Nazi Conscience*, 148–49.

8. Ibid., 161–62.

9. Ibid., 5.

10. Ibid., 72–73.

11. Ibid., 89.

12. Gellately, *Hitler's True Believers*, 320.

13. Koonz, *Nazi Conscience*, 2–3.

14. Ibid., 273.

15. Gellately, *Hitler's True Believers*, 317.

16. Koonz, *Nazi Conscience*, 9.

17. Ibid., 12–13.

18. Ibid., 14.

19. Ibid., 27.

20. Ibid., 31.

21. Ibid., 100.

22. Gellately, *Hitler's True Believers*, 317–18.

23. Koonz, *Nazi Conscience*, 102.

24. Sarah Ann Gordon, *Hitler, Germans, and the "Jewish Question"* (Princeton, NJ: Princeton University Press, 1984), 201–208.

25. Ulrich Herbert, ed., *National Socialist Extermination Policies: Contemporary German Perspectives and Controversies* (Oxford: Berghahn Books, 2000), 23.

26. Koonz, *Nazi Conscience*, 44.

27. Ibid., 165–66.

28. Ibid., 178.

29. Ibid., 192–93.

30. Ibid., 259.

31. Ibid., 272.

32. Nicholas Stargardt, *The German War: A Nation under Arms, 1939–1945* (New York: Basic Books, 2015), 244, 257–58.

33. David Bankier, *The Germans and the Final Solution: Public Opinion under Nazism* (Oxford: Blackwell, 1992), 102.

34. Koonz, *Nazi Conscience*, 15.

35. Ibid., 35.

36. Stefan Immerfall, "Courage and Conformity in Comparative Perspective—Nazi Germany and Beyond," paper presented at the Thirty-Fifth Congress of the International Institute of Sociology, Krakow, Poland, November 16, 2001, pp. 2–4.

37. Michael Selzner, "Psychistorical Approaches to the Study of Nazism," *Journal of Psychohistory* 4, no. 2 (1976): 215–24.

38. Immerfall, "Courage and Conformity in Comparative Perspective," 2–4.

39. Ibid., 11–13.

40. Ibid.

41. Ibid.

42. Ibid.

43. Ibid.

44. Michael Geyer, "Etudes in Political History: Reichswehr, NSDAP and the Seizure of Power," in *The Nazi Machtergreifung*, ed. Peter Stachura (London: Allen & Unwin, 1983), 101–23.

45. Omer Bartov, *Hitler's Army: Soldiers, Nazis and War in the Third Reich* (Oxford: Oxford University Press, 1994), 143.

46. Jürgen Förster, "Complicity or Entanglement? The Wehrmacht, the War, and the Holocaust," in *The Holocaust and History: The Known, the Unknown, the Disputed, and the Reexamined*, ed. Michael Berenbaum and Abraham J. Peck (Bloomington: Indiana University Press, 1998), 270.

47. Richard J. Evans, *In Hitler's Shadow: West German Historians and the Attempt to Escape the Nazi Past* (London: I. B. Tauris, 1989), 59.

48. Bartov, *Hitler's Army*, 49.

49. Förster, "Complicity or Entanglement?," 273–74.

50. Antony Beevor, *Stalingrad: The Fateful Siege, 1942–1943* (New York: Viking, 1998).

51. MacGregor Knox, "1 October 1942: Adolf Hitler, Wehrmacht Officer Policy, and Social Revolution," *Historical Journal* 43, no. 3 (2000): 801–25.

52. Allan Millett and Williamson Murray, *A War to Be Won: Fighting the Second World War, 1937–1945* (Cambridge, MA: Belknap Press, 2000), 141.

53. Jean-Jacques Frésard, *The Roots of Behaviour in War: A Survey of Literature* (Geneva: International Committee of the Red Cross, 2004), 27.

54. Hannes Heer, *Tote Zonen: Die Wehrmacht an der Ostfront* (Hamburg: Hamburger Edition, 1999), 312.

55. Gellately, *Hitler's True Believers*, 326.

56. Christopher Browning, *Ordinary Men: Reserve Police Battalion 101 and the Final Solution in Poland* (New York: Harper Perennial, 1998), 48.

57. Koonz, *Nazi Conscience*, 260.

58. Neitzel and Welzer, *Soldaten*, 35.

59. Ibid., 77.

60. Ibid., 80.

61. Ibid., 122.

62. Ibid., 127.

63. Ibid., 137.
64. Ibid., 149.
65. Ibid., 145.
66. Ibid., 146.
67. Ibid., 226.
68. Ibid., 232.
69. Ibid., 234–35.
70. Ibid., 272.
71. Ibid., 318.
72. Ibid., 319.
73. Ibid.

Chapter 29

Neo-Nazis in Germany Today?

HOW HAVE GERMANS CHANGED SINCE 1945?

The media repeatedly spotlights and justifiably scandalizes far-right or "neo-Nazi" demonstrations and acts of violence taking place in Germany. Should such events be read as proof that the country is still, or becoming again, racist? To better discern to what extent Germans might be pro-Nazi or xenophobic in the twenty-first century, a number of key historic developments from 1945 to the present need to be addressed.

After the Cold War ended and the East and West were reunited in 1990, Germany rose to become the foremost leader in Europe. However, there exists a persistent undercurrent of xenophobia in Germany that has led to incidents of aggression ranging from mob attacks to mass murders. Notably, a significant portion of this violence has occurred in the East or has been carried out by individuals from former East Germany. According to the Federal Ministry of the Interior, in 2014 almost half of the 130 reported antiforeigner crimes in Germany occurred in the East, despite the fact that only 17 percent of the population lives in the "New States."[1] This chapter also aims to examine the policies and development in the "Two Germanys" since their reunification, particularly with respect to xenophobia.

Following the crushing of Hitler's National Socialist regime in 1945, the Allied Powers attempted a denazification of the German *Volk* and led the drive to bring NS criminals to justice. Both the Allies and the Germans faced the challenge of safeguarding freedom and democracy, as well as dealing with the moral burden of National Socialism, the Holocaust, and widespread devastation in the country. The western regions of Germany received support from their Allies, but the Soviet-occupied zone faced greater difficulties. The resulting Cold War led to the establishment of two German states with different political ideals and mutual animosity.[2]

JUSTICE AND DENAZIFICATION IN WEST GERMANY

After the war ended, it was not challenging for interregnum officials to repeal the laws of the previous regime, erase its symbols and slogans from public life, remove unwanted books from Germany's libraries, eliminate swastikas from forms and paperwork, and rename streets.[3] However, the significant challenge ahead was to alter the mind-set and beliefs of not only the millions of members of the National Socialist Party and its various organizations but also the rest of Germany's citizens who had been indoctrinated by Hitlerian propaganda for twelve years.

Aside from the well-known Nuremberg Trials, which coordinated the hearings of twenty-one leaders and 177 military defendants, over one hundred thousand Germans and Austrians across Europe were held responsible for their involvement in Third Reich crimes. These numbers account for only those who were convicted out of nearly four hundred thousand Germans and Austrians who were detained on suspicion of committing National Socialist crimes or war crimes.[4]

While legal proceedings such as those at Nuremberg or the Dachau Trials for crimes against humanity were judicial hearings of specific crimes, denazification would have to use a different methodology. The first aim was to politically cleanse German society and ensure that those who had been active in applying the ideology of the NS regime were barred from important posts in society and state institutions. The German Law 104 for Liberation from National Socialism and Militarism of March 5, 1946, established five

Figure 29.1.   The main defendants at the Nuremberg Trials (1946). *Alamy 2A25Y3M*

Figure 29.2. One of the Dachau trials (1946). *Alamy BNHW5G*

categories for the classification of Germany's citizens: major offenders, offenders, lesser offenders, followers, and exonerated persons.[5]

As the truth about the appalling conditions in concentration camps within Germany as well as the mass extermination in the Reich's death camps in Eastern Europe came to light and the public was shown shocking film footage, ideas of shared guilt and the possibility of collective punishment for the German people began to emerge. The populace as well as returning soldiers were forced to confront the reality that millions of individuals, including six million Jews, nearly half a million Sinti and Roma, hundreds of thousands of hospital patients, three million Soviet prisoners of war, and at least 130,000 non-Jewish Polish civilians, had been killed as a result of war crimes and crimes against humanity. Faced with these disturbing truths, many individuals attempted to deny responsibility or sought leniency by claiming that they had been "seduced" by the regime's promises and placing all the blame on the "major war criminals."[6]

In order to project a truthful representation of National Socialism on the German population as part of the postwar denazification efforts, the Allies launched a psychological propaganda campaign with the aim of developing a German sense of collective responsibility.[7] With the support of the German press, which fell under Allied control, as well as posters and pamphlets, a program was carried out by which ordinary German citizens were informed of the horrors of the concentration camps. Posters were propagated, displaying images of concentration camp victims matched to texts such as "You Are Guilty of This!"[8] or "These Atrocities: Your Fault!" Thousands of Germans who lived near concentration camps in Germany were led through the camps to witness with their own eyes the crimes that had been committed by the regime that these people had supported. In addition, several films, such as *Die Todesmühlen* (The Death Mills), were produced with the aim of disclosing to the German public the reality of the concentration camp system.

In March 1946, the Allied Powers turned responsibility for denazification over to the German authorities. The accused had to provide detailed and truthful information about their political biography, including membership in the National Socialist Party or any other affiliated organization. The sanctions imposed included fines, forced retirement, or even confinement to a labor camp. Due to the scarcity of incriminating documents, an overwhelming majority of cases were classified in the fourth category of "followers." Only 1.4 percent of the accused undergoing denazification were classified "major offenders" or even "offenders."[9]

In the early period of denazification, the Allies' aim was to investigate every suspect and hold every supporter of National Socialism accountable. Soon, however, they realized that the number of suspects and the lack of qualified personnel simply made this goal unrealistic. It was also reasoned that pursuing denazification too thoroughly would hinder the creation of a functioning, economically efficient, democratic society in Germany. The Morgenthau Plan had recommended that the Allies construct a postwar Germany devoid of industrial means and reduced to a level of subsistence farming. The plan was soon deemed impracticable because of its excessive punitive measures that were likely to engender German anger and rebellion.[10]

Within a few years, a more important consideration that led to the tempering of the denazification effort in the West was the need to prevent the German population from turning to Communism.[11] As the Cold War commenced, Great Britain and the United States began to view West Germany as a crucial ally, and denazification was rapidly trimmed down in an effort to foster amicable relations between the occupying forces and the local population. Contemporary American critics of denazification decried it as a "counterproductive witch-hunt" and a failure. In 1951 the provisional West German government granted amnesties to lesser offenders and terminated the program.[12] Many convicted criminals were pardoned, and doctors guilty of the murder of patients returned to their medical careers. Former National

Socialist judges and even members of the terror apparatus were allowed to resume employment in the police force or public service.[13]

THE GERMAN FEDERAL REPUBLIC FROM 1949 TO 1990

In 1945 defeated Germany was split into four occupation zones, controlled by the United States, Great Britain, France, and the Soviet Union. In 1948, the Soviet Union blocked western access to Berlin, prompting the western powers to form a new federal state in the three western occupation zones. This new state, known as the Federal Republic of Germany (FRG), was established in May 1949 with its capital in Bonn. "West" Germany was initially governed by a provisional constitution, and Konrad Adenauer, a Christian Democrat, was appointed as its first chancellor. Prior to 1933, Adenauer had held prominent positions in the political hierarchy of the Weimar Republic, which led to his exclusion and persecution by the National Socialist regime.

The first president of the newly established Germany was Theodor Heuss, a liberal politician who had previously worked as a political journalist. Throughout Hitler's regime, Heuss had maintained close relationships with a network of liberals and established contact with the German resistance toward the end of the war, although he was not an active resister himself. While both Adenauer and Heuss shared a deep disdain for National Socialism, the new government shifted the nation's focus from denazification to recovery, guiding the country from the devastation of war toward becoming a productive and prosperous nation that fostered amicable relations with its former adversaries, including France, the United Kingdom, and the United States.

During the period from 1949 to 1959, when many Germans sought to forget about the National Socialist past, Heuss used his position as federal president to draw attention to the crimes of the NS era and bring it into West German national political discourse. With no electoral pressures, he addressed the "collective shame" of the Third Reich era, the value of the legacy of the German resistance, and the genocide of German and European Jewry. He regarded accepting the burden of the nation's recent past as a sign of bravery, responsibility, and patriotism, and avoiding it as an act of cowardice and a betrayal of German moral obligations.[14]

In 1948, as part of a scholarly survey, West German adults were posed the question, "Do you believe that National Socialism was a good idea that was executed poorly?" The results were striking, with 57 percent responding in the affirmative, 28 percent in the negative, and 15 percent being undecided. Nearly four decades later, in 1985, the same German scholars studied the viewpoints of individuals born prior to 1932 and discovered that 56 percent of respondents acknowledged having faith in National Socialism at some point, 32 percent denied having held any such beliefs, and 11 percent "had no recollection."[15]

Although Adenauer's government generally prioritized Germany's future over its past, a significant number of suspects had yet to face trial. By the late 1950s, West German prosecutors and scholars estimated that approximately one hundred thousand individuals had played some role in the devastation of European Jewry. From 1945 to the mid-1980s, Allied and then West German courts accused 90,921 individuals of committing war crimes or crimes against humanity. Among them, 6,479 were found guilty, with 12 being executed, 160 sentenced to life in prison, 6,192 given extended prison terms, 114 paying fines, and 83,140 cases being closed without any convictions.[16]

Although denazification and punishing National Socialist criminals or collaborators ceased being top priorities for West German leadership by the 1960s, *Vergangenheitsbewältigung* continued to be a significant concern. This compound German noun describes the process of facing and overcoming the past, which remained an ongoing task that the West German leadership considered essential. Further discussion of this topic will follow later.

THE GERMAN DEMOCRATIC REPUBLIC FROM 1949 TO 1990

The postwar Communist debate on the memory of the Jews took place during the period between the end of Hitler's rule and the beginning of the Cold War, a time of self-searching and adjustment known as the Nuremberg interregnum. The German Communists and Soviet occupation authorities considered Soviet suffering, subsequent triumph, and the narrative of Communist martyrdom as the central aspects of postwar commemoration. For many of them, the memorialization of the Holocaust loomed as an unwelcome competitor for the limited resource of postwar recognition. The preference for Communist "fighters" over Jewish "victims," the emphasis on Soviet suffering and redemptive victory at the expense of the Holocaust, and the delayed and subsequently rejected requests for restitution payments to Jewish survivors were all discouraging signs for Jewish Communists and their non-Jewish comrades.[17]

Many East Germans perceived the Russians' "liberation" of the eastern part of the country in 1945 as an ignominious injustice. While the Soviets primarily used denazification statutes to detain National Socialist officials, they also arrested a significant number of Germans, including women and children, who had no involvement in National Socialism in any administrative or other capacity. Many Germans were detained for extended periods without trial or subjected to unfair trials resulting in extremely severe sentences, often involving forced labor. The Soviets imprisoned at least 130,000 Germans on the grounds of denazification directives in so-called Special Camps, where at least 43,000 individuals perished.[18]

The East German government (GDR) claimed to be an antifascist state and thus exempt from the need to confront the specter of Third Reich history—since there could be no place for xenophobic hatred in such a state. The puppet government, as part of its indoctrination themes, allegedly underwent a radical antifascist and democratic transformation, which it referred to as an *antifaschistisch-demokratische Umwälzung*, a radical antifascist, democratic turnaround. This mind-set asserted that complete denazification, anti-imperialism, and genuine democratization were only possible in Germany under Soviet control. As a consequence, the West German government was landed with the status of National Socialist Germany's successor state, leading to the difficult task of addressing the damaging legacy of the former dictatorship.[19]

The German Democratic Republic addressed the national guilt of the Third Reich through the propagandic promotion of a new national identity emphasizing antifascism and resistance to oppression while celebrating local heroes. It also attempted to minimize the role and responsibility of East Germans during the National Socialist era by underlining their victimization under Hitler's regime. In addition, the GDR implemented reparations programs, compensated victims, and established memorials and museums to commemorate them. Despite these measures, the government faced international criticism for its handling of the NS regime's legacy, with some accusing it of failing to take sufficient responsibility for East Germans' role in Hitler's authoritarian regime.

The GDR viewed fascism as a form of capitalist exploitation, with anti-semitism and racism considered secondary or incidental manifestations. Consequently, East German representations of concentration camp life under National Socialism did not focus on racial persecution, whereby Jews, Sinti, and Roma were largely excluded from commemorative representation. During remembrance ceremonies, the pogrom was primarily associated with Communist bravery, while Jewish suffering was considered a secondary concern.[20]

Given that for four decades the GDR benefited from a supposedly international-minded government, the question arises as to why xenophobic violence is more prevalent in the East of Germany today. In contrast, during the same period and after the war, successive generations of West Germans became significantly less racist, while their East German counterparts became increasingly xenophobic.[21]

Prior to the collapse of the Soviet Union in 1989, the GDR had brought in a significant number of Mozambican and Vietnamese contract workers.

However, the East German government imposed administrative controls that isolated these fifteen thousand Mozambican workers from civil society. They were sequestered in buildings on the outskirts of cities, and those who violated regulations faced being sent home. Female contract workers who became pregnant were given only two options: either terminate the pregnancy or return home. These policies contributed to around 60 percent of East Germans stating that they had no contact with foreigners and little knowledge about them.[22]

SINCE THE 1990 REUNIFICATION: GERMANY'S IMMIGRANT POPULATION

To address the labor shortage in postwar West Germany, the German Federal Republic began inviting Turkish guest workers in 1961. While some returned home, many stayed, resulting in a growing population of individuals in Germany with Turkish roots. As of 2020, estimates vary between 3.5 and 7 million people of Turkish descent living in Germany, a large percentage of whom were born in the country.

Following the dissolution of the Soviet Union, emigration from its successor states surged in the 1990s. Between 1990 and 1999, Germany welcomed around 1.63 million ethnic Germans and 120,000 Jews from the former Soviet Union.[23]

In 2015 and 2016, a significant influx of refugees fleeing conflict and terrorism in Syria, Afghanistan, and Iraq arrived on Europe's shores, sparking fear and uncertainty regarding who would provide asylum and how to integrate these individuals. Despite this, German Chancellor Angela Merkel remained resolute and declared in August of that year, "We can do this!" Germany received more than one million first-time asylum applications, and five years later, over half of these refugees had secured employment: in Germany's "Old States," public backing for immigration remains strong.[24]

Though the 2015–2016 immigrant surge drew worldwide attention, the country has long been a major immigrant destination. Over 15 percent of the eighty-three million people living in Germany today are foreign born, a number that increases to 20 percent if the German-born children of immigrants are included. Since the early 2000s, Germany has experienced a significant policy shift toward recognizing its status and becoming a country that aims at the integration of newcomers and the recruitment of skilled labor migrants. This approach to immigration and immigrants has been tested, however, amid the massive humanitarian inflows that began in 2015 and which have stoked heated debate.[25]

JEWS IN GERMANY TODAY

Out of the approximately 250,000 Jewish displaced persons who passed through Germany in the postwar period, roughly 10 percent opted to stay in the country. The largest and most noticeable group of Jews living in Germany immediately after the war were those who were Eastern European displaced persons. They were accompanied by a small cohort of German Jews, approximately fifteen thousand of whom were liberated in 1945, some from hiding and others from concentration camps. Many of these German Jews had minimal prior contact with Jewish communities before 1933 and had survived due to the protection of a non-Jewish relative.

Despite these difficulties, a significant number of Jewish communities were established in the postwar years. The Jewish community of Cologne even resumed activities before the end of the war, in April 1945. By 1948, over one hundred Jewish communities had been established, with a total membership of about twenty thousand people. The Jewish population in Germany was thus divided into two distinct groups: a large number of Eastern European displaced persons who came to Germany by chance and often expressed a desire to depart as soon as possible, and a smaller group of German Jews who had been wholly assimilated and had connections to their non-Jewish surroundings.[26]

Between 1993 and 2021, around 219,000 Jews, including their partners and children, immigrated to Germany from the former Soviet Union.[27] Though it is unclear how many remained in Germany, some experts assess the number of Jewish or part-Jewish residents of Germany to be around 225,000 today, an estimate that remains difficult to confirm. Though only ninety-two thousand Jews officially belong to the official Jewish community,[28] it is safe to say, however, that Germany's Jewish community is now the third largest in Europe, after those of France and Great Britain.[29]

Starting in 1957, the Federal Republic of Germany has provided funding for half of the costs associated with ensuring the safety and monitoring of deserted Jewish cemeteries within the country. In 2020, the government approved a subsidy of twenty-two million euros to the Central Council of Jews in Germany for the execution of structural and technical safety measures in Jewish facilities throughout the nation. Furthermore, the council is in charge of conserving the cultural heritage of German Jews, as well as carrying out social and integration initiatives. The government provides an annual donation of thirteen million euros to support these endeavors.[30]

STOLPERSTEINE

German stumbling stones, *Stolpersteine* in German, are small, commemorative brass plaques that are embedded in the sidewalks of German cities and towns. They are designed to commemorate the victims of the Holocaust, particularly Jews who were deported and murdered by the National Socialists during World War II.

The stumbling stones were created by the German artist Gunter Demnig in 1992. Each plaque is about ten centimeters by ten centimeters (4 in by 4 in) and is engraved with the name, date of birth, and fate of a victim of the Holocaust. The plaques are placed outside the last known address of the person being commemorated, creating a visual representation of the scale of the tragedy and the extent to which it affected local communities.

The stumbling stones are designed to make people stop and pay attention as they walk through their neighborhoods and to remind them of the horrors of the Holocaust that took place on the very streets they walk on every day. The stones also encourage people to reflect on the lives of those who were targeted and to consider the impact of discrimination and prejudice on individuals and communities.

The *Stolpersteine* project has spread across Germany and to other countries in Europe, with over seventy-five thousand plaques installed as of 2021. While some controversy surrounds the placement of the plaques, with some arguing

Figure 29.3.   Stumbling stones on a German street. *Alamy AY4TRH*

that they are inappropriate for public spaces, many people believe that they are a powerful and necessary reminder of the atrocities of the Holocaust and of the importance of remembering and honoring its victims.

POSTREUNIFICATION: WHAT ABOUT THE "NEO-NAZIS"?

East Germany's ongoing xenophobia causes significant repercussions in today's society, especially for nonwhite foreigners. The GDR's social identity was earmarked by fixed boundaries that established citizens' inclusion in, or exclusion from, society. The image of what it means to be (or to appear) German is still constrained by a very specific set of characteristics.[31]

The German neofascist movement has been predominantly concentrated in East Germany since the latter half of the 1990s, displaying an expanding organizational network and gaining increasing traction in local and federal elections. The success of these parties can be attributed to their tendency to offer facile solutions to intricate issues, and their position on the fringe allows them to make lofty promises without the constraints of governing.[32]

On a political level, two far-right parties stand out in modern Germany. The first is the Alternative for Germany (AfD), a far-right political group known for its opposition to the EU and to immigration. It experienced a decline in the national vote share in the 2021 federal elections but remains the largest party in some parts of eastern Germany.[33] In March 2022, the AfD was classified by the German Federal Office for the Protection of the Constitution as a suspected right-wing extremist group and a threat to democracy, allowing for ongoing surveillance.[34]

The unexpected success of the AfD in eastern Germany is primarily attributable to post-1990 events and experiences rather than an inherent xenophobia. Given their weaker economy, limited job opportunities, and lower wages compared to the western states, it is an observable fact that East Germans feel dissatisfied with the Berlin government. Much of their industry is owned by entities from the West or abroad, and many of their once-thriving communities have become ghost towns after numerous East Germans moved to the western states in the early 1990s seeking better employment opportunities. The prospect of heightened competition in the job market and the social upheaval that resulted from the influx of refugees in 2015 and 2016 have undoubtedly drawn many East Germans to the AfD, a party that vowed to defend their rights and livelihood.[35]

These circumstances, coupled with inferior representation compared to their western counterparts, have spurred East Germans to stage protests. The location and organizational source of all rallies in Germany, often not

Figure 29.4.   Far-right demonstration in Dresden. *Alamy AYRFEC*

emphasized in media reporting, reveal that a majority of right-wing rallies are indeed held in the eastern part of Germany, with significantly higher participation rates than in the West. The rallies largely focus on the topic of refugees and issues of asylum, immigration, and exclusion of Muslims, with 80 to 85 percent of all rallies covering these issues.

Established in 1964, the National Democratic Party of Germany (NPD) is the second-largest far-right party in contemporary Germany, espousing a more radical stance of neo-Nazism and ultranationalism. Although efforts were made to outlaw the party, in 2017 the Federal Constitutional Court declined the petition to prohibit it, asserting that the NPD lacked the capability to undermine democracy in Germany. In the 2021 federal elections, the NPD garnered approximately 1 percent of the nationwide vote.

The creation and dissemination of pro-Nazi materials is prohibited under German law. Despite this, such paraphernalia has been illegally imported into the country for many years. Even though neo-Nazi music bands such as Landser have been banned in Germany, counterfeit copies of their albums produced in the United States and other nations continue to be circulated in the country. German neo-Nazi websites frequently rely on Internet servers located in Canada and the United States. They often employ symbols that resemble the swastika and incorporate other NS emblems, such as the sun cross, wolf's hook, and black sun.

ISLAMOPHOBIA OR HOSTILITY TO MUSLIMS?

The Bundeszentrale für politische Bildung (Federal Agency for Political Education) defines "Islamophobia" as the fear of Islam as a religion. However, what we are currently witnessing in numerous European nations is not so much a fear, criticism, or hatred of Islam as a faith but rather a feeling of resentment to those who follow the religion, namely, Muslims. In other words, the term "hostility to Muslims" is more appropriate to describe the attitudes prevalent in Germany today, akin to the antisemitic sentiments of the first half of the twentieth century.

On a statistical level, according to a study of the Leibnitz Institute for Social Sciences in 2003, about 70 percent of respondents rejected the statement, "Muslim culture definitely fits into our Western world." But likewise, the majority of respondents, 65 percent, rejected the statement, "I am more suspicious of people of Muslim faith." According to these results, there are both empirical as well as theoretical reasons for making a clear distinction between the dislike of Islam and hostility toward Muslims.

The survey also revealed that just under half of people in Germany agree with the statement, "The many Muslims here sometimes make me feel like a stranger in my own country." The 2020 Leipzig Authoritarianism Study found that just under half of people in Germany feel like strangers in their own country due to the presence of Muslims, and at least 25 percent believe that Muslim women should not be allowed to immigrate. In eastern Germany, the latter figure is even higher, around 40 percent. Furthermore, more than half of Germans perceive Islam as threatening.[36]

Anti-Muslim discrimination is a serious problem in Germany, and it manifests itself in various forms of Islamophobia. This includes negative attitudes and prejudices toward Muslims and "Islam" in various areas of life, including the job and housing market, education, and public spaces. Studies have also shown that anti-Muslim discrimination has a real impact on the job market, particularly for Muslim women who wear headscarves. A 2016 study by the Research Institute on the Future of Work (IZA) found that headscarf-wearing Muslim women with Turkish names had to apply four times as often as equally qualified applicants without headscarves and with German names to be invited for an interview. Islamophobic crimes are also a serious concern in Germany, with reports of attacks on mosques and other religious institutions. In 2020, authorities registered at least 901 Islamophobic crimes nationwide, some of which were attacks on religious institutions and places of worship. In 2019, the German Ministry of the Interior listed ninety-five attacks on mosques.[37]

The German government and civil society organizations have taken strong measures to combat the spread of neo-Nazism and far-right extremism. German authorities are vigilant and have taken significant steps to address hate speech, xenophobia, and any attempts to undermine the country's democratic principles. It can be said that, keenly aware of its historical stigma, Germany is making sincere and concerted efforts to expose the perpetrators of the National Socialist regime and to warn younger and future generations of the dangers of extremist policies.

VERGANGENHEITSBEWÄLTIGUNG: COMING TO TERMS WITH THE PAST

Following 1989, East Germans were confronted with the realization that elder National Socialists had also found refuge in the GDR after the war. They also discovered that antisemitism and neofascism were not alien to the "first Socialist State on German soil" and that some of their own grandparents may have been less innocent than they had professed.[38]

The East German government did not exhibit the same level of antisemitic ideology as the National Socialist regime that preceded it; however, it did not demonstrate the expected level of sympathy or compassion that might be expected from any German government following the Holocaust. This indifferent attitude was evidenced by the unfounded accusations during the GDR's anticosmopolitan campaigns as well as by the government's failure to provide adequate recognition and compensation to Jewish survivors and to pursue a comprehensive program of trials for National Socialist crimes during the 1950s.[39]

In the post–World War II years, despite some political leaders suggesting that public discussion of Jewish matters should have occurred in the Soviet occupation zone, it was, as we witnessed, in the western zones and, later, in West Germany where antisemitism and the Holocaust became a central topic of public discourse. The West German government provided financial restitution to Jewish survivors, established relations with Israel, and prioritized the memory of the Holocaust in national politics. In contrast, GDR leaders kept the Jewish question on the margins of narratives of the NS era, refused to provide restitution or support to Israel, and even supported Israel's adversaries.[40]

West Germany, on the other hand, made restitutions to victims and their families under the German Restitution Law, with the equivalent of 7.5 billion euros paid out and an additional 1.25 billion euros granted under a German-Israeli agreement in 1962. The world having projected an image of collective guilt on the Germans in general, and on West Germans in particular, today's third generation finds itself in the challenging position of having to regularly face and often accept negative social comparisons concerning Germany's history, even though they were born long after the events.[41]

Remembering the National Socialist regime itself has a patchy history in West Germany. Until the 1960s, the topic usually drew a general silence, and people neither wanted to know or hear about their own crimes or lack of action. The situation began to change when the country's younger generation started questioning—and accusing—their elders. In 1979, the American television series *Holocaust* was viewed by millions of people in West Germany. Amazingly, at that time, the term "Holocaust" was still unknown to most Germans. The series exerted a tremendous impact and long-lasting effect on German society.[42] Not only have citizens of West Germany gradually assumed greater accountability for the persecution of Jewish people, but in 1990 the GDR issued a formal apology to the Jewish people and to Israel for the role that many East Germans played in the atrocities committed by the NS regime during World War II. This apology was seen as a significant gesture of reconciliation and an important step toward healing past wounds.[43]

Germany's collective shame is not just a set of characteristics but also a process of evolving toward a more positive and acceptable identity. The National Socialist past of Germany and Austria, like many other nations' histories, is an ongoing legacy that shapes their political and social culture and influences their identity and self-image. The political and moral choices made by Germans in response to their historical legacy have become a significant story of our time, particularly as European unification brings former adversaries together in the shadow of the two world wars.[44]

In West Germany, the common tendency was to attribute National Socialist crimes to elite organizations like the SS, rather than considering the possibility that ordinary Germans may have been involved. According to the theologian and politician Wolfgang Ullmann, in the western part of the country, the belief was that antisemitic crimes had been committed in the name of Germans rather than by them. By blaming the Holocaust on specific elite organizations, it was possible to suggest that antisemitism was not a widespread issue and to absolve Germans of responsibility. However, the Auschwitz trials in Frankfurt in the early sixties created waves of interest, as did the showing of *Schindler's List* in 1994.[45]

In 1995 the Hamburg Institute for Social Research launched a review of the twentieth century's history, which was characterized by unparalleled devastation. The project aimed to commemorate the fiftieth anniversary of the end of World War II and provide insight into this tumultuous era. The project's exhibition was successful, particularly in generating controversy and sparking debates, not only in Germany but in other countries as well. The researchers chose to focus on the Wehrmacht, the Reich's largest military organization, believing that the theme would provide valuable insight into the functioning of NS Germany and its violent regime.

Apart from the exhibition, the project leaders organized lectures, conferences, and discussions that were aimed to present the history of violence to a wide audience. The exhibition focused on the involvement of the Wehrmacht in acts of mass murder in Eastern Europe that did not comply to the more traditional form of warfare. Within a couple of years, nearly one million people had visited the exhibition in thirty-two cities throughout Germany and Austria, generating both approval and controversy. Center-left parties supported and organized the exhibition, while center-right parties generally opposed it. In 1997, when the exhibition was shown in Munich, the extreme right-wing staged vehement protests that were countered by anti-neo-Nazi demonstrations implemented by left-leaning groups.[46]

REMEMBRANCE AND EDUCATION

The year 1995 was also highlighted by ceremonies to mark the fiftieth anniversary of the end of the NS regime. German political leaders, along with thousands of participants, traveled to former National Socialist concentration camps, in both the east and west of Germany, to recall the crimes of the Third Reich and to speak out for human rights in the present.[47] Since 1996,

Figure 29.5. Anti-Nazi demonstration in Essen. *Alamy END3GE*

January 27 has been recognized as a nationwide, legally established day of remembrance in Germany. The choice of date marks the day on which the Auschwitz extermination camp and the two adjoining Auschwitz concentration camps were liberated by the Red Army in the last year of World War II. Flags of mourning are hoisted on public buildings on this day and many events, such as readings, theater performances, and church services promote the memory of the crimes of the National Socialists. The day of remembrance also serves to draw attention to current trends of antisemitism, xenophobia, and misanthropy.

Education in Germany about National Socialism and the Holocaust has long been well established. All German states provide comprehensive coverage of these topics in either history or social sciences classes, and they are mandatory subjects in the eighth, ninth, or tenth school years. Additionally, the German education board encourages schools to arrange visits to places of remembrance or education, such as concentration camps or interpretive centers, in Germany or other countries.[48]

In the 1960s, former concentration camp sites in West Germany were opened to the public as places of remembrance and education. Over time, their educational offerings have expanded significantly, drawing an increasing number of German and international visitors, including many school groups. For example, the Dachau Concentration Camp Memorial Site receives nearly one million visitors annually, with one-third of them being student groups.[49]

Since the early 1990s, Berlin's Topography of Terror exhibitions have shed light on the crimes committed in Germany and throughout Europe by the Gestapo and the other various branches of the SS, as well as by the police. The Topography of Terror also administrates the former Tempelhof Airport site and Berlin-Schöneweide's Dokumentationszentrum NS-Zwangsarbeit (National Socialist Forced Labor Documentation Center).

In 1999 the Dokumentation Obersalzberg center was opened in Berchtesgaden as a place of learning and remembrance relating to the history of Obersalzberg and the National Socialist dictatorship. In addition, the center presents a broader picture of the entire period, from the troubles of the post–World War I Weimar Republic through to the end of World War II. It offers a wealth of material and insights related to National Socialist ideology, propaganda, war crimes, and the Holocaust. The center conducts tours for a wide range of visitors, in particular to German school groups, Germany's adult population, and members of the German armed forces. The annual number of visitors to this well-structured didactic center is between 145,000 and 170,000.[50]

The Institute of Contemporary History, originally called the German Institute of the History of the National Socialist Era, was established in 1949 following a suggestion by the Allied forces, with the goal of analyzing contemporary German history. The Obersalzberg center, located near Hitler's former home and headquarters and below his Eagle's Nest, was the institute's pioneering initiative. The institute is funded by the German federal government as well as several states.

In 2001 a documentation center with similar educational goals as that of Obersalzberg opened its doors at Nuremberg's former party rally grounds. Also, adjacent to Nuremberg's Courtroom 600, where the world-famous 1946 Nuremberg Trials took place and which is open to the public, another informative interpretive center invites visitors not only to understand the historic importance of the legal proceedings against the National Socialist perpetrators but to see the broader picture of their regime of terror.

The Munich Documentation Center for the History of National Socialism, established in 2015, serves as a facility for education and remembrance. It documents and addresses the crimes of the National Socialist dictatorship and their origins, manifestations, and contemporary consequences. The permanent exhibition explores the history of National Socialism in Munich, the city's role in the terror apparatus, and its efforts to confront its past after 1945. The center's educational concept and exhibition are founded on the principle of acknowledging, learning about, and comprehending the history of this location. The Documentation Center prompts visitors with two key questions: What does this have to do with me? And why should this still concern me today?[51]

The centers cited above are just a few examples of many. Several more worthy of mention include the former Order Castle Vogelsang IP, which provides excellent education about the SS organization; Wewelsburg Castle's informative coverage of the SS organization; the Berlin Story Bunker's "How Did Hitler Happen?"; and the many concentration camp memorial sites throughout Germany.

These numerous sites play a crucial role in edifying young Germans as well as those who may not have had the opportunity to learn about the history of the National Socialist regime and its catastrophic impact on Germany and the world. The comprehensive information available in English at these centers and memorial sites enables visitors from all over the world to gain a deeper understanding of the various aspects of these historical themes.

At all these centers in Germany and Austria the informative and educational content is presented in both an honest and unflinching way in its depiction of the grievous history of the National Socialist regime. Both Germany and Austria have made a concerted effort to confront their past and ensure that future generations understand the atrocities that were committed, both in Germany and abroad. Today, Germans are actively working to come to terms with the misguidance and crimes of their forefathers, and the country is emerging as a leader in the fight for racial equality and humanitarian policies.

The didactic content offered at these sites is a powerful reminder of the horrors that occurred before and during World War II and is a testament to the strength and resilience of the German people. By refusing to whitewash or rewrite history, Germans have shown a deep commitment to learning from the past and working toward a fairer future. As a result, the long years of finger-pointing at Germany are hopefully a thing of the past, and instead, mankind can focus on learning from this terrifying and sobering history.

By preserving the sordid memories of the Third Reich's dictatorial regime, Germany's history serves as an ongoing reminder and a dire warning to future generations. It admonishes us to sidestep the dangers of fascism and extremism, to remain aware of the devastating consequences of racism and bigotry, and to ever remember the importance of standing up for what we consider to be morally right, even in the face of overwhelming opposition. By continuing to learn from the past, humankind can help shape a more humane and more equitable future for all.

NOTES

1. Brandon Tensley, "Why Are Former East Germans Responsible for So Much Xenophobic Violence?," *Washington Post*, October 2, 2015.

2. Michal Kopecek, *Past in the Making: Historical Revisionism in Central Europe after 1989* (Budapest: Central European University Press, 2008), 59–71.

3. Alliierten Museum, "Denazification," https://www.alliiertenmuseum.de/en/thema/denazification/.

4. Norbert Frei, permanent exhibit, Topography of Terror Documentation Centre, Berlin, December 7, 2020.

5. Alliierten Museum, "Denazification."

6. Permanent exhibit, Topography of Terror Documentation Centre, Berlin, December 7, 2020.

7. Morris Janowitz, "German Reactions to Nazi Atrocities," *American Journal of Sociology* 52, no. 2 (September 1946): 141–46.

8. Harold Marcuse, *Legacies of Dachau: The Uses and Abuses of a Concentration Camp, 1933–2001* (Cambridge: Cambridge University Press, 2008), 61.

9. Ibid.

10. Frederick Taylor, *Exorcising Hitler: The Occupation and Denazification of Germany* (New York: Bloomsbury, 2011), 119–23.

11. Ibid., 97–98.

12. James L. Payne, "Did the United States Create Democracy in Germany?," *Independent Review* 11, no. 2 (Fall 2006): 209–21.

13. Permanent exhibit, Topography of Terror Documentation Centre, Berlin, December 7, 2020.

14. Jeffrey Herf, *Divided Memory: The Nazi Past in Two Germanys* (Cambridge, MA: Harvard University Press, 1997), 380.

15. Gellately, *Hitler's True Believers*, 318–19.

16. Herf, *Divided Memory*, 335.

17. Ibid., 381.

18. Bill Niven, *Facing the Nazi Past: United Germany and the Legacy of the Third Reich* (London: Routledge, 2002), 41.

19. Tensley, "Why Are Former East Germans Responsible?"

20. Niven, *Facing the Nazi Past*, 22–23.

21. Tensley, "Why Are Former East Germans Responsible?"

22. Ibid.

23. Barbara Dietz, "German and Jewish Migration from the Former Soviet Union to Germany: Background, Trends and Implications," *Journal of Ethnic and Migration Studies* 26, no. 4 (2000): 635–52.

24. Sekou Keita and Helen Dempster, "Five Years Later, One Million Refugees Are Thriving in Germany," Center for Global Development, December 4, 2020, https://www.cgdev.org/blog/five-years-later-one-million-refugees-are-thriving-germany.

25. Victoria Rietig and Andreas Müller, "The New Reality: Germany Adapts to Its Role as a Major Migrant Magnet," Migration Policy Institute, August 31, 2016, https://www.migrationpolicy.org/article/new-reality-germany-adapts-its-role-major-migrant-magnet.

26. Michael Brenner, "In the Shadow of the Holocaust: The Changing Image of German Jewry after 1945," United States Holocaust Memorial Museum, January 31, 2008.

27. "Jüdische Einwanderung nach Deutschland nach 1989," Lernen aus der Geschichte, March 15, 2016, http://lernen-aus-der-geschichte.de/Online-Lernen/Online-Modul/9136.

28. World Jewish Congress, "Germany," https://www.worldjewishcongress.org/en/about/communities/de.

29. Berman Jewish DataBank, "2020 World Jewish Population," https://www.jewishdatabank.org/databank/search-results?search=World+Jewish+Population.

30. Federal Ministry of the Interior and Community, "Strengthening the Jewish Community in Germany," July 6, 2018, https://www.bmi.bund.de/SharedDocs/kurzmeldungen/EN/2018/07/zentralrat-der-juden.html.

31. Tensley, "Why Are Former East Germans Responsible?"

32. Kopecek, *Past in the Making*, 59–71.

33. Frank Decker, "Wahlergebnisse und Wählerschaft der AfD," Bundeszentrale für politische Bildung, December 2, 2022, https://www.bpb.de/themen/parteien/parteien-in-deutschland/afd/273131/wahlergebnisse-und-waehlerschaft-der-afd/.

34. "German Court Rules Far-Right AfD Party a Suspected Threat to Democracy," *Guardian*, March 8, 2022, https://www.theguardian.com/world/2022/mar/08/german-court-rules-far-right-afd-party-a-suspected-threat-to-democracy.

35. Emily Schultheis, "East Germany Is Still a Country of Its Own," *Foreign Policy*, July 7, 2021.

36. Armin Pfahl-Traughber, "Bundeszentrale für politische Bildung," Bundeszentrale für Politische Bildung, June 17, 2019, https://www.bpb.de/themen/rechtsextremismus/entgrenzter-rechtsextremismus-2015/202684/armin-pfahl

-traughber-die-besonderheiten-des-nsu-rechtsterrorismus-im-internationalen-kontext
/.

37. *Zeit Online*, February 8, 2021.

38. Kopecek, *Past in the Making*, 59–71.

39. Herf, *Divided Memory*, 384–85.

40. Ibid., 3.

41. E. Dresler-Hawke and J. H. Liu, "Collective Shame and the Positioning of German National Identity," *Psicología Política* 32 (2006): 131–53.

42. Christoph Hasselbach, "Holocaust Remembrance in Germany: A Changing Culture," *Deutsche Welle*, January 27, 2019, https://www.dw.com/en/holocaust-remembrance-in-germany-a-changing-culture/a-47203540.

43. Dresler-Hawke and Liu, "Collective Shame."

44. Ibid.

45. Niven, *Facing the Nazi Past*, 137.

46. Ibid., 143–44.

47. Herf, *Divided Memory*, 367.

48. Deutscher Bundestag, "Die Verankerung des Themas Nationalsozialismus im Schulunterricht in Deutschland, Österreich, Polen und Frankreich," September 18, 2018, https://www.bundestag.de/resource/blob/577838/057659f45ba3ae2fc1ba10aca4f1da91/WD-8-091-18-pdf-data.pdf.

49. "Jeder Schüler soll ein ehemaliges KZ besuchen," *Süeddeutshe Zeitung*, June 7, 2018, https://www.sueddeutsche.de/bayern/gesetzentwurf-jeder-schueler-soll-ein-ehemaliges-kz-besuchen-1.4004537.

50. Sven Keller, Albert A. Feiber, and Eva-Maria Zembsch, *Dokumentation Obersalzberg, Jahresbericht 2018* (Munich: Institut für Zeitgeschichte, 2019), 6.

51. NSDOKU Munich, "About Us," https://www.nsdoku.de/en/about-us/the-nsdoku.

Index

Trambauer, Heinrich, 297
Tresckow, Henning von, 253
Triple Alliance, 267–68
Triumph of the Will (film), 94, 178–79, 180, 341
Troche, Theodor, 199, 200
Troost, Gerdy, 162
The Tunnel (film), 17–18

Ullmann, Wolfgang, 373
ultramontanism, 288–89
U.S. Holocaust Memorial Museum, 107, 260

Venice, 103, *308*
Vergangenheitsbewältigung and the past, 364, 372–74
Versailles Treaty, 27, 39, 42, 85, 121; Hitler as denouncing, 43, 152, 182, 183, 295, 344; military limits imposed by, 61, 179; as punishment for Germany, 29, 30–32, 51, 265; shame and humiliation of, 186, 246, 340
Victims of the Past (film), 175
Vienna, 4, 23, 80, 81, 283, 284, 332; Academy of Fine Arts, 7, 10, 17, 22; antisemitism in, 13–16, 18, 107–8; high society of, 3, 12–13; Hitler in, 7, 10–20, 38, 72, 75, 87, 155, 173, 225, 282; Imperial Regalia stored in, 197, 198, 201; Jewish citizens of, 12, 13, 15, 226, 232; opera houses, *16,* 94
Völkischer Beobachter (periodical), 51, 121, 285
Volk ohne Raum (People Without Space), 187–89
Volksempfänger (People's Radio), 125, 139, *166*
Volkskörper (racial corpus), 143, 144
Volkssturm (film), 177
Volkswagen, 60, 61, 66, 132, 139

Wagner, Richard, 6, 10, 76, 87–90, 91, 170, 178, 284
Wagner, Siegfried, 89
Wagner, Wieland, 89
Wagner, Winifred Williams, 89–90
Wandervogel youth movement, 50, 135
Wannsee Conference, 235
Wartenburg, P. G. Y. von, 249
Wehrmacht (armed forces), 61, 120, 135, 138–39, 189, 233–34, 253, 299, 324, 350–51, 373–74
Weimar Republic, 42, 44, 60, 63, 80, 111, 130, 165, 175, 205, 207, 252, 301, 347; division and disorder in, 34–35, 47, 121, 210, 211, 246, 313, 375; Ebert as first president, 29–30; establishment of, 28–29; freedoms allowed under, 150, 213; National Socialism, arising during, 29, 34; NS disdain for, 113, 319, 363; Rentenmark as currency, 32–33; weakness in, 53, 247, 343; Weimar Constitution, 55; women, faring during, 311–12; WWI military victims, commemorating, 297
Weinberg, Gerhard, 260, 262, 263, 278n52, 278n70
Weisse Rose resistance movement, 250
Weltanschauung (world view), 30, 42; of Hitler, 20, 41, 130, 259; of National Socialist Party, 209, 319, 332; propaganda use and, 93, 189
Welzer, Harald, 352
West Germany, 359, 360–66, 372, 373, 375
Weyler, Valeriano, 217
White Rose group, 250
Wiedemann, Fritz, 155
Wilhelm I, Emperor, 197
Wilhelm II, Emperor, 24, 27, 28, 34, 195
Wilson, Woodrow, 27, 28, 31
Winter Relief of the German People (WHW), 63

About the Author

David Harper was born in New York and grew up in a multicultural household with British, Indian, and American influences in Paris, France. He identifies as a "European American," and his family played an active role in the Allied war effort, with his aunt being executed by the SS at Dachau for her involvement in the Franco-British resistance.

Since 1987, Harper has worked as a tour guide in Germany, specializing in lecturing on the historical significance of Obersalzberg, also known as Hitler's Mountain, in Berchtesgaden. His research for his first book, a guidebook on Berchtesgaden's history and culture, led him to deepen his knowledge of the historical events that took place on the mountain during the Third Reich. He became an authority on the subject and was accredited to conduct educational tours at the Dokumentation Obersalzberg interpretive center.

Harper has spent over thirty-five years giving lectures on World War II themes and the Third Reich in Germany, France, Belgium, Austria, Poland, and Italy. He has participated in documentaries and has sought to address misconceptions and clichéd notions about what happened in Germany during Hitler's reign.

Harper's other works include *Your Complete Guide to Berchtesgaden* (1995, 2005) and *We Rubies Four* (coauthor) (2011).

www.ingramcontent.com/pod-product-compliance
Lightning Source LLC
Chambersburg PA
CBHW030253100426
42812CB00002B/427